and STRANGE HAPPENINGS IN THE BIBLE

AN ENGINEER'S STUDY OF SCRIPTURE

ROBERT C. BRENNER

Brenner Books • San Diego, CA

"Now we see the world dimly.
Then we shall know the truth."
QUOTE BASED ON 1 CHRONICLES 13:12

"But these miracles have been written so that you will believe
that Jesus is the Messiah, the Son of God,
and so that you will have life by believing in Him."
JOHN 20:31

Supernatural & Strange Happenings in the Bible
An Engineer's Study of Scripture

PUBLISHED BY:
Brenner Information Group
P.O. Box 721000
San Diego, CA 92172–1000
(858) 538–0093
www.brennerbooks.com

Book design by TLC Graphics, *www.TLCGraphics.com*
Cover: Tamara Dever; Interior: Erin Stark

Cover photo: ©iStockphoto.com/Irantzu_Arbaizagoitia

Printed in the United States of America

ISBN 978-1-930199-76-7

*This book is dedicated to all
who seek the truth with open minds.
May you find answers, understanding,
and comfort as you read* Supernatural
& Strange Happenings in the Bible.

Table of Contents

CHAPTER TWO
Power Over People

CHAPTER SEVEN

Preface

Supernatural & Strange Happenings in the Bible

HERE'S A BOOK FOR BOTH CHRISTIAN AND NON-Christian readers. It's about the supernatural and the mysterious. And it's about the mystical protection and punishment that existed way back then and that still exist today. Its story format makes this book easy to read and absorb.

The goal of *Supernatural & Strange Happenings in the Bible* is to identify every mention of things supernatural and mysterious recorded in Scripture. It was written so intelligent readers can research those things that interest them most. It is not intended to be a treatise challenging every religious and scientific position out there. Instead, this book is intended to be the "beginning" of your journey of discovery. I wrote it to provide direction, understanding, and hope to a fearful world.

During my research, I found 550 Bible verses that relate to supernatural events. Of these, 394 are records of unique incidents. Some of these incidents defy our standards of logic and reality, but in the world of the supernatural and spiritual, is this not expected?

Books of the Bible

OLD TESTAMENT

Genesis	2 Chronicles	Ezekiel
Exodus	Ezra	Daniel
Leviticus	Nehemiah	Hosea
Numbers	Esther	Joel
Deuteronomy	Job	Amos
Joshua	Psalms	Obadiah
Judges	Proverbs	Jonah
Ruth	Ecclesiastes	Micah
1 Samuel	Song of Songs/	Habakkuk
2 Samuel	Solomon	Haggai
1 Kings	Isaiah	Zechariah
2 Kings	Jeremiah	Malachi
1 Chronicles	Lamentations	

NEW TESTAMENT

Matthew	Ephesians	2 Peter
Mark	Colossians	1 John
Luke	1 Thessalonians	2 John
John	2 Thessalonians	3 John
Acts [of the	1 Timothy	Philemon
Apostles]	2 Timothy	Jude
Romans	Titus	James
1 Corinthians	Philippians	Revelation
2 Corinthians	Hebrews	
Galatians	1 Peter	

Acknowledgments

I WROTE THIS BOOK, BUT IT TOOK A TEAM OF DEDicated professionals and supporters to make *Supernatural & Strange Happenings* a reality. So, I want to thank the following terrific people:

To Rev. Dr. Donald J. Brenner for counseling and encouraging me and then vetting my manuscript against Hebrew and Greek writings of the Old and New Testaments.

To Barbara Sherburne of the Scopists Support Group (Yahoo forum) for voluntarily providing proofreading and editing services. She made my writing much stronger, and I appreciate her dedication and perseverance on this lengthy project.

To Cynthia Frank of Cypress House for graciously coaching me and sharing her publishing strategies and techniques.

To Tami Dever and Erin Stark of TLC Graphics for creating the cover and interior layout of this book. I especially appreciated their constructive criticism where warranted.

To my wife and family for patiently enduring many hours seeing me with my head down and fingers typing on the keyboard—totally engrossed in the project.

And finally to the many readers who provided feedback and encouragement as I embarked on this challenging assignment.

Each of you played a major role in this project. You made a difference, and I appreciate your being a part of this process. Thank you, and God bless all of you.

Introduction

THE BIBLE DESCRIBES THE HISTORY OF MANKIND and the relationship our ancestors had with a supreme being that we call "God." The Bible also tells us what happened when people didn't live within moral and ethical guidelines. It's a book about the interactions between mankind and God. And it describes supernatural and strange happenings.

Over 2,000 years have passed since events described in the Bible occurred. This book can amaze the most ardent futurist. It can also frighten the fearful. Yet it can comfort everyone who seeks to understand its content and meaning. It makes life and living worthwhile.

The Bible is an accounting of multiple dimensions, things unseen, extraterrestrial beings, levitation, teleportation, supernatural transfigurations, strange transformations, and absolute control. Matter is converted, it's moved, and it's made to live. The dead are raised to life, and the living are instantly destroyed. Fire comes from the sky to earth and goes from earth to the sky. Massive armies are suddenly destroyed. The weak are made strong, and the powerful are made weak. A hand appears and writes on a wall. A decorated box emanates power that can kill people who touch it, yet doesn't harm certain individuals. An iron ax head floats from the bottom of a river up to the surface where it's retrieved. And two people walk on the top of a deep lake. Clouds surround a voice, and a column of smoke and fire leads a nation of over two million people through the hot desert for 40 years. Food mysteriously appears and clothes and sandals never wear out. Plants are engulfed in flames, but don't burn. Men move about in a hot, fiery furnace, yet aren't consumed—even their clothes aren't burned. Loud voices come from nowhere, yet everywhere.

In my research I marveled at the power unleashed through spoken words. I read how the raging sea was immediately calmed by a command, and I read about powerful forces that controlled people, animals, matter, nature, and even life and death.

I read how a disgruntled family rebelled and was swallowed up by the earth that opened, dropped them in, and then covered them as the ground closed about them. I read about a man who vanished before the eyes of an official from the royal court of Ethiopia to be instantly teleported to a village 12 miles away. I read about the sun standing still in the sky for a full day, and how the sun's shadow moved on the stairs of a sundial opposite normal, and reports of animals talking to people. I learned about individuals and large armies that suddenly died or were killed by supernatural forces. I also read about people who died and were brought back to life.

And I learned about unidentified flying objects, demons, ghosts, spirits, magicians, mediums, monsters, giants, other dimensions, and the unseen.

As an engineer and amateur scientist, I've always been interested in things I don't fully understand. The Bible is no exception. So, over the past 10 years, I've studied the Scriptures in great detail. My goal was to analyze events, situations and people and to collect and categorize strange happenings and amazing accounts. My research was to help myself and others like you understand the fascinating mysteries contained in this book. I realized that there must be some reason why the Bible has been around longer than any other book in history. And I wanted to find out why.

In the following chapters I will share fascinating events recorded in history, frozen in time for today's generation to read and wonder. What was most amazing about my research was the ease in which Bible history has been made more acceptable and understandable after watching movies and TV programs such as "Independence Day," "Close Encounters of a Third Kind," "Star Trek," "Star Trek: Voyager," "Sightings," "X-Files," "Dark Skies," "Unsolved Mysteries," "Touched by an Angel," "Paranormal State," "Ghost Hunters," and "Ghost Whisperer."

It also helped my understanding of the mysteries recorded in Scripture after I researched the other dimensions subtly described in the Bible. When I read about these amazing things, I better understood how much of the Bible was possible. I learned during my own research that the Bible is an amazing document full of hidden messages and meanings. Only today are some of these becoming known to us.

By reading and studying this great Book for yourself, you'll come to understand how a stern and demanding God punished those who failed to follow His rules, saved people who believed and trusted in Him, and provided a savior to give us hope of salvation for our own future. I think there is much more to be discovered as God guides us toward mankind's final days on this earth. And I'm no longer afraid.

The information to follow reflects the results of this engineer's study and analysis of Scripture. See for yourself that mysteries are indeed being solved. Marvel as God enables science and technology to uncover secrets in our Bible.

There are literally hundreds of strange events mentioned in the Bible. I expanded on some of these in this book. They occurred in the lands that today we call Arabia, Egypt, Iran, Israel, Jordan, Syria, and Turkey. As you read each story, I'll tell you where and when the event occurred. You'll learn the location of villages, cities, mountains, and rivers in the land area we know as the Fertile Crescent. At the end of each chapter you'll find references to all the supernatural and amazing events that I found during my research.

As you read *Supernatural & Strange Happenings in the Bible*, set a Bible near you so you can look up and read for yourself what I will describe. Each of the events and incidents in this book came from the Bible. I wrote them from the perspective of a person with a technical background. I did all the research I could to explain the scenario for each story, then I had each of my examples vetted (verified) based on the original Hebrew and Greek writings.

Study this fascinating book for yourself. Check out what I will describe. Analyze it for yourself. Then draw your own conclusions about the fascinating facts and strange happenings described here and in the Bible.

I hope you find *Supernatural & Strange Happenings in the Bible* interesting and fascinating. For me, this has been a challenging yet enlightening, project. Now it's ready for you to enjoy. Get set for an exciting reading and learning experience. You are about to embark on an amazing journey of discovery.

Is the Bible True?

Are the stories found in the Bible true? Did they really happen? There are those who say that every word in the Bible is true. They believe that men guided by God wrote the words that became the books of the Bible.

Then there are those who believe that the Bible is probably right, but they doubt some of it, saying that writers can make mistakes, so these scribes likely wrote what they thought was accurate.

A third group claims that the Bible is totally false, that the things described in this book never happened. They feel the Bible is one big fairytale.

These perceptions are another reason why I wrote this book. By focusing on events recorded in Scripture, I researched and then described what I discovered regarding each event. Once the information was collected, and studied, I wrote about my findings. My technical editor checked my words against the original writings in Hebrew and Greek and compared and contrasted the original words with my own research notes. I've documented the results in this book, and now I leave it up to you to accept or deny what I've written.

What surprised me most in this process was how close my research matched the original Old Testament Hebrew and original New Testament Greek writings.

Slowly science is beginning to accept the existence of God. Recently a French physicist at the University of Paris-Sud won the £1M Templeton Foundation prize for predicting the reality of a "hypercosmic" god—a being who exists outside our physical universe.

Studies of the King James Bible using a letter sequence analysis (Equidistant Letter Sequences) are showing that the Bible is based on divine guidance.

Science now recognizes the existence of God and is beginning to confirm the accuracy of the Bible.

Science also accepts the reality of additional dimensions. The Bible and other ancient Hebrew writings recognized this thousands of years ago. Perhaps mankind is at a point where we can all learn and understand the marvelous facts described in the Bible. Read on and see if you agree.

Organization of This Book

After identifying over 550 Bible verses referring to super-natural incidents or events, I organized the information into specific manifestations of power. A number of the verses describe things that are also described in other books of the Bible. For example, the great flood that wiped out all mankind except eight people is described in the books of Genesis, Matthew, Hebrews, and First and Second Peter. And the story of Moses parting the Red Sea is described in Exodus, Psalms, and Hebrews.

So I collected all verses that describe the same event and created a composite list of the events by subject providing references to any related verses. In this way a single subject listing could have three or four reference locations in the Bible. Then I organized a list of specific and unique events. This reduced the list to 194 specific incidents. These 194 were then associated with the power exhibited. I identified each type of power so I could compare and contrast incidents based on like powers.

Next I organized the various powers into unique categories: power over matter, power over people, power over life and death, power over demons, power over nature, and power over animals. I added two special categories to cover the power of prophecy, and other paranormal realities such as magicians, mediums, ghosts, dragons, monsters, sea serpents, other dimensions, and the unseen.

Then I organized each power category listing all the relevant verses, and provided stories that demonstrate each power. In some cases, an incident falls under several categories. I selected the category that best fits the incident and added a complete listing of all the relevant events and incidents at the end of each chapter. The result was a set of examples each focusing on a specific power. This is how the book you now hold became reality.

CHAPTER ONE

Power Over Matter

FROM THE MOMENT GOD SPOKE AND CREATED OUR world, mankind has felt the power of His presence. This power is exhibited in a number of ways. One is a force that caused matter to change, move, appear, and disappear. This power, this force, created a pillar of cloud that protected and led people in a mass migration. At times it shot fire out of the cloud to punish evil people. This supernatural force also caused fire to come down from the sky, or to flash up into the sky. It made walking sticks turn into snakes and a dry wooden rod sprout and grow leaves and fruit overnight. It caused people to levitate, change their appearance, and teleport from one place to another. It enabled people to walk on the surface of deep water, prison chains to fall loose and gates to mysteriously open. It also caused water to flow where it never flowed before. It made food multiply so vast groups could eat their fill leaving more leftovers than the original amount of food. It caused instant infestations of insects and deadly disease. It caused tumors to appear and a face to shine so bright the person required a veil just to be seen by others. It caused water in the seas and rivers to part so people could walk across on dry ground. It produced tongues of fire, and it produced a rainbow of promise.

The Bible describes this power as it relates to select people and select groups. Thus we read about angels, messengers of the Lord, men of God, prophets, apostles, kings, generals, and people like Abraham, Moses, Aaron, Joshua, Saul, Samuel, Sampson, David, Solomon, Elijah, Elisha, Jesus, Peter, and the whole Israelite nation.

I found 136 verses in the Bible that deal with power over matter. In the stories to follow, I'll elaborate on important examples of this force. At the end of this section, you'll find a list of all the relevant incidents that were discovered during my research.

The Genesis of Life: Creation and the Beginning of History

In the beginning God created the heavens and the earth.

GENESIS 1:1

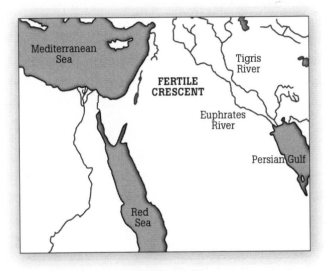

GENESIS 1:1-31
Location: Fertile Crescent | **Historical Time:** The beginning of time

TO VIEW MAPS ONLINE:
Copy this link into your browser and press Enter/Return
www.britannica.com/EBchecked/topic/205250/Fertile-Crescent
ancienthistory.about.com/od/neareast/ss/110708ANE_10.htm

WHEN DID THE WORLD BEGIN? HOW DID IT ALL START? WAS there a big bang in the universe and suddenly there we were? What is the universe? How was it formed? Was there a being out there that one day decided to make a world? Where was "out there?" Is there a God? Where did God come from? And why are we here?

These questions have challenged philosophers, historians, scholars, scientists, engineers, religious researchers, and even skeptics for centuries. There are many hypotheses yet none can prove beyond a shadow of doubt how our world began. We can however, see evidence of creation everywhere. And based on substantial evidence, we can conclude that there is a supreme being, and this being is controlling the destiny of all of us. We call this being "God."

In the first part of the last century, a German physicist, Dr. Albert Einstein, postulated that matter can neither be created nor destroyed. He showed mathematically that energy is equal to mass times the speed of light squared. Energy and mass are equivalent. They are different forms of the same thing. Mass is matter. Therefore, according to Einstein's Theory of Special Relativity, matter can be turned into energy, and energy can be turned into matter. If God is energy, then God can indeed create matter from nothing, using just energy and the speed of light. It's a classic case of intelligent design. Therefore from a scientific standpoint, God created matter. He created the heavens, the cosmos, the moon, sun, and stars, and the earth. He also created living creatures and living humans. And so our world began.

Eyewitness accounts of life during the creation period were passed down from Adam and Eve to subsequent generations until a learned man was tasked to write a testimony of this in a document called "Genesis."

Research shows that Moses was responsible and directed by God to create Genesis, the first book of the Bible. Moses collected the verbal and written accounts of creation and then wrote the book of Genesis under divine guidance. We now believe that he used the words of Adam, Noah (son of Lamech and an 8th generation grandson of Adam), Noah's three sons (Shem, Ham, and Japheth), Terah (Shem's son, and the father of Abram/Abraham, and an 8th generation grandson of Noah), Ishmael (Abraham's first born child), Isaac (Abraham's son by Sarah), Esau and Jacob (sons of Isaac), and Joseph (son of Jacob) to produce this historical document. According to the Bible, Moses was trained in the "wisdom of the Egyptians" and could read cuneiform writings on clay tablets and Hebrew on papyrus and animal skins. Some believe Moses carried the information with him and wrote Genesis during the 40 days he was up on Mount Sinai.

As an engineer with an inquisitive mind seeking the truth, I decided that my best approach is to simply present what the Bible says and let you decide.

This scientific study of the supernatural nature of the Bible begins in the book of Genesis where we read about the beginning of our world. The name Genesis comes from the Greek word for "origins." Essentially it's a book about the beginning of the universe, the earth, and its inhabitants.

The King James translation of the Bible starts with the words *"In the beginning God created the heavens and the earth"* (Genesis 1:1). Some later interpretations made the word "heavens" singular, but the original Hebrew writings say "heavens." The first thing that struck me was that God created "heavens," not just "heaven." Some scholars believe that the good and bad angels battled it out and the evil angels were ousted here, before anything else was created.

The next things I noticed were the words "earth," "formless," "empty," "darkness over the surface of the deep," and the "Spirit of God" hovering "over the waters" (Genesis 1:2).

Then Genesis describes the awesome power of a supreme being we call "God." Just by speaking, matter was formed, molded and shaped. In Genesis 1:3, 9, 11, 14, 20, 24, and 26 we read, *"Then God said, 'Let there be...' So there was...."*

Creation is a fascinating series of events. Even evolutionists marvel when science continues to uncover more facts about how our world began and confirms that intelligent design (divine creation) is not only possible but plausible. While skeptics scratch their heads and agnostics look on in amazement, each year more events, people, and places described in the Bible thousands of years ago are confirmed and acknowledged.

The entire scientific world was recently jolted by the discovery that the *Higgs boson* ("bow-sahn") or *"God particle"* is real. Theorized in 1964 by British physicist Peter Higgs, he and teams of other physicists in America and Belgium, conducted research over the past 45 years to actually find a Higgs boson subatomic particle. On July 4, 2012, scientists announced that the existence of the Higgs boson was confirmed in two independent tests by over 6,000 scientists. This subatomic particle is the building block of all matter. Like a force field, the Higgs boson is the invisible sticky force that holds our universe together and produces mass. It is the link between energy and matter, and it confirms Einstein's Special Theory of Relativity. The discovery of the Higgs boson completes the Standard Model of particle physics, the equivalent of the Periodic Table in chemistry. This discovery opens a new era of technology and development just as Newton's laws of gravity led to basic equations of mechanics and made the industrial revolution possible.

It has already revolutionized communications. When Higgs boson research began, scientists created the

ARPANET, a network forum for advanced research projects. This evolved into the Internet and the World Wide Web.

Today, new findings and discoveries like this are rapidly coming as "those things hidden in the Bible" are being made known to us. And we're learning that scientific and archeological discoveries consistently prove that events reported in the Bible actually occurred as recorded thousands of years ago.

Eleven times in the first chapter of Genesis, God used words to cause change and produce matter. He spoke and it was so. (Genesis 1:3) *"Then God said...,"* and there was light (the first day). (Genesis 1:6) *"Then God said ...,"* and the waters covering the earth parted into water above and below with a sky and a real horizon (the second day). (Genesis 1:9) *"Then God said ...,"* and the water under the sky came together to form dry land with water and earth. (Genesis 1:11) *"Then God said...,"* and the earth produced vegetation. (It was the third day.) (Genesis 1:14) *"Then God said ...,"* and stars, the moon and the sun appeared in the sky to separate day from night (the fourth day). (Genesis 1:20) *"Then God said ..."* and sea creatures and flying birds appeared. On this same day, *"God blessed them and ..."* they were able to reproduce. (It was the fifth day). (Genesis 1:24) *"Then God said...,"* and living animals appeared on the earth. (Genesis 1:26) *"Then God said...,"* and a male was formed out of the dust of the earth and made in God's own image.

Then God created a female from part of man to be a companion for the male, someone to be his partner in life. The man called her "woman" because she was taken out of him. *"God blessed them ...,"* and they were able to reproduce their own kind and were charged with ruling the fish, the birds and all the animals on earth. *"God said...,"* and humans were able to eat the plants with seeds and fruit from the trees, thus sustaining life. It was the sixth day of creation. (Genesis 2:2) On the seventh day, God rested. He blessed this seventh day and made it holy to set an example for mankind to follow.

When did the world begin? For decades the Christian, Jewish, and secular world have argued over when the earth was actually formed. I remember heated arguments over whether the earth began millions of years, tens of thousands of years, or just several thousand years ago. Since I am prone to evaluate all hypotheses, I formed the opinion that all sides are right. God has His own time line. To Him a day can be a thousand years.

As God gives us answers, we continue to fill in the puzzle of our existence. The earth itself can indeed be a million years old. What is this but a blink of an eye to a supreme being who controls all aspects of time? The mass of what we call earth could have been in space for eons, gradually hardening into shape with land drying out and even dust appearing.

God made man out of this dust and blew life into his nostrils. This made man live. This could have occurred 10,000 years ago. Or it could have been 30,000 years ago as ancient Sumerian writings suggest. (There is a Sumerian list of kings claiming that these kings ruled the Sumerian people about 30,000 years before the Great Flood, but ancient scribes tended to embellish and lengthen time periods, particularly how long a ruler was in power, so we're not really sure.)

In my research I found information that the Sumerian culture was the first of its kind, and it existed from 3100 to 2100 BC. In the book *A History of Israel*, Colman Mockler, Distinguished Professor of the Old Testament and writing under the pen name Walter Kaiser, compiled a table listing the approximate dates of the chronology of Israel's history. In the table, he shows the oldest date for the ancient world to be between 8500 BC and 7500 BC (what he calls the "Pre-Pottery Neolithic age). Another source claims the earth is about 4,000 years old and puts the catastrophic flood that covered the earth at around 2600 BC in the Bronze Age. Take your choice: ancient, or really ancient!

But let's get back to the creation story. Initially the earth was covered with a canopy of fog that protected the planet from the intense sun and provided a mist that kept the earth cool. It didn't rain, so there were no plants or bushes on the land. Underground water seeped up out of the earth and dampened the entire surface of the planet. The land part of earth was one huge supercontinent. During a symposium on continental drift in 1927, this supercontinent was named *Pangaea*.

Once God made man, He made a beautiful, tranquil, and peaceful park called the "Garden of Eden" with trees that bore delicious fruit. He told man that he could eat the fruit of any tree in the garden except from two trees in the center of the park. One was the Tree of Life, and the second was the Tree of Knowledge of Good and Evil. The first gave immortality. The second gave wisdom.

God put man in charge of the garden and all animals and living things that He created. Man was told to farm the land and care for it. God gave him a helpmate that the man called "Eve," and they were both made responsible for managing God's creation.

God formed a river in the Garden of Eden to water the land. As the river flowed out of the Garden, it divided into four rivers: the Pishon, the Gihon, the Tigris, and the Euphrates.

The land area from the Nile River in Egypt, up along the eastern Mediterranean (encompassing the Jordan River in Israel), and the land that today we know as Syria, Jordan, Turkey, Iraq, Armenia, Kuwait, and Iran (including the Tigris and Euphrates Rivers) forms a half-moon shape that was called the "Fertile Crescent." Civilization began somewhere in this Fertile Crescent. The word "Eden" means "fertile plain" in Sumerian. Eden means "delight" in Hebrew. It means "fruitful, well-watered" in Aramaic.

We're not certain where the original Garden of Eden was located. For years, archeologists thought that the Garden of Eden was between the northern end of the Tigris and Euphrates or somewhere in this vicinity. In an online search I found at least 10 suggested locations: northern Iran, eastern Turkey, southern Iraq, northeast Africa, Lumeria (a continent that sunk in the Indian Ocean), the Seychelles, the South China Sea, Israel near Jerusalem, the American state of Missouri, and even Mars (for those "far out" researchers).

Current satellite photos have shown a set of dry riverbeds in the region of Israel and Lebanon that may actually be the original site of these four rivers. There is considerable support for this location because of the historical importance of this area and the comment by Ezekiel (Ezekiel 28:13-14) when he said of Jerusalem, "You were in Eden, the garden of God."

Other satellite photos show the existence of "fossil rivers" (dry riverbeds) in Iran and Armenia (in the Caucasus region of Eurasia).

An accurate identification is still to be determined. The Great Flood of Noah's day was such a worldwide catastrophe that the topography of the whole earth changed. The supercontinent of Pangaea split into several continents with volcanoes, earthquakes, and rampant severe weather. These events changed the landscape of earth. It's likely that the Garden of Eden is now buried under many feet of sediment (or water).

Research continues, but it does strongly suggest that man appeared in the Fertile Crescent, Adam and Eve were the first humans, and these two people created the whole human race.

Genesis 3:1 says that there was also a serpent in this garden. This serpent could talk, and some think it could walk. Rabbi David Fohrman, director of the Hoffberger Foundation for Torah Studies and adjunct professor at John Hopkins University, wrote in *Jewish World Review* that this primal serpent walked and talked. Others think the serpent was actually a dragon or gecko-like creature. And still others claim the serpent was a fallen angel.

The Jewish Zohar (Book of Spendour) describes this serpent as standing upright on two hind legs. Ancient Egyptian carvings show the serpent as a slender biped standing just taller than a human.

We don't know for certain, but, since this reptile was actually Satan, it would be easy for Satan to change his physical look and action. The serpent was the personification of evil. It was crafty and tempted Eve to eat fruit from the Tree of Knowledge of Good and Evil. When she did, she gave some to Adam, who also ate the fruit. Thus sin entered their lives and Adam and Eve recognized that they were naked. They fell from grace and were banned from the Garden of Eden. From this point on, the woman experienced pain in childbirth, the land outside the Garden was difficult to cultivate, and plants grew thorns.

To prevent their getting to the Tree of Life, God placed an angel on the east side of the garden (from where they were expelled) with a flaming sword that flashed back and forth.

Adam and Eve lost their beautiful garden home because of sin and were forced to settle on lands outside the Garden. To the east of the Garden, Adam and Eve tended flocks of animals and raised crops.

Bible scholars believe they settled on the "Plain of Sumer" (or Shinar) in what is now Armenia. There they began the first family, starting with Cain and Abel and then other children. The Sumerians were the first group or civilization to form.

According to Genesis 4:16, after Cain killed Abel, he moved away from Adam and Eve and lived in the land of Nod further to the east of Eden. In Hebrew, Nod means "to wander." Adam and Eve had more children and so did Cain.

As the population of the earth grew, people initially communicated orally, passing down verbal stories about their ancestors and "life back then." Gradually the people began to communicate in writing, too. The first form of writing consisted of wedge-shaped impressions in clay. Wedge (cuneia) writing became the Cuneiform of ancient civilizations. In Hebrew, the word "write" means "to dig" or "cut in." Abraham, Isaac, and Jacob wrote in Cuneiform. Clay tablets found in Egypt contain Cuneiform letters carved in clay back around 1400 BC. Eventually papyrus replaced clay as the writing surface. Moses took all of this into account when he compiled the book Genesis.

Civilizations developed and went away as men and women progressed in their relationship with God and with each other. And it all happened because God first commanded it to be. Words produced matter from nothing. And so the genesis of life occurred.

Against the Gods: Devastating Plagues Strike Egypt

*The Egyptians will know that I am the Lord
when I use my power against Egypt.*
EXODUS 7:5

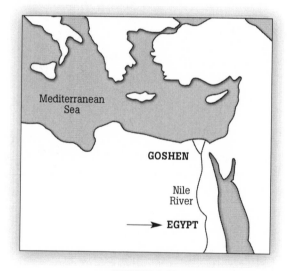

EXODUS 6–11
Location: Egypt | **Historical Time:** Late Bronze Age – ca 1445 BC;
Another reference says 1391–1271 BC
TO VIEW MAPS ONLINE:
Copy this link into your browser and press Enter/Return
en.wikipedia.org/wiki/File:Ancient_Egypt_map-en.svg

FOR THE ISRAELITES, LIFE IN EGYPT SINCE JOSEPH WAS
Grand Vizier—second in command to the pharaoh—had
changed greatly. The Pharaoh and the friendly people that
Joseph and Jacob lived among had all died and joined

their ancestors. During their lives the population of Israelites had grown significantly since the 70 who first migrated south with Jacob. The generations of Jacob and Joseph were gone, but the number of Israelites continued to increase, and they became their own nation within the kingdom of Egypt. This worried the next pharaoh (Seti I?). He wasn't familiar with Joseph, so he organized the male Israelites into work battalions as conscripts. Later he made them unpaid slaves.

Moses had been born to an Israelite couple named Amram and Jochebed. The pharaoh thought there were too many Israelites, so he gave these people increasingly more difficult physical tasks. He was trying to significantly slow their birth rate. Instead of dying from overwork, they thrived.

Finally, he ordered that all the newborn Hebrew boys be killed at childbirth. Fear swept through the Israelite nation. Moses' mother, Jochebed, hid baby Moses and then, when three months old, placed him in a waterproof basket and set him adrift in the bulrushes along the Nile. The basket was discovered by the pharaoh's daughter (the Jewish Midrash [Lev. R. § 1] called the foster mother of Moses Bithiah), and she adopted the baby. Moses' sister Miriam was watching and offered to find someone to care for the baby. The mother of Moses, Jochebed, was recruited and raised her own child in the royal house of the pharaoh without their learning her real identity.

Moses was educated in the pharaoh's palace by the best teachers from around the known world and grew to be an educated and intelligent man. But he was still a "foreigner" adopted into the royal court. One day he saw an Egyptian taskmaster beating an exhausted slave and Moses interceded, killing the Egyptian.

The next day Moses discovered that his action had become known and the pharaoh had decided to kill him, so he fled to Midian across the Red Sea. There he came to the rescue of seven young women shepherdesses who were being harassed by a band of rude shepherds. These women were daughters of Reuel (or Raguel), priest of Midian and sisters of Hobab. They tended a large flock of Reuel's sheep. Moses married Zipporah, one of the daughters of Reuel, and Hobab became his brother-in-law. Moses lived with the family there in Midian for 40 years. Scholars believe that Jethro and Reuel were the same person, or a sibling of Hobab. Moses helped tend the flocks of Jethro and the rest of the Reuel family.

In the meantime, the pharaoh died and the Hebrew slaves in Egypt came under increasingly harsh treatment involving backbreaking labor and unbearable beatings. God heard their cries and used Moses to help free them from bondage.

Moses was on Mount Horeb tending the flocks of Jethro, when he came upon a bush that was on fire but not being consumed. God was in the bush. It was a theophany (manifestation of God), and God told Moses to remove his sandals because that was a holy place. Moses did, and then God commanded him to return to Egypt to bring the Israelites out and up to the land promised to the descendants of Abraham.

Overcoming his fear, Moses and his older brother Aaron went to Egypt to confront the pharaoh and demand the release of over a million Israelite slaves. Moses was charged with getting the pharaoh to release the Israelites, but a speech impediment prevented him from talking clearly.

Aaron was a skilled orator and Levite priest, so Aaron was selected to go with Moses and do most of the talking.

They went to the pharaoh and asked him to release the Hebrew people so they could go into the desert to worship and sacrifice to their God. But Israelite slaves made up a large part of the market economy in Egypt and the arrogant pharaoh was unwilling to let them go. These slaves worked for free and were fed just enough to keep them strong so they could work hard, long hours on construction and farming projects. He didn't think these two men and their Hebrew God posed a significant threat to his political and economic status and power. He remained hard-nosed and unbending.

So Moses and Aaron began to display the power of God to the pharaoh by turning their walking sticks into snakes. Pharaoh's magicians did the same thing with their walking sticks. Although Aaron's snake swallowed the vipers of the Egyptian magicians, the pharaoh's determination to maintain the status quo held, and Moses and Aaron were dragged away from his presence and thrown out of the palace.

This initiated a series of plagues over the next 12 months that God used to humble an arrogant pharaoh and directly challenge and defeat the gods of Egypt.

Egyptian society was polytheistic. They worshiped many gods, and there was a god for everything. There were over 80 gods that they believed controlled life and living in Egypt. Upper and Lower Egypt were comprised of a number of regions, and each region also had its own gods, so in all there were over 2,000 gods in the country. It was against these false gods that the God of Israel acted. God chose to hit the Egyptians where they were most vulnerable: through their water, their land, their animals, their food supply, and finally their firstborn children. He demonstrated that the Egyptian gods were powerless against the God of Israel.

God brought 10 plagues to Egypt. He caused them in His own time. All but three were announced to the pharaoh before they began. The first three directly involved the Nile River. One involved power over matter, six involved power over nature, one centered on power over animals, one involved power over people, and two involved power over life and death.

POWER DEMONSTATED IN THE 10 PLAGUES

PLAGUE 1: Power over Matter (Nile River Turns into Blood)

PLAGUE 2: Power over Nature (Overrun by Frogs)

PLAGUE 3: Power over Nature (Gnats, Fleas, and Lice)

PLAGUE 4: Power over Nature (Swarms of Biting Flies)

PLAGUE 5: Power over Life & Death (Livestock Die)

PLAGUE 6: Power over People (Boils and Open Sores)

PLAGUE 7: Power over Life & Death (Deadly Hail)

PLAGUE 8: Power over Nature (Locusts)

PLAGUE 9: Power over Nature (Complete Darkness)

PLAGUE 10: Power over Life & Death (Firstborn Die)

Nile River Turns Into Blood

All the water in the river turned into blood.
EXODUS 7:20

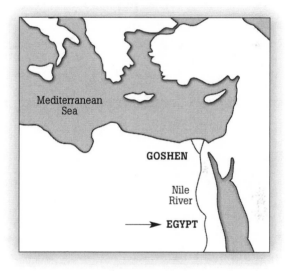

Mediterranean
Sea

GOSHEN

Nile
River

⟶ **EGYPT**

EXODUS 7:14–25
Location: Egypt | **Historical Time:** Late Bronze Age – ca 1445 BC
TO VIEW MAPS ONLINE:
Copy this link into your browser and press Enter/Return
en.wikipedia.org/wiki/File:Ancient_Egypt_map-en.svg

ALTHOUGH EGYPT IS BORDERED BY THE MEDITERRANEAN
Sea at the north, Libya on the west, Sudan on the south,
and Israel and Jordan on the east today, back then the
main population of Egypt lived in an area less than 30
miles wide and situated along the Nile River. In one place
the country was only two miles wide.

The Nile was the source of life for Egypt. The black soils deposited along its banks were very good for growing crops and made Egypt the breadbasket of the ancient world. Life and commerce revolved around this waterway, and it was critical to the success of the Egyptian nation.

The Nile is over 4,000 miles long (the longest river in the world). It originates south of the equator, flows northward through northeastern Africa through Upper and Lower Egypt into the delta area and out into the Mediterranean Sea.

In ancient times, there were no bridges over the Nile so water travel developed rapidly. The average width of this river is 1.7 miles (2.8 km). It's 4.7 miles (7.5 km) across at its widest point (near Edfu) and only 383 yards (350 m) at its narrowest place, the Silwa Gorge near Aswan.

Water depth averages between 26 and 36 feet (8-11 m), and 300 cubic meters of water discharge from the Nile into the Mediterranean each day.

Commerce, crops, people, and animal life depended on this river. So it had its own gods who were worshiped by the people.

Hapi was the spirit of the Nile. Hapi was the lord of the fish and birds, and even the marshes. The water in the Nile represented the bloodstream of the god Osiris, who controlled the underworld. The Egyptians also had a god for the hippopotamus (Tauret), for life in the Nile (Nu), and for the equatorial sources of the river (Khnum).

Bible scholars think the first plague involving the Nile occurred in June. In front of the pharaoh and his officials down by the river, Moses held out his walking rod and struck the surface of the river. Before their eyes the water immediately turned into blood. I didn't find historical data to explain how much river became blood, whether it was all the way from the headwaters near the equator down to where it empties into the Mediterranean, but that it occurred is significant.

This was a direct challenge to the gods who controlled this great waterway and a significant insult to the people and leadership of Egypt.

Microorganisms in the water can sometimes turn the Nile water reddish, but not into actual blood. In other parts of the world, this reddish condition is called the *"red tide."*

When the Nile turned a reddish color (red tide), marine life still lived and fish continued to be caught for food. But when it turned into blood during this plague, all the marine life died. The river stank and the banks and shorelines were covered with dead fish. Even the crocodiles and hippos had to abandon the river for cleaner waters.

Pharaoh's magicians duplicated the plague in a small way by turning water in some containers into blood and then back into water. But they couldn't turn the blood in the huge Nile River back into water. Still, their act was enough for the pharaoh to dismiss the plague and return to his palace.

This plague lasted seven days.

Over a 12-month period, 10 plagues affected Egypt and broke the arrogance and resistance of the pharaoh. These plagues were devastating to the leadership and people of Egypt. Their families, land, and economy were decimated. All of their gods had been proven powerless against the God of Israel. Egyptian morale was crushed and the Egyptians wanted these slaves to leave their country and get out of their lives.

When the pharaoh's son died that fateful night of the final plague, he gave in and told the Israelites to leave. It was after midnight. The Israelites quickly packed up everything they owned including foods they were preparing for meals. They even wrapped bread dough in clothes and carried it on their shoulders. (Later, during their sojourn away from Egypt, they baked and ate the bread they had taken with them. This began the tradition of eating unleavened bread during the eight-day celebration of Passover.)

Around 600,000 men on foot, plus women and children, and other non-Israelites departed with all their possessions. Historians estimate that two million people trudged out from the delta area of Lower Egypt and walked toward Sinai in the east, beginning an exodus that would last 40 years.

They left an Egypt destroyed by the power of God. But the judgment on Egypt had just begun. Worse calamity was to occur when the pharaoh changed his mind one last time and went after the fleeing Israelites.

Pillar of Cloud and Fire Leads a Nation

*And the Lord went before them by day
in a pillar of a cloud, to lead them the way;
and by night in a pillar of fire, to give them light.*
EXODUS 13:21

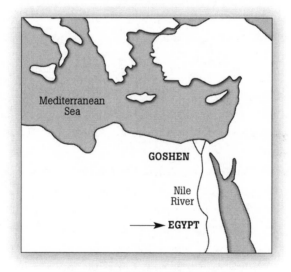

EXODUS 13:17–22; EXODUS 40:38
Location: Egypt to Palestine | **Historical Time:** Late Bronze Age – ca 1446 BC
TO VIEW MAPS ONLINE:
Copy this link into your browser and press Enter/Return
en.wikipedia.org/wiki/File:Ancient_Egypt_map-en.svg

THE ISRAELITES HAD BEEN IN EGYPT FOR 430 YEARS. HERE at the end of the Bronze Age, there were about three million Egyptians in Egypt. But there were almost four million

Israelites in the country. So there were more Israelites in Egypt than Egyptians.

Many were nautical people, sailing deep draft ships around the known world and trading with other nations. According to the late Walter Baucum, author of *Bronze Age Atlantis*, about half of them left Egypt before the Exodus and spread throughout the western Mediterranean. They became a nautical empire of sea peoples.

Those who remained in Egypt were made slaves to the pharaoh. This was when Moses entered the history of Israel and challenged the pharaoh and gods of Egypt to free the slaves from bondage.

When an exasperated pharaoh finally gave up and told Moses to get the Israelites out of Egypt, the largest mass migration in history began. Over two million people with animals and personal possessions began moving out of the Nile Delta and east toward the deserts of what is called Arabia today.

They traveled to Etham, a region on the edge of the wilderness, near one of the northern fingers of the Red Sea—the Gulf of Suez or the Gulf of Aqaba. (The Gulf of Aqaba is the most likely place.) East of here (in the Arabian Peninsula) there were no traveled roads or well-marked paths to follow, so God provided a visible guide in the form of a pillar of smoke and fire that mysteriously appeared (Exodus 13:21).

What was this pillar cloud? How big was it? What did it do? And how long was it present?

It was huge. It needed to be seen by several million people. It formed in front of the Israelites. As I tried to visualize a group this size, I looked for historical gatherings that were this large.

Civil rights leader Rev. Dr. Martin Luther King led 250,000 to 300,000 people in his March on Washington on August 28, 1963. Conservative celebrity Glenn Beck spoke to 300,000 to 500,000 people at his Restoring Honor rally in Washington, D.C. on August 28, 2010. Photos of these two events showed crowds that stretched almost a mile long and a quarter mile wide.

Based on my research, the supernatural pillar and cloud probably looked like a 150-foot column with a wide cloud base. According to Josephus writing in the book *Antiquities,* King Uzziah ruled Jerusalem in 791 BC. He had many towers built that were one hundred and fifty cubits high (a cubit was about 1.5 feet, so the towers were about 225 feet tall). The pillar of the Exodus needed to be seen from over a mile away, so it was also quite tall—150 feet high was tall enough. But this pillar moved.

The pillar of cloud served several purposes. It was a visible sign that God was present with the Israelites, and it protected them from the weather.

During the day, it took the form of a column of smoke. At night flashing fire could be seen in the cloud. God was present in this cloud. They called it the *Shekinah* (shuh kigh nuh), the place where God dwelled. Its continual presence showed the people that God was there protecting them. It moved as God willed and showed them the direction to follow.

The base also protected the people from the harsh elements and stifling heat there in the desert (1 Cor. 10). Its shade was said to contain moisture that cooled the people and the animals, protecting them from the scorching sun.

As the Israelites hurried to get away from a pharaoh who might change his mind about letting them go, they traveled day and night. At night, the cloud shined brightly bathing the path of the people in fire light.

The cloud was both supernatural and spiritual. This divine escort gave comfort and was a reminder that God was constantly with them. Blowing wind could not scatter or disperse it.

They traveled south and camped in Etham, but the cloud pillar moved from the encampment and led the people back toward Pi Hahiroth, the place where the reeds grow. Pi Hahiroth means a "mouth of water" in Hebrew. Here the shoreline of the Red Sea was shaped like an open mouth giving the area its name.

Red Sea Suddenly Parts for Crossing

Then Moses stretched out his hand over the sea.
All night long the Lord pushed back the sea with
a strong east wind and turned the sea into dry ground.
The water divided, and the Israelites went
through the middle of the sea on dry ground.
EXODUS 14:21, 22

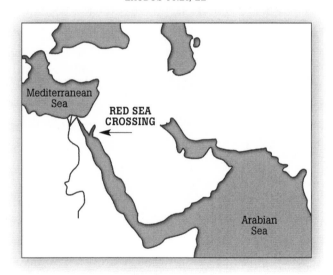

EXODUS 14:13-31
Location: Red Sea | **Historical Time:** Late Bronze Age – ca 1446 BC
TO VIEW MAPS ONLINE:
Copy this link into your browser and press Enter/Return
www.bible.ca/archeology/bible-archeology-maps.htm

ACROSS THE FINGER OF THE RED SEA, THE ISRAELITES could see Mount Tiran and the traditional home of the god of Baal-Zephon, the sea and storm god. From Pi Hahiroth to Mount Tiran was 19 km (about 12 miles) of open water.

Egyptian spies watched the Israelites go from Etham back toward Pi Hahiroth and assumed they had become confused and lost, afraid to venture into the wilderness and blocked by the open sea. They reported to the pharaoh that this was a good time to attack and destroy the Israelite nation.

The pharaoh regretted his decision to let the Israelites go. So he assembled a huge army consisting of all 600 of his royal chariots and all the other chariots in Egypt. He gathered 50,000 horsemen and over 200,000 infantry. Then they set out for Pi Hahiroth to get his slaves back.

Moses and the people arrived at Pi Hahiroth near the shore of the Red Sea. Not far from Pi Hahiroth was a watch-tower called Migdol. Pharaoh and his huge army raced toward Pi Hahiroth, and Israelite lookouts saw the huge dust created by the approaching Egyptians and reported to Moses. They were worried that all of them would soon perish. The Israelites were trapped, but God had another plan. He allowed the Egyptian force to race toward the Israelites.

Then the tall column of smoke and fire moved from in front of the Israelites and positioned behind them, standing between the terrified Israelites and the approaching Egyptians. There it stood as a silent column of power, its base wide and dark. Night came and the fire in the cloud lit up the scene. The Egyptians were closing. To them the bottom of the pillar looked like a broad cloud of darkness. On the side facing the Israelites it looked like fire light. The Egyptians stopped, and both sides stood their ground with the pillar of cloud between them.

Moses told the people to not be afraid. God was about to show them His power, and they would soon never see these Egyptians again. Inwardly Moses was fearful and cried out to God. God told him to stop praying and start doing. He told Moses to get the people moving toward the shoreline and the open water of the Red Sea. Then he told Moses that once there, he was to raise and hold his walking staff over the water. God said He would divide the water so the nation of Israel could pass through the sea on dry ground. He also told Moses that the Egyptians would be stubborn and follow the Israelites out onto the seabed where they would be defeated.

Suddenly a strong east wind began blowing in the faces of the fleeing Israelites, pushing the deep water back and holding both sides of the sea apart so the seabed could dry out. Stirred on by the command of God, the entire nation of Israel began crossing over the sea on dry land between two tall walls of water. The seabed had a slope from the shoreline down to about 50 feet below sea level and then up on the opposite side, so the walls of water in the center of the passage were pretty tall.

It was about 12 miles across and the Israelites could move along at only two to three miles an hour. Remember that they had children, mothers with babies, cattle, and sheep so the movement was slow. They traveled all night.

As the Israelites were reaching the eastern shore of the gulf, the Egyptians moved into the parted sea and followed cautiously. They felt something supernatural about the cloud of fire ahead of them, but they moved ahead. The hot winds from the desert to the east blew down through the trench formed by the two walls of water but the cloud did not break up or dissipate in the wind. Instead it followed slowly behind the escaping Israelites.

Two significant supernatural things occurred during this event. First, the sea stayed parted all night long—for about six hours. Second, a cloud of fire and smoke accompanied, led, and protected the people as they moved over a dry seabed. God's power over matter was being visibly demonstrated to the Israelites and to the Egyptians.

Wall of Water Collapses on Army

The water flowed back and covered Pharaoh's entire army as well as the chariots and the cavalry that had followed Israel into the sea.

EXODUS 14:28

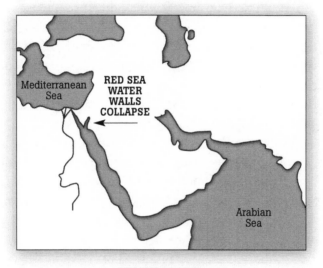

EXODUS 14:23-31
Location: Red Sea | **Historical Time:** Late Bronze Age – ca 1446 BC
TO VIEW MAPS ONLINE:
Copy this link into your browser and press Enter/Return
www.bible.ca/archeology/bible-archeology-maps.htm

AS THE GRAY LIGHT OF DAWN APPEARED IN THE EAST, THE last of the Israelites reached the eastern shore of the gulf. Then the Shekinah cloud suddenly moved around the Israelites and positioned on shore at the side of the nation of Israel.

I can just imagine the feeling Pharaoh had upon seeing his prey up out of the dry sea floor on land and ready to escape into the wilderness beyond. With a shout of anger he ordered his army to attack. A quarter of a million soldiers surged ahead, eager to finish off the former slaves. Yes, that's 250,000 men!

They got closer and could see their prey on the shore ahead. But suddenly the seabed became soft and the wheels of the chariots began to bog down snapping from the axles and stranding the chariots where they stuck. The horses of the cavalry slipped and fell, dumping riders onto the muddy seabed. The Egyptians recognized that the Lord was fighting for Israel and they frantically began to retreat. Sloshing through the deepening mud, they struggled to get back to the Egyptian side of the gulf.

Then from the cloud, God told Moses to stretch out his hand and hold his walking stick out over the sea. Moses did and the wind abruptly stopped, allowing the walls of water to collapse. As the morning sun burst out over the scene, the entire Egyptian force was deluged by the sea. Pandemonium changed to panic. The Egyptians were trapped at the bottom of 10 to 50 feet of seawater. Covered by the deep water, the pharaoh and his entire army drowned. Many bodies washed up on the shore near Moses confirming that no one had survived and was left to harm them. Wild jubilation broke out as the people of Israel celebrated and sang praises to God.

They had escaped the bondage in Egypt. And the cloud was still there with them. More of their sojourn lay ahead as they moved out into the desert and all the way to the Promised Land.

Pillar Cloud
Continues to Appear

*In all their travels, whenever the column of smoke
moved from the tent, the Israelites would break camp.
But if the column didn't move, they wouldn't break camp.*

EXODUS 40:36

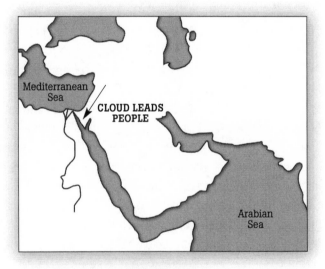

Mediterranean
Sea

CLOUD LEADS
PEOPLE

Arabian
Sea

EXODUS 13–21
Location: Arabian Peninsula | **Historical Time:** Late Bronze Age – ca 1446 BC
TO VIEW MAPS ONLINE:
Copy this link into your browser and press Enter/Return
en.wikipedia.org/wiki/Arabian_Peninsula

THE ISRAELITES WERE SAFELY AWAY FROM THE EGYPTIAN
threat. But they still faced dangers and disappointments.
The cloud moved over in front and led the nation into the
Desert of Shur at the north end of the Sinai Peninsula.
They walked for three days without finding water. And

they began to complain. Finally they came to Marah, a place with water, but the water was bitter. Moses tossed some wood into the bitter pool, and the water instantly became sweet and drinkable.

As the people quenched their thirst and tended to their flocks and herds, Moses told the people what God commanded regarding laws and rules for them to follow. He explained that if they obeyed God, they would never have to suffer any of the diseases inflicted on the Egyptians.

The cloud moved leading the people to Elim. The oasis here had 12 springs and 70 palm trees, so they camped here until the cloud moved again. And so began around three years of traveling, making and then breaking camp as they headed toward Canaan led by the cloud of glory.

At Mount Sinai, the Israelites constructed a special tent with a tabernacle for offering sacrifices to God. The Shekinah cloud entered the tent and moved outside only when it was time for the people to move along on their sojourn. Numbers 9 describes how the cloud covered the tabernacle with the Tent of Meeting from evening until morning. It appeared like a cloud of smoke during the day and as fire during the night. When it moved, the Israelites broke camp and followed the cloud.

The cloud led them to Rephidim near Mount Horeb where God instructed Moses to strike a rock releasing water for the people to drink. Two months after they had left Egypt, Moses' father-in-law, Jethro, the priest of Midian, located them in the desert and brought Moses' wife and sons to him. Jethro helped Moses organize the nation into groups with appointed leaders who would resolve minor issues between the people. Moses would hear the difficult cases and judge after getting direction from God.

Numbers 12 describes an incident where Miriam and Aaron became jealous of the wife Moses chose and were severely chastised by God speaking out of the cloud at the entrance to the Tent of Meeting. When the Shekinah cloud moved away from the tent, Miriam had become leprous and the leprosy afflicted her for seven days.

According to the Jewish Seder 'Olam ix, the cloud left when Aaron died and the Ark of the Covenant became the substitute dwelling place of God. It was carried ahead of the Israelites by priests until the Philistines took the ark away from the sinful Hebrews. Then God left the Ark and dwelling place. But the cloud of Shekinah was always there, unseen until God wanted to make it visible.

When the Israelites reached the Promised Land about 1406 BC, the cloud of Shekinah no longer led the Hebrew nation from place to place. But it did appear periodically to chastise, punish, or inform the Israelite people. It was present when major incidents occurred.

Around 570 BC during the exile of the Israelites to Babylon, the prophet Ezekiel (Ezekiel 1:1-28) saw a great cloud come out of the north with a stormy wind (Ezekiel 1). It was bright and fire continually flashed in it. Ezekiel 1:28 confirms that this cloud was a visual appearance of the likeness of the glory of the Lord.

According to the Bible, the Shekinah cloud appeared several more times (around 33 AD). In the New Testament, Luke 9:29 describes the transfiguration of Christ. The appearance of Jesus changed and his clothing became bright white. Two men appeared and began talking with Jesus about his pending departure. Peter, John and James saw them and suggested to Jesus that they make three tabernacles: one for Jesus, one for Moses, and one for Elijah.

A cloud overshadowed them and they became frightened as it covered them. But a voice from within the cloud told them that Jesus was the Son of God. The voice commanded them to listen to Him. Then the cloud and Moses and Elijah disappeared and Jesus stood alone with the apostles.

The next time a cloud is mentioned in the New Testament is in Acts 1:9 when Jesus ascended into heaven. After talking with the apostles, Jesus was taken up into a cloud, and they no longer could see him. Suddenly two men in white were standing by them. They told the apostles that Jesus will come back from heaven in the same way that they saw him leave. He will come back in a Shekinah cloud (Acts 1:11).

Strange Food (Manna) Provides Daily Food

... in the morning, there was a layer of dew around the camp. When the dew was gone, the ground was covered with a thin layer of flakes like frost on the ground.

EXODUS 16:13-14

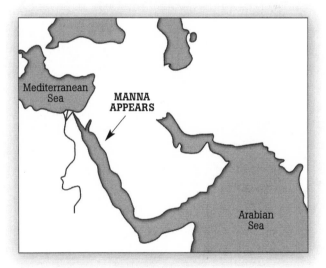

Mediterranean Sea

MANNA APPEARS

Arabian Sea

EXODUS 16:13-26
Location: Arabian Peninsula to Jordan River
Historical Time: Late Bronze Age – ca 1446 BC
TO VIEW MAPS ONLINE:
Copy this link into your browser and press Enter/Return
en.wikipedia.org/wiki/Arabian_Peninsula

WHILE THE ISRAELITES CONTINUED THEIR EXODUS, THEY often complained about their condition. God patiently provided for their needs.

When their food ran out, He sent meat in the form of quail. Then He provided food for baking. Each morning (except on the Sabbath) the Israelites found the ground covered with a thin layer of flakes that looked like frost. It was edible and tasted like coriander seeds. The Israelites used it to make wafers of sweet-tasting food. They called it "manna." In Hebrew, manna means "What is it?"

They collected and ate manna for the next 40 years. Manna last appeared on the ground the morning after celebrating the Passover at Gilgal, a new town in the Jericho plain of the Promised Land. From then on no more manna appeared, and they ate crops and produce that grew there in Canaan. *(Joshua 5:12)*

Commandments Etched on Stone Tablets

Then He gave him the two tablets with His words on them, stone tablets inscribed by God Himself.
EXODUS 31:18

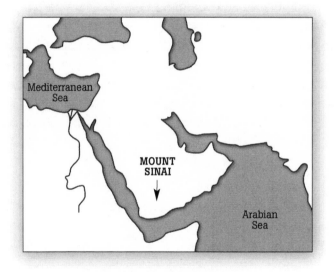

EXODUS 31:18; EXODUS 32:15-19
Location: Arabian Peninsula Mount Sinai
Historical Time: Late Bronze Age – ca 1446 BC
TO VIEW MAPS ONLINE:
Copy this link into your browser and press Enter/Return
en.wikipedia.org/wiki/Mount_Sinai

MOSES WAS UP ON MOUNT SINAI FOR 40 DAYS AND 40 nights getting specific instructions from God. God wrote His law in the form of 10 Commandments on both sides of two stone tablets. He gave the tablets to Moses so he could share these laws with the Israelites and teach them His rules for life and living.

Moses started back down the mountain carrying the tablets, but when he reached the base of Mount Sinai, he found that his brother Aaron, had allowed the people to revert to idolatry. They had constructed and were worshiping a golden calf.

In a fit of rage, Moses threw the tablets down smashing them on the ground *(Exodus 32:19)*. Then he smashed the idol of the golden calf into tiny pieces, ground it into powder, scattered the powder on the pool of water nearby, and then made the people drink the water. God was also angry and planned to destroy the sinful people, but Moses pleaded with God not to destroy these "stiff-necked" people. God let the people live (unless they further disobeyed his commands), but he specified how they were to act.

Wooden Ark
has Power
to Heal or Destroy

And I have set there a place for the ark, wherein is the covenant of the Lord, which He made with our fathers, when He brought them out of the land of Egypt.

1 KINGS 8:21

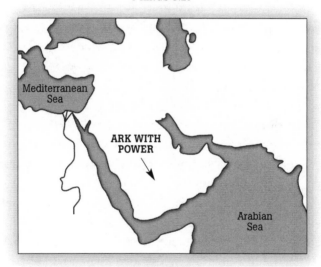

I KINGS 8:21

Location: Arabian Peninsula | **Historical Time:** Iron Age – ca 1271–586 BC

TO VIEW MAPS ONLINE:

Copy this link into your browser and press Enter/Return

www.bible.ca/archeology/bible-archeology-exodus-route-straits-of-tiran.htm
www.biblepages.web.surftown.se/ho06.htm
en.wikipedia.org/wiki/The_Exodus

WHAT IS THE ARK OF THE COVENANT? WHAT DOES IT LOOK like? What does it contain? Why was it made? And where is it now?

Many people think that the Ark was likely destroyed in 586 BC along with the temple in Jerusalem. But they don't know for sure. If the original Ark were to be found, church leaders claim that the discovery would be interesting but not spiritually significant. To them perhaps, but for the rest of the 6.4 billion people on our planet, this discovery would be a colossal event, because it would confirm Bible truth and shatter atheistic myths about the existence of God. It would rattle the Islamic world to its core, and it would bring millions back into favor with God.

In the movie *Raiders of the Lost Ark*, Harrison Ford makes a comment that finding the Ark would be the most significant archeological discovery in history. And he was correct. The Ark represents God's light to the whole world. It held mysterious powers then, and this may still be true today.

While Moses was leading the Israelite nation away from Egypt toward the Promised Land up on the western side of the Jordan River, God made a covenant with these, His chosen people. He told them that if they trusted and obeyed Him, they would never suffer diseases like the Egyptians did during the plagues leading up to the Hebrew release from slavery. God told them that He would protect and care for them.

Twice He wrote his commands (Ten Commandments) on stone tablets. The first set of tablets were broken when Moses returned from up on Mount Sinai and found the people worshiping a golden calf instead of God. The second set of commands were placed inside a special chest or ark.

God became so angry at the sinful behavior of the Israelites that He told Moses that He would leave these people to die there in the wilderness and no longer protect and guide them. Moses begged God to remain with them, and He did, but only after a special tent and dwelling place had been built.

The tent was the Tabernacle, the temple in which only the priests of God could enter and offer sacrifice. The dwelling place of God was at the top of a gold-covered wooden box called the Ark of the Covenant.

The Tabernacle tent had two rooms. The outer room (Holy room) was entered throughout the year by priests from the tribe of Levi. In this outer room, the priests worshiped, prayed, and sprinkled sacrificial blood toward the inner room. This innermost room was called the "Holy of Holies," and it was here that the Ark of the Covenant was kept. Once a year, on the Day of Atonement (Yom Kippur), the "high priest" would enter and sprinkle sacrificial blood on the top of the Ark on behalf of the sins of the Israelite people.

God commanded Moses to have the craftsman Bezalel build an ark out of acacia (shitta) wood. This Ark would hold the commands and promises of God. It contained an agreement between God and the nation of Israel. If the people would obey and worship God, they could enjoy the peace and protection that only God can provide. But if they sin, they would suffer dearly. So the Ark was associated with judgment and wrath. And it had mysterious power to destroy or to heal.

The Ark of acacia wood was 45 inches (2.5 cubits) long, 27 inches (1.5 cubits) wide, and 27 inches (1.5 cubits) deep. The wood was covered inside and out with gold, and the box had a gold molding around it. A gold ring (possibly iron with gold plating) was connected to each corner at the bottom of the box, and two acacia poles were carved and slid into each set of rings so the Ark could be lifted and carried along by the priests as the Israelites moved from place to place.

The lid on top the Ark was made from pure gold. This lid was called the "Throne of Mercy" or "Mercy Seat." The statues of two angels were hammered out of a single piece of gold and placed on the Mercy Seat so the angels were at each end facing one another. Their wings touched and overshadowed the throne. God dwelled on the Mercy Seat during the exodus of the people of Israel.

Inside the Ark, Moses placed three things: the stone tablets containing the Ten Commandments, a golden bowl containing manna, and Aaron's walking staff that had budded overnight and produced almonds.

The stone tablets are called the "Tables of Testimony." They describe what God is like and how He wants us to live. They are the basis for God's covenant with Israel. It would not take long for the Israelites to break this covenant when they disobeyed God's commandments and they suffered for this. God never breaks His agreements.

The Golden Pot of Manna was a vessel that contained a tenth of a bushel (an omer) of manna collected from the ground. Exodus 16 describes how God sent manna six days a week with the early morning dew. It had to be gathered quickly because the hot sun would evaporate most of the manna and any residue would breed worms and smell. Manna looked like white coriander seed. It was said to taste like wafer biscuits made with honey. The Golden Pot of Manna in the Ark was a memorial to future generations showing how God cared for His people during the difficult exodus sojourn in the desert.

Aaron's rod was proof that God wanted his priests to come from the tribe of Levi. Numbers 17 says that the Israelites were complaining and arguing over who should lead them in worship and sacrifice. Moses had a rod marked for each of the 12 tribes placed before the Ark so God could tell them which tribe would be selected to serve as priests. Aaron was the leader of the Levites. Overnight Aaron's rod sprouted with blossoms and ripe almonds. Aaron had been selected.

God told Moses to place Aaron's rod inside the Ark of the Covenant to show which tribe God had chosen for priestly duties.

Moses also wrote God's covenant in a book and placed it in the side of the Ark. This book was called the "Book of the Covenant" or "Book of the Law." Some believe this Book also contained the story of Genesis, the beginning of history. It disappeared years later when the Ark was taken from the Israelites by the Philistines.

Next Moses had other furnishings made for the "tent of the words of God's promise" (the Tent of Meeting)—a Table of Shewbread complete with plates, dishes, bowls, and pitchers, an Altar of Incense, and a Seven-Branched Lamp-stand (Menora). All were covered with gold.

God had Moses institute a strict protocol for entering and conducting affairs within the tabernacle tent. This was the beginning of a formal ritual for offerings and worship.

Exodus 13:21 describes how God led the Israelites from inside a column of smoke during the day and a column of fire at night. These columns were constantly present while the Tabernacle Tent (Tent of Meeting) and the Ark of the Covenant were being built.

Once the Tabernacle and Ark were dedicated to God, the column of smoke filled the tent. There was fire in the smoke at night, but the tent never burned. When the smoke moved out and away from the tent, the Israelites broke camp and followed the column of smoke. When the smoke entered the tent and remained inside, the Israelites would pitch their tents and stay.

God resided on the Mercy Seat between the two cherubim there on the Ark in the Holy of Holies inner room. Only the high priest could approach the Ark and prepare it for being transported once the column of smoke had moved outside. And then only the Levite priests could carry the Ark of the Covenant as the nation of Israel wandered in the wilderness. God kept them wandering about in the desert for 40 years and waited for their generation to age and die. At the same time, He was teaching them how to live. They were told to pass these guidelines down to their children. Some followed God's guidelines for living. Others turned away and suffered for their actions. Many were (and still are) a stubborn people.

Priests carried the Ark ahead of the Israelite army led by Joshua as they crossed the parted Jordan River and claimed the land promised them by God. And the Ark was carried in front of the Israelite armies as they went into battle. It was called the "Lord of Armies." God used the Ark to show the people that without Him they could not win, but with God, they would be victorious over any enemy. This enabled Joshua and the Israelite army to defeat the forces of 31 kings. The Israelites with their God struck fear in the hearts of everyone they faced causing many to seek peace with Israel. God didn't want the Israelites to intermarry with their enemies, but they did, and this continually introduced temptation and sin among the Israelite nation.

Each time the Israelites settled in a place, the Ark was placed back inside the Holy of Holies. These people had it made, but sin continued to turn them aside. Since the people were unable to keep their part of the agreement, God promised to make a new covenant. This covenant was to send His son Jesus to die for the sins of all people. Jesus would be the sacrificial offering enabling our forgiveness from sin.

But Jesus would not come for 1500 years. So once a year the high priest entered the Holy of Holies and offered a sacrifice to God praying for forgiveness for the sins of Israel.

We don't know when God left the Mercy Seat on the Ark, but sin and corruption among the Israelites caused Him to let them move along without Him. Their lives involved sin, then repentance, then sin again. He gave them choice, and they chose sin.

While in Shiloh, corruption and sin became rampant among the priesthood. God sent prophets to warn all of the people that their focus should be on Him. Samuel was one of these prophets. He served in Shiloh and continually told the people to rid themselves of their idols and return to worshiping God. But the people had hardened their hearts against God and didn't listen.

Over the years, the Israelites lost the meaning of the Ark of the Covenant and felt that just its presence alone would bring them victory in any battle. However, God no longer went with them, and they began to lose battle after battle. One day the Philistines defeated the Israelites and took the

Ark of the Covenant. The Bible doesn't say whether Levite priests were forced to carry the Ark into Philistine territory, but this is likely.

The Philistines took the Ark to Ebenezer at Ashdod, and into a house where Dagon, the idol of their sun god, stood. In 1 Samuel 5, the Bible describes how the statue of Dagon was overturned during the first night and was eventually broken apart when the idol was righted and again placed near the Ark. The Philistines finally understood the power of this box and saw the Ark as a serious source of trouble. They began to regret having taken the Ark.

They sent the Ark to the town of Gath, but all the men in Gath came down with a skin disease (like radiation burn). They took the Ark to Ekron about 35 miles to the west of Jerusalem, but the people there refused to let the Ark stay. So for seven months, the Ark was passed from place to place around the Philistine territories, and each time the Ark remained in a location, the people there got sick—possibly radiation sickness.

Eventually the Philistines decided to give the Ark back to the Israelites. After discussions with Jewish priests, the ark was placed on a wagon harnessed to some cattle. Then the cattle were released to go where they willed. The cattle departed without being driven and pulled the Ark to Beth-shemesh (house of the sun) on the border between the territory of the Philistines and that of the Israelites. Scholars think that Beth-shemesh is now called "Ain Shems."

Word spread rapidly that the Ark of the Covenant was there, and thousands of Israelites gathered to see it. The people were not to look inside, but several of them lifted the Mercy Seat lid and the energy that emanated killed 70 people. The Mercy Seat lid was closed and the people of Beth-shemesh refused to keep the Ark there.

Levite priests from Kirjath-Jearim took the Ark to a man named Abinadab so his son Eleazar could watch over the Ark. For several years, Abinadab and his son cared for the Ark. They were not harmed in any way by being near the Ark. In fact, while the ark remained there for the next 20 to 40 years, the lives of Abinadab and his family were significantly better because it was there.

Meanwhile, the prophet Samuel became the Judge of Israel. He eventually got the Israelites to destroy their idols and worship God. When they did, Israel began to win battles with the Philistines, and the Philistines stopped attacking and coming over the borders into Israelite territory.

But then sin entered the lives of the Israelites again, and they demanded to be led by a king like the other nations and not by a judge. God permitted Samuel to anoint Saul as the first king of Israel. But Saul was sinful, so God had Samuel anoint David as the new king. David was from the tribe of Judah. He wanted to follow the covenant made with God. He took over the land where Jerusalem now stands and brought 30,000 people with him to take the Ark from the home of Abinadab to the new city of Jerusalem.

David and thousands of Israelites rejoiced, sang, and played music while two of Abinadab's sons walked along the carriage containing the Ark and driving the animals pulling the Ark toward Jerusalem. But the carriage leaned as it passed through a rut in the road, and one of the men, Uzzah, touched the Ark as if to steady it. Uzzah was killed instantly.

The huge crowd was terrified, and David took the Ark to the house of Obed-edom, a Levite of the family of Koath and a Gittite from Gath, instead of into Jerusalem. God blessed Obed-edom and his family because they faithfully cared for the Ark. Apparently they enjoyed good health and became wealthy because of their service. When David heard how God blessed this family, he brought the Ark to Jerusalem and placed it in a Tabernacle Tent (much like the tent that Moses had used).

David wanted to build a permanent temple in which to keep the Ark and temple furnishings, but he had sinned, so God told David that not he but his son Solomon would build the Temple. Solomon did. He had the Temple designed and built according to the same pattern as the Tabernacle of Moses' time. It took seven years to complete the Temple.

But Solomon, too, fell into sin and allowed idolatry to spread throughout Israel. After Solomon's death, the Israelite nation split into two. King Jeroboam led the 10 tribes of the northern kingdom. And King Rehoboam led the southern two tribes (Benjamin and Judah). Kings came and went, and the sinful ways continued until one of the priests of King Josiah of the southern kingdom found the Book of the Law that Moses had placed in the side of the Ark. The king's scribe read it aloud, and Josiah became terrified because the Book exactly described the curses that the people experienced because they had not obeyed God. Josiah had the Book read to all of his people. Then he renewed the covenant with God and they destroyed the idols and tried to obey God (2 Kings 23). The last time the location of the Ark of the Covenant was described was during this reformation under King Josiah (2 Chronicles 35).

But the destiny of the Ark had already been decided. Josiah's predecessor, Hezekiah, had shown representatives of Babylon the treasures of Israel including the gold-covered Ark, and they remembered.

When Josiah's grandson Zedekiah became king, Nebuchadnezzar, King of Babylon, told Zedekiah that if he surrendered Israel authority to Babylon, the Israelites could live in peace and Zedekiah could remain as king instead of the brother of Nebuchadnezzar. Zedekiah accepted this offer, but later broke the agreement. This led to the siege of Jerusalem in about 586 BC.

The Babylonians built a siege wall all around Jerusalem. It was built just beyond the reach of the weapons of that time, and it prevented anyone from entering or leaving the city. Soon starvation and death ravaged Jerusalem.

The prophet Jeremiah repeatedly advised Zedekiah to honor his agreement with Nebuchadnezzar, but he refused. It was during this siege that the Ark of the Covenant disappeared. The last mention of the Ark is in Jeremiah 3:16.

Eventually Jerusalem was taken by Babylon, and Zedekiah was blinded and taken captive. The leaders of the Jews were forced to bow down outside the ruins of Solomon's Temple with their backs to the temple ground and to worship the sun that rose from the east.

All of the riches of Jerusalem were taken to Babylon, but the Ark of the Covenant was not listed among the treasures. Seventy years later the treasures were returned to Jerusalem, but the Ark had disappeared. Where is the Ark of the Covenant?

Four possible locations have been identified:

1. Mount Nebo on the east (Jordanian) bank of the Jordan River.

2. Near Qumran on the west bank of the Jordan River and near the Dead Sea.

3. Saint Mary's of Zion church in the Ethiopian town of Axum.

4. Beneath Jerusalem in a stone-carved tunnel in Mount Moriah.

The last option seems most likely because Jerusalem was under siege just before the Ark disappeared. The Babylonians would not allow anything to be taken out of the city, and they certainly would have detected Jewish priests carrying a heavy, gold-covered box out of Jerusalem. So the Jewish priests must have hidden the Ark within the siege walls.

In 1982, amateur archeologist Ron Wyatt claimed to have found the actual site where Jesus was crucified. He didn't realize how important this site would become in pointing to the Ark of the Covenant—the missing symbol of God for the whole Israelite world.

Wyatt found what some believe is the site where Jesus was crucified down in Jeremiah's Grotto, a steep gorge cut through Mount Moriah. He noticed what appeared to be dried blood around and down in the hole that held the wooden cross of Christ. A sample of this substance was tested and confirmed that it was indeed blood. A deep earthquake crack ran through the hole for the cross, and the dried blood could be seen leading down into the crack.

With the help of a tiny Arab man, Wyatt found a small entrance to a chamber about 20 feet below the site of the crucifixion. Upon wiggling through the entrance into the chamber, the man became terrified and refused to go back, so Wyatt had to find another way in. He did, and in this chamber Wyatt found what he believes is the missing Ark of the Covenant.

The first thing he noticed upon crawling into the chamber was rock piled almost to the roof of the room. As he moved rocks aside, he found dry, rotted wood on top of animal skins. Under the skins he noticed something shiny. This turned out to be the Table of Shewbread. He also found the Seven Branch Candlestick, the Altar of Incense, and a large sword (possibly used by Goliath). And then he found a stone casing with a lid that was slightly ajar. On top of the casing was the same dried blood he had noticed around the crucifixion hole 20 feet above.

Shining his flashlight down into the opening in the cement casing, Wyatt saw a chest of beaten gold. He believed that he had found the Ark of the Covenant.

Jeremiah's Grotto is under the control of the Muslims, and Wyatt made four visits to the chamber. But word got out about what he may have found, and he was not allowed to return to complete his exploration. In fact, the Muslims who control that portion of Jerusalem have placed Islamic burial sites throughout the grotto preventing further archeological digs. Wyatt was told by "messengers" whom he met that the time was not yet right for the world to see the Ark.

Sadly, Wyatt got cancer and died in 1999 before his findings could be widely reported. (Perhaps from being too close to the Ark?) In the recent book *Confrontation— The Battle Between the Ark of the Covenant and the Mark of the Beast* by Rebecca Samsing, the experiences of Ron Wyatt are described in detail. The book recalls how a Roman soldier had stuck a spear into the side of Jesus after he had died releasing blood and water. The blood ran down the cross, and into the hole where the cross was mounted. When the earthquake shook the area at the death of Jesus, the blood continued down the crack running through the crucifixion hole and onto the lid of the Ark of the Covenant.

In Moses' time, animal blood was used as a sacrifice. In Jesus' time, His blood was used as the sacrifice, so finding dried blood on the top of the container holding the Ark of the Covenant is significant. Only the high priest could put blood on the Ark as a sacrifice to God. Jesus is our high priest.

The old covenant contained in the Ark and on the Tablets has been replaced by the new covenant contained in Jesus Christ who gave His life for all of our sins so we can enjoy eternal life.

I believe that we are very close to the time when the Ark and the Tablets will be revealed to the world. And other "secrets" of the Bible will soon be made known. To some, these are frightening times, but to me, these are exciting times, exciting indeed.

Jordan River Parts Making Path for Dry Crossing

... as soon as the priests who carried the ark reached the Jordan and their feet touched the water's edge, the water from upstream stopped flowing.

JOSHUA 3:15

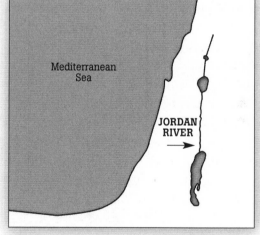

Mediterranean Sea

JORDAN RIVER

JOSHUA 3:1–17; JOSHUA 4:1–18
Location: Jordan River
Historical Time: Late Bronze Age – 1600–1400 BC, ca 1406 BC
TO VIEW MAPS ONLINE:
Copy this link into your browser and press Enter/Return
en.wikipedia.org/wiki/File:JordanRiver_en.svg

JOSHUA LED THE PEOPLE OF ISRAEL AWAY FROM SHITTIM on the eastern side of the Jordan where they camped. It was spring and the Jordan was at its seasonal flood stage. Three days later, the Ark of the Covenant was brought out of the Tent of Meeting and the people knew that this was the day they would cross the Jordan and enter the lands of Canaan. (Joshua 3:4) Joshua told the people that the priests should walk with the Ark about 1,000 yards in front of the rest of the people. As soon as the priests reached the Jordan at an overflow area of the river, they stepped into the water and immediately the water stopped flowing from upstream all the way from near a town called Adam in the vicinity of Zarethan downstream to the Salt Sea (Sea of the Arabath).

The riverbed quickly dried and the priests carried the Ark into the middle of the Jordan and stood there while the entire nation of Israel passed by and into Canaan. Then God told Joshua to have one man from each of the 12 tribes select a large stone from near the priests who stood holding the Ark (Joshua 4:4). Each man was to take his tribe's stone across to the Canaan side. These stones became "standing stones" commemorating the place where the nation crossed the Jordan. The stones were placed at Gilgal, very near where they crossed.

Joshua had the people stack another 12 stones in the middle of the Jordan where the priests stood. According to Joshua 4:9, these standing stones are still there.

Then the people of the Israelite nation watched as the priests moved the rest of the way across the Jordan. Joshua ordered them to come up out of the Jordan. As recorded in Joshua 4:18, immediately upon setting their feet on the shore the waters of the Jordan began flowing again at flood stage. Even water is subject to the plan of God.

Jericho City Walls Collapse at Loud Sound

So the troops shouted very loudly when they heard the blast of the rams' horns, and the wall collapsed.

JOSHUA 6:20

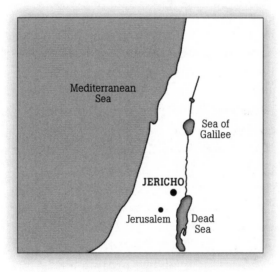

JOSHUA 6:2-25
Location: Jericho in Canaan
Historical Time: Late Bronze Age – Proposed time periods:
1600–1400 BC/ca 1550 BC/ca 1406 BC

TO VIEW MAPS ONLINE:
Copy this link into your browser and press Enter/Return
en.wikipedia.org/wiki/Jericho

JERICHO "THE CITY OF PALM TREES," HAD BEEN INHABITED for thousands of years. It was the ancient site of lunar deity worship. Carbon dating shows that this Canaanite city was destroyed sometime in the late Bronze Age about 1550 BC (between 1617 and 1530 BC). And Jericho would be the first city in Canaan to be taken by the people of God.

Once the Israelites had crossed the Jordan into Canaan, Joshua prepared to take Jericho for God. Now the city of Jericho was put in lockdown at night. No one came in or left. (Joshua 2:1) During the day, Joshua sent two spies from Shittim to check out the defenses of Jericho. Before the gates were closed for the night, they entered the house of a prostitute named Rahab. Her house was built in the city wall. She knew the Israelites were going to attack Jericho. The king in Jericho heard that she had two men in her house and sent soldiers to look for them, but she hid them up on her roof under stalks of flax laid there to dry in the sun.

When the king's soldiers came to her house to inquire about the strangers, she told them the men had left just before the city gates were closed for the night. The troops went out of the city to look for them.

The spies stayed on the roof until late at night. Then they came down into the house and spoke with the woman. She told them the whole city was terrified of the Israelites. She asked the spies to remember her kindness in hiding them. She took out a scarlet cord (rope) to let them climb out a window and down to the ground outside the wall. She told them to hide in the hills outside Jericho for three days until the troops looking for them returned. Then they could go on their way back to Joshua and the army of Israel.

They told her to hang the scarlet cord outside the window in the wall and to gather her whole family inside the house. Even though Rahab was a prostitute, she had a good relationship with her family and convinced her father, her mother, brothers and sisters and all who belong to them to gather in her home. They waited there for the attack by the army of Joshua.

The spies reported back to Joshua and Joshua instructed his troops to spare Rahab and her family when Jericho was taken. They were also ordered not to take any of the "devoted things" in the city. He said that all the gold, silver, bronze, and iron articles would become part of the treasury of the Lord.

Then he ordered his army to move out. As Joshua approached Jericho (Joshua 5:13), he saw a man standing in the roadway with a drawn sword. Joshua asked him if he was for them or for the people of Jericho. The man said, "Neither." Then he told Joshua that He was the Commander of the army of the Lord.

Joshua laid face down on the ground in reverence. He asked what message there was for him. Joshua was told to remove his sandals because the ground there was holy. Joshua did and then the Lord told Joshua how to take the city.

Joshua gave orders and the priests picked up the Ark of the Covenant and began marching in a path around Jericho. Following behind an armed advance guard, seven priests carried trumpets just in front of the priests who carried the Ark. Another armed guard followed the priests carrying the Ark. Standing off behind them was the huge army of Joshua.

When Joshua ordered the priests and armed guards to "Advance," the trumpet players began blowing on the trumpets while stepping forward. The group said nothing. Only the sound of trumpets filled the air. They circled the city once, and then they returned to their encampment near Joshua's troops. This process was repeated every day for six days.

On the seventh day, the parade of advance guards, priests with trumpets, priests carrying the ark and armed rear guards marched around the city seven times. As they finished the seventh circling of Jericho, Joshua told them to "shout" loudly.

They did, and the walls of Jericho began to crumble. The wall in front of Joshua's army collapsed and every man charged through the opening. In a short time they took over the city.

There have been cases of matter being destroyed by sounds and certain frequencies. In 1 Samuel 4:5 the people of Israel shouted with joy at seeing the Ark, and the earth rang with echoes. The incident at Jericho may well be one of those cases. This could have been how God destroyed Jericho. The city was indeed destroyed.

The men of Joshua killed every living thing in Jericho except Rahab and her family. All the other residents died regardless of sex or age. Joshua's army also killed the cattle, sheep, and donkeys. Nothing was left living except those whom God spared (specifically, Rahab and her family).

Then Joshua told the two spies to bring Rahab and her family outside the ruined city. They did, and Joshua had Rahab and her family relocated safely to a place outside of Jericho. Then Joshua had the whole city burned to the ground.

Rahab was spared because she believed in what the Israelites were doing, and she hid the two spies Joshua had sent. She lived among the Israelites from that day on.

Ditches Suddenly Fill with Water, Ending Famine

You will not see wind or rain, but this valley will be filled with water. In addition, He will put Moab at your mercy.

2 KINGS 3:17, 18

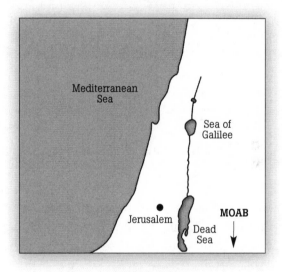

2 KINGS 3:4–27
Location: Moab, a mountainous strip of land alongside the eastern shore of the Dead Sea
Historical Time: Iron Age – 900–800 BC
TO VIEW MAPS ONLINE:
Copy this link into your browser and press Enter/Return
en.wikipedia.org/wiki/Moab

WHEN KING AHAB OF ISRAEL DIED AND JORAM BECAME king, King Mesha of Moab reneged on an agreement to provide male lambs and wool to the king of Israel for protecting them. So King Joram of Israel prepared to fight Moab. King Jehoshaphat of Judah joined King Joram, as did the king of Edom. They took an indirect route to Moab by going south and then up through the desert of Edom. After seven days they ran out of water for the troops and animals. They became frantic. Fortunately Elisha was in the area.

The three kings went to Elisha for advice about getting water and being successful in their battle against Moab. Elisha told them that he wouldn't even give them the courtesy of an audience with him if it weren't for King Jehoshaphat of Judah. Then Elisha told them to get someone to play music for him. Elisha went into a higher state of consciousness as the musician played, and he prophesied to the three kings.

He said that there would not be wind or rain, but the ditches in the valley would be filled with water. With that the troops and animals could drink their fill. Elisha said this was simple for God, but the Moabites would also be delivered into their hands. He told the three kings that they would defeat and capture every walled and important city in Moab. They would cut down every good tree, seal all the wells, and place rocks on every good piece of land.

The next morning was sunny and water began flowing from Edom, inundating the countryside. All were refreshed with the water. Then the alliance of kings moved up to the border of Moab and prepared to invade from the east. The Moabites standing at their eastern border saw the bright sun reflecting on the water and thought that it looked like red blood. They concluded that the three kings had argued, fought, and destroyed each other. The Moabites decided to rush over to where the three kings and their army had died and take the goods left from the battle.

However, when the Moabites rushed into the Israelite camp, the troops of the three kings rose up and attacked the surprised Moabites. The Moabites fled and the troops of the three kings followed them into Moab and killed much of the Moabite army.

Then Israel went after the rest of the Moabites. Just as predicted, they tore down the cities and threw rocks on every good field. They sealed the water wells and cut down all the good trees. Then they attacked the stone walls of Kir Haraseth (city of pottery) where King Mesha of Moab had taken refuge. Israelite catapult operators began a fierce bombardment of the city with rocks, but the city was well fortified and essentially impregnable.

The king of Moab took 700 men with swords and tried to break through to the king of Edom, but they could not. Jewish scholars believe that the Moabites captured the son of the king of Edom and sacrificed him as a burnt offering on the wall. The Edomites blamed the Israelites for the death of the boy and the coalition split apart. There was great indignation against Israel, and the Edomites returned to Edom while King Joram and King Jehoshaphat ended the campaign unsuccessfully.

Historians have suggested that the forces of Israel and Judah feared Chemosh, the Moabite god, and gave up victory even though it was well within their grasp. King Joram and King Jehoshaphat did not believe that God would give them victory over the people of Chemosh. After this event the Moabites and the Israelites were bitter enemies. Later Kir Haraseth was destroyed by the Babylonians.

Today, Kir Haraseth is called Khirbet Karnak. Its located 11 miles east of the Dead Sea and 50 miles diagonally southeast of Jerusalem on the eastern side of the Dead Sea.

Iron Axe Head Levitates off River Bottom

Elisha cut a stick and threw it there, and made the iron float.
2 KINGS 6:6

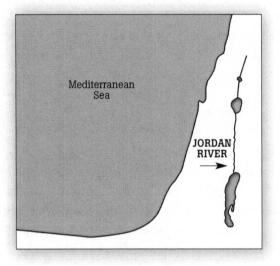

2 KINGS 6:4-7
Location: Jordan River
Historical Time: Iron Age – 900–800 BC/ca 850 BC
TO VIEW MAPS ONLINE:
Copy this link into your browser and press Enter/Return
en.wikipedia.org/wiki/File:JordanRiver_en.svg

IT WAS THE IRON AGE AND ELISHA, SON OF SHAPHAT, WAS a popular preaching prophet. He was from a farming family in the upper Jordan valley and trained under the prophet Elijah. The selection of Elisha by Elijah is described in 1

Kings 19:16-21. Elisha was gentle, diplomatic, and soft-spoken. He performed a number of miracles during his life and is believed to have started schools for prophets at Bethel, Gilgal and Jericho. He was an advisor to several kings and actually anointed Jehu as king of Israel. Elisha had a large following of students. He lived in Gilgal, near the Jordan River, and every day he met with his students, teaching them and prophesying what God told him to share.

The King James Version of the Bible calls them the "company of the prophets." God's Word to the Nations calls them the "disciples of the prophets." These apprentice prophets lived and studied in a learning community.

One day, some of these students came to Elisha and said that the place where they were meeting and staying was too small for their growing group. They suggested to Elisha that they go down to the banks of the Jordan River and cut some logs so they could build a larger dwelling.

At this time, the climate was semi-tropical and the banks of the Jordan were lined with great trees interspersed with shrubbery. The Jordan had plenty of water for drinking, washing, and bathing. So this was a good place to construct a rough shelter.

Elisha was invited to go with them to get logs for the dwelling. He did, and Elisha watched as the disciples/students began to cut down trees. As one of them swung an axe at a tree trunk, the iron axe head came off its handle and flew out over the Jordan and sank to the bottom. The man cried out, "Oh no, master! It was borrowed!"

Iron implements were rare and expensive. The Bronze Age gave way to the Iron Age about 1200 BC. It lasted until 600 BC, so Elisha lived during the Iron Age. The problem was that the Israelites didn't have knowledge of smelting the iron ore in the presence of carbon to produce carburized iron (steel) that was usable. Copper melts at 1100 degrees, but iron melts at 1550 degrees and no furnaces in the land of the Israelites could heat iron ore hot enough to cause it to melt. The Philistines mastered the technology, so they were the providers of iron implements and iron weapons. In this way they controlled other tribal groups, especially the Israelites. Nevertheless, some iron implements did get into the hands of the Israelites. But these implements were jealously guarded and not readily loaned. Thus there was an imperative for the disciple/student to recover the iron axe head quickly.

Elisha asked the student where the axe head had fallen into the water. The man showed Elisha the spot and Elisha cut off a piece of wood and tossed the wood into the water at the same spot where the axe head had sunk. The axe head floated to the surface and over near where they stood. "Pick it up," Elisha said. The man did and re-attached it to the axe handle.

Iron axe heads do not float, so Elisha had the power to levitate the heavy object up off the river bottom, bring it to the surface, and move it over to where they stood on the riverbank.

When the log cutting was done, the axe was returned to its owner, but everyone present recognized that Elisha was the man who could raise objects by levitation.

SIDENOTE:

The Roman Catholic Church has a "patron saint" called Saint Joseph of Cupertino who is the Patron Saint of air travelers. This Italian friar lived between 1603 and 1663. He was nicknamed "The Flying Friar" since it's believed that he could levitate. (Sources: en.wikipedia.org/wiki/Joseph_of_Cupertino and http://www.catholic.org/saints/saint.php?saint_id=72))

Jesus Levitates up into a Cloud

While he was blessing them,
he left them and was taken up into heaven.

LUKE 24:51

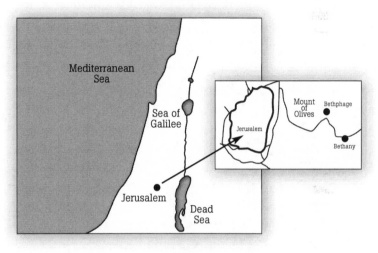

LUKE 24:51
Location: Mount of Olives | **Historical Time:** ca 34 AD
TO VIEW MAPS ONLINE:
Copy this link into your browser and press Enter/Return
www.frugalsites.net/jesus/gethsemane.htm

ANOTHER EXAMPLE OF LEVITATION OCCURRED AT THE Ascension of Jesus on a mountaintop near Bethany. Jesus led his disciples to the place and gave them last-minute instructions and assignments. Then He stretched out His arms and hands and blessed them. They watched in amazement as Jesus began to rise into the air. He levitated up and up and all the way into the clouds of heaven.

Man Vanishes and Reappears Twelve Miles Away

...the Spirit of the Lord suddenly took Philip away.
The official didn't see Philip again. Philip found
himself in the city of Azotus.

ACTS 8:39, 40

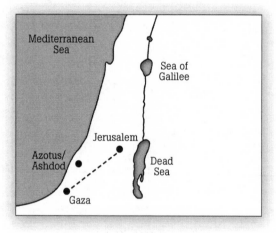

ACTS 8:39–40
Location: Road from Jerusalem to Gaza | **Historical Time:** ca 30 AD
TO VIEW MAPS ONLINE:
Copy this link into your browser and press Enter/Return
www.sacred-destinations.com/israel/jerusalem-map
www.sacred-destinations.com/israel/israel-map
www.ccel.org/bible/phillips/CP051GOSPELMAPS.htm
bibleatlas.org/jerusalem.htm

THIS INCIDENT OF TELEPORTATION CONCERNS PHILIP, A
follower of Jesus. Philip was one of seven men whom God
chose to become a leader of the early church. He became
known as "Philip the Evangelist."

Acts 8:26 describes how an angel told Philip to go down a desert wilderness road leading south from Jerusalem to Gaza. As he walked along, a chariot began to approach from behind. Riding in the chariot was an Ethiopian man, who was a high-ranking official in charge of all the treasures of Queen Candace of Ethiopia. He was returning to Ethiopia after worshiping in Jerusalem, and he was reading the words of the prophet Isaiah.

As the chariot with its Ethiopian rider was passing, a spirit voice told Philip to keep up with the carriage. So Philip began to run alongside. He could hear the Ethiopian man reading aloud. Philip asked him, "Do you understand what you are reading?"

The official turned toward Philip and said, "How can I unless someone guides me?" Then he invited Philip to sit in the chariot with him so Philip could explain the words of Isaiah.

Philip climbed into the chariot and told the Ethiopian official that Isaiah had written about Jesus and what He would do for mankind. The Ethiopian man was impressed. When the two travelers came near some water on the side of the road, the official stopped the chariot and asked Philip if he could be baptized right then, right there in that water. Philip assured him that he could, and they climbed down from the chariot and walked into the water where Philip baptized the man.

As they stepped up out of the water, Philip suddenly vanished from before the Ethiopian's eyes. He instantly reappeared in Azotus, a small city about 12 miles away. Was there teleportation in the first century? You bet!

Jesus Teleported into the Desert

At once the Spirit brought Him into the desert.
MARK 1:12

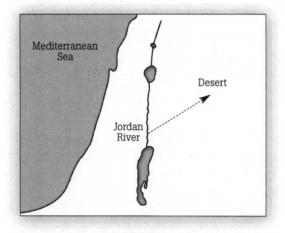

MARK 1:12–13
Location: Jordan River and desert | **Historical Time:** ca 30 AD
TO VIEW MAPS ONLINE:
Copy this link into your browser and press Enter/Return
http://en.wikipedia.org/wiki/File:JordanRiver_en.svg

IMMEDIATELY AFTER JOHN HAD BAPTIZED JESUS IN THE Jordan River, and the Holy Spirit came down to Him as a dove, Jesus was taken (teleported) by the Spirit out to the desert. Here Satan tempted Him for 40 days. Angels took care of Him.

After this experience, Jesus began to select and call his disciples. His ministry was about to begin. He also began performing impressive miracles.

Jesus and Fishing Boat Teleported to Shore

Immediately, the boat reached the shore where they were going.

JOHN 6:21

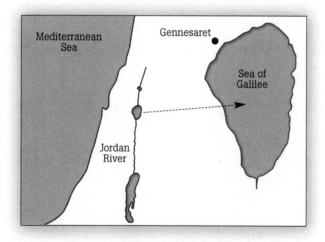

JOHN 6:15-21; MATTHEW 14:22-36; MARK 6:45-56
Location: Sea of Galilee | Historical Time: ca 30 AD
TO VIEW MAPS ONLINE:
Copy this link into your browser and press Enter/Return
en.wikipedia.org/wiki/Sea_of_Galilee
emp.byui.edu/SATTERFIELDB/Galilee/default.htm
www.bible-history.com/geography/ancient-israel/sea-of-galilee.html

ANOTHER INCIDENT OCCURRED WHEN JESUS WAS NEAR
the northwestern shore of the Sea of Galilee (Lake Gennesaret). He walked out over the surface of the water to
meet a boat that the disciples were trying to paddle to the

other side of the large lake. They were fighting a strong wind and had only been able to row three or four miles (of the eight miles across), but the moment Jesus got into the boat, the wind stopped and the boat and occupants were immediately teleported to Gennesaret on the northeastern shore of the lake.

They still had about four miles to row when this supernatural event occurred.

UFOs, Elijah, Fiery Chariots, and Oh My!

*As they continued walking and talking, a fiery chariot
with fiery horses separated the two of them,
and Elijah went to heaven in a windstorm.*

2 KINGS 2:11

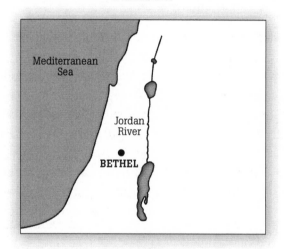

2 KINGS 2:1-11
Location: Bethel and Jordan River | **Historical Time:** ca 875 BC
TO VIEW MAPS ONLINE:
Copy this link into your browser and press Enter/Return
blog.eteacherbiblical.com/wp-content/uploads/2008/01/judah-and-israel.gif

IS IT POSSIBLE UNIDENTIFIED FLYING OBJECTS (UFOS)
existed 3,000 years ago? Could teleportation and extraterrestrial travel have occurred before the birth of Christ?
There are those who think they did and it could. They
believe that the Bible describes spacecraft that can appear,

disappear, move in any direction, and whisk away at the blink of an eye. Read the following. Then you decide. We begin many years before the birth of Jesus. During the days of King Ahaziah (around 875 BC), Elijah was a powerful prophet. He is one of the dominant figures in Bible history during this period. Elijah is as well-known as Moses. He came from Tishbe, the capital of Samaria, the homeland of the northern tribes of Israel. Elijah was a native of Gilead and grew up in the wilderness, mountains, and ravines of what is called Syria today. His hair was thick and long, and he wore sheepskin or coarse camel hair tied at the middle with a leather belt.

According to biblical records, Elijah had a fiery zeal and was often at odds with King Ahab, the reigning king of Israel, because he confronted the king and his son, the co-regent king Ahaziah about their sins. Through his wicked wife, Ahab instituted worship of the false idol Baal, and infant sacrifices throughout Israel. And Elijah called them on this. These kings were powerless to kill Elijah because he was so prominent and influential. Elijah accurately predicted a long drought and performed a number of important miracles including raising the dead, causing a jar of flour and a jug of oil to stay full. Elijah also brought fire down from heaven when he challenged the wicked priests who worshipped Baal to show if their idol god was more powerful than the God of Elijah. The fire that Elijah called down consumed an altar and a sacrifice on Mount Carmel. Later Elijah used fire from heaven to destroy two military groups each comprised of an officer and 50 soldiers. These actions earned Elijah the nickname "Prophet of Fire."

Elijah had been on Mount Horeb (where Moses received the law) and knew that his departure was imminent. Elijah had traveled to Mount Horeb, where Moses was buried. Some biblical historians feel that he met Moses there and they became heavenly friends, appearing together on a mountain at the transfiguration of Jesus (Matt 17:3).

A teacher of prophets, Elijah, anointed prophet-apprentice Elisha to succeed him. On the appointed day, Elijah and Elisha went to Bethel. There Elijah tried to get Elisha to remain behind and not accompany him further, but Elisha insisted that he go with Elijah. Some scholars feel that Elijah may have felt that Elisha was not quite ready to take over.

Elijah had been operating schools in Bethel and Jericho, teaching new prophets how to enter a state where they could prophesy. So as I read 2 Kings 2:1-6, it seemed to me that Elijah was cautious about giving Elisha full reins as a prophet.

Nevertheless, Elisha was adamant that he was going with Elijah all the way to his departure point. So Elijah allowed this and they went on to Jericho together.

The two men walked together down to the banks of the Jordan River. Fifty disciples followed but stood at a distance because they knew that God was going to take Elijah from them on that day. It's interesting that the Bible says "all" of Elijah's students also knew that their teacher was going to be taken away that day. It was as though this was common knowledge among the prophet community.

Elijah and his successor, Elisha, stood together on the west bank of the Jordan. Elijah rolled up his coat (mantle) and struck the surface of the river. Instantly, the Jordan parted and the two prophets walked across on a dry riverbed. As they crossed, Elijah asked Elisha what he'd like him to leave him. Elisha asked for a double share of Elijah's spirit. Elijah told him that if he saw him taken to heaven, then Elisha would indeed have twice the power of Elijah.

After they crossed and had stepped out of the riverbed onto the bank on the east side, the water being held back upstream began flowing downstream again, and the water in the river returned to its flood stage condition. Soon it was again deep and rushing downstream past where the two prophets stood.

Elijah and Elisha walked away from the bank of the river. They hadn't gotten far when what is described in 2 Kings 2:9-11 as a "fiery chariot with fiery horses" swooped down between the men. It happened so fast.

Elijah was whisked aboard and taken up into the sky in a roaring, rumbling craft that produced a whirlwind around Elisha standing in awe there on the ground. The fiery cloud that led the Israelites during the Exodus was again present and Elisha knew that the power of God was behind all that was happening.

Elijah was the second person in Bible history who went to heaven without experiencing death. Enoch was the first.

Elijah's coat fell to the ground as he was swooped up, and that was all that remained of the senior prophet. In a matter of seconds, Elijah was gone and Elisha stood alone.

When Elijah and the chariot had gone up and out of sight, Elisha tore his robe in two. Then he picked up Elijah's coat and walked back to the east bank of the Jordan. At the water's edge, Elisha struck the surface of the water with Elijah's coat. Nothing happened. Elisha struck the water a second time, and the river water parted just as it had for Elijah. Elisha walked across the Jordan on a dry riverbed to where the astounded student prophets were standing. Elisha began performing miracles, and he became the leading proponent of God from that time forward.

Elisha and the Fiery Chariots at Dothan

The mountain around Elisha was full of fiery horses and chariots.
2 KINGS 6:17

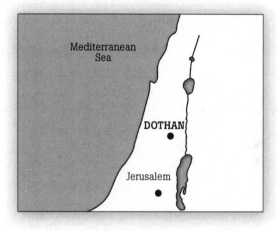

2 KINGS 6:8–20
Location: Dothan | Historical Time: ca 860 BC
TO VIEW MAPS ONLINE:
Copy this link into your browser and press Enter/Return
bibleatlas.org/dothan.htm
www.keyway.ca/htm2000/20000807.htm
www.bible-history.com/
www.ibiblemaps.com/m008.html

THERE ARE SEVERAL OTHER INCIDENTS OF FIERY CHARIOTS recorded in the Bible. In 2 Kings 6, you can read about a confrontation between the king of Aram and King Jehoram of Israel. The king of Aram learned that Elisha was telling the king of Israel everything that the Aramean king was saying. This was how the Israelites were able to avoid a confrontation with the Aramean army. The king of Aram wanted to stop Elisha.

The Aramean king was told that Elisha was in the small city of Dothan north of Samaria and about 15 miles west of the Jordan River. So the king of Aram sent an army to Dothan to find and apprehend Elisha. The Aramean troops arrived at night and surrounded Dothan. The residents of Dothan could hear and see the Arameans surrounding their city and they became terrified. Elisha's servant cried out in fright, "Master, what should we do?"

Elisha told him not to worry. He explained that the Israelites had more forces on their side than the Arameans had on theirs. Apparently Elisha knew that a large, unseen army surrounded them all – Dothan and the Arameans. Then Elisha prayed that God would open the eyes of the servant and the people of Dothan so they could also see the powerful forces on God's side. God did, and suddenly the people trapped in Dothan saw fiery chariots and fiery horses at the top of every mountain and hill surrounding the city.

2 Kings 6 goes on to explain that Elisha prayed and the army of Aram were suddenly blinded and needed to be led. They were led south to Samaria, capital of the Northern Kingdom of Israel.

Then Elisha prayed that their eyes would be opened, and they were. They found themselves no longer blind, but helpless in the middle of Samaria. The king of Israel asked Elisha if the Arameans should be killed. Elisha told him not to kill these men, but to instead give them food and water, then set them free to return to Aram. After these men went back to their homes, the Arameans no longer raided Israelite territories.

Ezekiel and His UFO Encounters

In the center of the cloud I saw what looked like four living creatures....Something like a dome was spread over the heads of the living creatures.

EZEKIEL 1:5 AND 1:22

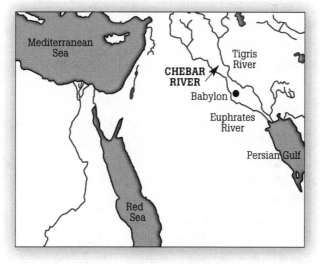

EZEKIEL 1:5, 22
Location: Chebar River in Babylon | **Historical Time:** ca 593 BC
TO VIEW MAPS ONLINE:
Copy this link into your browser and press Enter/Return
bibleatlas.org/chebar.htm
bible.cc/ezekiel/1-3.htm

EZEKIEL LIVED AROUND 590 BC. ELIJAH AND ELISHA LIVED around 880 BC, so almost 300 years had passed by the time Ezekiel experienced his own "fiery chariot." In writing his book, Ezekiel provided a vivid description of the "fiery chariots." As you read the description in Ezekiel 1, you will be amazed at the similarities between these fiery chariots and military hover and lift craft common today. Remember that the writers of 2 Kings and Ezekiel described their environment in terms familiar to them. Fiery chariots they could understand; hovercraft, UFOs and other strange unidentified objects they could not. They wrote from their own point of reference using their own terminology.

Ezekiel was the son of Buzi, a priest who lived during the Babylonian captivity of Judah. (Israel had been taken into captivity 120 years earlier.) Ezekiel was with the Israelites taken out of Jerusalem and held captive by Nebuchadnezzar in Babylon from 597 BC to around 570 BC (about 27 years). Bible scholars believe that Ezekiel was a disciple of Jeremiah. While Jeremiah preached to the people in Jerusalem, Ezekiel preached to the exiles in Babylon. Ezekiel is also believed to have known Daniel since Daniel had been living in the Babylonian palace there for nine years before Ezekiel arrived on the scene.

The book of Ezekiel describes seven visions that the prophet had between 593 and 571 BC. Jerusalem was destroyed in 586 BC and Ezekiel had predicted this event before it happened. Bible historians feel that all seven of Ezekiel's visions refer to God's judgment on Israel, His judgment on the nations that fought against Israel, and future blessings for His people.

Another school of thought claims that the book of Ezekiel describes visits by ancient astronauts who put us here and who are all around earth and its inhabitants as mostly unseen watchers. Occasionally these "watchers" appear as UFOs, walk-ins, or other visible spirits. In this book, I will present what I learned in my research on

Ezekiel and let you choose the meaning best suited to you at this time in your life.

Ezekiel was living with the exiles near the Chebar River in the Babylonian empire. This river is a wide boat canal branching off the Euphrates above the city of Babylon. The Chebar enabled water travel to and from the settlements along the Tigris River. These geographical sites are in what is now called Iraq.

Ezekiel was a prophet, and prophets often went into a trance-like state before they prophesied. This state produced a surreal experience that was real to the person there in the moment. Ezekiel did just that. The Bible calls it a vision. Prophets (and prophetesses) experienced visions and dreams. To them there was no distinction between the significance of each. The visions that Ezekiel saw were vivid and real. He wrote about them in the book that bears his name. Chapters 1 and 10 are the most challenging to our understanding of Scripture because these chapters describe in great detail the supernatural objects that Ezekiel saw.

In his first amazing vision, he saw a fiery chariot. It came out of an immense cloud flashing with light. The cloud came like a storm from the north. In the middle was a glowing metal craft. He described it as a gleaming vehicle emitting bright rays and raising up a dust cloud wherever it went. The craft had four wheels and could move in all directions including up, while making a great rushing sound. In the center under a dome were four living creatures.

Ezekiel described being taken aboard this craft from where he was standing on the side of the Chebar River and flown about 50 miles southwest to Tel Abib (Telabib), his residence while in captivity. He remained there for seven days, stunned by the experience. Then Ezekiel became outspoken and warned the people to change their ways or suffer the consequences.

During another supernatural experience, he saw what looked like a spirit in human form. From the waist down its body looked like fire. From the waist up it looked like glowing metal. This spirit took him by the hair and swept him off to Jerusalem to see the corruption of the temple and of the people. Ezekiel was then shown the coming destruction of Jerusalem and the temple, and he learned about the salvation that was to come.

In Ezekiel Chapter 10, he described being in the temple at Jerusalem and seeing a flying object with angels, wheels, and sound. It was associated with a divine cloud. The angels were the same living creatures he saw in the craft at the Chebar River. Was the "flying object" the same "fiery chariot" mentioned in 2 Kings 2 and 2 Kings 6?

Were the "fiery chariots" actually hovercraft or flying spacecraft as some have speculated? Were they "flown" by heavenly beings with power and direction that comes directly from God? Did Ezekiel and his predecessors Elijah and Elisha actually see UFOs? Only God knows. But Erich von Daniken wasn't the only person to postulate this. So have Chuck Misler, former medical doctor and coauthor of *Alien Encounters*, Zecharia Sitchin, author of *The Twelfth Planet*, and NASA engineer Josef Blumrich, author of *The Spaceships of Ezekiel*. Even Dr. Steven Hawking, one of the most brilliant scientists of our time, describes things and principles that exceed the imagination of most. Based on these facts and this analysis of Scripture, anything is possible in our amazing world.

They Walked on Water

When they had rowed three and a half miles, they saw Jesus approaching the boat, walking on the water.

JOHN 6:19

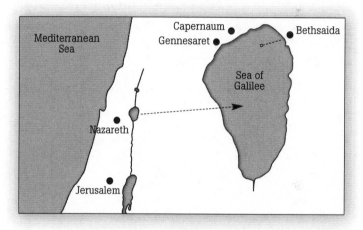

MATTHEW 14:22-36; MARK 6:45-56; JOHN 6:15-21
Location: Sea of Galilee | **Historical Time:** ca 30-33 AD

TO VIEW MAPS ONLINE:
Copy this link into your browser and press Enter/Return
en.wikipedia.org/wiki/Sea_of_Galilee
emp.byui.edu/SATTERFIELDB/Galilee/default.htm
www.bible-history.com/geography/ancient-israel/sea-of-galilee.html

JESUS WAS PREACHING AND TEACHING WITH HIS DISCIPLES. They were near Bethsaida on the northeastern shore of the Sea of Galilee., and a huge crowd had gathered to listen to Jesus. The time for the evening meal time approached. So Jesus made five loaves of barley bread and two small fish feed over 5,000 men plus women and children. After the meal 12 baskets of food scraps were collected.

Then Jesus told the disciples to sail across the lake ahead of him while He dismissed the crowd. He wanted time alone to pray (and to let His disciples get far out in the lake). Reluctantly they departed. They didn't realize another teaching moment was coming.

The Sea of Galilee is a large lake extending about 13 miles north to south in the center of Israel. It's shaped like a harp or oval with the wider side at the north end. It's also called Lake Gennesaret, Lake of Tiberius, Sea of Tiberius, and Lake of Galilee. Between four and eight miles wide it's 682 feet below sea level. The Jordan River enters at the northern end and exits at the southern end, eventually emptying into the Dead Sea 65 miles south. The depth of the Sea of Galilee reaches 200 feet. Nazareth is 20 miles west, Jerusalem is 70 miles to the southwest, and Caesarea on the shores of the Mediterranean is 55 miles west-southwest.

An ancient trade route and Roman road, the *Via Maris* linked Egypt with the northern areas of Anatolia, Mesopotamia, and Syria passing along the Sea of Galilee, through Tiberius on the western shore and up through Capernaum on the northern shore.

Winds funneling through the east-west Galilee hill country can increase quickly and transform the sea's calm and serene surface into a tempest of violent waves that can reach 10 in height.

Fishing was the primary industry along the Sea of Galilee and over 200 small fishing boats were active on the water at the time of Jesus. Historians believe the boat that the disciples used was about 26 feet long and seven feet wide with a single flat sail to aid in propulsion. The boat could hold up to 15 people.

In this incident, the disciples climbed into their small boat and rowed away from Bethsaida on the eastern shore and out into the lake as Jesus directed. But after they were out away from land, a westerly wind came up and blew against the small boatload of disciples trying to go from the northeastern to the northwestern shore (a distance of about seven miles). The wind got stronger and blew spray over the bow as they tried to move the boat forward. It was one of those sudden and furious storms common on this lake. Since their sail worked against them in that wind, it was likely lowered and the small boat was buffeted about as the disciples fought to use oars alone to move the boat forward.

As evening came their boat was just approaching the center of the lake and progress was very slow. The disciples became fearful. Other boats have been lost during storms out here, and they didn't want their boat to become swamped and capsize.

By the fourth watch (between 3:00 and 6:00 a.m.) the disciples had barely reached the halfway point on the lake, and they were exhausted.

Suddenly they saw to the east a figure walking toward them out on the surface of the water. It looked like the person was walking over a smooth carpet of grass. They became terrified and thought they were seeing an apparition. They crouched down in the boat and shouted out in fear, "It's a ghost!"

As the figure came closer, they began to scream, but Jesus spoke firmly, "Take courage! It is I. Do not be afraid."

The disciples were shocked to hear the figure talk. It sounded like Jesus, their teacher. Peter was the first to reply, "Lord, if it is you, tell me to come to you on the water." Jesus calmly replied, "Come."

With faith overpowering his apprehension, Peter stepped out over the transom of the boat and stood on the dark surface of the water. The water there was over 100 feet deep. The other disciples looked shocked. Here was their friend standing out of the boat on the surface of the deep sea completely immune to the forces of gravity and physics. He looked like he was standing on solid ground. And it was still quite dark that night. Then Peter began to walk out to Jesus. As long as he kept his focus on Jesus, he could walk easily over the surface of the deep water. (*Sometimes each of us must also step out of the boat and move forward based on faith alone.*)

Peter was doing fine, but then he was distracted by the wind and his focus was broken. He recognized where he was, and suddenly fear took hold. As he began to sink into the dark sea, Peter cried out, "Lord, save me!"

Jesus immediately took Peter's hand and raised him back up out of the water. Jesus reprimanded Peter saying, "You of little faith, why did you doubt?" Then Jesus took Peter to the side of the boat and they climbed aboard. Jesus commanded the wind to stop. It did, and immediately the seas became calm. The disciples exclaimed, "Truly you are the Son of God!"

According to John 6, the last half of their voyage was supernaturally accelerated, and in the blink of an eye the boat was suddenly at Gennesaret near Capernaum.

Morning arrived and people in the area discovered that Jesus was there. They brought sick and injured to Him, and He let them touch His robe making them well. As the power of God healed these people, the disciples looked on their teacher in awe reflecting on what they had witnessed. They had just watched Jesus and Peter walk on the surface of a deep lake, defying gravity and the howling wind. They had seen a supernatural event, and they knew that their teacher had powers far beyond what they could only imagine.

Transfiguration

ANOTHER AMAZING AND SUPERNATURAL PART OF THE Bible involves its descriptions of the transfigurations of people. To transfigure means to alter or change the form, shape, or appearance of a person or object. When the looks and features of people are changed, we call this "transfiguration." When the looks and features of objects are changed, we call this "transformation." In both cases, matter is altered. Transfiguration could include a sudden emanation of radiance from a person.

Let's look at transfiguration first. Transfigurations are depicted in recent Harry Potter movies such as *Harry Potter and the Chamber of Secrets,* Harry turned into Goyle. Also in this movie, Hermoine turned into a cat. So the concept of transfiguration is with us even today.

I found three transfigurations recorded in the Bible. In order of mention, they involved Moses, Jesus, and Stephen. Let's explore each of these.

The Face of
Moses Shined

*His face was shining from speaking
with the Lord, but he didn't know it.*
EXODUS 34:29

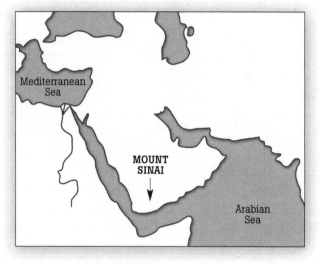

EXODUS 34:28-35; 2 COR 3:7-13
Location: Mount Sinai | **Historical Time:** ca 1500/1446 BC
TO VIEW MAPS ONLINE:
Copy this link into your browser and press Enter/Return
www.specialtyinterests.net/map_mt_sinai.html
www.arkdiscovery.com/mt__sinai_found.htm

THE FIRST TRANSFIGURATION RECORDED IN THE BIBLE
concerns the face of Moses during the exodus of the
Israelites back around 1500 BC.

After the first set of stone tablets were destroyed, Moses
went back up on the mountain where God made a second
set listing His commandments for living. Moses was up

there on Mount Sinai for 40 days. When he came down this time, he was holding the two tablets with God's commandments etched into the stone. And his face shined brightly.

The people said it shined like it did because Moses was in the direct presence of God. The brightness was so intense that Moses began wearing a veil to cover his face so the people wouldn't shun him in fear. He wore the veil until the intensity of the shining subsided. After a day or two, the brightness faded and his normal face color returned.

Each time Moses came into the presence of God his face began to shine. So while the Israelites were at Mount Sinai, his face periodically shined and he periodically wore a veil. Moses always took the veil off when he entered the Tent of Meeting to interface with God.

The Appearance of Jesus Changed

Jesus' appearance changed in front of them.
His face became as bright as the sun and
His clothes as white as light.
MATTHEW 17:2

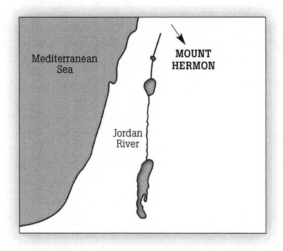

MATTHEW 17:1–9; MARK 9:2–8; LUKE 9:28–36
Location: Mount Hermon | **Historical Time:** ca 29–33 AD
TO VIEW MAPS ONLINE:
Copy this link into your browser and press Enter/Return
www.keyway.ca/htm2002/mthermon.htm
en.wikipedia.org/wiki/Mount_Hermon

THE MOST SIGNIFICANT TRANSFIGURATION INCIDENTS IN the Bible are those of Jesus. His appearance was transformed both before and after His death on the cross. In my research I found seven specific instances where Jesus looked different or radiated supernatural power.

Before Jesus was crucified, and about a week after Jesus first announced his pending death and resurrection, He took three of His disciples, Peter, James, and John up on a mountain (believed to be Mount Hermon). He wanted them near Him as He prayed.

While He prayed, they saw his appearance change. His clothing became dazzling white, and a radiance of divine emanated out from Him. His face became bright, like the sun.

A Shekinah cloud of glory overshadowed Jesus and the three disciples, and Moses and Elijah appeared in the bright cloud talking with Jesus. Although hundreds of years had elapsed since these prophets were alive (1500 BC and 850 BC), the disciples instinctively knew these ancient prophets. Moses represented the Law. Elijah represented prophecy and the fellowship of prophets.

Peter suggested that they construct three tents, one for each of them. Shelter or tabernacles were not necessary for the three, but immediately a voice from the cloud broke in saying, "This is My beloved Son in whom I am well pleased; hear ye Him."

There are scholars who believe that this Shekinah cloud was a theophany appearance of God associated with a commissioning. Moses saw the burning bush and was commissioned to go to Egypt and lead the Israelites out of bondage. Here Jesus was being commissioned to do what he was sent for—to die for the sins of all.

The disciples fell back in fear and turned their heads away from the sight, but Jesus touched them and told them not to fear. When they looked back at Jesus, Moses and Elijah were gone. Then Jesus led them back down the mountain.

Mary Thought He was a Gardener

... she turned around and saw Jesus standing there. However, she didn't know that it was Jesus.

JOHN 20:14

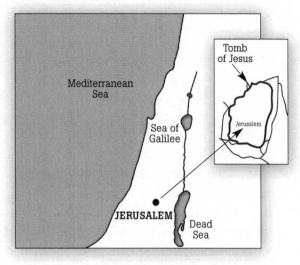

Mediterranean Sea

Sea of Galilee

JERUSALEM

Dead Sea

Tomb of Jesus

Jerusalem

JOHN 20:11–18
Location: Jerusalem | **Historical Time:** ca 29–33 AD
TO VIEW MAPS ONLINE:
Copy this link into your browser and press Enter/Return
www.sacred-destinations.com/israel/jerusalem-map
www.sacred-destinations.com/israel/israel-map
www.ccel.org/bible/phillips/CP051GOSPELMAPS.htm
bibleatlas.org/jerusalem.htm

THE MORNING AFTER JESUS WAS PLACED IN THE TOMB belonging to Joseph of Arimathea, Mary Magdalene, Mary, the mother of James, and Salome, cousin of the Virgin Mary, each started out for the tomb with spices to put on the body (Luke 23:55 – 24:1). They weren't sure who would roll the stone away from in front of the cave. It turned out not to matter.

When they arrived, Mary Magdalene and Mary, mother of James, found the stone rolled away and Jesus gone (Luke 24:2-9). Mary Magdalene rushed off to tell the disciples (John 20:1-2). Mary, mother of James, came near the tomb and saw an angel who told her that Jesus had risen from the dead (Matt 28:1-2). She rushed back to meet the other women following with spices.

Meanwhile, Peter and John arrived, looked into the tomb, and went to tell the others (John 20:3-10).

Mary Magdalene returned, crying, and saw two angels in the tomb (John 20:11-18). They asked her why she was crying and she told them that "they" had removed her Lord and she didn't know where He was placed. Then she turned around and saw a man standing near her. She thought this man was the gardener. (It was the transfigured Jesus.)

Jesus spoke to her, and she asked Him to tell her where the body of her Lord had been taken. She offered to go and get His body. Then Jesus spoke a single word, "Mary," and she knew it was Jesus. Mary said, "Rabbone" (Teacher), and she moved forward to hug Him. But He stopped her, and told her not to hold Him because He hadn't yet gone to the Father. He told her to go instead to His brothers and sisters and tell them He had risen. He told her to say, "I am going to my Father and your Father, to my God and your God." (John 20:17-18)

Then Mary Magdalene went to the disciples and told them what had happened and that Jesus had arisen from the dead.

Mary, the mother of James, returned to the tomb with the other women including Mary Magdalene and Joanna, another follower of Jesus. After this, Joanna became an apostle of Christ. The two angels at the tomb told these women that Jesus was alive. (Luke 24:5) (Mark 16:5)

Then the women left and went back into the city to tell all of this to the eleven disciples. Suddenly, Jesus met them and greeted them (Matt 28:9). They went up to Him, bowed down and took hold of His nail-pierced feet.

Jesus told them not to be afraid, but to tell the disciples to go to Galilee where they too would see Him in person (Matt 28:10).

Two Disciples on the Road to Emmaus

Then their eyes were opened and they recognized him,
and he disappeared from their sight.
LUKE 24:31

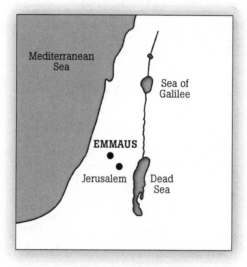

MARK 16:12–13; LUKE 24:13–33
Location: Emmaus | Historical Time: ca 29–33 AD
TO VIEW MAPS ONLINE:
Copy this link into your browser and press Enter/Return
en.wikipedia.org/wiki/File:First_century_palestine.gif
en.wikipedia.org/wiki/Emmaus_Nicopolis

WHILE TWO DISCIPLES (CLEOPAS AND ANOTHER FOLLOWER) were walking the seven miles from Jerusalem to their home in Emmaus, Jesus appeared and walked with them. His appearance was different, and they didn't recognize him. They told Jesus about the amazing resurrection (of

Him) that very morning. Then Jesus explained everything the Scripture said regarding the prophets and the suffering, death, and glory of Christ. It was getting late in the day, and they invited Jesus to stay with them.

A supper meal was set for them and while at their table, Jesus picked up the bread, gave thanks, broke it, and then began handing it to them. Suddenly the disciples recognized Jesus, and immediately Jesus vanished. The two men quickly stood up and rushed back to Jerusalem to tell the other disciples.

Jesus Appears to Ten Disciples Hiding in Galilee

Even though the doors were locked, Jesus stood among them and said, 'Peace be with you.'

JOHN 20:26

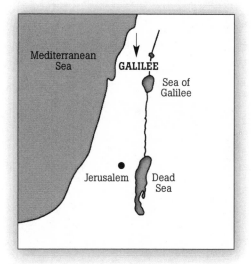

MARK 16:12–13; LUKE 24:36–48; JOHN 20:19–29
Location: Galilee | **Historical Time:** ca 29–33 AD

TO VIEW MAPS ONLINE:
Copy this link into your browser and press Enter/Return
en.wikipedia.org/wiki/Galilee
en.wikipedia.org/wiki/File:Ancient_Galilee.jpg
www.keyway.ca/htm2003/20030720.htm

TEN OF THE ELEVEN DISCIPLES WERE HIDING IN A HOUSE in the region of Galilee. (Nazareth and Tiberias are cities in Galilee.) Thomas was not with them yet. Although the front door was locked, Jesus appeared and spoke to them. He showed them his hands and side. Then he breathed on them with the Holy Spirit and opened their minds to understand the Scriptures. He instructed them to tell all nations to turn to God and change their ways and thinking.

Jesus Appears to the Doubting Thomas

*Still later Jesus appeared to the
eleven apostles while they were eating.*

MARK 16:14

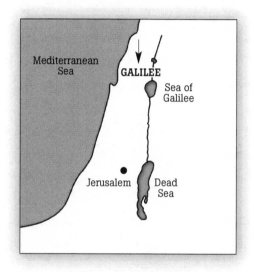

MARK 16:14; JOHN 20:24–29
Location: Galilee | **Historical Time:** ca 33 AD
TO VIEW MAPS ONLINE:
Copy this link into your browser and press Enter/Return
en.wikipedia.org/wiki/Galilee
en.wikipedia.org/wiki/File:Ancient_Galilee.jpg
www.keyway.ca/htm2003/20030720.htm

THE DISCIPLES WERE EATING A MEAL IN GALILEE WHEN
Jesus appeared in the room with them. He put them to
shame for doubting that He actually had risen and for
being too stubborn to believe those who had already seen
him alive.

Then Jesus focused in on doubting Thomas. He told him, "Put your finger here, and look at my hands. Take your hand and put it into my side [where a Roman soldier had stabbed Him with his spear]. Stop doubting, and believe." Thomas replied, "My Lord and my God!"

Jesus Gives Fishing Lesson to Disciples

*None of the disciples dared to ask Him who He was.
They knew He was the Lord.*

JOHN 21:12

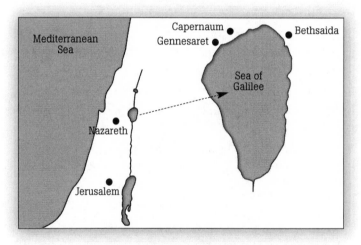

JOHN 21: 1-14
Location: Sea of Galilee | Historical Time: ca 33 AD
TO VIEW MAPS ONLINE:
Copy this link into your browser and press Enter/Return
en.wikipedia.org/wiki/Sea_of_Galilee
emp.byui.edu/SATTERFIELDB/Galilee/default.htm
www.bible-history.com/geography/ancient-israel/sea-of-galilee.html

SIMON PETER (PETER IS CALLED CEPHAS IN ARAMAIC), Thomas (called Didymus), Nathanael from Cana in Galilee, Zebedee's sons, and two other disciples were on the Sea of Galilee at night trying to catch fish with a net.

As the sun began to rise, Jesus appeared on the shore. The seven men didn't recognize Him because his appearance had changed. He asked them if they had caught any fish. They said they hadn't.

Jesus told them to put their net out on the right side of their boat and they'd catch some (fish). They did, and immediately the net filled with 153 large fish. It was so heavy they couldn't pull it in without tearing the net.

The disciple whom Jesus loved told Simon Peter that it was the Lord. The boat was 100 yards from shore when Simon Peter put back on his shirt, jumped into the water and waded out to help move the boat to shore.

As they reached the shore, they saw a loaf of bread and a campfire with a fish lying on the coals. Jesus told them to bring some of the fish they just caught and have breakfast with Him.

Peter pulled the net ashore and they took some of the fish and cooked them on the fire. They didn't recognize Jesus, but none of them dared to ask who He was, because they somehow knew He was the Lord.

Jesus took the bread, blessed it, and broke it, giving some to each of them. Then He did the same thing with the fish.

This was the third time that Jesus had appeared to the disciples since His resurrection.

Jesus Ascends into Heaven

While He was blessing them,
He left them and was taken to heaven.

LUKE 24:51

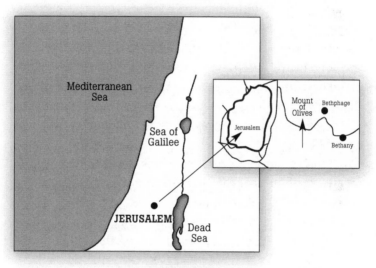

EXODUS 13–21
Location: Mount of Olives | **Historical Time:** Late Bronze Age – ca 34 AD
TO VIEW MAPS ONLINE:
Copy this link into your browser and press Enter/Return
www.frugalsites.net/jesus/gethsemane.htm

ACCORDING TO THE BOOK OF ACTS, JESUS APPEARED TO his disciples for 40 days teaching them and talking about the kingdom of God. After appearing to the 11 disciples in Galilee, Jesus told them He would meet them on a certain mountain near Bethany. (According to Acts 1:12, this was the Mount of Olives located about a half mile from Jerusalem.)

This would be His final appearance to them. When Jesus appeared, they bowed down to worship Him. The Bible records that some still had doubts about his identity. Jesus came near and told them that all authority in heaven and on earth had been given to Him. Then Jesus gave them power to cast out demons, heal the sick, speak other languages, and touch poisonous snakes and drink poisoned liquids without being harmed. He said wherever they go they should make disciples of the people of all the nations, baptizing them in the name of the Father, and of the Son, and of the Holy Spirit. He told them to teach people everything He had commanded. Then He told them that He would always be with them until the end of time.

They asked when He was going to restore the kingdom of Israel. He told them that they had no need to know when the Father will make things happen, but they would receive the power of the Holy Spirit and they should witness and testify about Him.

Then He raised His hands, blessed them, and ascended into (was immediately taken to) heaven through a Shekinah cloud where the Bible says God gave Him the highest position. By the time Jesus ascended into heaven, He had appeared to over 500 people.

According to Acts 1:10 two men (angels) in white clothing suddenly appeared in front of the disciples. They asked why the disciples were standing there staring up at the sky. The angels said that Jesus, who was taken to heaven, will return the same way they saw Him leave.

The disciples went back into Jerusalem and began their preaching ministry.

The Angelic Face of Stephen

Everyone who sat in the council stared at him and saw that his face looked like an angel's face....All who were sitting in the Sanhedrin looked intently at Stephen, and they saw that his face was like the face of an angel.

ACTS 6:15

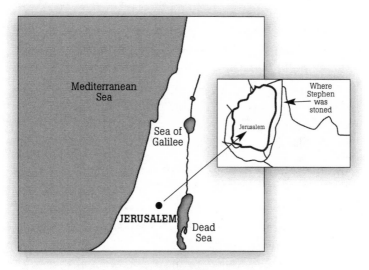

ACTS 6:15
Location: Jerusalem | **Historical Time:** ca 40 AD
TO VIEW MAPS ONLINE:
Copy this link into your browser and press Enter/Return
www.sacred-destinations.com/israel/jerusalem-map
www.sacred-destinations.com/israel/israel-map
www.ccel.org/bible/phillips/CP051GOSPELMAPS.htm
bibleatlas.org/jerusalem.htm

ANOTHER INSTANCE OF TRANSFIGURATION INVOLVED
Stephen. Stephen had strong faith and spoke openly about

the risen Lord. He also performed miracles, making the lives of the common people better.

But there were some men from the synagogue in Jerusalem who were angry with Stephen and his message. They argued openly with Stephen, but his wisdom and Spirit only made the other people in Jerusalem more supportive of the Christian movement. So these men conspired to destroy Stephen. They bribed others to say that Stephen said things that were blasphemous against Moses and God. They continuously lied and incited the people, the Jewish elders, and the "experts" in the law to turn on Stephen.

They seized Stephen and brought him before the Jewish council, the Sanhedrin. There these false witnesses stood up and openly lied about the things Stephen had said. (We see these same actions in many of our political debates and discussions today.)

As Stephen was being interrogated by the Council, the investigators began to stare at Stephen. His face and his whole demeanor had changed. He had a calm, serene, and innocent look. Sages say Stephen's face began to shine like the face of Moses had done 1,500 years earlier. Others say it had a radiance all of its own.

Then Stephen gave an accurate and eloquent testimonial on why he believed the teachings of the current Jewish leaders were wrong. This incensed the Council so much they became furious and lost their composure. They dragged Stephen out of the city and stoned him to death. Saul held the coats of the executioners. Saul would become a powerful persecutor of Christians, until the day he became a believer. On the day Stephen was executed, widespread persecution of all believers began.

Transformation of Matter

THE FINAL SUPERNATURAL PHENOMENON INVOLVING GOD'S power over matter is changing matter into something completely different. Three incidents immediately come to mind. In each case, matter was completely changed from one substance into another.

Wooden Walking Stick Changed into Snake

When Moses threw it on the ground, it became a snake.
EXODUS 4:3

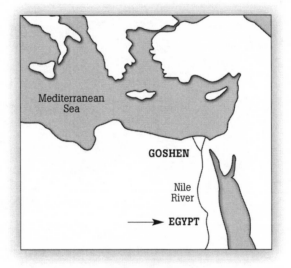

EXODUS 4:1–5; 7:10
Location: Egypt | **Historical Time:** ca 1500–1400 BC
TO VIEW MAPS ONLINE:
Copy this link into your browser and press Enter/Return
en.wikipedia.org/wiki/File:Ancient_Egypt_map-en.svg

BOTH MOSES AND AARON TURNED THEIR WALKING STICKS
(rods) into live snakes in front of the pharaoh in Egypt.

Nile River Changed into Blood

All the water in the river turned into blood.
EXODUS 7:20

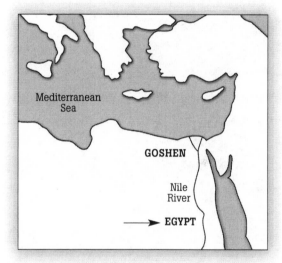

EXODUS 7:20; PSALMS 78:44; 105:29
Location: Egypt | **Historical Time:** ca 1500–1400 BC
TO VIEW MAPS ONLINE:
Copy this link into your browser and press Enter/Return
en.wikipedia.org/wiki/File:Ancient_Egypt_map-en.svg

THIS WAS THE FIRST PLAGUE TO AFFECT EGYPT AS MOSES and Aaron confront the pharaoh about freedom for the Israelites. Details are on page 15 at the beginning of this chapter.

Water Changed into Wine

But you have saved the best wine for now.

JOHN 2:10

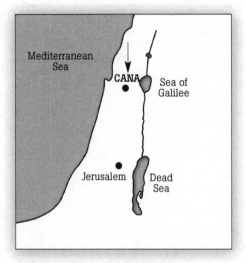

JOHN 2:1–10
Location: Cana | Historical Time: ca 30 AD
TO VIEW MAPS ONLINE:
Copy this link into your browser and press Enter/Return
en.wikipedia.org/wiki/Cana

JESUS CHANGED THE WATER IN SIX STONE JARS INTO 18 TO 27 gallons each of the best tasting wine at a wedding in Cana.

Summary

THIS HAS BEEN AN IN-DEPTH LOOK INTO DESCRIPTIONS OF power over matter as recorded in the Bible. You read how God has had His hand in the lives of humans ever since He created them. You read about matter that was changed, moved, levitated, teleported, made to appear, made to vanish, and made to protect and destroy. This power was and still is absolute. Regardless of how you look at the Bible, from any perspective, from any ideological position, this is, and continues to be, an amazing and powerful book.

It contains much more than you thought before you started reading about power over matter and comparing what I've written with your own copy of the Bible. If you now look at the Bible in amazement and a strong interest in learning more, my goal has been achieved. And there are many more discoveries to be made. Read on.

Relevant Verses in Chapter One

Incidents Involving Power over Matter

APPEARANCE: Jesus Appears to Doubting Thomas
Location: Galilee
Verses: John 20:26, 27
Jesus asked doubting Thomas to put hand into wound on side.

APPEARANCE: Angel Appears to Jesus
Location: Garden of Gethsemane
Verse: Luke 22:43
Angel appears and gives Jesus strength while praying in the Garden of Gethsemane before being arrested and later crucified.

APPEARANCE: Angel Appears to Man (Gideon)
Verse: Judges 6:12
Gideon is visited by an angel.

APPEARANCE: Angel Appears to Man (Zechariah)
Verse: Luke 1:11
Zechariah is visited by an angel.

APPEARANCE: Angel Appears to Manoah and his Barren Wife
Location: Mahaneh Dan, between Zorah and Eshtaol
Verses: Judges 13:1–24

Angel told woman she would become pregnant and give birth to a son, who would become a Nazarite. Before this, his wife could not have children. She gave birth to a boy and named him "Sampson."

APPEARANCE: Angel Appears to Mary
Verse: Luke 1:26
Announce pregnancy and coming birth of Jesus.

APPEARANCE: Angel Appears to Roman Officer
Location: Caesarea
Verse: Acts 10:3
Roman army officer, Cornelius of Caesarea, gets vision and sees an angel. He's told to send for Simon Peter and to bring him there.

APPEARANCE: Angel Appears to Shepherds
Location: Bethlehem
Verse: Luke 2:8
Announces Jesus' birth, and then an army of angels appear.

APPEARANCE: Angel Appears to the Two Women Named Mary

Location: Jerusalem
Verses: Matthew 28:1-7;
Luke 24:4-8
Angels were there at Jesus'
resurrection.

APPEARANCE: Angel Tells
Joseph to go to Egypt
Location: Bethlehem
Verse: Matthew 2:13
Angel appeared and told
Joseph to take Jesus and Mary
to Egypt since Herod plans to
kill the child.

APPEARANCE: Angel Tells
Joseph to Return from Egypt
Location: Egypt
Verse: Matthew 2:19
When Herod died, an angel
appeared to Joseph in a dream
telling him to return to Israel.

APPEARANCE: Angels Appear
to Mary at Tomb of Jesus
Location: Jerusalem,
Tomb of Jesus
Verse: John 20:11
Two angels are in tomb of
Jesus when Mary of Magdala
enters tomb.

APPEARANCE: Angels Suddenly
Appear to Disciples
Verses: Acts 1:10, 11
At the Ascension of Jesus.

APPEARANCE: Angels Suddenly
Appear to Shepherds
Verse: Luke 2:8
Announcing Jesus' birth.

APPEARANCE: Appearance of
Jesus Changed/Transfigured
Location: Tomb of Jesus
Verse: John 20:15

Jesus was not recognized by
Mary. She thought Jesus was
the gardener. Jesus spoke her
name and she immediately
recognized Him.

APPEARANCE: Armed
Messenger Appears to David
Verses: 1 Chron 21:15-27
Messenger causes deadly
plague.

APPEARANCE: Cloud Appears
Verses: Matthew 17:1-8
Pillar of cloud and fire appears
and envelops group at
transfiguration of Jesus.

APPEARANCE: Giants
Location: Fertile Crescent
Verse: Gen 6:2
Fallen Angels appeared
on earth as giants.

APPEARANCE: Flaming Torch
Appears
Verse: Gen 15:17
Abram asked God for a sign.

APPEARANCE: Flashing Light
Appears
Verse: Acts 9:3
Saul was suddenly bathed in
flashing light.

APPEARANCE: God Appears
in Human Form
Location: Road outside
Jericho
Verse: Joshua 5:13
At Jericho Joshua sees
theopony with drawn sword.

APPEARANCE: God Appears
to Abraham
Verses: Genesis 17:15-19

Told him Sarah at 90 would have Isaac.

APPEARANCE: God Appears to Abram
Verse: Genesis 16:1
Is told of many descendants, name now Abraham.

APPEARANCE: God Appears to Solomon
Location: Jerusalem
Verses: 1 Kings 9:1–9; 2 Chron 7:12–22
At night to talk about future.

APPEARANCE: Hand Appears and Writes on Rock Wall
Verses: Daniel 5:1–29
During a party of King Belshazzar of Babylon.

APPEARANCE: Jesus Appears Alive to Mary from Magdala
Verses: Mark 16:9, 10
At Jesus' resurrection.

APPEARANCE: Jesus Appears Alive to the Two Women Named Mary
Verses: Matthew 28:9,10
See Resurrected Jesus.

APPEARANCE: Jesus Appears
Verse: Acts 1:3
Spends 40 Days with the Apostles (former disciples).

APPEARANCE: Jesus Appears to Disciples on Road to Emmaus
Location: Road to Emmaus
Verse: Mark 16:12
Risen and transfigured Jesus appeared to two disciples walking to their village home in the country near Emmaus. They didn't recognize Him as He did not look the same.

APPEARANCE: Jesus Appears to Fishing Disciples
Location: Sea of Galilee
Verse: John 21:4
Jesus was not recognized when He appeared to the disciples fishing in the Sea of Galilee. His appearance had changed and they didn't recognize Him, but then they knew it was Him.

APPEARANCE: Jesus Appears to Many after Resurrection
Verses: 1 Cor 15:3–8
Paul tells who saw Jesus after.

APPEARANCE: Jesus Passes through Wall to Appear to Disciples
Location: Jerusalem
Verse: John 20:19
Jesus appeared to disciples behind locked doors.

APPEARANCE: Jesus Suddenly Appears to Disciples
Verses: Luke 24:36–46
Jesus appeared to disciples behind locked doors.

APPEARANCE: Manna Mysteriously Appears and Sustains Millions
Verses: Exodus 16:2–5, 13
Manna from heaven appeared.

APPEARANCE: Messenger Appears to Woman
Verse: Gen 16:7
Told Hagar she would have Ishmael.

APPEARANCE: Messenger of God Appears
Verses: Gen 21:14–21
Messenger of God talked with Hagar.

APPEARANCE: Messenger of the Lord Appears
Location: Mount Moriah
Verse: Gen 22:15
A Messenger of the Lord appeared and told Abraham he'd have many descendants.

APPEARANCE: Messenger of the Lord appears to Moses
Location: Mount Horeb
Verse: Exodus 3:2
In burning bush

APPEARANCE: Spirit Appears as a Dove
Verses: Matthew 3:13–17
Jesus was baptized in the Jordan by John.

APPEARANCE: The Cloud
Verses: Exodus 13:20–22
Tall column of smoke and fire leads Israelites during Exodus.

APPEARANCE: Transfiguration of Stephen
Verse: Acts 6:15
Stephen's face changed during interrogation.

APPEARANCE: Transfigured
Verses: John 20:14–18
Mary from Magdala didn't recognize Jesus.

APPEARANCE: Transfigured Jesus Appears
Verses: Matthew 28:16–20
Sends disciples to Galilee.

APPEARANCE: Transfigured/Appearance ChangedVerse: Mark 16:12
Disciples didn't recognize Jesus.

APPEARANCE: Unidentified Flying Object
Verses: 2 Kings 2:9–11
Suddenly appears and separates Elijah and Elisha.

APPEARANCE: Unidentified Flying Objects
Verse: 2 Kings 6:16
Surround enemy of Elisha and Israelites at Dothan.

APPEARANCE: Angel Appears
Location: Horeb
Verses: 1 Kings 19–1–18
Provides Elijah food and drink preparing him for 40 days and nights of travel to Horeb the mount of God.

APPEARANCE: Messenger of the Lord Suddenly Appears to Balaam
Location: road from Pethor on the Euphrates River to Moab
Verses: Numbers 23:31
Donkey spoke to Balaam and suddenly Balaam could see the Messenger of the Lord standing in the road with his sword drawn.

APPEARANCE: Moses and Elijah Suddenly Appear
Location: believed to be Mount Hermon
Verse: Matthew 17:1;
Mark 9:2–13; Luke 9:28–36

With Jesus in front of Peter, James, and John. Jesus' appearance changed. His face became bright as the sun, and His clothes became white as light. Suddenly Moses and Elijah appeared and began talking with Jesus about his approaching death. A bright cloud overshadowed the group, and a voice came out of the cloud.

ARK: Wooden Box Has Power to Heal or Destroy
Verse: 1 Kings 8:21
Ark of the Covenant.

BATTLE SIGN: Dew Becomes Sign of Pending Victory
Verses: Judges 6:37–40
Gideon and wool.

BLINDED: Man Blinded by the Light
Verse: Acts 9:8
Saul blind for three days.

CLOUD: Supernatural Cloud Fills Temple
Verse: 1 Kings 8:10
Divine Shekinah cloud of power inside temple.

CLOUD: Cloud of Smoke Covers Meeting Place
Verse: Exodus 33:9; Exodus 40:34
Tent of Meeting covered over.

CLOUD: Column of Smoke and Fire Leads People
Verses: Exodus 13:21; 40:38
During Exodus through desert.

CREATION: God Creates Day and Night
Verse: Gen 1:3
The First Day.

CREATION: God Creates Garden of Eden
Verse: Gen 2:26
Garden with fruit trees and river.

CREATION: God Creates Heaven and Earth
Verse: Gen 1:1
Sky and planet.

CREATION: God Creates Horizon
Verse: Gen 1:6
The Second Day.

CREATION: God Creates Human
Verse: Gen 1:26
To rule over the earth, the fish, the birds, and animals that crawl.

CREATION: God Creates Land and Sea
Verse: Gen 1:9
The Third Day.

CREATION: God Creates Lights in the Sky
Verse: Gen 1:14
Sun, moon, and stars created on Fourth Day.

CREATION: God Creates Living Creatures
Verse: Gen 1:24
Domestic and wild animals, and crawling animals created on Sixth Day.

CREATION: God Creates Man
Verse: Gen 2:7
From the dust of the earth.

CREATION: God Creates Swimming and Flying Creatures
Verse: Gen 1:20
The Fifth Day.

CREATION: God Creates Vegetation
Verse: Gen 1:11
Plants and fruit trees with fruit and seeds.

CREATION: Woman Made from Rib of Man
Verse: Gen 2:21
God took rib of man and created woman.

DISAPPEARANCE: Jesus Becomes Invisible and Passes through Hostile Crowd
Location: Jerusalem
Verse: John 8:59
Angry Jews picked up stones to throw at Jesus, but He suddenly became unseen ("was concealed") and passed through the hostile crowd in the courtyard of the temple in Jerusalem. (New International version says "Jesus hid himself, slipping away from the temple grounds.") (King James Bible says "but Jesus hid himself, and went out of the temple, going through the midst of them, and so passed by.")

DISAPPEARANCE: Jesus Disappears in Shekinah Cloud
Verse: Acts 1:9
Cloud covered Jesus and he disappeared.

DISAPPEARANCE: Manna Stops
Verse: Joshua 5:12
Daily food suddenly stops after 40 years once Israelites reach Promised Land.

DISAPPEARANCE: Messenger Burns Offering Then Disappears
Location: Ophrah, a city in the tribal lot of Manasseh, west of Jordan River
Verse: Judges 6:20, 21
Messenger touches food with staff instantly burning Gideon's offering. Then the messenger disappeared.

DISAPPEARANCE: Messenger Disappears in Flames
Location: between Zorah and Eshtaol
Verse: Judges 13:20
God's "messenger" disappeared before the eyes of Manoah and his wife in flames of burnt offering rising up toward the sky.

EARTH: Earth Opens & Swallows Family
Verses: Numbers 16:1–31
Korah challenges Moses' authority.

EARTHQUAKE: Earthquake Shakes Meeting Place
Verse: Acts 4:31
Apostles and Holy Spirit.

FIG TREE: Fig Tree Cursed and Is Destroyed
Verse: Matthew 21:18
Jesus destroyed fig tree with no fruit.

FIRE: Fire Comes Down from the Sky
Verse: 1 Chron 21:26
Consumes David's offering on the altar.

FIRE: Fire Comes Down from the Sky
Verses: 2 Kings 1-9
Elijah calls down fire to kill officer with 50 soldiers.

FIRE: Fire Comes Down from the Sky
Verses: 1 Kings 18-1-39
Elijah challenged 450 ungodly prophets.

FIRE: Fire Comes Down from the Sky
Verse: Job 1:16
Job was told his flocks and servants burned up.

FIRE: Fire Comes Down from the Sky
Verses: 1 Kings 8:62-66
At Temple dedication in Jerusalem.

FIRE: Fire Consumes Offering
Verse: Judges 13:19
An angel caused fire to consume offering.

FIRE: Fire from Rock Burns Offering
Verses: Judges 6:20-21
When Messenger touched food with staff.

FIRE: Sudden Fire from Cloud Consumes Sacrifice
Verse: Leviticus 9:23
Fire from cloud of smoke.

FOOD: Food Multiplies
Verse: 2 Kings 4:42
Elisha fed 100 people.

FOOD: Food Multiplies
Verses: Matthew 15:32-38
Jesus fed over 4,000 people.

FOOD: Food Multiplies
Verses: Matthew 14:15-21
Jesus fed over 5,000 people.

FOOD: Food Supply Never Ends during Famine
Verses: 1 Kings 17:8-16
Elijah and flour and oil never run out.

FOOD: Oil Containers Continue to Fill
Verses: 2 Kings 4:1-7
Elisha keeps oil jars full for poor widow.

FOOD: Poisoned Food Made Edible
Verses: 2 Kings 4:38-41
Elisha made poisoned pottage safe to eat.

FOREVER WEAR: Clothing and Shoes Don't Wear Out
Verse: Deuteronomy 8:4
Clothes and sandals never wore out during 40-year Exodus.

HEALING: People Healed Just by Touching Cloth
Verse: Acts 19:11
Cloth that touched Paul's skin heals.

HEALING: Touch Restores Sight
Verse: Acts 9:18
Ananias heals Saul's blindness as scales fall off.

HEALING POWER: Special Power Given to Disciples
Verses: Mark 16:17–19
Jesus gave them power to heal.

HOLY SPIRIT: Tongues of Fire
Verse: Acts 2:3
Holy Spirit enters disciples at Pentecost.

IDOL: Idol Smashed in Presence of Ark
Verses: 1 Sam 5:1–5
Ark in Philistine temple of Dagon.

LEVITATION: Sunken Axe Head Levitates
Verse: 2 Kings 6:5
Elisha floats axe head out of Jordan River.

LEVITATION: Transfigured Jesus Ascends to Heaven
Verse: Mark 16:19
Jesus ascends from mountaintop.

PLAGUE: Sudden Darkness Halts Sun Worship
Verse: Exodus 10:21
Exodus Ninth Plague.

PRISON: Angel Opens Prison Cell Door
Verse: Acts 5:19
Peter and other apostles led out of prison.

PRISON: Prison Chains and Gate Suddenly Open
Verses: Acts 12:1–19
Peter's prison cell filled with light.

PRISON: Prison Doors Suddenly Open
Verses: Acts 16:24–40
Paul and Silius prisoners during earthquake.

SOUND: Sudden Sound Causes Panic, Siege Abandonment, and Flight
Verses: 2 Kings 7:5–20
Supernatural sounds like approaching army panic huge army

SOUND: Sudden Sound Fills House
Verse: Acts 2:1
Pentecost, sound like a violently blowing wind.

SOUND: Sudden Sounds Collapse City Walls
Verses: Joshua 6:2–20
Walls of Jericho collapse.

SPROUTING: Dry Walking Stick Sprouts Ripe Almonds Overnight
Verses: Numbers 17:1–10
Aaron's rod blossoms.

SUN STILL: Sun and Moon Stand Still
Verse: Joshua 10:13
Joshua chased down the fleeing Amorites.

TABLETS: Stone Tablets Etched by God
Verse: Deut 10:1
God wrote Ten Commandments on stone.

TELEPORTATION: Enoch Taken Directly to Heaven
Location: unknown

Verse: Gen 5:21
Enoch went directly to heaven when he was 365 years old.

TELEPORTATION: Jesus and Fishing Boat with Crew Teleported to Shore
Location: Sea of Galilee
Verse: John 6:21
Jesus got in the boat and it immediately "reached" shore 4 miles away.

TELEPORTATION: Jesus ascends into Heaven
Verse: Luke 24:51
The ascension of Jesus.

TELEPORTATION: Jesus taken by Satanic Spirit
Verses: Matthew 4:1–11
Into desert to be tempted for 40 days.

TELEPORTATION: Man Abducted and Teleported to Third Heaven
Verses: 2 Cor 12:2–4
Paul told the people of Corinth about a follower of Christ who was snatched away to the third heaven 14 years earlier. The third heaven is one of the 10 dimensions described in the Bible.

TELEPORTATION: Philip Teleported 12 Miles
Location: Azostus
Verses: Acts 8:26–40
Philip explains writings of Isaiah to Ethiopian eunuch and high-ranking official in charge of all treasures of Queen Candace of Ethiopia. Official was riding in carriage from Jerusalem to Gaza. After talking with Philip, they stopped and official was baptized by Philip in some water alongside the road. When they stepped out of the water, Philip suddenly disappeared and reappeared in the village of Azotus, 12 miles away.

TEMPLE CURTAIN: Temple Curtain Suddenly Rips in Two
Verse: Matthew 27:45
Occurs when Jesus died on the cross.

TRANSFIGURATION:
Appearance of Jesus Changes (Transfigured)
Location: believed to be Mount Hermon
Verses: Matthew 17:1–8; Mark 9:2–13; Luke 9:28–36
Peter, James, and John watch Jesus' appearance change. His face became bright as the sun, and His clothes became white as light. Suddenly Moses and Elijah appeared and began talking with Jesus about his approaching death. A bright cloud overshadowed the group, and a voice came out of the cloud saying, "This is my Son, whom I have chosen. Listen to him!" The next day, Jesus spoke with the three disciples and led them down the mountain.

TRANSFIGURATION: Jesus' Transfiguration/Sudden Appearance
Verses: Matthew 17:1-8
Jesus' features change.

TRANSFIGURATION: Stephen's Face Transfigured
Location: Jerusalem
Verse: Acts 6:15
Stephen is being interrogated by Jewish Council when they began to stare at Stephen. His face looked like that of an angel.

TRANSFIGURED: Moses' Face Shined
Verses: 2 Cor 3:7-13
Paul described how Moses' face shined.

TRANSFORMATION: Aaron's Wooden Staff Becomes Live Snake
Verse: Exodus 7:10
Aaron turned staff into snake.

TRANSFORMATION: Moses' Wooden Staff Becomes Live Snake
Verse: Exodus 4:3
Moses turned staff into snake.

WATER: Earth Splits Open and Water Gushes Out
Location: Lehi
Verse: Judges 15:18, 19
Sampson at spring of En Hakkore.

WATER: Jesus Walks on Water
Verses: Matthew 14:24-31
Jesus walked on surface of Sea of Galilee.

WATER: Jordan River Parts for Huge Group to Cross
Verses: Joshua 3:13-16
Joshua with Ark at Jordan River.

WATER: Jordan River Water Parts for Elijah
Verses: 2 Kings 2-1-8
Elisha and Elijah cross Jordan River.

WATER: Jordan River Water Parts for Elisha
Verse: 2 Kings 2:14
Elisha took two tries to part Jordan River.

WATER: Peter Walks on Water
Verses: Matthew 14:24-31
Peter walked on water out to Jesus.

WATER: Sea Parts for Large Group to Cross
Verses: Exodus 14:21-31
Red Sea separated during Exodus.

WATER: Strikes Rock Releasing Water
Verse: Numbers 20:1
Moses struck rock and water came out.

WATER: Water Changed into Wine
Verses: John 2:1-10
Jesus was at a wedding celebration in Cana.

WATER: Water Flows from Rock Struck by Wooden Staff
Verse: Exodus 17:6
Moses gets water out of rock.

WATER: Water from Well of Beer-elim Sustains a Nation
Verses: Numbers 21:13–18
Moses and Exodus.

WATER: Water in Nile Turns into Blood
Location: Egypt
Verses: Exodus 7:14–25
The First Plague.

WATER: Water Made Pure
Verses: 2 Kings 2:19–22
Elisha and water at Jericho.

WATER: Water Suddenly Becomes Drinkable
Verse: Exodus 15:25
Wood used to make bitter water sweet.

WATER: Water Suddenly Fills Ditches
Verses: 2 Kings 3:1–22
Elisha in wilderness of Edom.

WATER WALKING: Jesus and Peter Walk on Water
Location: Sea of Galilee
Verses: Matthew 14:24–31; Mark 6:44–56; John 6:15–21
The disciples were crossing the Sea of Galilee against the wind to go to the western side ahead of him. Jesus walked out to them over the water. Then Peter walked out to Jesus on the water. A strong wind came up, Peter lost courage and began to sink into the sea. Jesus saved Peter, and then commanded the wind to stop blowing. It did, and the boat continued across the Sea of Galilee to Bethsaida in Gennesaret. There Jesus allowed sick people to touch his clothes, making them well again.

CHAPTER TWO

Power Over People

THE BIBLE ALSO DESCRIBES POWER OVER PEOPLE and power over groups. Thus we read about angels, messengers of the Lord, men of God, prophets, apostles, kings, generals, Abraham, Moses, Aaron, Joshua, Saul, Samuel, Sampson, David, Solomon, Elijah, Elisha, Jesus, Peter, and the whole Israelite nation.

I found 103 incidents in the Bible that deal with power over people. In the stories to follow, I'll elaborate on important examples of this force. At the end of this chapter, you'll find a list of all the relevant incidents that were discovered during my research.

King's Finger and Arm Instantly Paralyzed

But the arm that he used to point to the man of God was paralyzed so he couldn't pull it back.

1 KINGS 13:46

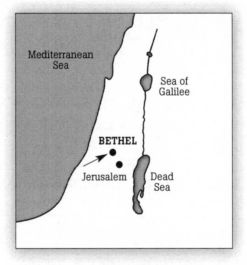

1 KINGS 13:1-5
Location: Bethel | **Historical Time:** ca 931 BC
TO VIEW MAPS ONLINE:
Copy this link into your browser and press Enter/Return
blog.eteacherbiblical.com/wp-content/uploads/2008/01/judah-and-israel.gif

WHEN JEROBOAM BECAME KING OF ISRAEL, HE VIOLATED God's command for a single altar at Jerusalem and established new centers of worship at Dan and Bethel. He also took on the role of a priest while in Bethel by beginning to offer a sacrifice on the altar. But a man of God from Judah stepped forward and condemned the altar. Speaking directly to the altar, the man of God declared, "O altar, altar, this is what the Lord says: 'There will be a son born in David's family line. His name will be Josiah. Here on you, Josiah will sacrifice the priests from the illegal worship sites who offer sacrifices on you. Human bones will be burned on you.'" This prediction regarding Josiah came true 300 years later.

Then the man of God spoke to the people standing there. He said, "This is the sign that the Lord will give you: You will see the altar torn apart. The ashes on it will be poured on the ground."

King Jeroboam became furious. He pointed to the man of God across the altar from him and commanded, "Arrest him."

Before his guards could take the man of God into custody, King Jeroboam's pointing arm became paralyzed out from his body. And just as suddenly, the altar was torn apart and the ashes from past offerings were poured on the ground.

The king realized that he was dealing with something far more powerful than he. King Jeroboam asked the man of God to pray to his God that he could use his arm again. The man prayed and the king's arm suddenly began working again.

Like a bully who was beaten, King Jeroboam then wanted to befriend the man of God. He told the man to go with him to his home where he could eat and drink. The humbled king also said he had a gift for the man of God.

But the man of God was not to be swayed. He told Jeroboam that even if the king gave him half of his palace, he would never eat or drink there with him. He told the king that the Lord had commanded him not to eat or drink or return on the same road he took to get there. Then the man of God turned and left Bethel on another road, leaving King Jeroboam with the knowledge that the Lord of this man of God was far more powerful than he, the king, would ever be.

Gehazi Lies and Suddenly Gets Leprosy

When he left Elisha, Gehazi had a disease that made his skin as flaky as snow.

2 KINGS 5:27

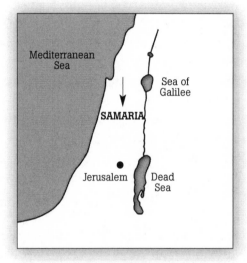

Mediterranean Sea

Sea of Galilee

SAMARIA

Jerusalem

Dead Sea

2 KINGS 5:19–27
Location: Near Jordan River in Samaria | **Historical Time:** ca 860 BC
TO VIEW MAPS ONLINE:
Copy this link into your browser and press Enter/Return
en.wikipedia.org/wiki/File:JordanRiver_en.svg

ELISHA HAD JUST ENABLED NAAMAN, THE COMMANDER OF the Aramean king's army, to be cured of a skin disease [leprosy] by washing in the Jordan River seven times. The healthy commander wanted to give Elisha a gift for his kindness, but the prophet declined. Naaman insisted, but Elisha still refused.

So Naaman asked for as much dirt as a pair of mules could carry back with him. He asked the Lord of Elisha to forgive him when he went to the temple of Rimmon to allow his king to lean on his arm as the king worshipped the idol at Rimmon and when he had to bow down before the idol with the king.

Elisha understood and told the commander to go in peace. So Naaman and his men departed.

But Gehazi, the servant of Elisha felt Naaman should have left the gift. He wanted something for himself. In his greed, Gehazi hurried after Naaman. When the commander saw the servant running after him, he stopped his troop and came down from his chariot to speak with Gehazi.

Naaman asked, "Is something wrong?"

Gehazi replied, "No. My master has sent me." Gehazi said that Elisha told him that two young men from the disciples of the prophets in the hills of Ephraim had arrived, and Elisha wanted to give them 75 pounds of silver and two sets of clothing.

Naaman immediately offered to give Gehazi 150 pounds of silver and two sets of clothing. Gehazi accepted, and Naaman had 150 pounds of silver placed in two bags that were tied shut. Then he had two sets of clothing given to Gehazi to carry back.

Gehazi took the gifts and departed. He went to Ophel in Samaria and "put the things away in the house." Then Gehazi dismissed the men who helped him carry the bounty, and he returned to Elisha.

When he arrived, Elisha asked Gehazi, "Where were you?"

Gehazi replied, "I didn't go anywhere."

Then Elisha sternly said to Gehazi, "I went with you in spirit when the man [Naaman] turned around in his chariot to speak to you."

Gehazi looked sheepish and began to feel quite uneasy. His master knew that he was lying.

Elisha continued, "How could you accept silver, clothes, olive orchards, vineyards, sheep, cattle, or slaves?"

Then Elisha said sternly, "Naaman's skin disease will cling to you and your descendants permanently."

Immediately Gehazi contracted leprosy. As he left the presence of Elisha, Gehazi's skin had become flaky like new-fallen snow. Gehazi had this skin disease for the rest of his life. Although 2 Kings 5:27 doesn't elaborate, we can only surmise that the children of Gehazi suffered the same fate.

Zechariah Unable to Speak until Baby is Born

When he [Zechariah] did come out [of the Temple], he was unable to speak to them.
LUKE 1:22

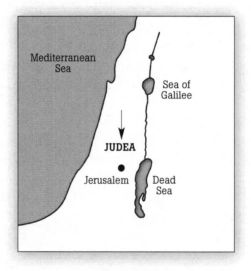

LUKE 1:5–64
Location: Mountain region of Judea | **Historical Time:** ca 1 BC
TO VIEW MAPS ONLINE:
Copy this link into your browser and press Enter/Return
en.wikipedia.org/wiki/Judea
people.usd.edu/~clehmann/pir/judaea.htm

HEROD WAS KING OF JUDEA. IN HIS COUNTRY THERE LIVED a priest named Zechariah. This priest and his wife, Elizabeth, were faithful to God and followed His commands and regulations perfectly. But they had no children and often prayed for a family of their own.

One day, Zechariah was performing his priestly duties burning incense in the Lord's temple while the people prayed outside.

Suddenly an angel appeared at the end of the altar frightening Zechariah. The angel said, "Don't be afraid, Zechariah! God has heard your prayer."

Then the angel told Zechariah that he and his wife would have a son. He will be named John, and John will be the pride and joy of the couple. He said, "Many people will be glad that he was born. As far as the Lord is concerned, he will be a great man."

The angel went on to tell Zechariah that John will never drink wine or any other liquor, and John would be filled with the Holy Spirit even before he was born. He said that John would bring many people back to God, and John would have the same spirit and power as Elijah did years before. The angel said that John would change parents' attitudes toward their children and cause disobedient people to accept the wisdom of those with God's approval. In this way, John would prepare the people for the coming of the Lord.

Zechariah was skeptical about becoming a father. He asked the angel, "What proof is there for this? I'm an old man, and my wife is beyond her childbearing years."

The angel sternly replied, "I'm Gabriel! I stand in God's presence. God sent me to tell you this good news." Then he said, "But because you didn't believe what I said, you will be unable to talk until the day this happens. Everything will come true at the right time."

While Zechariah was being reprimanded by Gabriel, the people outside the temple were waiting and wondering why Zechariah was taking so long to finish making the offering. They were amazed when he finally came out but could not speak. They quickly knew that he had seen a vision. From that moment on, Zechariah could motion and write, but he could not speak.

After his priestly duties were complete, Zechariah went home. Elizabeth became pregnant. She had a difficult time handling this at her age and didn't go out in public for five months. Then she accepted her condition and said, "The Lord has done this for me now. He has removed my public disgrace."

In her sixth month of pregnancy, God sent the angel Gabriel to Nazareth over in Galilee. Gabriel visited Mary, a virgin promised in marriage to Joseph, a descendant of David. During the conversation with Mary, Gabriel told her that her cousin, Elizabeth was already six months pregnant. Gabriel said that people told Elizabeth she couldn't have a child at her age, but nothing was impossible for God.

After Gabriel left, the young virgin Mary hurried to the mountain region of Judah and the home of Zechariah and Elizabeth. When Mary greeted her cousin, the baby inside Elizabeth kicked and Elizabeth was filled with the Holy Spirit.

The two women became very close, and Mary stayed with Elizabeth for three months. Then Mary returned to Nazareth while Elizabeth took the baby to full term.

Then the baby boy was born, and the relatives and neighbors of Elizabeth celebrated the joy of Zechariah and his wife. But for nine months Zechariah had not been able to speak a word.

When the baby was eight days old, he was taken to the temple for circumcision and naming. Everyone thought he would be named Zechariah after his father, but Elizabeth said, "Absolutely not! His name will be John."

Friends there said, "But you don't have any relatives with that name!" So they motioned for Zechariah for direction. Zechariah asked for writing material and wrote, "His name is John."

The friends were amazed, but even more amazed when Zechariah immediately began to speak and praise God [Luke 1:57-64]. Just as Gabriel had said, Zechariah's ability to speak returned once baby John had arrived.

Blinded by the Light
(Saul to Paul)

When he opened his eyes, he was blind.
ACTS 9:8

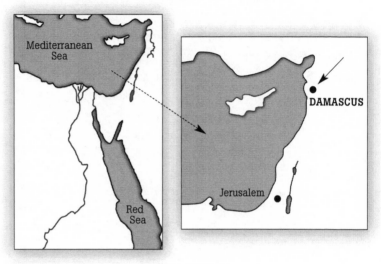

ACTS 9:1–18; 22:11
Location: Road to Damascus | **Historical Time:** ca 33 AD
TO VIEW MAPS ONLINE:
Copy this link into your browser and press Enter/Return
en.wikipedia.org/wiki/Damascus

SAUL WAS THE JEW WHO HELD THE COATS OF THE MEN who stoned Stephen. After this event, Saul became a fanatic in his persecution of Christians. He consistently threatened to murder those who followed The Way (believed in Jesus Christ as Savior).

Saul went to the chief priest in Jerusalem asking for a letter to all synagogue leaders authorizing Saul to arrest any man or woman who followed the way of Jesus Christ. The letter gave him permission to apprehend these followers and imprison them in Jerusalem. So Saul set out on his mission to find and persecute Christians. His hatred of Christians made him arrogant, powerful and well-known.

He traveled throughout Judea and Samaria including up north beyond the Sea of Galilee. He went past Mount Hermon and entered on the road toward Damascus about 120 miles northeast of Jerusalem when a supernatural event occurred.

Acts 9:3 says that as he was approaching Damascus, a bright light from heaven suddenly flashed causing him to fall to the ground. Then Saul heard a voice say, "Saul! Saul! Why are you persecuting me?"

Saul asked who was speaking. The voice said, "I'm Jesus, the one you're persecuting." In verse 5, Saul is ordered to get up and go into Damascus where he would receive instructions.

The men with Saul were flabbergasted. They saw the bright flash, and they heard the voice, but they didn't see anyone.

Saul opened his eyes and realized that he was blind. The men with Saul helped him to his feet and led the completely humiliated (former) Christian persecutor into the city. They took him to the house of Judas on Straight Street.

For three days, Saul remained there sitting alone in blind darkness. He didn't eat, and he didn't drink. He could only reach out with his hands and feel the material around him and hear the voices of those with him. Saul felt all alone in his misery. Here was a mighty man reduced to a helpless and powerless human in the instant of a bright flash of light.

A follower of the Way (Christian believer) named Ananias lived there in Damascus and at night God came to Ananias in a vision. The Lord called him by name and Ananias answered, "Yes, Lord."

Ananias was told to get up and go to the house of Judas on Straight Street and ask for a man named Saul from the city of Tarsus. The Lord told Ananias that Saul was praying at that moment and Saul has had a vision of a man named Ananias who would place his hands on him and restore his sight.

But Ananias was frightened. He told the Lord that he's heard that Saul had done many evil things to the believers in Jerusalem. Ananias knew that Saul was there with authority from the chief priests to arrest and imprison anyone who calls on His name.

In Acts 9:15, the Lord says, "Go! I've chosen this man [Saul] to bring my name to nations, to kings, and to the people of Israel." He said He would show Saul how much he has to suffer for the sake of His name.

Then Ananias went to the house and came immediately to Saul. Ananias told Saul, "Brother Saul, the Lord Jesus, who appeared to you on your way to Damascus, sent me to you. He wants you to see again and to be filled with the Holy Spirit."

With that, Ananias placed his hands on Saul, and immediately something like fish scales fell from Saul's eyes, and he could see again.

Saul stood up and was baptized. Then he ate and regained his strength. For the next several days, Saul began telling the people in the synagogues that Jesus was truly the Son of God.

The people were amazed. The Jewish leadership was furious. Here was the one who had destroyed everyone caught worshipping the one named Jesus in Jerusalem, and who had come to Damascus to arrest these worshipers and take them prisoner to the chief priests in Jerusalem. Now he was preaching that Jesus was the Messiah.

They planned to murder Saul and watched the city gates day and night. But Saul found out about their plot and escaped Damascus when some of his disciples lowered him in a basket down from an opening in the city walls.

Saul went to Jerusalem speaking boldly with the power and authority of the Lord. Jews there also tried to murder Saul, so his disciples took him to Caesarea and then to Tarsus. Barnabas, another believer, came to Tarsus to find Saul.

They met and together went to Antioch were they met with the believers there for a whole year. It was here that the disciples were called "Christians" for the first time.

In 34 AD, Barnabas and Saul sailed to Cyprus (also called the "Island of Dan"). According to Acts 13:9, we read that Saul is now becoming known as Paul.

Paul confronts an evil astrologer at Paphos on Cyprus, who was trying to dissuade the governor of Cyprus from believing Paul. Paul blinds the man. From this time on, Saul is called Paul.

Paul performed many miracles and became one of Christianity's most important apostles. He made three significant missionary trips between 40 AD and 59 AD. During his first trip, the followers of Jesus became known as "Christians."

As described in Acts 28:8, Paul healed Sergius Paulus, the father of Paulus, governor of Cyprus, of a fever and dysentery. He drove a demon out of a woman servant; he caused the Holy Spirit to enter 12 disciples in Ephesus, enabling them to speak in tongues; he healed people who put their hands on handkerchiefs and aprons that had touched him; and he raised a young man in Troas named Eutychus who had died.

Eutychus had fallen asleep and fell backwards out of an open third floor window during a lengthy group discussion of Scripture led by Paul. The fall killed him, but Paul brought him back to life. Other than being embarrassed, Eutychus was alive. The discussions continued. Eutychus ate with the others and then returned home after sunrise, while Paul continued on his missionary journey.

Saul was an ardent persecutor of those who believed in Jesus' resurrection, and he was an even stronger supporter and bold and outspoken speaker as Paul, the friend and brother of the growing Christian movement.

People and Animals Suddenly Get Boils

All of the livestock of the Egyptians died,
but none of the Israelites' animals died.
EXODUS 9:7

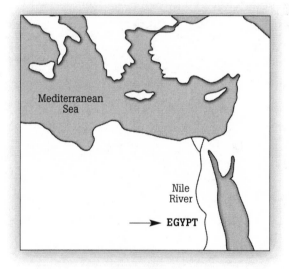

EXODUS 9:1-7
Location: Egypt | Historical Time: Late Bronze Age – ca 1445 BC
TO VIEW MAPS ONLINE:
Copy this link into your browser and press Enter/Return
en.wikipedia.org/wiki/File:Ancient_Egypt_map-en.svg

IN THIS SIXTH PLAGUE LEADING UP TO THE RELEASE OF
the Israelite slaves from bondage in Egypt, God told Moses
to pick up a handful of ashes from a kiln near the pharaoh.
As the pharaoh watched, Moses threw the ashes up into
the air. The ashes immediately became a fine dust that rap-

idly spread throughout Egypt causing boils on the Egyptians and their animals. The boils became open sores.

Even the Egyptian magicians could not stop the plague, and they all suffered. Still the pharaoh refused to budge.

Moses Talks with God on Mount Sinai

*Then Moses went up the mountain to God,
and the Lord called to him.*
EXODUS 19:36

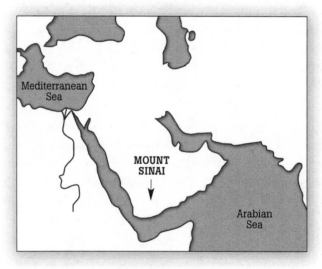

EXODUS 19:1-25
Location: Mount Sinai | **Historical Time:** Late Bronze Age – ca 1446 BC
TO VIEW MAPS ONLINE:
Copy this link into your browser and press Enter/Return
en.wikipedia.org/wiki/Mount_Sinai

AT MOUNT SINAI, MOSES WENT UP AND TALKED WITH GOD. Then he told the people what God had said. He told them to make ready to meet God. As the Israelites approached the base of the mountain, the cloud and column moved up and spread out over Mount Sinai. The entire mountain was covered with smoke; the Lord was present in the cloud and in the fire.

The people were told not to approach or touch the edge of the cloud or they would die. God told Moses to bring Aaron, Nadab and Abihu, his eldest sons, and 70 of the elders up into the foothills of the mountain.

From down below, the people looked up and saw the fiery smoke, the dark cloud with the lightning, and they heard the loud thunder. Then God gave the leaders of the Hebrews laws to live by. These laws covered the treatment of people, property rights, the three Festivals, laws for living with others, and laws about listening to God's Messenger.

Moses placed Aaron in charge of the leaders and sent all the leadership down to the people. Then Moses went on up into the cloud. Moses stayed up there for 40 days and 40 nights getting specific instructions. God told Moses to construct a wooden ark in which to keep the tablets. It would be called the "Ark of the Covenant." He also told Moses to have the people make a Tent of Meeting with an inner and outer room. He instructed them to make a three-foot Table to hold plates, dishes, pitchers, bowls, and a lamp stand with six branches and seven lamps of pure gold.

Then God told him to have an altar made out of acacia wood and covered with bronze. All of these would be placed in the Tent of Meeting and only certain priests could go inside. God also established a 20% tax or an ounce of silver for everyone 20 and older. This tax was used to maintain the Tent of Meeting.

Finally God wrote His law on two tablets of stone, and Moses started back down the mountain carrying the tablets.

Jealousy of Miriam Results in Leprosy

Miriam was covered with an infectious skin disease.
NUMBERS 12:10

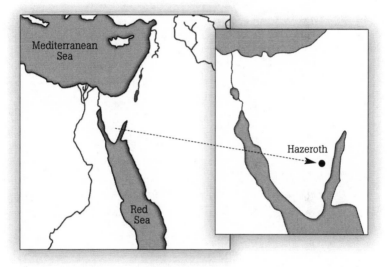

NUMBER 12:1–16
Location: Hazeroth | **Historical Time:** Late Bronze Age – ca 1446 BC
TO VIEW MAPS ONLINE:
Copy this link into your browser and press Enter/Return
bibleatlas.org/hazeroth.htm

WHILE THE ISRAELITES WERE CAMPED AT HAZEROTH, Miriam and Aaron became jealous of Moses because he had married a Cushite woman.

When they spoke out against Moses, all three (Moses, Aaron, and Miriam) were commanded to go to the Tent of Meeting. They did, and the Lord came down in a pillar of cloud (Shekinah) and positioned at the entrance to the tent. Aaron and Miriam were called forward and were severely chastised by God.

When the cloud moved away from over the tent, Miriam had become leprous. Aaron and Miriam were both sorry for their comments. Nevertheless, Miriam was required to stay out of the camp for seven days until her leprosy had gone away.

Then the exodus of the Israelite nation continued.

Paul Heals Father
of Maltese Governor

*Paul went to him, prayed, placed his hands on him,
and made him well.*
ACTS 28:8

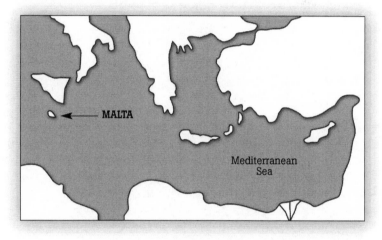

ACTS 28: 7–10
Location: Island of Malta | Historical Time: ca 59 AD
TO VIEW MAPS ONLINE:
Copy this link into your browser and press Enter/Return
en.wikipedia.org/wiki/Malta_(island)

PAUL AND HIS ROMAN GUARD WERE GUESTS OF PUBLIUS,
governor of Malta. When Paul learned that the father of
Publius was sick and suffering from fever and dysentery,
he went to the man and prayed over him. Then Paul placed
his hands on Publius' father and the father was immediately healed.

When the Maltese people heard about Paul's healing of
the father of the governor, they came to Paul asking him

to cure them. Paul had been a medical doctor so he likely used his medical skills as well as his divine skills to make them well.

Paul and his companions stayed on Malta for three months waiting for another Alexandrian grain ship. When it arrived, the local people gave the travelers plenty of provisions for their trip to Rome. He treated them with respect, and they treated him with respect.

Summary

IN THIS CHAPTER YOU SAW HOW GOD'S POWER OVER PEOPLE is absolute. He caused people to come down with disease. He made them blind, paralyzed, or unable to speak. And he healed them of their afflictions. He can still do these today.

In the next chapter, you'll read how God destroyed evil people while protecting and saving the innocent. You'll read about God's power over life and death.

Relevant Verses
in Chapter Two

Incidents Involving
Power over People

ABDUCTION: Abduction by
Angels
Location: by Chebar River
Verse: Ezekiel 11:22
Angels with wheels beside
them raised their wings.
Ezekiel was lifted by the Spirit
and taken back to Babylonia.

ABDUCTION: Prophet Abducted
Location: by the Chebar River,
and Jerusalem
Verse: Ezekiel 40:1
During a vision, Ezekiel was
taken to Jerusalem where a
man, who looked like he was
covered in bronze, described
the construction of the New
Temple of God.

ABDUCTION: Prophet Abducted
Location: by Chebar River,
then Jerusalem
Verse: Ezekiel 8:1
Ezekiel saw a humanoid. It
grabbed him by the hair on his
head and carried him up into
sky and over to Jerusalem so
Ezekiel could see the disgust-
ing things that the priests and
people were doing.

ABDUCTION: Prophet Abducted
Location: by Chebar River,
then Jerusalem
Verse: Ezekiel 11:1
Spirit lifted Ezekiel and
carried him off to the east gate
of the temple in Jerusalem.

AFFLICTION: Angels Blind
Hostile Crowd
Location: Sodom and
Gomorrah
Verse: Genesis 19:8
Two angels visited Lot in
Sodom to warn him of the
pending destruction of the
city. A group of homosexuals
tried to break into Lot's house
to get at the angels and were
blinded. Then the angels told
Lot to take his family and
leave Sodom immediately.

AFFLICTION: Angel Makes
Man Unable to Speak
Location: Mountain region
of Judea
Verse: Luke 1:18
Zechariah questions the angel
Gabriel and asked for proof
that his wife, Elizabeth, would
have a child. Gabriel told

Zechariah that he stood in God's presence and was sent to tell him this good news. But because he didn't believe, he would be unable to talk until after the baby was born. Immediately Zechariah became unable to speak.

AFFLICTION: Astrologer Blinded
Location: Antioch, Cyprus
Verse: Acts 13:11
Saul (also known as Paul) and Barnabas are in Cyprus preaching. The governor of the island, Sergius Paulus, sent for them so he could hear the word of God. Elymas, an astrologer, opposed Barnabas and Saul and tried to distort their words so the governor wouldn't believe. Paul confronts Elymas and told him he'd become blind for a while. Suddenly Elymas could no longer see. The governor then listened to and believed the teachings of Paul and Barnabas.

AFFLICTION: Boils, Blisters, and Swelling Suddenly Appear
Location: Egypt
Verses: Exodus 9:8–11; Psalms 78:47, 48
Exodus Sixth Plague – Afflicts Egyptians and their animals. Outbreak of blain affected Egyptians, not Israelites.

AFFLICTION: Curse Occurs Instantly
Location: Hebron
Verse: 2 Samuel 3:29

David put a curse on Joab and his family.

AFFLICTION: Hip Dislocated by Touch of Angel
Location: at Jabbok River on east side of Jordan River almost opposite Jerusalem
Verse: Genesis 32:22
Jacob is on his way to meet his brother, Esau, after many years, but he is wary. He sends his family across a shallow part of the Jabbok River, but remains the night on his side. A man appears (believed to be from God), who wrestles with Jacob all night long. Neither could overpower the other, so the man touched Jacob's hip, dislocating it. Jacob still wouldn't release his hold on the man. Jacob told the man that he won't let go until the man blesses him. The man does and changes Jacob's name to "Israel."

AFFLICTION: Instant Blindness
Location: Dothan
Verse: 2 Kings 6:18
Arameans surrounded the Israelites in Dothan while Elisha prayed. When the Aramean army attacked Dothan, all of them were instantly blinded and were led away by the Israelites with Elisha, and eventually released.

AFFLICTION: Instant Leprosy
Location: Tiphsah

Verses: 2 Kings 15:5–7; 2 Chron 26:16–23

King Uzziah of Judah (also known as Azariah) ruled 52 years in Jerusalem. He became powerful and proud and became unfaithful to God. He violated temple rules and went into the temple to burn incense, against the rights reserved for the priests, who descended from Aaron. Uzziah became angry when challenged about his right while holding an incense burner in his hand. Suddenly an incurable leprosy broke out on his forehead. The priests rushed Uzziah out of the temple, but the skin disease spread. Uzziah was barred from the Lord's Temple and lived in a separate house from his family until he died. His son, Jotham, was placed in charge of the royal palace and governed Judah.

AFFLICTION: Instant Paralysis
Location: Bethel
Verses: 1 Kings 13:1–6
Man Paralyzed after Pointing at Messenger – King Jeroboam pointed a finger at a Man of God and his arm and hand were instantly paralyzed extended and pointing.

AFFLICTION: Instant Skin Disease
Location: Egypt
Verse: Exodus 4:6
Moses put his hand in his shirt. Then he brought it out and it had a skin disease. He put it in and out again and the skin was healthy.

AFFLICTION: Lies Results in Plague
Location: Egypt
Verses: Genesis 12:10–20
Famine drove people to Egypt where food was still abundant. Abram (Exalted Father) deceived the pharaoh regarding his wife, Sarai, and a terrible plague struck the pharaoh and his household.

AFFLICTION: Lying Man Instantly Gets Skin Disease
Location: Samaria
Verse: 2 Kings 5:26
Gehazi solicited gifts from Naaman and then lied to Elisha. He immediately got permanent leprosy. His skin remained flaky and white like snow the rest of his life.

AFFLICTION: Saul Blinded by the Light
Location: Damascus
Verses: Acts 9:8; Acts 22:11
Saul suddenly became blind and could not see for three days.

AFFLICTION: Woman Criticizes Moses and Suddenly Gets Leprosy
Location: Hazeroth
Verses: Numbers 12:1–16
Miriam became jealous and criticized Moses for his choice of a wife. Miriam immediately

got leprosy, an infectious disease. After begging for mercy, she was placed in isolation for seven days while the disease went away and her skin cleared.

BARREN MADE FERTILE: Long-Time Barren Woman Becomes Pregnant
Location: Ramathaim Zophim in mountains of Ephraim
Verses: 1 Sam 1:20, 2
Hannah prayed at the temple and promised to dedicate her first boy to God's service if she could become pregnant. Eli blessed her. Hannah and Elkanah did have a son, Samuel, and he became a highly respected man of God.

BARREN MADE FERTILE: Prayer Enables Childbearing
Location: Geher in the Negev, between Kadesh and Shur
Verses: Genesis 20:1–7, 17–18
Abraham prayed and God healed King Abimelech, his wife and his slaves so they could produce children.

EVICTED: First Humans Kicked out of Their Home
Location: Fertile Crescent
Verse: Gen 3:23
God kicked Adam and Eve out of the Garden of Eden setting it off limits to them. He placed angels with a flaming sword in the garden to block the way to the Tree of Life.

FACE SHINES: Face of Moses Shines Brightly
Location: at foot of Mount Sinai; another reference said it was about 15 miles SE of Rephidim
Verse: Exodus 34:29
After meeting with God, Moses' face shined so bright, he wore a veil to keep from frightening the people.

GOD SEEN: Israelite Leadership See God
Location: Mount Sinai; another reference said it was about 15 miles SE of Rephidim
Verse: Exodus 24:9
Aaron, Nadab, Abihu, and 70+ leaders of Israel all see God.

GOD SEEN: Man Sees God
Location: Mount Sinai; another reference said it was about 15 miles SE of Rephidim
Verse: Exodus 33:18
Moses saw the back of God as He passed by up on Mount Sinai.

GOD SEEN AND HEARD: Power of God Seen and Heard
Location: Mount Sinai
Verse: Exodus 20:18
God demonstrated His power before Moses and the people at Mt Sinai. Israelites see and hear power of God.

GOD SPEAKS: Voice Calls in Night
Location: Shiloh
Verse: 1 Samuel 3:4
The voice of God called Samuel

four times during the night and told him that Eli would be punished for not stopping his sons from their sins.

GOD TALKED: God Speaks to Abram
Location: Canaan
Verses: Genesis 15–17
God spoke to Abram in Canaan.

GOD TALKED: God Speaks to Jacob
Location: Jacob: Beersheba; Joseph: Egypt
Verse: Genesis 46:2
While at Beersheba, God commanded Jacob to go to Egypt where Joseph was living.

GOD TALKED: God Speaks to Man
Location: Besor
Verse: 1 Samuel 30:8
David spoke to God and was told to pursue and defeat the Amalekites to get his captured family back.

GOD TALKED: God Speaks to Moses
Location: Mount Sinai (Another reference said it was about 15 miles SE of Rephidim)
Verse: Exodus 19:20
God came down from Mt Sinai and called for Moses to come up on the mountain.

GOD TALKED: God Talks with Adam and Eve
Location: Fertile Crescent
Verse: Genesis 3:8

God walked around in the garden during the cool of the night and called to Adam. Then speaks to Adam and Eve.

GOD TALKED: Voice from Heaven Speaks
Location: Jerusalem
Verse: John 12:28
Mysterious voice spoke to Jesus and to Greeks standing by Jesus.

GOD WRITES ON STONE:
God Etches on Two Tablets of Stone
Location: Mount Sinai (Another reference said it was about 15 miles SE of Rephidim)
Verse: Exodus 32:15
Moses walked down off Mount Sinai carrying two stone tablets that had been etched by God on the front and back. On them was written the 10 Commandments for living.

HEALING: Ananias Restores Sight to Saul
Location: Damascus
Verses: Acts 9:18; Acts 22:12
A disciple in Damascus named Ananias came to Saul at Judas' house on Straight Street. Ananias told Saul that Jesus, who appeared to him on the road to Damascus, wanted Saul to see again and be filled with the Holy Spirit. Saul had been blind for three days. Ananias placed his hands on Saul and immediately something like fish scales fell from

Saul's eyes. Saul could see again. He stood up and was baptized and became known as Paul.

HEALING: Blind Man Healed by Touch
Location: Pool of Siloam near Jerusalem
Verses: John 9:1-7
Jesus mixed His saliva with dirt and smeared it on the eyes of a blind man instructing him to wash off his eyes in the Pool of Siloam. The man did, and he could see for the first time in his life.

HEALING: Festering Boil Cured with Fig Cake
Location: Jerusalem
Verse: 2 Kings 20:6
Festering boil on King Hezekiah cured when Isaiah instructs him to place a fig cake directly on the boil.

HEALING: Good Energy Emanates from Ark
Location: Gath
Verses: 1 Chronicles 13:12-14
Family of Obed Edom received blessings and good energy from the Ark.

HEALING: Father of Governor Healed by Touch
Location: Malta
Verses: Acts 28:3-6
Paul healed the father of Publius, governor of Malta. The father was suffering from fever and dysentery. Paul prayed, placed his hands on the sick man, and made him well. Then Paul healed other sick people on the island.

HEALING: Healed by Touching Object
Location: unknown
Verse: Acts 19:11
People would take handkerchiefs and aprons that had touched Paul's skin and place them on the sick, curing them or causing evil spirits to leave them.

HEALING: Healing and Demons Exorcized
Location: Jerusalem
Verses: Acts 8:4-8
Philip performed miracles, cast out evil spirits, and cured people, who were paralyzed and lame.

HEALING: Healing Authority - Casting out Demons
Location: near Capernaum
Verses: Matthew 10:5; Mark 6:13; Luke 9:1
Jesus gave authority to 12 apostles and they cured the sick by pouring oil on them and cast demons out of people.

HEALING: Healing Authority
Location: Capernaum
Verse: Matthew 10:1
Jesus gave His 12 apostles the authority to force evil spirits out and to cure every disease and sickness.

HEALING: Healing Touch and Voice

Location: Phoenicia, district of Tyre and Sidon
Verse: Mark 7:32
Jesus cured deaf man with speech defect. Put His fingers into man's ears and then spit on fingers and touched man's tongue. Then Jesus said, "Ephphatha" ("Be opened").

HEALING: Healing Touch Restores Sight
Location: Capernaum
Verses: Matthew 9:27–30
Jesus touched the eyes of two blind men immediately restoring their sight.

HEALING: Jesus Gives 70 Other Disciples Power to Heal
Location: on road to Jerusalem
Verse: Luke 10:9
Jesus appointed 70 other disciples (some manuscripts say 72) and sent them out in pairs to do mission work. He gave them power to heal the sick.

HEALING: Jesus Healed Blind, Disabled, and Lame
Location: Decapolis
Verses: Matthew 15:30–31
Jesus is on mountain alongside Sea of Galilee meeting people bringing lame, blind, disabled, and mute people unable to speak. He cured them all.

HEALING: Jesus Heals 10 Men with Leprosy
Location: border between Samaria and Galilee on way to Jerusalem
Verses: Luke 17:11–19
Jesus met 10 men with a skin disease as He walked along the border between Samaria and Galilee. He told them to show themselves to the priests. As they went, one saw he was healed. He was a Samaritan and turned back to thank and praise God. Jesus told him to go home. His faith had made him well. (Doesn't tell what happened to the other nine men.)

HEALING: Jesus Heals Blind Man
Location: near Jericho
Verses: Matthew 20:29; Mark 10:46–52; Luke 18:35–43
Jesus healed blind beggar named Bartimaeus just outside Jericho. Matthew 20:29–34 says He healed two blind men sitting alongside the road just outside Jericho.

HEALING: Jesus Heals Crippled Man at Bethesda
Location: Jerusalem
Verses: John 5:1–9
Jesus spoke and healed a man who had been an invalid for 38 years at the Pool of Bethesda near the Sheep Gate in Jerusalem.

HEALING: Jesus Heals Epileptic Man
Location: near Caesarea Philippi
Verses: Matthew 17:14–18; Mark 9:17–27; Luke 9:37–43

Man's epileptic son suffers from a demon that causes seizures, foaming at mouth and grinding of the son's teeth. The disciples were unable to force the spirit out. Jesus ordered the demon out of the boy and it immediately left. Jesus told disciples that this kind of spirit could only be forced out by prayer.

HEALING: Jesus Heals Man Who Was Blind and Mute
Location: unknown
Verses: Matthew 12:22–32; Mark 3:20–30; Luke 11:14–23
Jesus cast out demon that possessed a man and restored his sight and ability to speak.

HEALING: Jesus Heals Man with Dropsy
Location: Peraea
Verses: Luke 14:1–4
Jesus encountered a man swollen with fluid retention (dropsy) at the home of a prominent Pharisee. Jesus took hold of the man, healed him, and sent him on his way.

HEALING: Jesus Heals Man with Paralyzed Hand
Location: in synagogue in Capernaum
Verses: Matthew 12:9–14; Mark 3:1–6; Luke 6:6–11
Jesus healed a man with a paralyzed hand by telling him to hold out his withered hand. The man did and his hand became normal. Pharisees began plotting to kill Jesus.

HEALING: Jesus Heals People and Drives Out Demons
Location: Capernaum
Verses: Matthew 8:14–18; Mark 1:32–34; Luke 4:40–41
While at Peter's house, Jesus used His voice to force evil spirits out of possessed people and cure everyone who was sick. He wouldn't let demons speak because they knew who He was.

HEALING: Jesus Heals Serious Skin Disease
Location: synagogue in Galilee
Verses: Matthew 8:1–4, Mark 1:40, Luke 5:12–14
Jesus heals man with serious skin disease by reaching out, touching him and commanding him to be healed.

HEALING: Jesus Heals Severed Ear
Location: Garden of Gethsemane
Verses: Luke 22:47–51; John 18:10
While Jesus was being arrested, one of the disciples cut the ear off Malchus, a servant of the chief priest. Jesus told the disciples to stop resisting. Then He touched the servant's ear and instantly healed him.

HEALING: Jesus Heals the Blind and Lame
Location: Jerusalem
Verses: Matthew 21:14; Mark 11:15–19; Luke 19:45–48

After throwing moneychangers out of the temple courtyard, Jesus healed blind and lame people.

HEALING: Lame Man Healed by Peter
Location: at temple gate in Jerusalem
Verses: Acts 3:1–8
Each day a lame man would be taken to the Beautiful Gate in the temple courtyard to beg. Peter and John were going there for three o'clock prayer. Peter told a man, "Through the power of Jesus Christ from Nazareth, walk!" He took hold of the man's right hand and helped him up. Immediately the man's feet and ankles became strong, and he went with Peter and John into the temple courtyard walking, jumping, and praising God.

HEALING: Lame Man Healed by Voice
Location: Lystra
Verse: Acts 14:8
Paul healed a lame man in Lystra, a small town in modern Turkey (now called Klistra). The crowds began to call Barnabas "Zeus" and Paul "Hermes." Paul and Barnabas tried to stop them from sacrificing to the idols Zeus and Hermes, and a riot broke out.

HEALING: Leper is Miraculously Healed
Location: Samaria

Verses: 2 Kings 5:1–19
Elisha healed Naaman, commander of the Aramean king's army, of skin disease by telling him to wash seven times in the Jordan River. He did and he was healed of leprosy.

HEALING: Man Suddenly Able to Speak Again
Location: mountain region of Judea
Verses: Luke 1:57–64
Zechariah's wife, Elizabeth, gave birth. When the child was eight days old, he was taken to the temple to be circumcised. Mary said his name should be John (and not Zechariah after his father). Zechariah was asked his opinion. He motioned for a writing tablet and wrote the name "John" on it. Suddenly he was able to speak again. Then Zechariah began to prophesy about John the Baptist.

HEALING: Paralyzed Man Healed by Voice
Location: Lydda, northwest between Joppa and Jerusalem
Verse: Acts 9:32
Peter healed Aeneas of Lydda who was paralyzed and had been confined to a cot for eight years.

HEALING: People Healed by Touching Clothes of Jesus
Location: near Sea of Galilee
Verses: Matthew 14:22–36; Mark 6:56; John 6:15–21
Sick people came or were

brought to the marketplace so they could touch the edge of Jesus' clothes and be healed. Everyone who touched His cloak was cured.

HEALING: People Healed in Peter's Shadow
Location: Jerusalem
Verses: Acts 5:12–15
People placed sick and diseased where shadow of Peter would fall on them as he passed by. Each person in the shadow was cured.

HEALING: People Instantly Cured
Location: Galilee
Verse: Matthew 4:23
Jesus cured every disease and sickness.

HEALING: Touch Heals Woman of Bleeding
Location: Gennesaret
Verses: Matthew 9:20–22; Mark 5:22; Luke 8:43–45
Woman suffering for 12 years with chronic hemorrhage touched the edge of Jesus' cloak and is immediately healed. Jesus felt power go out of him.

HEALING: Touch Heals Woman of Fever
Location: Capernaum
Verses: Matthew 8:14–18; Mark 1:29–31; Luke 4:38–39
Jesus healed Peter's mother-in-law of fever. He touched her hand and the fever went away.

HEALING: Touch of Jesus Heals Blind Man
Location: Bethsaida
Verse: Mark 8:22
Jesus healed blind man at Bethsaida. Spit into man's blind eyes and placed his hands on him. Applied hand touch twice until man saw clearly.

HEALING: Touch of Jesus Heals Leper
Location: Galilee
Verses: Matthew 8:2; Mark 1:40–45; Luke 5:12–16
Jesus healed a man with leprosy, a serious skin disease, by reaching out and touching him.

HEALING: Jesus Touches and Heals People
Location: near Capernaum
Verses: Mark 3:10; Luke 6:17–19
Jesus cured diseased people who touched Him, and He subjugated and cast out demons. Power came out of Him and He healed the sick people.

HEALING: Voice of Jesus Heals Paralyzed Man
Location: Capernaum
Verses: Matthew 9:1–8; Mark 2:1–12; Luke 5:18–26
Jesus healed a paralyzed man brought to Him on a stretcher (cot) lowered through a hole in the roof.

HEALING: Voice of Jesus Heals Paralyzed Man
Location: Hill of Hattin, Capernaum
Verses: Matthew 8:5–13; Luke 7:1–10
Jesus healed the paralyzed servant of a Roman army officer (Centurion) by speaking "Go! What you believed will be done for you." At that moment the servant was healed of palsy.

LANGUAGES: Different Languages Suddenly Occur
Location: Plain of Shinar in Babylonia
Verses: Genesis 11:1, 5–9; Isaiah 13:1
The people tried to build a tower into heaven at Babble, but their language turned into "babble" halting the tower construction. New languages caused people to move apart and spread out over the earth.

PLAGUE: Locusts Suddenly Appear
Location: Egypt
Verses: Exodus 10:1; Psalms 78:46; Psalms 105:34
Exodus Eighth Plague – Locusts appeared and ate the vegetation in Egypt.

RAPTURE: Jesus Describes Rapture in End Times
Location: unknown
Verses: Luke 17:34–36
Jesus describes rapture to disciples.

SOUND: Unidentified Object Produces Sound
Location: by Chebar River
Verse: Ezekiel 1:24
Craft sounded like rushing water and thunder.

SOUNDS: Supernatural Sounds Cause Enemy to Panic, Abandon Siege, and Flee
Location: Samaria
Verses: 2 Kings 7:5–20
Aramean army (Syrians) blockade Samaria causing severe food shortages. During the night, the Aramean army heard the sounds of chariots, horses, and a large army. They thought the king of Israel had hired the Hittites and Egyptians to attack them. They panicked and fled at twilight (dusk) leaving their camp, their tents, horses, donkeys, food, water, and possessions intact for the starving Samarians to take. When the Arameans abandoned their camp and the besieged Israelites recovered all the Aramean possessions, flour and barley prices nosedived.

SPIRIT: Evil Spirit Enters Judas
Location: Jerusalem
Verses: Matthew 26:14–16; John 13:27
Satan became a "walk–in" and entered Judas, son of Simon Iscariot, causing him to betray Jesus. Judas agreed to betray Jesus for 30 pieces of silver.

SPIRIT: Holy Spirit Fills Believers
Location: Jerusalem
Verses: Acts 8:14–17
Apostles Peter and John placed hands on Samaritan believers causing them to receive the Holy Spirit.

SPIRIT: Job Sees Spirit Pass By
Location: Fertile Uz
Verse: Job 4:12
Job sees spirit pass in front of him causing his hair to stand on end.

SPIRIT: Spirit Causes Men to Speak in Tongues
Location: Ephesus
Verse: Acts 19:8
Paul was in Ephesus and baptized about 12 disciples there. When Paul placed his hands on them, the Holy Spirit came upon them, and they began talking in other languages.

SPIRIT: Spirit Enters Prophet
Location: by Chebar River
Verse: Ezekiel 2:2
Spirit entered Ezekiel and stood him on his feet. Ezekiel sees hand stretched out toward him and holding scroll. Scroll had funeral songs, songs of mourning, and horrible things about future written on it.

SPIRIT: Spirit Enters Prophet and Stands Him Up
Location: by Chebar River
Verse: Ezekiel 3:24
Spirit entered Ezekiel and stood him on his feet once again.

SPIRIT: Spirit in Unidentified Object lifts up Ezekiel
Location: by Chebar River
Verse: Ezekiel 3:12
Spirit in strange craft lifts Ezekiel up. Ezekiel heard loud thundering voice of the Spirit, the noise of the wings of the living creatures touching, the noise of the wheels beside them, and a loud rumbling.

SPIRIT: Spirit Leads Judge
Location: in Canaan, possibly near Jerusalem
Verses: Judges 3:9–11
Faithful judge had help from a Spirit to lead the Israelite people through 40 years of peace.

SPIRIT: Spirit Takes over Saul
Location: unknown
Verse: 1 Samuel 19:23
God's spirit (walk–in) takes over Saul's body and mind.

STRONG MADE WEAK: Strong Man Loses All Strength after Haircut
Location: Gaza
Verses: Judges 16:4–22
Sampson lost his supernatural strength when his long hair was cut off. In weakness, he was blinded and made a beast of burden.

STRONG MADE WEAK:
Voice Causes People to fall to Ground
Location: Garden of Gethsemane in Kidron Valley near Jerusalem
Verses: John 18:5–6

Roman soldiers and Jewish religious leaders came to the Garden of Gethsemane in the Kidron Valley to arrest Jesus. They asked if He was Jesus of Nazareth. Jesus said, "I am He." The crowd immediately backed away and fell to the ground.

SUPER STRENGTH: Sampson Releases 300 Foxes with Burning Torches into Grain Fields
Location: Lehi
Verse: Judges 15:4
Sampson caught 300 foxes. He tied their tails together in pairs, attached a burning torch to each pair, and set the foxes loose to burn the Philistine grain fields.

SUPER STRENGTH: Strong Man Easily Breaks Ropes
Location: Lehi
Verses: Judges 15:12-14
Sampson allowed 3,000 men of Judah to tie him up and hand him over to the Philistines. He broke the strong ropes tying him up like strings burned in a fire.

SUPER STRENGTH: Strong Man Pulls Temple Columns Down
Location: Gaza
Verse: Judges 16:30
Blinded Sampson was brought out into the courtyard of the Temple of Dagon for all the Philistine people to ridicule as the man who killed so many of them but was then blinded and weak. They didn't notice

that his hair had grown out. Sampson pulled down the columns holding up the temple collapsing it and killing about 3,000 Philistine men and women.

SUPER STRENGTH: Strong Man Rips City Gates Completely off Hinge Posts
Location: Gaza
Verses: Judges 16:1-13
Sampson pulled the city gates, posts, and securing bars off the entrance to the city.

SURVIVAL: Man Survives 40 Days on Mountain without Food or Water
Location: Mount Sinai (Another reference said it was about 15 miles SE of Rephidim)
Verse: Exodus 24:18
Moses was alone on Mount Sinai for 40 days and nights.

UFO: Unidentified Flying Object Described
Location: by Chebar River
Verses: Ezekiel 10:1-21
Ezekiel described unidentified flying object as saucer with angels and "person dressed in linen" inside.

UFO: Unidentified Object Described
Location: by Chebar River
Verses: Ezekiel 1:28
Dome on craft looked like throne of sapphire. Humanoid figure from waist up looked like glowing bronze with fire;

waste down looked like fire. Bright light surrounded figure; looked like rainbow in clouds. Isaiah heard figure speak to him.

UFO: Unidentified Object Appears to Fly
Location: by Chebar River
Verse: Ezekiel 1:15
Ezekiel describes flying craft.

UFO: Unidentified Object Appears to Man
Location: by Chebar River
Verse: Ezekiel 1:4
(600-500 BC – Persian Empire) Cloud with glowing metal center appears to Ezekiel.

VIRGIN BIRTH: Jesus Born to Virgin in Bethlehem
Location: Bethlehem
Verses: Matthew 2:1; Luke 2:6
Caesar Augustus ordered a census of the Roman Empire while Quirinius was governor of Syria. Joseph took Mary to Bethlehem where she delivered a baby in a stable. He was named Jesus.

VISION: Apostle Has Vision
Location: Joppa
Verses: Acts 10:9, 11:5
Peter has vision of sky opening and a large linen sheet filled with four-footed animals, reptiles, and birds lowered to the ground. Three times Peter has same vision.

WISDOM: Man Asks for Wisdom and Gets Supernatural Mental Gift
Location: Gibron
Verses: 1 Kings 3:4-14; 2 Chronicles 1:1
King Solomon asked for wisdom to lead and was given supernatural mental skills.

CHAPTER THREE

Power Over Life and Death

I FOUND OVER 76 VERSES IN THE BIBLE THAT DEAL with power over life and death. In the stories to follow I'll elaborate on important examples of this force. You're going to learn about the death of people and large groups. You'll read about a family that was swallowed up by the earth, how deadly fire came down from the sky and how fire came out of a huge pillar of cloud. You'll also marvel at how the dead are restored to life and how one man bypassed death on his way to heaven. At the end of this section, you'll find references to the verses covering all the relevant incidents that were discovered during this research.

Enoch Never Dies, Transports Directly to Heaven

Enoch walked with God;
then he was gone because God took him.
GENESIS 5:24

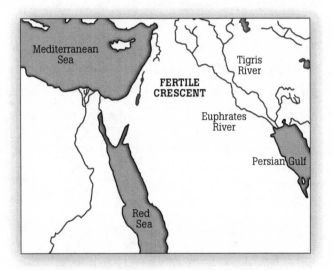

GENESIS 5:18–24; HEBREWS 11:5; JUDE 1:14–15
Location: Fertile Crescent | **Historical Time:** ca Creation + 800 years
TO VIEW MAPS ONLINE:
Copy this link into your browser and press Enter/Return
www.britannica.com/EBchecked/topic/205250/Fertile-Crescent
ancienthistory.about.com/od/neareast/ss/110708ANE_10.htm

IN GENESIS 5, YOU CAN READ THE FAMILY GENEALOGY from Adam to Noah including the life of Enoch. To put it in perspective, Enoch was born when Adam was 622 years old—during the antediluvian period before the Flood when people lived for around 900 years.

After Enoch was born Adam lived another 318 years and saw his great-great-great-great-grandson (Enoch) grow up there in the Fertile Crescent where they lived. Just imagine the family reunions they must have had back then! Enoch was from the seventh generation after Adam.

When he was 365, Enoch was taken by God directly to heaven. His father, Jared, was 527 and would live for another 435 years.

Enoch had a number of sons and daughters. The Bible says that "Enoch walked with God." Genesis 5:22 tells us that this closeness to God occurred after the birth of Methuselah. Methuselah lived a long life—969 years—and became the longest-living human. He was born when Enoch was 65, so we can only surmise that something happened relative to that birth that caused Enoch to re-evaluate his life and devotion. From that moment on, Enoch became very close to God. The Bible doesn't say Enoch "followed" God; it says Enoch "walked with" God. They were friends.

Enoch was given the power to prophesy. As a seer, he told people around him that God would come with thousands of angels to judge the wicked in the world.

For 300 years, Enoch remained faithful to God, his friend and confidant. Meanwhile the population of earth was increasing rapidly. Wickedness was growing as well. Yet Enoch kept his life spotless as the world around him became increasingly sinful.

According to Genesis 5, when the time had come, and 987 years after the birth of Adam and 365 years after his own birth, Enoch, the faithful man, was suddenly taken away by God. He never died.

In my research, only two other persons were teleported to heaven without first dying: Elijah (2 Kings 2:11) and a follower of Christ, who was teleported to the third heaven during Paul's time (2 Corinthians 12:2).

Livestock
Suddenly Die

All the livestock of the Egyptians died,
but none of the Israelites' animals died.
EXODUS 9:6

EXODUS 9:1-7
Location: Egypt | Historical Time: Late Bronze Age – ca 1445 BC
TO VIEW MAPS ONLINE:
Copy this link into your browser and press Enter/Return
en.wikipedia.org/wiki/File:Ancient_Egypt_map-en.svg

THIS FIFTH PLAGUE AFFECTED THE DOMESTIC ANIMALS IN
Egypt. After getting direction from God, Moses went to the
pharaoh and repeated his demand to let the Israelites go.
He said if he refused, then God would bring a terrible pestilence on Egyptian livestock including the horses, donkeys,

camels, cattle, sheep, and goats. He further said that no animals belonging to the Israelites would be affected or die. Horses and cattle are sacred and highly prized in Egypt. This plague directly attacked the Egyptian gods Apis, Bast, Hathor, Khnum, Ptah, and Re.

Bible scholars think that swarms of insects from the fourth plague became carriers of the infectious and usually fatal bacteria Bacillus anthracis. This had already killed the fish and the frogs. This plague has been described as Murrain, rinderpest, and pestilence in the ancient writings. The key point is that these afflictions occurred at a specific time and affected specific animals.

Moses said that the Egyptian livestock in the fields would die the very next day, and this happened precisely as Moses had said. All the livestock of Egypt that were out in the fields mysteriously died. Not some, but all of them in the fields died. None of the Egyptian livestock that were kept inside died. And none of the Israelite livestock in Goshen (in fields or buildings) were affected.

Deadly Hail Kills Egyptians

All over Egypt the hail knocked down everything that was out in the open. It struck down people, animals, and every plant in the fields and destroyed every tree in the fields.

EXODUS 9:25

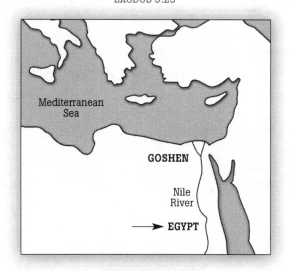

EXODUS 9:13-35
Location: Egypt | **Historical Time:** Late Bronze Age – ca 1445 BC
TO VIEW MAPS ONLINE:
Copy this link into your browser and press Enter/Return
en.wikipedia.org/wiki/File:Ancient_Egypt_map-en.svg

BIBLE SCHOLARS BELIEVE THAT THIS PLAGUE OCCURRED in January when flax and barley are ripe and ready for harvesting. This seventh plague was the first to directly affect human life.

Under God's direction, Moses went to the pharaoh early in the morning. He told the pharaoh that the next plagues would affect him personally as well as his officials and the rest of the Egyptian people. Through Moses, God told the pharaoh that He could have killed him and his people at any time and at any place. But He wanted to show the pharaoh His power and make Him known throughout the land. He told the pharaoh that he was still blocking the Israelites from leaving, so at this time tomorrow, He would send the worst hailstorm to ever occur in Egypt. This was unusual since hail was extremely rare there. And a storm such as this coming at an appointed time was beyond belief.

This plague was against Nut, the goddess of the sky. According to Egyptian lore, Nut was the mother of Osiris, Hathor, Set, Isis, and Nephthys. Also targeted were Shu, the wind god of the atmosphere, Horus, the sky god of Upper Egypt, and Isis and Seth, gods that protected the crops.

Moses told the pharaoh to have all the livestock and possessions brought inside away from the risk of exposure to hail. Some in the pharaoh's court listened and quickly brought servants and animals inside. Others were as arrogant as the pharaoh and ignored Moses.

At the appointed time, Moses lifted his staff up toward the sky, and lightning, thunder, rain, and deadly hail came down on Egypt. The hail was huge. It struck people, animals and plants, even destroying trees in the field. The flax and barley crops were destroyed. Yet no hail came down on Goshen.

For the first time, the pharaoh publicly recognized the God of Israel. The pharaoh sent for Moses and Aaron and said, "This time I have sinned." He said he would obey and let the people go. Then he asked Moses to pray that the God of Israel stop the hail storm.

Moses told the pharaoh that as soon as he was out of the city, he would spread out his hands in prayer, and the thunder and hail would stop. Moses did as he said he would, and the storm immediately stopped.

But as soon as the rain, hail, and thunder stopped, the pharaoh reneged on his word again and refused to let the Israelites go.

Death of Firstborn Sons and Animals

*At midnight the Lord killed every firstborn
male in Egypt from the firstborn son of the Pharaoh
who ruled the land to the firstborn son of the
prisoner in jail, and also every firstborn animal.*

EXODUS 12:29

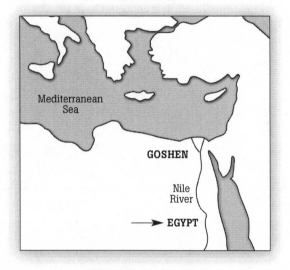

EXODUS 11:1-10; 12:1-36
Location: Egypt | **Historical Time:** Late Bronze Age – ca 1445 BC

TO VIEW MAPS ONLINE:
Copy this link into your browser and press Enter/Return
en.wikipedia.org/wiki/File:Ancient_Egypt_map-en.svg

THIS 10ᵀᴴ PLAGUE WAS THE FINAL JUDGMENT ON THE gods
of Egypt, on the pharaoh, and on the Egyptian people. It
was more devastating than all the other plagues. And it
was selective. It destroyed only the firstborn male children
and animals.

For the people, the death of the firstborn robbed the family estates of accepted inheritance since the firstborn son inherited the family's holdings when a father died. So the families of Egypt were crippled legally and emotionally. Even worse was the sudden loss of Egypt's children and future leaders.

A wave of death was about to be let loose over all Egypt. To preserve and teach the Israelites, God had Moses instruct the people in how to mark their exterior door frames so death would pass by their homes.

Moses was told to have each Hebrew family put the blood of a sacrificed lamb or goat on the top and sides of the exterior doorframes to their houses. The painting of blood was to be done at dusk.

Historical sages say that not all Israelites believed Moses and Aaron. Some of them had been worshiping Egyptian gods, so God needed to punish them too. They didn't participate in the brushing of blood on the door frames.

At midnight, death visited the homes of all the Egyptians and others who failed to mark their door frames. The firstborn male children in these families and their firstborn male animals immediately died. The pharaoh's own son died, and he was grief-stricken.

The Bible says that the anguish of crying could be heard all over the land (except in Goshen). In Goshen, the firstborn sons of the Israelites who had marked their doorframes were unharmed. There was great jubilation the next day and an annual celebration of the event became part of Jewish tradition. Thus began the *Festival of Passover*.

The pharaoh called for Moses and Aaron while it was still night and told them to leave at once. He told them to take the people, flocks, and herds with them. Then strangely, he asked Moses to bless him. He now understood that the God of Israel was far more powerful than the gods of Egypt. And thus began the Exodus of the Hebrew people out of Egypt into the desert and eventually to the Promised Land.

Sudden Fire
from Cloud
Consumes Two Men

*A fire flashed from the Lord and burned them,
and they died in the presence of the Lord.*
LEVITICUS 10:2

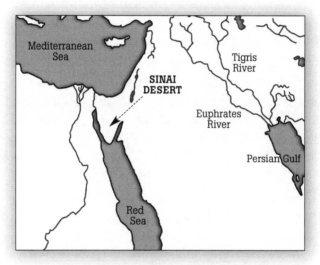

LEVITICUS 10:1-7; NUMBERS 3:1-4
Location: Sinai Desert, desert of Paran, Kadesh/Kadesh Barnea
Historical Time: Late Bronze Age – ca 1400 BC
TO VIEW MAPS ONLINE:
Copy this link into your browser and press Enter/Return
en.wikipedia.org/wiki/Sinai_Peninsula

AFTER THE TENT OF MEETING WAS CONSTRUCTED, THE
priests were given strict rules on how they could approach
and enter this structure. If they failed to follow these rules,
the punishment was severe.

Leviticus 10:2 describes the fate of Aaron's sons and apprentice priests Abihu and Nadab. They disobeyed God by bringing an activated incense burner to the Tent of Meeting. While they were offering the unauthorized incense in the Lord's presence, a hot stream of fire suddenly flashed out of the cloud at the Tent of Meeting and consumed both of them. They died while still in their linen robes. Aaron was speechless.

Moses had the sons of Aaron's uncle Uzziel come to the Tent of Meeting and take the bodies of Abihu and Nadab to a place outside the camp.

Then Moses told Aaron and his other sons, Eleazar and Ithamar, that they should not mourn for Abihu and Nadab. He said that the other members of the congregation could mourn and cry over these two dead men, but Aaron, Eleazar, and Ithamar must not mourn or they will die and God will become angry with the whole congregation.

Moses further said that these three men must not leave the entrance to the Tent of Meeting or they, too, would die. God demanded obedience. They obeyed God and Moses.

Instant Death for Spreading Lies

So the men Moses sent to explore the land died in front of the Lord from a plague.
NUMBERS 14:36

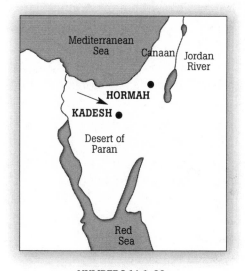

NUMBERS 14:1–38
Location: Desert of Paran, Kadesh
Historical Time: Late Bronze Age – ca 1440 BC

TO VIEW MAPS ONLINE:
Copy this link into your browser and press Enter/Return
www.lds.org/scriptures/bible-maps/map-2?lang=eng
www.keyway.ca/htm2002/20020429.htm
www.bible.ca/archeology/bible-archeology-exodus-route-wilderness-of-paran.htm

THE DESERT OF PARAN (SOUTHEASTERN JORDAN TODAY) was hot and dusty as usual. Moses sent 12 spies including Joshua and Caleb into Canaan to gather intelligence on the land, the people, and their capability. The scouts that

Moses sent up along the east side of the Jordan and into Canaan had reported back. Only two of the spies, Caleb and Joshua, urged Moses to lead the Hebrews ahead into the Promised Land. They told Moses that the land was there to be taken. They advised Moses and Aaron to take Canaan for the Lord.

The other 10 spies were afraid and convinced most of the Israelites that they should not move ahead into the Promised Land as God had commanded. They said that Canaan was full of milk and honey (according to Numbers 13:23, it took two men to carry a single cluster of grapes on a pole), but the Canaanites were giants, with large armies, and fortified cities. They said this land could not be taken.

The people immediately became terrified and cried out all night long. They complained because they were brought to the border of Canaan and did not die in Egypt or in the desert during their Exodus. They decided to choose another leader and go back to Egypt to be slaves.

Most of the Israelites whined and they all began talking of stoning Moses and Aaron to death.

Then they saw a bright shining light at the Tent of Meeting. God was speaking with Moses. He wanted to exterminate all of the Israelites, but again Moses interceded and begged for their lives. God forgave them their rebelliousness, but told Moses that none of those there 20 years and older except Caleb and Joshua would enter the Promised Land (not even Moses and Aaron). God also said that He let them explore and enjoy the Promised Land for 40 days, so for the next 40 years the whole nation would suffer– one year for each day.

Then the 10 spineless spies who had lied were instantly killed of a plague right before God, Moses, Aaron and the rest of the Hebrews.

Moses told the people to turn around and head back into the desert, but they didn't want to go. They refused to heed God's command and decided to stay there. They planned an attack on the Amalekites and Canaanites, but were soundly defeated at Hormah. Then they accepted their fate and looked to the Shekinah cloud for direction.

The cloud moved south and began leading the Israelite nation back out into the wilderness. Thus began 40 years of wandering. By the time 40 years had passed, all of the Israelites 20 years and older at the start had died in the desert except Joshua and Caleb. Even Moses and Aaron died out there. And all this occurred because some of the spies lied to Moses.

Earth Opens and Swallows Family

As soon as he had finished saying all this, the ground under them split, and the earth opened up to swallow them, their families, the followers of Korah, and all their property.

NUMBERS 16:31

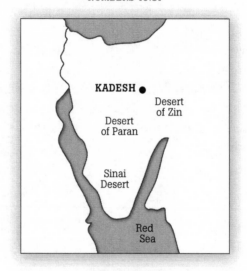

NUMBERS 16:1-36
Location: Desert of Paran, Kadesh, Desert of Zin
Historical Time: Late Bronze Age – ca 1440 BC

TO VIEW MAPS ONLINE:
Copy this link into your browser and press Enter/Return
www.lds.org/scriptures/bible-maps/map-2?lang=eng
www.keyway.ca/htm2002/20020429.htm
www.bible.ca/archeology/bible-archeology-exodus-route-wilderness-of-paran.htm

NUMBERS 16 DESCRIBES A REVOLT BY A LEVITE PRIEST named Korah and his followers. It was around 1460 BC, and the huge Hebrew nation was slowly migrating back into the hot deserts toward the south. As they did, the grumbling continued incessantly and increasingly.

Four influential Levites, Korah, Dathan, Abiram, and On, came to Moses with 250 other officials to confront Aaron and challenge Moses. They claimed that "all" of the Hebrews were holy, so Moses should not be allowed to be the holy leader of the entire nation and the only one who could meet directly with God. They wanted to be high priests so they could approach God themselves, instead of serving God in the outer area of the Tent of Meeting.

The Bible doesn't tell us what happened to On, but God singled out Korah, Dathan, and Abiram for punishment. We assume that On met the same fate as his fellow dissenters.

Moses turned the issue over to God and he was instructed to tell Korah and his followers to bring incense burners to the front of the Tent of Meeting the following morning. As the sun was rising and giving light to a new day, Dathan and Abiram refused to come and remained in their tents. But Korah and his 250 followers did come to see Moses. Moses told Korah to have the 250 followers put hot coals and incense in their burners. Then Korah and Aaron started their incense burners.

Numbers 16:19 says that the glory of the Lord appeared at the entrance to the Tent of Meeting. God told Moses to move away from these grumbling men and their possessions because He was going to destroy them. Korah became terrified and ran back to where his family had their tents. The 250 other dissenters stubbornly remained with their incense burners in front of the Tent of Meeting.

Moses and a large group of Israelites followed Korah back to his family and their tents. Apparently they lived next to Dathan and Abiram. Then Moses told the Hebrew people to move back away from the tents of Korah, Dathan, and Abiram and not to touch anything that belonged to them. Dathan and Abiram were standing in front of their tents with their wives and children. Korah was hiding inside his tent.

Moses told the assembly that if these grumbling men and their families die a natural death, then God isn't offended with their grumbling. But if God opens the earth and swallows them and their possessions, and they go down alive into their graves, then these men have treated the Lord with contempt.

At that moment, the ground rumbled and the earth split open. A huge tear in the earth appeared in front of the people. All of the Israelites were terrified as the huge crack widened. Then Korah, Dathan, Abiram, and all of their families and property were suddenly swept into the crack falling down into the blackness. Then the ground began to close over the screaming dissenters. The rest of the Hebrews witnessing this horror began to run away from the screams of the dying, as the cracked earth moved back together. The crack closed. When it was over, there was no trace that Korah, Dathan, Abiram, and their families had ever existed. In the place where they once lived there was only sand, gravel, and desert stones.

Meanwhile the 250 followers of Korah were standing in front of the Tent of Meeting. Suddenly fire swept out from inside the cloud and burned all of them to death. They too died for their stubborn attitudes.

From that time on only Aaron and his Levite descendants were allowed to come near the presence of God with burning incense. Anyone else who came near would die.

God is serious about respect and obedience. And His justice was harsh on those Israelites who refused to obey His commands. All the people were condemned because they couldn't or wouldn't accept their role in the family of God.

We too are sinners. We grumble, we covet, and we sometimes don't honor God as we should. This is why God sent Jesus to die for our sins. He knew that we couldn't make it without Jesus. By being open to Jesus as the Savior, the Holy Spirit will help us believe and be saved from eternal damnation. The early Jews didn't have Jesus, and they didn't have anyone to explain this part of God's plan. We do. So wise people will stay on course and live according to God's will. We too should cheerfully accept the role that God currently gives us in this life. He wants us to be the best at what we do while praising and obeying Him.

Plague Kills over 14,000 Rebellious People

Aaron took his incense burner and ran into the middle of the assembly, because the plague had already begun.

NUMBERS 16:47

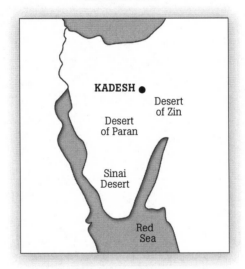

KADESH ●

Desert of Zin

Desert of Paran

Sinai Desert

Red Sea

NUMBERS 16:43–60
Location: Desert of Paran, Kadesh, Desert of Zin
Historical Time: Late Bronze Age – ca 1440–1406 BC

TO VIEW MAPS ONLINE:
Copy this link into your browser and press Enter/Return
www.lds.org/scriptures/bible-maps/map-2?lang=eng
www.keyway.ca/htm2002/20020429.htm
www.bible.ca/archeology/bible-archeology-exodus-route-wilderness-of-paran.htm

THE DAY AFTER KORAH AND HIS FAMILY WERE SWALLOWED up by the earth, the whole congregation of Israelites rebelled against Moses and Aaron. God's wrath came out of the cloud and a deadly plague immediately began sweeping through the mass. Moses told Aaron to quickly run through the crowd with a lighted incense burner. Aaron ran to a point between the people who had dropped dead and the still living. He stood there, and the plague stopped. In its path 14,700 had died.

The Israelites continued their wandering. Sometime later Aaron died, and his son Eleazar was given his priestly garments and the responsibility of high priest. Moses continued on and saw the Promised Land from the top of Mount Nebo to the east of the Jordan before he too died. Then Joshua took command and led the Israelites into Canaan.

Snakebite Protection: The Bronze Serpent

Make a [bronze] snake, and put it on a pole.
Anyone who is bitten can look at it and live.
NUMBERS 21:8

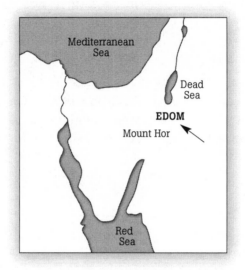

NUMBERS 21:4-9
Location: Desert road from Mount Hor to Red Sea and around Edom
Historical Time: Late Bronze Age – ca 1391 BC
TO VIEW MAPS ONLINE:
Copy this link into your browser and press Enter/Return
bibleatlas.org/mount_hor.htm
bible.cc/numbers/21-4.htm

MOSES AND THE ISRAELITES MOVED FROM MOUNT HOR
going around Edom through the Wilderness of Zin to get
to the Red Sea. The Israelites began to complain again.
They said they had tired of eating manna—that it was
"awful food." God became angry with them.

According to Numbers 21:6, God sent poisonous snakes to bite the people. Many of them died. The people realized they had sinned (again) and came to Moses asking him to pray that the snakes be taken away.

God didn't do this. Instead He told Moses to make a bronze snake and mount it on a pole. Then anyone who was bitten by a snake could simply look at the pole, and they would not die. They still got bitten, but they no longer died from the bites. The pain of the bite was intended to remind them of their sin.

They brought the snake pole with them into Canaan and called it "Nehushtan" (2 Kings 18:4). Years later they burned incense to it. Finally King Hezekiah of Judah crushed the bronze snake and stopped this practice.

Fire from Heaven Kills Officer and Fifty Soldiers

*Then fire came down from heaven
and burned up the officer and his 50 men.*

2 KINGS 1:10

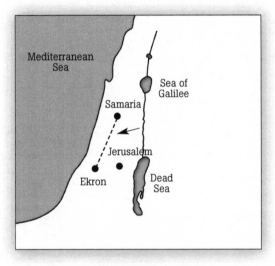

2 KINGS 1:1–18
Location: Samaria | Historical Time: ca 875 BC

TO VIEW MAPS ONLINE:
Copy this link into your browser and press Enter/Return
en.wikipedia.org/wiki/Samaria
www.gods-word-first.org/bible-maps/samaria-map.html

AHAZIAH, KING OF SAMARIA, FELL THROUGH A WINDOW
lattice in an upstairs room of his palace and was injured on the
stone floor below. He sent messengers to Ekron to ask Baalzebub, the god of Ekron, if he would recover from his injury.

An angel told Elijah to meet the messengers. Elijah met the messengers and asked if they sought advice from Baalzebub because they didn't think there was a god in Israel. Then Elijah told them what God said regarding King Ahaziah. Elijah said, "You will not get up from the bed you are lying on. Instead, you will die there." Then Elijah left them.

The messengers returned to the king, and the king asked why they returned so quickly. They said a man came to see them on their way to Ekron. The man told them to return to the king and tell Ahaziah what he had said.

The king was infuriated and said, "What was the man who told you this like?" They described him, and King Ahaziah exclaimed, "That's Elijah from Tishbe!"

So the king sent one of his officers (a captain) with 50 men to get Elijah and bring him to the king.

The captain and his troops found Elijah sitting on top of a hill. The arrogant officer said, "Man of God, the king says, 'Come down.'" They expected Elijah to obey the king before that of God. But Elijah remained on the hill and replied, "If I'm a man of God, fire will come from heaven and burn up you and your 50 men.

Suddenly fire came down from heaven and incinerated the officer and his 50 men. How did this happen? Was the "fire" a hot beam emanating from something (a craft) in the sky above? Did the fire come out of another dimension? Was there something above them that was unseen? There is no mention of the people around Elijah seeing anything in the sky. Yet fire suddenly came out of the sky and burned 51 people to death.

The king sent a second detachment comprised of another captain with 50 men to get Elijah. And the same thing happened again. Elijah was ordered to come down.

He refused and told them if he was a man of God, fire would come down and burn this detachment up.

Immediately fire came down from heaven, and this military troop was also burned to death. Strange. Strange indeed. The king sent a third detachment. The captain of this troop knew what had happened to his previous two colleagues, so he fell on his knees in front of Elijah. He acknowledged the power of God over people, but he had to obey the king, too (or at least make the attempt).

Notice that Elijah remained calm and in control of each situation. Faced by a large group of trained soldiers, the prophet was not afraid for his life. Did he have a larger contingent of protectors surrounding him unseen by the soldiers at the foot of the hill?

The captain begged Elijah, "Man of God, please treat my life and the life of these 50 servants of yours as something precious. Fire has come from heaven and burned up the first two officers and their men. But treat my life as something precious."

The unseen angel with Elijah told him, "Go with him. Don't be afraid of him." So Elijah got to his feet, walked down the hill and went with the officer to see the king.

Before the king, Elijah boldly spoke, "This is what the Lord says: 'You sent messengers to seek advice from Baalzebub, the god of Ekron. Is this because you think there is no god in Israel to seek?'"

He looked King Ahaziah straight in the face and said, "You will not get up from the bed you are lying on. Instead you will die there."

And he did. Ahaziah died, and Jehoram succeeded Ahaziah because he had no son. Jehoram was Ahaziah's brother. Both were the sons of Ahab.

Dead Man Lives after Touching Elisha's Bones

... when the body touched Elisha's bones, the man came back to life and stood up.

2 KINGS 13:21

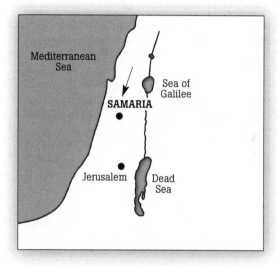

2 KINGS 13:20–21
Location: Samaria | Historical Time: ca 850 BC
TO VIEW MAPS ONLINE:
Copy this link into your browser and press Enter/Return
en.wikipedia.org/wiki/Samaria
www.gods-word-first.org/bible-maps/samaria-map.html

THE PROPHET ELISHA HAD DIED. HE WAS GIVEN A MAGNIF-
icent funeral and buried in a tomb in Samaria.

The Northern Kingdom of Israel was weak, and the country was vulnerable. The enemies of Israel sensed their weakness and began to attack, rob, and kill the Israelites whenever and wherever they could.

As spring arrived, a small group of mourners were taking a prominent dead man to be buried down in the valley where Elisha's tomb was located. Suddenly, they spotted a raiding band of Moabites approaching.

In panic they raced up to the nearest tomb (that of Elisha), rolled the stone door aside and threw the body inside so they could hide. As soon as the dead man's body touched the bones of Elisha, the corpse immediately came to life and the man stood on his feet.

Imagine the surprise when the man found himself alive and next to the bones of the prophet. Here is a situation where the spiritual presence of Elisha remained by his corpse. The divine power of Elisha was there even after his death.

Angel Destroys
185,000 in One Night

*The Lord's angel went out and killed
185,000 soldiers in the Assyrian camp.*
2 KINGS 19:35

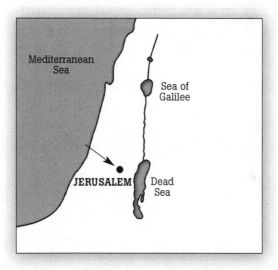

2 KINGS 19:35; 2 CHRONICLES 32:1–22; ISAIAH 36:1–22; 37:1–38
Location: Jerusalem | **Historical Time:** ca 729 BC
TO VIEW MAPS ONLINE:
Copy this link into your browser and press Enter/Return
www.sacred-destinations.com/israel/jerusalem-map
www.sacred-destinations.com/israel/israel-map
www.ccel.org/bible/phillips/CP051GOSPELMAPS.htm
bibleatlas.org/jerusalem.htm

THE NORTHERN TRIBES OF ISRAEL HAD BEEN OVERCOME
by Sargon, king of Assyria, in 722 BC, and virtually all of
the ruling classes including the leadership and landowners
were exiled 450 miles northeast to the upper end of the
Fertile Crescent.

Sargon repopulated Samaria with Babylonians and other Assyrians. These colonists and their descendants came to be known as "Samaritans."

When Sargon died, his son Sennacherib became king and attacked and captured the fortified cities of Judah. Only Jerusalem remained. King Sennacherib sent his commander in chief, his quartermaster, and his field commander with a large army to put Jerusalem under siege.

King Hezekiah of Judah offered to pay a tribute to King Sennacherib if they would go away and leave Jerusalem alone.

The king of Assyria demanded 22,500 pounds of silver and 2,250 pounds of gold. Hezekiah collected all the wealth they could amass and gave it to Sennacherib, but it was not enough. The Assyrians wanted more, and the siege continued.

Eliakim, master of the palace in Jerusalem, Shebna, the scribe, and Joah, the royal historian, came out of the city and met the field commander to negotiate terms. The commander taunted them and said that no city in Judah had withstood the power of Assyria. The field commander spoke in Hebrew so the Jews on the walls of Jerusalem could hear his words. He said that King Hezekiah could not protect them. He said if they would come out and make peace with Assyria, they would be taken to a country where each of them would eat from their own grapevine and fig tree and drink from their own cistern. He said that they would go to a country with grain and new wine, bread, olive trees, and honey.

The people of Jerusalem were silent. Eliakim, Shebna, and Joah tore their clothes in grief and went back into the city. They told King Hezekiah what was said, and he, too, tore his clothes. Then he put on sackcloth and went into the Temple to pray. He sent Eliakim, Shebna, and the leaders of the priests to the prophet Isaiah, who was also there inside the city.

Isaiah told the visitors to tell King Hezekiah not to worry. He said that God would put a spirit in Sennacherib that will cause him to believe a rumor and return to his own country where he'll be assassinated.

Meanwhile, the field commander of the Assyrian army went back to King Sennacherib, who was now fighting against Libnah. Sennacherib had heard that King Tirkakah of Sudan was coming to fight him, and he became anxious to overpower Jerusalem so he could focus on Tirkakah.

Sennacherib sent letters to Hezekiah saying that the God they trust would not rescue them. He reminded Hezekiah of the many other countries and kingdoms that Assyria had taken. They had worshipped idols, and Sennacherib destroyed their wooden and stone statues. Now he was after the God of Judah.

Hezekiah took the letters from the messengers, read each, and spread them out in front of God in the Lord's temple. Then he prayed for divine intervention to rescue Jerusalem and show Assyria that He alone is the Lord God.

Isaiah sent a message to Hezekiah telling him that God has heard his prayer and that Sennecherib will never come into Jerusalem. He said that God will shield the city and rescue it for the sake of Isaiah and for the sake of His servant David.

And then a supernatural event occurred. During the night, an angel went through the enemy camp and killed 185,000 Assyrian soldiers. In the morning the Judeans looked out over the walls of Jerusalem and saw all the corpses.

The Greek historian Herodotus describes a sudden retreat of the Assyrians. He said a massive plague of deadly mice appeared. The mice gnawed the arrows, quivers, and leatherwork on the Assyrian shields. The Bible doesn't mention the plague of mice. It simply says that an angle of God killed 185,000 Assyrians in one night. The point is: God's rescue was sudden, and it was deadly to Assyria.

King Sennecherib returned home to Ninevah, where his sons assassinated him just as Isaiah had prophesied.

Back to Life: "Tabitha, Get Up!"

Tabitha opened her eyes, saw Peter, and sat up.
ACTS 9:40

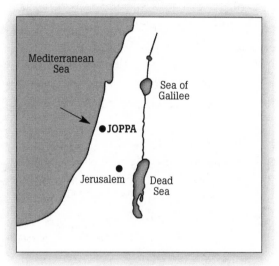

ACTS 9:36–42
Location: Joppa | **Historical Time:** ca 34 AD
TO VIEW MAPS ONLINE:
Copy this link into your browser and press Enter/Return
www.bible-history.com/geography/ancient-israel/joppa.html
bibleatlas.org/joppa.htm

TWO DISCIPLES CAME TO PETER IN LYDDA AND BEGGED him to hurry to Joppa to help a faithful woman named "Dorcas" in Greek ("Tabitha" in Hebrew).

Tabitha was a kind and generous woman who gave to the poor and was consistently helping the needy. She became sick and died when she was not ready. Now it was she who needed help.

Peter immediately went with the disciples to Joppa. When he arrived at the home of Tabitha, he was taken upstairs where Tabitha's body lay. Her body was prepared and waiting for burial.

A number of widows were in the room crying. They showed Peter the articles of clothing that Tabitha had made for them.

Peter asked all of them to leave the room. Then he turned toward the corpse, knelt and prayed, and then stood up and said, "Tabitha, get up!"

Immediately Tabitha opened her eyes, saw Peter and sat up. Peter took her hand and helped her to her feet. She was alive!

Peter called the believers in the house, especially the widows, to come to him. Then he presented the resurrected Tabitha to the people. The news of Tabitha's return to life spread rapidly through Joppa, and many people became believers in the Lord.

Peter remained in Joppa for a few days, staying with Simon, a leatherworker.

Dead Man Brought Back to Life

[Jesus] shouted, "Lazarus, come out!"
JOHN 11:43

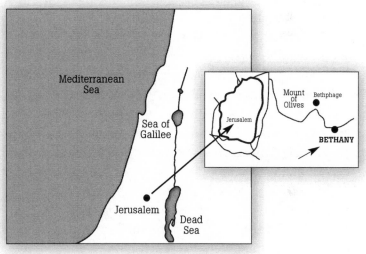

JOHN 11:1–53
Location: Bethany | **Historical Time:** ca 33 AD
TO VIEW MAPS ONLINE:
Copy this link into your browser and press Enter/Return
www.bible-history.com/geography/ancient-israel/bethany.html

JESUS MADE SPECIAL FRIENDS DURING HIS MINISTRY ON earth. Three who were especially close to Him were Mary, Martha, and their brother, Lazarus. They lived in Bethany, a small village on the eastern side of the Mount of Olives about 20 miles from the northern end of the Dead Sea and just a few miles east of Jerusalem.

I've not found any records of what these sisters and their brother did in Bethany or about their parents, but Mary, Martha, and Lazarus were dear friends of Jesus. He often visited with these three people when He was in Bethany. According to John 11:2, a day or two before the Passover meal, Mary poured perfume on Jesus' feet and then dried them using her own hair.

About a month before Jesus was to be crucified, He had gone across the Jordan and was staying in Perea, the place where John the Baptist had baptized so many people a few years earlier. Perea was about 22 miles to the east of Bethany over by the Dead Sea.

While Jesus was there, his friend Lazarus became seriously ill. Lazarus' sisters were terribly worried and sent a messenger from Bethany to find Jesus and tell Him that their brother was very sick.

The messenger found Jesus on the east side of the Jordan near where the river flows into the Dead Sea and told Him about Lazarus. But Jesus did not immediately leave for Bethany. Instead He stayed there at the Jordan for two more days. Another teaching moment was coming. During this period, Lazarus died.

Jesus knew this had happened and told his disciples that they would now go back to Bethany in Judea. He told them that Lazarus was dead, and they were going to Lazarus so they (the disciples) could grow in faith. It took several days to walk to Bethany.

When Jesus and his disciples approached Bethany and the house of the grieving family, a crowd was with Mary and Martha comforting them on the loss of their brother, Lazarus. Martha heard that Jesus was approaching and went out to meet Him. In her grief, she told Jesus that her brother would not have died if He had been there. Then she said that even so, she knows that God would give Jesus whatever He asks.

Jesus told Martha that her brother would come back to life. She thought that He meant returning to life on the last day. But Jesus meant that very day.

Now understand this: Lazarus had been dead for four days and his human body was beginning to decompose (the Bible calls it "becoming corrupt"). Back then, when a person died, the body was covered with perfume and wrapped in linen cloth. Then it was placed in a tomb and a stone was rolled in front of the opening. With life gone out of it, the cells in the body immediately began to die and decompose. Since the family did not embalm the body, after four days, the decaying corpse began to smell. The stone that blocked the entrance to the tomb contained the strong odor.

The Jews also believed that when a person dies, the soul hovers over the body until the third day, when corruption (decomposition) begins. Then the soul takes flight.

When Jesus came to the house of Mary, Martha, and Lazarus, Martha went inside and whispered to her sister that the "Teacher" was there and was calling for her. Mary quickly rose and rushed out to meet Jesus. She knelt at His feet and told Him the same thing that Martha had said—that Lazarus would not have died if He had been there. Mary was crying profusely, as was everyone else with her.

Jesus felt the grief of the sisters and asked where they had placed the body of their brother Lazarus. They asked Jesus to come with them and see. As the grief-stricken group moved off toward the tomb, the tears of the suffering sisters touched Jesus so much that He also wept. As a human, He felt the pain of losing a beloved person. And the depth of grief of the two sisters moved Him deeply.

The tomb was a cave with a stone covering the entrance. Jesus commanded that they take the stone away from the entrance. Martha told Jesus that it had been four days since Lazarus had been dead and that her brother's body must surely smell.

Jesus looked at her and said, "Didn't I tell you that if you believe, you would see God's glory?" The stone was moved away. Jesus looked up and spoke to His Father, thanking God for hearing Him.

Then Jesus looked straight into the darkness of the tomb and shouted loudly, "Lazarus, come out!"

The crowd stood in hushed silence as the powerful teacher stared at the tomb. Suddenly a figure appeared in the opening to the tomb. It was Lazarus. He had strips of cloth wound around his body, feet, and hands, and his face was wrapped with a cloth. But the moving body showed that Lazarus was alive. He staggered out of the cave, barely able to move forward with all the wrappings around him.

Jesus commanded the people to free Lazarus by removing the burial cloths constraining him. Lazarus was washed clean, dressed in fine clothes, and returned to his astounded yet ecstatic sisters. He could talk, move, and even eat. He had indeed been raised from the dead.

No record has been found describing the secrets that Lazarus may have learned in the world beyond, but legend has it that the first question Lazarus asked after his resurrection was whether he must die a second time. Jewish tradition suggests that when he was told that he would die again, Lazarus became sad and was said to have never smiled again.

The word about Lazarus' resurrection spread quickly, and even more of the Jewish people began to follow Jesus. The leaders of the Jewish council were infuriated. The chief priests immediately began planning to kill Jesus. They also began planning to kill Lazarus because he was the reason that so many people were abandoning the influence of the Jewish leadership and were following Jesus.

Jesus continued his ministry in and around the countryside, healing and preaching. It was the beginning of Passion Week on the Sunday that Jesus made his triumphant entry into Jerusalem. Each evening on Sunday through Wednesday of that week, Jesus stayed with Mary, Martha, and Lazarus. On Thursday evening, He celebrated the Last Supper with His disciples in Jerusalem. Then Jesus spent the night praying in the Garden of Gethsemane. In the wee hours of the night, Judas and a crowd of Roman soldiers and Jewish leaders arrived to arrest Jesus. The next three days set the stage for the future of the whole world.

Jewish history reports that Mary, Martha, and Lazarus were present at the crucifixion when Jesus died and the ground shook, the sky became dark, dead believers came out of tombs around Jerusalem, and the huge curtain in the temple ripped in two. These three followers were also present when Jesus began to appear to others after His own resurrection.

The resurrection and then ascension of Jesus turned the Jewish world upside down. The common people were all talking about Jesus, the savior of the world. And the Jewish priests and their cohorts were quickly losing control over the Jewish people. And lose control was something they did not want.

Jewish leaders wanted to kill all the followers of Jesus, but Roman law forbade this. Only a Roman had the authority to kill a Jew. But the Roman authorities did not prevent the Jewish leaders from capturing all the Christians they could and setting them adrift in boats and ships without means of control or propulsion, letting their ships float wherever the current carried them, hoping the watercraft would capsize and sink with all the hated followers.

Thus it was that Joseph of Arimathea and a group of dedicated believers were set adrift off the western coast of Palestine out into the Mediterranean Sea. Water entering the Mediterranean from the Nile and other rivers emptying into it flows west toward the Strait of Gibraltar and out into the Atlantic. Any watercraft on the surface of this sea would float toward the Strait of Gibraltar.

The Mediterranean is known for sudden and severe storms with high seas and blowing winds. The Jewish leadership felt that it wouldn't be long before the watercraft would be flooded and sink with all on board. It's reported that on one small ship were Joseph of Arimathea, Mary, Martha, and their brother, Lazarus.

The Jewish leaders felt this group wouldn't last a week out on the water. They didn't count on the skills of Joseph of Arimathea. He had grown up with the Phoenicians and had made a number of sea cruises on the Mediterranean. He was an accomplished seaman.

Joseph apparently fashioned a rudder and guided their ship over to the southern coast of France. So Joseph, Lazarus, and his sisters were safe in France. There the ship was properly outfitted with a better rudder, oars and a sail. Then they left France and sailed out through the Strait of Gibraltar and up to Glastonbury, England. Here they established the first Christian church above ground. Glastonbury quickly filled with converts, and baptisms, and teaching thrived.

As the Christian congregation in England grew, missionary trips were made back to Europe. Among the first missionaries to go out from Glastonbury were Mary, Martha, and their brother, Lazarus. They sailed to Marseilles on the southern coast of France where Lazarus was made Bishop of the Christian church in France. He held the Bishopric post for seven years and is believed to have died in France. And, as reported in *The Coming of the Saints* by Taylor, the two sisters, Mary and Martha, went with Lazarus and lived out their lives in France, preaching and teaching about Jesus.

Jesus' Execution and Supernatural Resurrection

... He said, 'It is finished!' then He bowed His head and died.
JOHN 19:30

She turned around and saw Jesus standing there.
JOHN 20:14

He's not here. He has been brought back to life!
LUKE 24:5

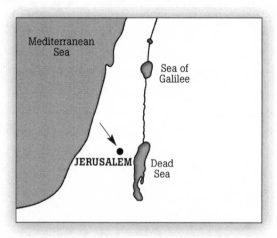

MATTHEW 26:30–28:20; MARK 14:26–16:20;
LUKE 22:39–24:53; JOHN 18:1–21:25
Location: Jerusalem | **Historical Time:** ca 34 AD
TO VIEW MAPS ONLINE:
Copy this link into your browser and press Enter/Return
www.sacred-destinations.com/israel/jerusalem-map
www.sacred-destinations.com/israel/israel-map
www.ccel.org/bible/phillips/CP051GOSPELMAPS.htm
bibleatlas.org/jerusalem.htm

THE LIFE, DEATH, AND RESURRECTION OF JESUS CHRIST validates the entire Bible. He is the alpha to the omega. From the very beginning to the very end, God has been implementing a plan for the Jewish nation and for all of us. Jesus played an important part in this drama.

After a Passover supper in which He confronted Judas, the betrayer, Jesus took the remaining disciples up on the Mount of Olives to a quiet park called the "Garden of Gethsemane." Jesus had completed his ministry, and now He was preparing for the most important part of His life on earth.

He had been telling His followers that He was soon going to be put to death, but He would come back to life in three days. They were afraid or too stubborn to accept His words, and Simon Peter vigorously denied the prophecy, but Jesus rebuked him and told Peter that he would deny knowing Jesus three times before He died.

There in the peaceful garden, Jesus took Peter, James, and John away from the group and began to pray. It was night and they were alone. He had always lived a lonely life. He could never get in mischief or play like the other children in Nazareth because He was special; He was the Son of God. He never sinned, and He refused all temptation that came His way. So he had few friends throughout his life. Even He and His siblings weren't close. His disciples were the closest friends He had. And here they were about to experience a traumatic event that would change their relationship forever.

The disciples kept falling asleep, but Jesus kept praying. He was taking on all the sins of the entire world, and He was beginning His difficult journey of suffering right there in the Garden. The stress was horrible. As physicist and Christian writer, Lambert Dolphin described in his excellent article, *"Six Hours in Eternity"* (Source: www.ldolphin.org/sixhours.html) Jesus endured terrible emotional and spiritual torment.

Jesus' earthly father, Joseph, had died many years earlier, and now His heavenly Father was abandoning Him to let Him take on the sin and guilt of all humans.

He asked His Father to take Him out of this situation. Jesus said, "Father, if it's possible, let this cup of suffering be taken away from me." Then the obedient Son continued, "But let your will be done rather than mine."

He went over to His sleeping disciples and asked them to stay awake and pray that they won't be tempted to abandon Him. Then He went away from them to pray a second time. In this prayer He said if the cup of suffering cannot be taken away, then let His Father's will be done. His cry to His Father was one of deep desperation and despair.

According to Luke 22:43 an angel came to strengthen Jesus before He prayed a third time. He was in such mental and spiritual anguish that perspiration poured out of his pores like blood.

Then Jesus woke his sleepy disciples and told them to get ready because the one who betrayed Him was coming. He was still speaking when the sounds of an approaching crowd caught their attention. The crowd included a troop of soldiers, chief priests, their guards, and Pharisees, the leaders of the Jews. Many were carrying swords and clubs. Judas was with them. He greeted Jesus, and some of the men came forward to arrest Him.

Suddenly Peter stepped out and drew his sword. He swiped at the first man cutting off the ear of the servant of the chief priest. I envisioned it barely hanging alongside his head by a piece of skin.

Jesus told Peter to put his sword away. He said that if He wanted He could call on His Father to send over 12 legions of angels to help Him, but this would not fulfill prophecies in the Scriptures. And He was there to do just that. Jesus healed the servant's ear and then was taken into custody.

As you read the accounts of the trial and treatment of Jesus, you can see that He was hated by the Jewish leadership. They railroaded Him using false accusations and dirty politics. It was a mock trial that even the Roman authorities could not stop.

When he was condemned to die by crucifixion, Jesus was ordered scourged and He was beaten by the Roman executioners with whips that had barbs on the end. The skin on His back was ripped to shreds. Then a crown of sharp thorns was violently forced down over His head, and a purple-red cape was placed over Him by the mocking and jeering Roman soldiers. With blood streaming down His body, a 100 pound beam was placed on His shoulders. It would be used as the cross beam at his execution. Jesus was pushed and beaten along a narrow street through the city to the place of execution on the hill called Golgatha (the Skull).

Once in front of the pole for the cross, Jesus was stripped of what was left of His clothes, and He was nailed to the cross. His arms were stretched out on the cross beam, and spikes were driven through the base of his hands in the area of the carpal tunnel. This caused excruciating pain. It also prevented the nails from pulling out through the skin of the hands when His body hung on the cross.

Next His legs were bent and one foot was placed over the other. A long spike was driven through His feet to impale them to the vertical wood of the cross.

It was nine o'clock on Friday morning. With Jesus firmly nailed to the wooden cross members, the cross was raised vertical and its base lowered into a deep hole in the ground. The cross stood solidly upright as Jesus the man tried to find a comfortable position. None could be found, and the suffering intensified.

It was difficult to take in air or to raise His body up to exhale. So Jesus hung there as some family members and curious onlookers and the Roman soldiers watched Him slowly die.

One of the two other men being crucified alongside Jesus said He should not be there—that unlike them, He committed no crime. The man asked Jesus to remember him when He got into His kingdom. Jesus told the man he would be there with Him in paradise that same day.

Several medical experts have written white papers on what likely happened in the body of Jesus as He suffered on the cross. Physically His body was so damaged the heart was failing and He was dying of asphyxiation because He was steadily losing the ability to breathe.

At noon an erie darkness came over the land. Jesus was dying, and all His family and followers could do is watch in horror.

Just before three o'clock, Jesus cried out, "My God, My God, why have you abandoned Me?" Some of the people standing in front of Him thought He was calling Elijah. Then Jesus said, "I thirst." A man got a sponge, soaked it in vinegar, and offered it to Jesus. The others there said to stay back and leave Jesus alone. They mocked Jesus saying let Elijah save Him.

One of the soldiers put the vinegar-soaked sponge on a hyssop stick and touched the sponge to Jesus' mouth. Jesus tasted the vinegar, then looked up and said, "It is finished" and died.

At that moment, the earth shook and rocks were split open and the huge curtain in the temple ripped in two from top to bottom. The tombs of others who had died opened and many holy people came back to life. When the man, Jesus, died and gave up the ghost, He immediately went up against the devil and all the demons, fallen angels, and powers of evil in the universe. And He completely overpowered all of them.

Since Saturday was a day of worship, Jewish leaders asked that all executions be over before then, so the soldiers checked the bodies of all those hanging on crosses. If they found anyone still alive, they took a club and broke their legs above the ankle. This would cause them to sink down, held only by the nails through their hands. Suffocation and death began immediately. The two men who were crucified with Jesus still lived so their legs were broken, and they died.

But when they came to Jesus, the soldiers found that He was already dead. One of them took a spear and stabbed Jesus in the side up into the heart area. Jesus' body didn't respond and blood and water came out confirming his death. Then they stood back so each body could be taken down by friends or relatives and buried. Jesus hung there until his uncle arrived to claim the corpse.

Joseph of Arimathea was the uncle of Jesus, a member of the Jewish Council, and Minister of Mines for the

Roman government. That evening he arrived from Arimathea and asked and got permission from Pilate to take the body of Jesus for burial. He and Nicodemus took Jesus's body with 75 pounds of a myrrh and aloe mixture to a new tomb that Joseph had purchased. Soldiers, Jews, priests, Mary Magdalene, and Mary the mother of Jesus followed Joseph and Nicodemus to the tomb. The terrified disciples were hiding.

Joeseph and Nicodemus wrapped the body of Jesus with strips of linen soaked in the fragrant myrrh and aloe. Pilate directed that soldiers roll a huge stone in front of the tomb and guard the tomb all night to keep any of Jesus' followers from taking the body.

On Saturday, a seal was placed on the stone and the guard continued. The next morning the women began arriving to put spices on the body. To their surprise, they found the stone rolled away and the tomb empty. Jesus had risen, and the world has never been the same since.

He appeared to his disciples and to over 500 people over the next 40 days. Then the disciples were given the Holy Spirit and power to preach the good news that Christ had risen. All who believed were told they would be saved from eternal damnation. Those who didn't would realize another end.

As C.S. Lewis wrote in his book, *Mere Christianity*, "The same fires which heal, purify and warm the righteous are the consuming, everlasting burnings of Gehenna—where beings who refused to become the human persons they were designed to be must finally endure the "backside" of God's love—which is hell."

Paul Unhurt by Bite of Poisonous Snake

The snake bit Paul's hand and wouldn't let go.
ACTS 28:3

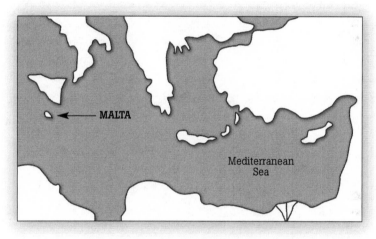

ACTS 28:1-6
Location: Island of Malta | **Historical Time:** ca 59 AD
TO VIEW MAPS ONLINE:
Copy this link into your browser and press Enter/Return
en.wikipedia.org/wiki/Malta_(island)

PAUL AND THE REST OF THE PRISONERS OF THE ROMANS had gotten to shore after their ship ran aground and was wrecked on Malta. The people on the island didn't speak Greek, but they showed Paul and the others kindness. They started a fire to warm the survivors from the cold and rain.

Paul gathered more wood to put on the fire. When he laid the sticks and branches on the burning fire, a poisonous viper came out of the wood and bit Paul on his hand.

The snake would not let go, and the island dwellers thought Paul was a murderer and was being punished. But Paul shook the snake off into the fire and nothing happened to him. The bite area did not swell up and Paul did not fall down dead from the poison.

The Maltese people who observed this concluded that Paul was some form of god.

Summary

THIS HAS BEEN AN IN-DEPTH LOOK INTO THE BIBLE'S description of power over life and death. You read about the death of individuals, groups, and even armies. You read about Korah and his family getting swallowed up by the earth. You read about deadly fire coming down from the sky and flashing out of a pillar of cloud. And you read how Lazarus was raised to life days after he had died. Then you read about Enoch, the man who never died and how Jesus died and rose again. In the relevant verses that follow, you can find other instances of power over life and death. In the next chapter you'll read about God's power over demons.

Relevant Verses in Chapter Three

Incidents Involving Life and Death

AFTERMATH: End Times
Location: Travelers Valley to the East of the Dead Sea
Verse: Ezekiel 39:8
Verse describes cleanup after end time war. Gog and whole army will be buried in Travelers Valley east of the Dead Sea. It will take seven months to bury all the dead. Birds and animals will feast on the corpses.

ANGEL KILLS: Angel Kills Attacking Army of 185,000
Location: Jerusalem
Verses: 2 Kings 19:1–36; 2 Chronicles 32:1–22; Isaiah 36:21–37
Sennacherib and his Assyrian army surrounded King Hezekiah of Judah, and his people including Isaiah. Hezekiah and Isaiah prayed, and overnight an angel exterminated 185,000 Assyrian soldiers, officials and commanders.

ANGEL KILLS: King Killed by Angel
Location: Jerusalem
Verse: Acts 12:23
King Herod let people call him a god and an angel suddenly appeared and killed Herod. His body was eaten by maggots.

ANGEL STOPS SACRIFICE: Child Sacrifice Stopped by Angel
Location: Mount Moriah near Jerusalem
Verse: Genesis 22:8
Abraham's sacrifice of his son Isaac was stopped by "Messenger of the Lord."

ANIMAL KILLED: Strength to Kill Lion
Location: Kabzeel, Moab
Verses: 2 Samuel 23:20; 1 Chronicles 11:11, 20, 22
Giant Benaiah killed a lion in a pit.

ANIMAL KILLS: Lion Stands Guard by Donkey
Location: On road from Bethel
Verse: 1 Kings 13:21
Man of God is killed. Lion stands by live donkey and dead Man of God. Does not kill or eat donkey.

ANIMALS KILL: Lions Kill Captives until They Worship God
Location: Samaria

Verse: 2 Kings 17:25
Lions killed pagan captives of Assyria in Samaria who failed to worship God. Once they worshipped God, they were no longer killed.

ANIMALS KILL BOYS: Bears kill 42 Disrespectful Boys
Location: On road from Jericho to Bethel
Verses: 2 Kings 2:23–25
Mocking boys taunted bald Elisha, Elisha cursed them and two bears rushed out of trees and tore the irreverent boys apart.

ANIMALS KILLED: Livestock in Egypt Suddenly Die, Others Unaffected (Exodus 5th Plague)
Location: Egypt
Verse: Exodus 9:6

COMPLAINERS DIE: Quail Suddenly Appear But Bring Plague
Location: Kibroth Hattaavah – Graves of Those Who Craved Meat
Verses: Exodus 16:8, 11–13; Numbers 11:31, 34; Psalms 78:26–30; Psalms 105:39–42
Israelites complained of diet without meat. In the evening God sent a huge flock of quail 3 feet deep in evening, but before complainers could swallow a mouthful of meat, they died of plague.

CONCEPTION: The Immaculate Conception of Jesus
Location: Nazareth

Verse: Matthew 1:18
Mary discovered she was pregnant but had never slept with Joseph or any man.

DEAD MAN SPEAKS: Dead Conjured Up for Conversation
Location: Endor
Verse: 1 Samuel 28:11
Mystic seer brought Samuel back from the dead to talk with King Saul. Samuel told Saul he and his sons would die the next day.

DEATH BY FIRE: Fire Suddenly Consumes 250 Rebels
Location: Ephraim
Verses: 2 Chronicles 13:1–18
Complainers who rebelled against Moses with Korah and offered incense are suddenly burned to death by fire.

DEATH BY FIRE: Fire Suddenly Kills Complainers
Location: Desert of Paran
Verses: Numbers 11:1; Psalm 78:21
Fire consumed complaining people. The place where they died was called "Taberah" (Fire).

DEATH BY PLAGUE: Plague POWER OVER LIFE AND DEATHSuddenly Kills Spies
Location: Desert of Paran
Verse: Numbers 14:36
"So the men Moses sent to explore the land died in front of the Lord from a plague." Spies who complained about giants in Canaan suddenly

died from plague. Joshua and Caleb not affected.

DEATH OF MOSES: God Buries Dead Man
Location: Mount Nebo at top of Pisgah
Verses: Deuteronomy 34; Jude 9
When Moses died after seeing the Promised Land, he was not buried by the Israelites. God, not man, buried Moses. The archangel Michael argued with the devil over the body of Moses. Satan never got the body of Moses, and Moses later appeared in bodily form with Elijah at the transfiguration of Jesus.

DEATH PREVENTION: Bronze Serpent on Pole Prevents Death from Snakebite
Location: Along road from Mount Hor to the Red Sea in Wilderness of Zin **Verses:** Numbers 21:6; 2 Kings 18:4; John 3:14; 1 Corinthians 10:9
Poisonous snakes appeared and began to bite the complaining Israelites. God told Moses to place an image of a bronze snake on a pole. Anytime someone was bitten, the victim could look at the bronze snake and they would not die.

DIDN'T DIE: Enoch Never Died, Teleported to Heaven
Location: Fertile Crescent
Verses: Gen 5:18-24; Hebrews 11:5; Jude 1:14-15
Verse explains that Enoch pleased God and was taken away (teleported) to heaven at age 365 without dying.

DIDN'T DIE: Snatched Away to Third Heaven
Location: Corinth
Verses: 2 Cor 12:2-4
Paul told the people of Corinth about a follower of Christ who was snatched away to the third heaven 14 years earlier. The third heaven is one of the 10 dimensions described in the Bible.

DOUBT KILLS: Prophet Predicts Death for Questioning Servant
Location: Samaria
Verses: 2 Kings 7:2, 20
King's servant questioned the food prophecy of Elisha and was told he would die. When the Arameans abandoned their camps and the people recovered all their loot, flour and barley prices nosedived. The king's servant was in charge of the gate at Samaria when the people stormed out to get the food. He was trampled to death as predicted.

EAR RESTORED: Severed Ear Immediately Healed
Location: Gethsemane, Mount of Olives
Verses: Luke 22:47-51; John 18:10
While Jesus was being arrested, one of the disciples cut off the ear of Malchus, a servant of the chief priest. Jesus told the disciples to stop resisting those who

came to arrest him. Then he touched the servant's ear and healed him.

ENEMY DEFEATED: Attacking Israelites Defeated by God
Location: Mount Zemaraim
Verses: 2 Chronicles 13:1–18
King Jeroboam of the Israelites rebelled and attacked King Abijah of Judah. When the priests of Judah blew their trumpets and the people of Judah shouted, God attacked Jeroboam and all Israel in front of Abijah and Judah.

ENEMY DEFEATED: Attacking Sudanese Defeated by God
Location: Zephathah Valley
Verses: 2 Chronicles 14:8–15
King Asa of Judah asked God to help him defeat the invading army of Zerah. Judah had 300,000 Judeans and 280,000 Benjaminites against the Sudanese with one million men and 300 chariots. In the Zephathah Valley at Mareshah, the Lord attacked the Sudanese army in front of Asa and Judah. The Sudanese fled and many were killed.

ENEMY DEFEATED: Battle Won While Spear Held over People
Location: Ai
Verses: Joshua 8
Joshua defeated the Canaanites at Ai while holding out his spear.

ENEMY KILLED: Invading Armies Defeated by God
Location: Beracah at end of Ziz Pass near Jeruel Desert
Verses: 2 Chronicles 20:13–26
King Jehoshaphat was told to lead the armies of Judah into battle against the Ammonites, Moabites, and people of Mount Seir, but they would not actually fight because God would fight for them. The Lord set ambushes for the invaders. Then the Ammonites and Moabites attacked the people from Mount Seir and annihilated them. Next they fought with each other and destroyed one another. No invader escaped.

ENEMY KILLED: Strength to Kill 800 Enemies
Location: Unknown
Verses: 2 Samuel 23:8; 1 Chronicles 11:11, 20, 22
Josheb killed 800 men.

ENEMY KILLED: Strong Man Attacks and Kills 30 People
Sampson killed 30 Philistines.
Location: Ashkelon
Verse: Judges 14:19

ENEMY KILLED: Strong Man Kills 1,000 with Jawbone
Location: Ramath Lehi
Verse: Judges 15:15
After breaking the ropes tying him, Sampson killed 1,000 men using the jawbone of an ass. The place was called Ramath Lehi (Jawbone Hill).

ENEMY KILLED: Strong Man Kills Enemy by Striking Hip and Thigh

Location: Lehi
Verses: Judges 15:6–8
When the Philistines learned what Sampson had done with the foxes, they burned his wife and her father to death. Sampson attacked the Philistines and slaughtered them by striking their hips and thighs.

ENEMY KILLED: Strong Man Pulls Temple Columns Down
Location: Gaza
Verse: Judges 16:30
Blinded Sampson was brought out into the courtyard of the Temple of Dagon for all the people to ridicule as the man who killed so many of them but was then blinded and weak. They didn't notice that his hair had grown out. Sampson pulled down the columns holding up the temple, collapsing it and killing about 3,000 Philistine men and women.

ENEMY KILLED BY GIANT:
Super Strong Man Kills 300 Enemy Soldiers
Location: Unknown
Verses: 1 Chronicles 11:11, 20, 22
A giant man in the army of David, Jashobeam, used a spear to kill 300 enemy soldiers.

ENEMY KILLED BY GIANT:
Strength to Kill 300 Men
Location: Valley of Rephaim
Verses: 2 Samuel 23:18; 1 Chronicles 11:11, 20, 22
Giant man Abishai used his spear to kill 300 men.

FATAL DISEASE: Evil King Suddenly Gets Fatal Disease
Location: Near Jerusalem
Verse: 2 Chronicles 13:20
King Jeroboam of Israel was defeated by God and struck with sudden death from a languishing disease he contracted after his attack on Judah.

FATAL FOOT DISEASE: Stubborn King Gets Fatal Foot Disease
Location: Judah
Verses: 2 Chronicles 16:12–14
King Asa contracted foot disease that got progressively worse. Instead of asking God for help, he had doctors look after him. He died.

FATAL TUMORS: Tumors Suddenly Kill Men
Location: Ashdod and then Gath
Verses: 1 Samuel 5:6–12
Philistines in Ashdod got deadly tumorous hemorrhoids (emerods) from being in the presence of the Ark. The Ark was taken from Ashdod to Gath, and the people there began to be covered with tumors.

FIRE DOESN'T BURN: Men in Fiery Furnace Not Burned
Location: Babylon
Verses: Daniel 3:19–33
Shadrach, Meshack, and Abednego refuse to worship 90-foot statue built on order of King Nebuchadnezzar. Command was that anyone who didn't bow down and

worship idol when sound of instruments was heard would be thrown into blazing furnace. King orders furnace to be heated to seven times normal and the three men were thrown in. Flames so hot, the men who threw the three into the furnace were burned to death from the heat. Four men were then seen in the flames. The three men and a fourth that looked like "a son of the gods." Shadrach, Meshack, and Abednego were seen untied and walking about in the fire. Nebuchadnezzar stood at the door to the furnace and commanded the three men to come out. They did, and the king saw that their bodies were not harmed. The hair wasn't singed, their clothes were not burned, nor did they smell of smoke.

FIRE KILLS: Sudden Fire Consumes Two Men
Location: Sinai Desert
Verses: Leviticus 10:1; Numbers 3:1–4
Judgment came to Aaron's sons, Nadab and Abihu. Fire killed Aaron's sons for burning coals and incense without permission. Fire flashed out from cloud and burned them to death. They died while still in their linen robes.

FIRE TO KILL: Power to Bring Fire
Location: Samaritan village

Verses: Luke 9:52–55
Disciples ask, "Should we bring fire down on village?" (James and John re: Samaritans)

GIANT KILLED: Giant Killed in Battle
Location: Gath
Verses: 1 Chronicles 20:4–8
Goliath's brother giant Lamni, from Gath, was killed by Elhanan, son of Jair.

GIANT KILLED: Six-Fingered Giant Killed in Battle
Location: Gath
Verses: 1 Chronicles 20:4–8
David's brother, Jonathan, killed a giant at Gath with six fingers on each hand and six toes on each foot. The giant was a descendent of Haraphah, Goliath's father, who lived in Gath.

GIANT KILLED: Small Boy Kills Defiant Giant with Slingshot
Location: Near Beit Fased in the Valley of Elah
Verse: 1 Samuel 17:4
A small unprotected shepherd boy, David, killed a much bigger and stronger 9'6" giant named Goliath with a smooth stone and a slingshot.

GIANT KILLED: Super Strong Man Kills Enemy, a Lion, and a Giant
Location: Unknown
Verse: 1 Chronicles 11:22
Giant Benaiah from Kabzeel killed two powerful soldiers from Moab. He also went into

a cistern pit and killed a lion on the day it snowed. Then he killed an 8-foot-tall Egyptian who attacked Benaiah with a spear like a "weaver's beam." Benaiah grabbed it away and killed the giant with his own spear.

HAIL KILLS: Deadly Hail Kills Retreating Army
Location: near Gibeon on slope of Beth Horon toward Azekah
Verse: Joshua 10:11
Hailstones rained down and killed the fleeing Amorite army.

JESUS CRUCIFIED: Innocent Man Executed by Jewish Leadership
Location: Jerusalem
Verses: Matthew 27:45–56; Mark 15:20–40; Luke 23:44–49; John 19:28–30
Jesus suffered humiliation and severe beatings. Then He was nailed to a wooden cross and crucified. At three Friday afternoon Jesus said "It is finished" and bowed His head and died.

KILLED WITH STICK: Man Kills 600 Enemy with Stick
Location: near the place where the Philistines camped when David fought Goliath (modern-day Beit Fased)
Verse: Judges 3:31
Shamgar killed 600 Philistines with a sharp stick used to prod animals along. Shamgar was one of the Judges; son of Anath.

LIES KILL: Deceivers Die for Cheating God
Location: Jerusalem
Verse: Acts 5:1
Ananias and his wife, Sapphira, sold property but held back part of money pledged to apostles. Peter confronted Ananias and Ananias dropped dead. Three hours later Sapphira arrived. She lied to Peter about how much money she and Ananias got for selling the land. Peter confronted her with the truth, and she too dropped dead.

LIES KILL: Lying Prophet Killed by Lion
Location: Road out of Bethel
Verses: 1 Kings 13:11–26
Old prophet disobeyed God by lying and was killed by a lion; torn apart; not eaten. Donkey that he was riding was not attacked by lion.

LION KILLED: Strong Man Kills Lion with Bare Hands
Location: Near vineyards of Timnah
Verse: Judges 14:6
Sampson killed a lion with his bare hands.

LOOK KILLS: Men Instantly Die When Look into Ark
Location: Beth Shemesh
Verses: 1 Samuel 6:19–21
As the Ark arrived at Beth Shemesh, the people placed it on a rock in the field of Joshua. Some of the people looked inside the Ark. and 70 of them were instantly killed.

LOOK KILLS: Woman Turned into Salt Pillar
Location: between Zoar and Sodom and Gomorrah
Verses: Genesis 19:24-28; Luke 17:28-32
Lot's wife looked back and turned into a pillar of salt.

PLAGUE: All Firstborn Suddenly Die – Exodus 10ᵗʰ Plague
Location: Egypt
Verses: Exodus 12; Psalm 105:36; Psalm 135:8; Psalm 136:10; Hebrews 11:28
At midnight all firstborn sons in Egypt died. Moses (Passover).

PLAGUE: Complaining Spies Die of Plague
Location: Desert of Paran
Verse: Numbers 14:36
Spies who complained about giants in Canaan suddenly died from plague. Joshua and Caleb were not affected.

PLAGUE: Deadly Plague Kills Rebels
Location: Desert of Paran
Verse: Numbers 16:41
Community of Israel complained to Moses and Aaron. A deadly plague instantly started sweeping through the complaining people. Aaron ran through the crowd carrying an incense burner. He ran to the front of the plague and stood between the dead and still living. The plague stopped as suddenly as it started, but 14,700 people died before it was over.

PLAGUE: Plague Instantly Stops upon Death of Couple
Location: Abel Shittim on plains of Moab
Verse: Numbers 25:26
Execution of adulterous man and woman instantly stops plague that had already killed 24,000 Israelites.

PLAGUE: Plague Kills 70,000
Location: Araunah between Dan and Beersheba, also Jerusalem
Verses: 2 Samuel 24:15-17; 1 Chronicles 21:14
King David sinned by ordering a census of Israelites to determine how many people he has in his kingdom. Messenger of God brings pestilence plague that killed 70,000 people of David from Dan to Beersheba.

PREVENTION: Deadly Boil Cured by Prophet
Location: Assyria
2 Kings 20:1-11, Isaiah 38:1-8
A festering boil was killing King Hezekiah, and he asked to be cured. Isaiah instructed him to place a fig cake on the boil. He did and was healed.

PREVENTION: Dying Boy Cured of Fever
Location: Cana and Capernaum
Verses: John 4:46-53
A government official in Cana had a son in Capernaum who was sick and dying with fever.

The nobleman went to Jesus and asked for help. At 7:00 p.m. (another source said 1:00 p.m.), Jesus told the official that his faith has made his son well. The next day, the official met servants from his home as he was returning to Capernaum. They told him that at exactly 7:00 p.m. (another source said 1:00 p.m.), the night before the fever left the boy and he was now fine.

PROTECTION: Power over Threat and Protection from Harm
Location: On road to Jerusalem
Verse: Luke 10:19
Jesus told the 70 disciples that neither snakes, scorpions nor anything else can hurt them.

RESURRECTED: Appearance after Resurrection
Location: Corinth
Verses: 1 Corinthians 15:3–8
Paul told people how Jesus died and rose again. He told them that Jesus appeared to Cephas (Aramaic name for Peter), then to the 12 apostles. Next he appeared to over 500 believers at one time. Then he appeared to James and then to all the apostles. Last of all Jesus appeared to Paul.

RESURRECTION: Jesus Predicts Three Days to Resurrection
Location: Synagogue in unknown location
Verse: Matthew 12:38
Jesus told the scribes and Phar-isees that just as Jonah was in the belly of the fish for three days, He would be in the heart of the earth for three days.

RESURRECTION: Jesus Rises from the Dead
Location: Jerusalem
Verses: Matthew 28:1–20; Mark 16:1–20; Luke 24:1–53; John 20:28–30
Immediately after returning to life, Jesus began appearing to His disciples and others. In the next 40 days, He would appear to over 500 people.

REVIVED: Dead Boy Brought Back to Life
Location: Zarephath
Verse: 1 Kings 17:21
Prophet Elijah restores life to widow's young.

REVIVED: Dead Boy Brought Back to Life
Location: Shunem
Verses: 2 Kings 4:8–37
Shunemite woman's son died from sunstroke. She rode 15 miles to Carmel to get Elisha. After holding out his staff to revive the boy and finding this unsuccessful, Elisha personally went to the boy. Elisha brought the boy back to life. Boy revived, sneezed seven times and was returned to his mother.

REVIVED: Dead Man Brought Back to Life
Location: Bethany
Verses: John 11:1–44

Jesus raised His friend Lazarus who had been dead for three days. "Lazarus, come out!" (Jesus, Lazarus, his sisters Mary and Martha)

REVIVED: Dead Man Brought Back to Life
Location: Troas or Philippi
Verses: Acts 20:7–12
Paul brought Eutychus back to life after he fell out of a second-floor window and was killed.

REVIVED: Dead Man Raised to Life
Location: Capernaum
Verses: Luke 7:12–16
Jesus raised dead man being taken by funeral procession at city of Nain. Man was only child of widow. Jesus took hold of coffin being carried by men of city and told the dead man to "... come back to life!" The man sat up and began to talk. Jesus gave him back to his mother.

REVIVED: Dead Man Touches Prophet Bones, Comes Alive
Location: Unknown
Verse: 2 Kings 13:20
Burial team hid a man they were burying from a Moabite raiding party by placing the body inside the tomb of Elisha. The body touched Elisha's bones, and the dead man awakened and stood up.

REVIVED: Dead Suddenly Come to Life
Location: Jerusalem
Verses: Matthew 27:45; Mark 15:33–38; Luke 23:44–49
At the moment Jesus died on the cross at Golgotha, the curtain in the temple ripped in two, the earth shook and rocks were split open. Tombs opened and dead believers came back to life.

REVIVED: Dry Bones of People Come Alive
Location: By Chebar River
Verse: Ezekiel 37:1
Ezekiel was taken by a Spirit to the middle of a valley filled with bones. Ezekiel was commanded to prophesy to the bones. As he did, a rattling noise occurred and the bones came together, ligaments formed, then muscles covered by skin. Then Ezekiel was commanded to prophesy to the breath, and breath entered the resurrected bodies. As they began to move, a very large army began to form.

REVIVED: Raised from the Dead
Location: Capernaum
Verses: Matthew 9:18–21; Mark 5:22, 35–41; Luke 8:44, 49–56
Jesus brought the dead daughter of Jarius, a synagogue leader, back to life by taking hold of her hand and saying "Talitha, koum!" ("Child, get up!").

SALVATION: End Times
Location: By Chebar River
Verses: Ezekiel 38:17–23

The end of time is described in detail.

SAMPSON AND THE FOXES: Strong Man Sets 300 Foxes with Burning Torches Attached to Tails Loose in Grain Field
Location: Lehi
Verse: Judges 15:4
Sampson caught 300 foxes. He tied their tails together in pairs, attached a burning torch to each pair, and set the foxes loose to burn the Philistine grain fields.

SIN KILLS: Death for Sin
Location: Corinth
Verses: 1 Corinthians 10:6–12
Paul reminded the people of Corinth what happened to the Israelites who left Egypt. Sexual sin resulted in 23,000 dying on one day. Some were killed by poisonous snakes.

SNAKEBITE DOESN'T KILL: Poisonous Snakebite Doesn't Kill
Location: Malta
Verses: Acts 28:3–6
Paul was bitten by a poisonous snake that bit his hand and wouldn't release. Paul shook the snake off into a fire and was unharmed.

STORM KILLS: Mysterious Storm Defeats Army
Location: Jabesh–Gilead
Verses: 1 Samuel 12:16–25
Saul defeated the Ammonites during a mysterious thunderstorm and rainstorm.

SURGERY SAVES LIFE: Quick Surgery on Son Saves Man from Death
Location: Egypt
Verses: Exodus 4:29–31
The Lord was going to kill Moses for disobedience regarding command for circumcision, but his wife, Zipporah, took a flint knife and circumcised her son and then touched the severed piece of skin to Moses' feet, calling Moses a "bridegroom of blood to her." The Lord immediately left Moses alone.

TOUCH KILLS: Man Instantly Killed When He Touched the Ark
Location: Perez–uzzah
Verses: 2 Samuel 6:7; 1 Chronicles 13:6–10
Uzzah died instantly after touching the sacred Ark of Covenant.

CHAPTER FOUR

Power Over Demons

THEY'VE BEEN CALLED "DEMONS," "EVIL SPIRITS," and the "unclean." These expressions refer to the fallen angels that were kicked out of heaven with Satan. To keep it simple, I'll just call them "demons." These entities serve Satan. They hate God, and they hate His people. They pleasure in causing pain, misery, and suffering.

Many times these demons are the cause of physical and mental illness. However not every illness is caused by demon possession.

Demons know that Jesus has total power over them. They know who Jesus is, and they are terrified at what Jesus can do to them. They constantly oppose the good angels for possession of God's people.

There is a battle occurring between the forces of good and the forces of evil. This battle is far from being just a physical one. It's also a battle against the rulers of the dark world, and against the principalities of the evil ones. They can make those whom they possess appear attractive and continuously seduce the unwitting into sinning and losing their self-respect and often their wealth, health, family, and friendships.

It's best to stay away from people who act sinful and who refuse to follow the rules for living laid out by God thousands of years ago. We call these "rules" the Ten Commandments. They provide sound principles for living a good, clean, happy, and healthy life. Storms and temptations may swirl all about you, but remember that God is stronger than all of them. God is indeed bigger than the "boogeyman."

The possessing demons will lose, but in the meantime, they leave human casualties and destroyed lives along the way because they cause havoc, pain, and misery wherever they settle.

I found 18 verses in the Bible that speak about demons. The power of demons is not trivial. It's serious, and it involves every one of us. In the stories to follow I'll elaborate on important examples of this powerful force and how it has been defeated. At the end of this section, you'll find a list of all the relevant incidents that were discovered during this research.

Apostle Pretenders Attacked by Demon

They tried to use the name of the Lord Jesus to force evil spirits out of those who were possessed.
ACTS 19:13

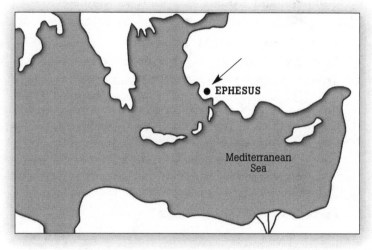

ACTS 19:13-20
Location: Ephesus | Historical Time: ca 60 AD
TO VIEW MAPS ONLINE:
Copy this link into your browser and press Enter/Return
en.wikipedia.org/wiki/Ephesus

DURING THE PERIOD PAUL WAS PREACHING AND DEBATING the reality of Christ's resurrection, there were Jews who pretended to be part of Paul's group. These Jews traveled about forcing evil spirits out of people. When they attempted their exorcisms, they tried to use the name of Jesus to achieve their goals. These Jews would say, "I order you to come out in the name of Jesus, whom Paul talks about."

One group of pretenders is mentioned in Acts 19—the seven sons of Sceva, a Jewish chief priest. They were in Ephesus attempting to rid a possessed man of an evil spirit. After they pronounced their words of exorcism, the demon possessing the man said, "I know Jesus, and I'm acquainted with Paul, but who are you?"

Then the possessed man attacked the seven brothers. It was a sudden and brutal attack, and the pretenders were beaten so badly, their clothes were ripped off, and they ran out of the house naked and wounded.

The Greeks and Jews living in Ephesus heard about this incident and were filled with awe at the name of the Lord Jesus. They began to speak very highly about Jesus Christ and many of them believed in the resurrected Lord.

A large number of them admitted their involvement with magical spells and in the occult. Many of them gathered their books on magic and the occult and burned them in front of the rest of their neighbors. The value of these books was estimated to be 50,000 silver coins.

These events caused the word of the Lord to spread and gain strength. God had used pretenders to send a powerful message to the people.

Jesus Casts Demon out of Woman in Synagogue

... she immediately stood up straight and praised God.
LUKE 13:13

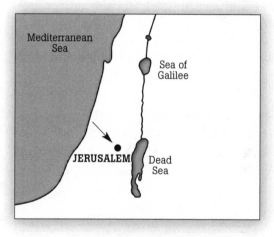

LUKE 13:10-13
Location: Jerusalem | **Historical Time:** ca 30 AD
TO VIEW MAPS ONLINE:
Copy this link into your browser and press Enter/Return
www.sacred-destinations.com/israel/jerusalem-map
www.sacred-destinations.com/israel/israel-map
www.ccel.org/bible/phillips/CP051GOSPELMAPS.htm
bibleatlas.org/jerusalem.htm

IT WAS THE DAY OF WORSHIP, AND MANY JEWS WERE IN the synagogue. One was a woman who had been possessed by a demon for 18 years. The evil spirit had disabled her such that she was hunched over and could not stand up straight.

Jesus saw her and called her to come to him. She hobbled over and Jesus looked her straight in the eyes and pronounced, "Woman, you are free from your disability." Then Jesus placed His hands on her, and she immediately stood up straight and praised God.

The leader of the synagogue was irritated with Jesus for healing on the day of worship. So this person told the crowd, "There are six days when work can be done. So come on one of those days to be healed. Don't come on the day of worship."

Jesus turned to this arrogant person and exclaimed, "You hypocrites! Do not each of you free your ox or donkey on the day of worship? Don't you then take it out of its stall to give it some water to drink?" Then He said, "Now, here is a descendant of Abraham. Satan has kept her in this condition for 18 years. Isn't it right to free her on the day of worship?"

The Jews who opposed Him felt ashamed, but the entire crowd was happy that Jesus was doing these miraculous things.

Demons Exorcised by a Stranger

Master, we saw someone forcing demons out of a person by using the power and authority of your name.

LUKE 9:49

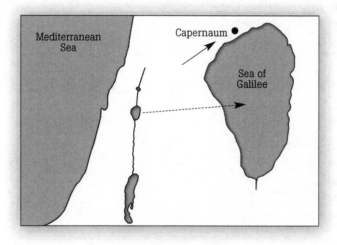

MARK 9:38–41; LUKE 9:49–50
Location: Capernaum | Historical Time: ca 30–33 AD
TO VIEW MAPS ONLINE:
Copy this link into your browser and press Enter/Return
bibleatlas.org/capernaum.htm
www.bible-history.com/geography/ancient-israel/capernaum.html
www.ccel.org/bible/phillips/CP051GOSPELMAPS.htm

THE DISCIPLES WERE WITH JESUS IN CAPERNAUM WHEN John came to Jesus and told him, "Master, we saw someone forcing demons out of a person by using the power and authority of your name. We tried to stop him because he was not one of us."

Jesus replied, "Don't stop him! No one who works a miracle in my name can turn around and speak evil of me."

Then Jesus made the statement that has been used by many tacticians throughout history, "Whoever isn't against us is for us."

Jesus told the disciples that whoever gives you a cup of water to drink because you belong to Christ will certainly not lose their reward.

Demons Forced out and into Swine

Jesus said to them, "Go!"
The demons came out and went into the pigs.
MATTHEW 8:32

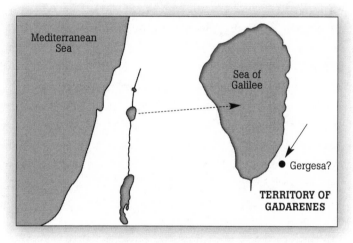

MATTHEW 8:20–33; MARK 5:1–13; LUKE 8:26–33
Location: Gergesa in territory of Gadarenes | **Historical Time:** ca 30–33 AD
TO VIEW MAPS ONLINE:
Copy this link into your browser and press Enter/Return
www.bible-history.com/geography/ancient-israel/gergesa.html
en.wikipedia.org/wiki/Gergesa

JESUS AND HIS DISCIPLES SAILED ACROSS TO THE EAST side of the Sea of Galilee to the territory of Gadarenes.

This area encompassed the Greeco-Roman city of Gardara to the southeast. Gardara was one of the Ten Cities of the Decapolis, an island of Greek and Roman culture with common language, culture, and political status in a primarily Semitic (Aramean, Jewish, and Nabatean) region. The cities were interconnected with good Roman roads in the area that is now Jordan.

As Jesus and his disciples stepped ashore, they were met by two men possessed by demons. Mark and Luke describe only one man since he was the more vocal of the two. They were living in burial caves in the hillside. These tombs were shunned by the local Jews because of the bones of the dead buried there. They considered the area unclean.

One of the men ran forward shouting at Jesus and his followers, "Why are you bothering me, Jesus, Son of the Most High God? I beg you not to torture me!"

The people in the area had kept him bound hand and foot with chains, but he had broken free. He was wild, and the locals felt that no one could tame or control him. He was fierce and often cut himself with stones mutilating his naked body and shrieking loudly. This man confronted Jesus and his followers. The second man apparently held back and observed.

The demons possessing these men knew that Jesus would cast them out. Jesus asked the man, "What is your name?"

The demons in the man replied, "Legion!" In the Roman army a legion is 6,000 soldiers.

The demons begged Jesus not to order them into the bottomless pit, a place of torment where the ministers of judgment are the "tormentors." They knew that Jesus was the Judge who would consign them to their doom.

There was a large herd of pigs feeding nearby on the mountainside. The demons begged Jesus to let them enter the swine. They said, "If you're going to force us out, send us into that herd of pigs."

Jesus allowed this and forcefully said, "Go!" The demons immediately came out and went into the swine. Then the whole herd of about 2,000 pigs suddenly turned and rushed down the hill over a cliff into the sea below where they all drowned.

The swine-herders who saw this incident ran into the nearby city and reported what had happened. The Jews didn't eat pork, but they had no problem selling pork to the Romans. Their willingness to provide forbidden meat to others was a violation of the Torah law. The death of the swine was a loss of income to the local people.

The Gadarenes rushed out of the city to see for themselves what had just occurred. They found Jesus standing over the man who was formerly possessed. He was quietly seated at Jesus' feet and was dressed. He was calm, lucid, and alert. The people were frightened. The same day they lost a source of income from pig sales two men had been freed from demon possession by Jesus. It was much to take in. And they weren't sure if the demons would return for vengeance. So they became fearful and asked Jesus to leave.

Without a word, Jesus turned and walked back to the boat with his disciples. One man followed Jesus and begged him, "Let me stay with you."

Jesus declined, saying, "Go home to your family, and tell them how much the Lord has done for you and how merciful He has been to you."

As the boat moved away from the beach, the man left and began telling everyone throughout the Ten Cities how much Jesus had done for him (Mark 5:20). Everyone who heard the news was amazed.

Jesus Exorcises Demon from a Canaanite Woman

At that moment her daughter was cured.
MATTHEW 15:28

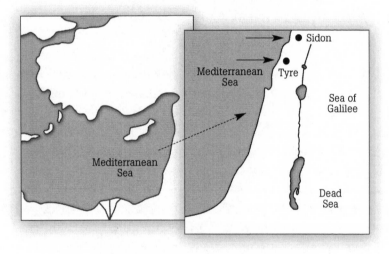

MATTHEW 15:21–29; MARK 7:24–30
Location: Region of Tyre and Sidon | **Historical Time:** ca 30–33 AD
TO VIEW MAPS ONLINE:
Copy this link into your browser and press Enter/Return
en.wikipedia.org/wiki/Tyre,_Lebanon
www.bible-history.com/geography/ancient-israel/tyre.html
en.wikipedia.org/wiki/Sidon
www.bible-history.com/geography/ancient-israel/sidon.html

THIS INCIDENT ILLUSTRATES THE FAITH AND DETERMINA-
tion of a Canaanite woman. Jesus was in the region of Tyre
and Sidon on the shores of the Mediterranean Sea. A Canaan-

ite woman came to Him begging Jesus to cast out a demon that was tormenting her daughter. She was from Syria-Phoenicia, and she shouted loudly, "Have mercy on me, Lord, Son of David! My daughter is tormented by a demon."

Jesus didn't answer, and she continued to shout. His disciples urged him to send her away. She was not Jewish, and, therefore, not part of the lost sheep of the nation of Israel.

As she persisted, Jesus turned to her and said, "I was sent only to the lost sheep of the nation of Israel."

She approached Jesus, bowed down, and said, "Lord, help me!"

Jesus tested her. He said, "It's not right to take the children's food and throw it to the dogs."

Undeterred, she replied, "You're right, Lord. But even the dogs eat scraps that fall from their masters' tables."

Jesus answered, "Woman, you have strong faith! What you wanted will be done for you." At that very moment, her daughter was cured.

Jesus Exorcises Demon from an Epileptic Son

*I command you to come out of him
and never enter him again.*
MARK 9:25

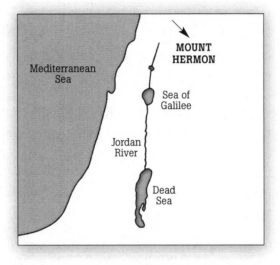

MATTTHEW 17:14–18; MARK 9:17–27; LUKE 9:37–43
Location: Mount Hermon | **Historical Time:** ca 30–33 AD
TO VIEW MAPS ONLINE:
Copy this link into your browser and press Enter/Return
www.keyway.ca/htm2002/mthermon.htm
en.wikipedia.org/wiki/Mount_Hermon

THE DISCIPLES WERE UNABLE TO FORCE AN EVIL SPIRIT
out of a boy suffering from epilepsy. A demon possessed
the boy, and he suffered severe seizures. He would foam
at the mouth and grind his teeth.

The boy's father brought him to Jesus. He explained that he had asked the disciples of Jesus to force the spirit out, but they didn't have the power to do it.

As soon as the demon saw Jesus, it threw the boy into convulsions, and the boy fell to the ground rolling around and foaming at the mouth.

Jesus asked the father how long his son had been like that. The father told Jesus that the boy had suffered like this since he was a child. He said the demon had often thrown the boy into the fire or into water as it tried to destroy him. The father asked Jesus to help them if it was possible.

Jesus told the father that everything is possible for a person who believes. Then the father cried out, "I believe! Help my lack of faith."

Jesus gave an order to the evil spirit, "You spirit that won't let him talk, I command you to come out of him and never enter him again!"

With a scream, the evil spirit shook the boy violently and came out. The boy lay on the floor looking as if he had died, and the people there said, "He's dead!"

But Jesus took the boy's hand and helped him to his feet. He could speak, and he never again suffered epileptic seizures.

Later, the disciples asked Jesus privately why they couldn't force the demon out. Jesus replied, "This kind of spirit can be forced out only by prayer." Jesus told them that they couldn't exorcise the demon because they still had too little faith. Then he said, "If your faith is [even] the size of a mustard seed, you can say to this mountain, 'Move from here to there,' and it will move. Nothing will be impossible for you." Their faith needed to become stronger.

Jesus Drives out Demons at Peter's House

He forced the evil spirits out of people with a command.
MATTHEW 8:16

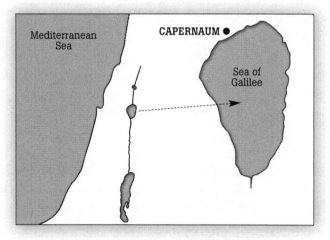

MARK 8:16–18; MARK 1:32–34; LUKE 4:40–41
Location: Capernaum | **Historical Time:** ca 30–33 AD
TO VIEW MAPS ONLINE:
Copy this link into your browser and press Enter/Return
bibleatlas.org/capernaum.htm

The disciples were with Jesus at Peter's house in Capernaum. Jesus had healed Peter's mother-in-law of fever, and she had gotten up and prepared a meal for everyone there.

In the evening many demon-possessed people were brought to Jesus. Jesus forced the evil spirits out of these people with a command.

Summary

THIS HAS BEEN AN IN-DEPTH LOOK INTO THE BIBLE'S description of power over demons. You read how a demon had attacked a pretend apostle and how Jesus went about driving demons out of the people. In the references below you'll find verses on Mary Magdalene and her possession by seven demons, and you'll see Paul describe a significant increase in demon activity in the Last Days. As I researched this subject, it became crystal clear that God is in charge. God has power over all demons and their various forms. And they know it.

Relevant Verses in Chapter Four

Incidents Involving Power Over Demons

AUTHORITY: Authority to Cast out Demons
Location: near Capernaum
Verses: Matthew 10:5; Mark 6:13; Luke 9:1
Jesus gave authority to 12 apostles and they cured the sick by pouring oil on them and cast demons out of people.

AUTHORITY: Special Power Given to Disciples
Location: Mountain near Bethany
Verses: Mark 16:17–19; Luke 24:50–51
After talking to the disciples, Jesus gave them power to cast out demons, to speak other languages, to touch poisonous snakes and drink poisoned liquids without being harmed, and to heal the sick. He also instructed them to go out and tell the news about Him and to baptize in His name.

DEMONS ATTACK: Demon Attacks Apostle Pretenders
Location: Ephesus
Verses: Acts 19:13–20
The seven sons of Sceva, a Jewish chief priest, tried to use the name of Jesus to force evil spirits out of those possessed. They did not know Jesus. An evil spirit told them it knew Jesus and Paul, but not them. Then the possessed man attacked them and beat them up so badly they ran out of the house naked and wounded.

EXORCISM: Demon–Possessed Blind and Mute Man Healed
Location: Capernaum
Verses: Matthew 12:22; Luke 11:14
Jesus cast out a demon possessing a man and restored the man's sight and ability to speak.

EXORCISM: Demons Obey Missionary Disciples
Location: On road to Jerusalem
Verse: Luke 10:17
The 70 disciples reported back to Jesus that even the demons obey them when they use the power and authority of His name.

EXORCISM: Healing and Demons Exorcized
Location: Samaria
Verses: Acts 8:4–8

Philip performed miracles, cast out evil spirits, and cured paralyzed and lame people.

EXORCISM: Healing Voice Exorcises Demon
Location: Mount Hermon
Verses: Matthew 17:14–18; Mark 9:17–27; Luke 9:37–43
Man's epileptic son suffered from a demon that caused seizures, foaming at mouth and grinding of the son's teeth. The disciples were unable to force the spirit out. Jesus ordered the demon out of the boy and it immediately left. Jesus then told the disciples that this kind of spirit could only be forced out by prayer.

EXORCISM: Seven Demons Cast out of Woman
Location: Magdala
Verse: Luke 8:2
Jesus exorcised seven demons from possessing Mary Magdalene.

EXORCISM: Touch Heals People
Location: near Capernaum
Verses: Mark 3:10; Luke 6:17–19
Jesus cured diseased people who touched Him and subjugated and cast out demons. Power came out of Him, and He healed all of them.

EXORCISM: Voice Command Exorcises Demon
Location: Capernaum
Verses: Mark 1:23, Luke 4:31–37
Jesus orders demon out of man in synagogue controlled by evil spirit.

EXORCISM: Voice Exorcises Demon
Location: Phoenicia, district of Tyre and Sidon
Verses: Matthew 15:22; Mark 7:24–30
Canaanite woman in region of Tyre and Sidon begged Jesus to cast out a demon tormenting her daughter. Jesus told the Syrophoenician Greek woman that because of her faith, her daughter was healed. Instantly her daughter was cured.

EXORCISM: Voice Heals People and Drives Demons Out
Location: Capernaum
Verses: Matthew 8:16–18; Mark 1:32–34; Luke 4:40–41
While at Peter's house, Jesus spoke to evil spirits, forcing them out of possessed people and curing everyone who was sick. He wouldn't let demons speak because they knew who He was.

EXORCISM BY STRANGER:
Demon Cast Out by Stranger
Location: Capernaum
Verses: Mark 9:38; Luke 9:49
Disciples told Jesus they saw a stranger force a demon out of a person using the power and authority of the name of Jesus. Jesus told them not to stop this because anyone who performs a miracle in His name can turn around and speak

evil of Jesus. Whoever is not against us is for us.

FOLLOWING DEMONS: End Times
Location: Ephesus
Verses: 1 Timothy 4:1–3
Paul describes conditions leading up to the last days. He talked about people who will deceive and follow the teaching of demons. They will speak lies disguised as truth and will try to stop many from getting married and from eating certain foods.

SPEECH PREVENTED: Demon Cast Out, Man Speaks
Location: Capernaum
Verse: Matthew 9:32
Jesus removes a demon that prevented a man from speaking.

SWINE: Demons Exorcised into Pigs
Location: Gergesa in territory of Gadarenes
Verses: Matthew 8:28–32; Mark 5:1–13; Luke 8:26–33
Jesus and disciples were on the shore at the east side of Sea of Galilee in the territory of the Gadarenes. A man (Matthew 8:28–32 says two men) possessed by demons came out of the tombs and shouted at the group. The demons knew that Jesus would cast them out, so they begged Jesus to send them into a nearby herd of pigs. Jesus said, "Go!" and the demons left the man and entered the swine. The whole herd of pigs then rushed down a cliff into the sea and drowned.

WOMAN POSSESSED: Demon Cast out of Woman
Location: Philippi in Macedonia, Greece
Verse: Acts 16:16
Paul casts demon out of possessed female servant who made money for her owners by telling fortunes. Owners dragged Paul and Barnabas (Silas) before Roman officials in Philippi of Macedonia.

WOMAN POSSESSED: Demon Cast out of Woman in Synagogue
Location: Synagogue in Judea
Verses: Luke 13:10–13
Jesus was teaching in the synagogue on the day of worship. A woman possessed by a demon was there. The demon had disabled her for 18 years so she was hunched over and could not stand up straight. Jesus called her over and told her she was free of her disability. Then He touched her, and she immediately stood up straight and praised God.

CHAPTER FIVE

Power Over Nature

THIS SECTION COVERS BIBLE REFERENCES TO power over nature (including the weather). I found 16 verses in the Bible that deal with this subject. In the stories to follow I'll elaborate on important examples of this force. You'll read about Noah and the Flood, the plagues that led up to the Exodus of the Hebrews out of Egypt, the sun and moon standing still during battle, and the sun's shadow moving in the opposite direction on the steps of a sundial. At the end of this chapter, you'll find a list of verses covering these and other relevant incidents that were discovered during my research.

Global Flood Kills
All but Eight People

Noah, make an ark.
GENESIS 6:14

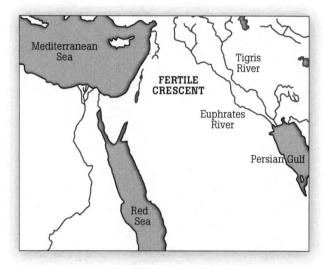

GENESIS 6:5–8:22
Location: Fertile Crescent | Historical Time: Early Bronze Age – ca 2600 BC
TO VIEW MAPS ONLINE:
Copy this link into your browser and press Enter/Return
www.britannica.com/EBchecked/topic/205250/Fertile-Crescent
ancienthistory.about.com/od/neareast/ss/110708ANE_10.htm

NOAH'S ARK IS ONE OF THE MOST FAMILIAR STORIES IN
the Bible. Ever since childhood most of us have heard or
read about the Great Flood and how Noah and his family
were saved from death in a floating boat while the rest of
civilization perished in waters that covered the earth. But
thanks to recent discoveries by geologists, archeologists,

and other scientists, much more has been made known concerning this dramatic event. This article will describe conditions before and after the Flood.

Noah was born during the Antediluvian Age, a time when the earth was covered with a thick layer of moisture. The Antediluvian Age (that period before the Flood) was a different world from that which we know today. Remember the description in Genesis about the earth that God created? He formed dry land. He placed a canopy of water vapor over the dry land. And He produced thousands of streams that flowed up out of the ground.

Scientists today believe that the water vapor canopy was a barrier about 6.5 feet (1-2 meters) thick. It protected the earth from the sun's radiation and provided the ultimate greenhouse effect for rapid growth of animals, plants, and people. This protective canopy was less than 100 feet above the ground.

There were no seasons. Water was abundant everywhere. And the plants that God gave man and animals for food grew thick. Besides protecting the earth from cosmic radiation, the water canopy produced a sub-tropical environment with conditions that were constantly humid and moist. Each evening the canopy would release a wet mist that drifted down and produced dew on the ground. Everything must have been constantly damp.

The temperature under the canopy was between a sweltering hot 143°F (335°K) over the equatorial regions (F for Fahrenheit, K for Kelvin) and a freezing cold -30°F (240°K) over the polar regions of the earth. (Yes, there were polar ice caps.) For comparison, water boils at just over 212°F (373°K) and ice melts at just over 32°F

(273°K). So, except for the poles, it was pretty warm and humid all the time.

It's now believed that all the "dry land" was one huge continent. There were no tectonic plates to move and shift thus producing other land masses. And there were no storms, wind, rain, hail, or severe weather patterns. There was a natural and continually renewing balance in this Antediluvian world. In 1927, scientists started calling this land mass "Pangaea."

The earth that Adam and Eve and their descendants inherited was like a huge tropical greenhouse. Lush vegetation was everywhere. They were never without food. Humans were vegetarians—vegans, if you will. They didn't eat meat until after the Flood.

With no cosmic radiation getting through the water canopy, the people were healthy, lived long, and grew to be quite tall. Today we'd call them giants. But back then, eight to 10 feet tall was common. (Some scholars believe that Noah and his family were also tall.)

Around the time of Adam, evil angels were kicked out of heaven and came to earth. They produced children with earthly women, and these children grew into giant humanoids called "Nephilim." Others were called "Rephaim."

Some researchers think that the "fallen angels" were both male and female. And they mated with many of the earth's inhabitants. Illicit unions between earthly men and female-like fallen angels is said to be the source of ancient legends such as the stories of Homer and the mythical demigods of Greece and Rome. But by crossing God-ordained boundaries for living, these fallen angels disobeyed the Creator and spread evil throughout the world.

Even though the inhabitants of earth were becoming increasingly evil, they were scientifically quite advanced. We are now learning that technology thrived before the Flood. Cain's children developed music and art. They played the lyre and pipe. They developed metalworking and science and industry. And they were able to forge instruments made of bronze and iron. (And we thought the Bronze Age began in 3200 BC and the Iron Age in 1200 BC.)

Being quite sophisticated, they likely built libraries and used technology superior to ours. The reality is that our current notion of "human progress" or the "advancement of man" is just an illusion. The world back then was very advanced.

Adam and Eve produced many children and their children in turn produced many more as the young earth began to be populated by humans. People lived long lives, so Adam and Eve actually saw many children, grandchildren, great grandchildren, and great great grandchildren before they died. Adam lived 930 years. Seven generations of his were alive when he died. With long lifespans, the world's population in Adam's time increased to about 120,000.

Noah was born over 1,000 years after Adam. His dad was Lamech. His grandfather was Methuselah, the longest-living human (969 years). When Methuselah died, Noah was 600 years old. So for 369 years, the grandfather of Noah was alive and participating in their family life. Methuselah and Lamech both died before the Flood began.

Noah was the father of Shem, Ham, and Japheth. (The descendants of Shem populated Asia, the descendants of Ham populated Africa, and the descendants of Japheth populated Europe.)

Estimates of the world population during the time of Noah vary from over 1 million to 7 billion. Regardless, this was a "lot" of people.

But the earth was a sinful place. All the crime, corruption, adultery, murder, and sexual deviation that occurs today was prevalent then, but even more so. Only Noah and his family lived lives free of the sin that permeated the world.

It was 2500 BC, and God had had enough. So 4,500 years ago, He decided to end His grand experiment and destroy all of humankind. But Noah, his wife, Naamah, and their three sons and their wives would be spared. Only eight individuals among all the people on earth would be allowed to live! Only eight people would survive the greatest water calamity in history!

Noah and his extended family lived near the Iraq/Iran border in what was to be called Mesopotamia. The Garden of Eden still existed somewhere to the south, but no one could go there. The original Tigris River flowed out of Eden.

God told Noah to build an ark, a huge ark. He was to build it on dry land, far from the ocean. Noah's father, Lamech, and his grandfather, Methuselah, were both alive when God told Noah to build the ark. They likely thought that Noah's neighbors were right: Noah was crazy.

But Noah persisted. For 120 years, he and his sons worked on the ark. Noah's grandfather, Methuselah, died 20 years before the ark was completed. And Noah's father, Lamech, died five years before the ark was finished. The only family Noah had left when the Flood came was his wife, his three sons and their wives.

Noah built the ark shaped like a ship, with a bow and a rounded stern. It was constructed of gopher wood (cedar) and cypress, and it was caulked inside and out with pitch (tar). The ark was huge—about 450 feet long (the length of one and a half football fields), 75 feet wide, and 45 feet high with three floors or decks. On one side was a large door. At the top was a small (18" high) window. Once closed up, the ark was snug and seaworthy.

The ark could hold 1.4 million cubic feet (about 522 railroad cars) of contents. Scientists estimate that it would take 188 railroad cars to hold a pair of each of the 17,600 species of animals presently known to man, so the extra space was for food, water, people, and waste. (For those of you who are farmers, just imagine cleaning out the stalls of this many animals!)

The top deck was for the people and food, the middle deck was for the animals, and the lower deck was for the waste deposits from the inhabitants. A number of heavy stone anchor weights were hung off each side of the ark to help maintain ballast stability.

Once the ark was completed, God told Noah to store food on board to feed the animals and birds. He and his sons did as they were instructed. Food was plentiful in their antediluvian world. Then God sent animals to Noah from every corner of the earth. He instructed Noah to bring the animals on board in male and female pairs (seven pairs of clean animals and birds and one pair of every unclean animal).

Clean animals have parted (cleft) hooves and chew cud. Pigs, for example, have parted hooves, but do not chew cud. Therefore, only one pair of pigs was taken on board. Camels chew cud but don't have parted hooves, so camels, too, are unclean, and only one pair was accepted. But cattle, sheep, goats, and deer have cleft hooves and chew cud, so they are examples of clean animals. Two pairs of each of these animals were selected.

One day the animals and birds began arriving, and they kept coming. God sent them in the proper pair order. Noah and his sons confirmed that the proper pairs were being allowed on board. The animals were not afraid of Noah. They walked obediently on board the ark.

Birds flew into the open door, seven pairs of male and female each. Even every kind of creature that crawls on the ground came to the ark. It's likely that young mammoths and small dinosaurs were included on the ark because we know that these animals lived and were wiped out sometime after the Flood.

Once Noah and his family and all of the selected animals, birds, and crawling creatures were on board, God shut the heavy door closing them up in their protective ship while condemning the rest of the world to die. The evil people outside the ark laughed and ridiculed Noah and his family.

Noah was told that in seven days the rain would come. And come it did. Biblical researchers believe it was February 17th about 2600 BC. A pitter-patter sound was heard on the top of the ark. Then heavy drops of water began to rain down. It had never rained before, so the sound of rain was new to everyone.

The people inside and outside the ark were amazed at this new weather change. But the rain became stronger, and the earth's protective canopy opened up pouring torrents of water down on the earth. Even more water began surging up from fountains in the ground. Water gushed up out of the ground and filled every low spot on earth. The water level got deeper, and the ark began to float. Noah saw that it was watertight. Outside, millions of people became terrified as they watched the water levels rise.

At first the people, animals, and crawling creatures who didn't get trapped at lower elevations moved up to higher ground, but it didn't take long for the water to get so deep that only the tops of the mountains were visible. And still the rain came. Finally the water covered the highest peaks on earth. The rain continued and didn't let up for 40 days and 40 nights.

Outside the ark, people and animals swam around screaming, shrieking, some cursing God. Eventually the world outside the ark became silent as all living creatures on earth drowned. Only Noah, his family and the animal survivors on the ark remained. As the sounds of the drowning died away, the eight survivors realized that they were all that remained of the human race. The ark floated about in the darkness.

Eventually the rain stopped and the sun came out. But there was no land to be seen. For 150 days, water covered the entire planet. Then a wind came up and began to push the seas, evaporating water and producing large white clouds. The fountains of the deep stopped flowing and the water began to recede.

According to Jewish accounts, on July 17th, five months after the beginning of the Flood, the bottom of the ark made contact with land on the mountains of Ararat nearly 17,400 feet above sea level, as we know it today. Although the keel of the ark had touched ground, water still covered the land, so Noah and his family patiently waited.

On October 1st, Noah looked out the window of the ark and saw the tops of mountains. Forty days later (around November 11th), Noah released a raven. This bird is a scavenger and is known to feed on dead animals. The raven did not return to the ark.

Noah also released a dove, but in a few minutes it came back to the ark. Noah waited seven more days, and on the morning of November 18th, he released the dove again. That evening, the dove returned carrying an olive leaf in its beak.

Noah waited another seven days, and on November 25th, he released the dove again. This time it did not return. It had found vegetation and food.

On January 1st, when Noah was 601 years old, he lifted a covering at the top of the ark, and he and his family looked out on a new world. The face of the land around them was dry, and the ark was firmly settled on the slope of the mountain.

But Noah did not come out from the ark. He was waiting for God's signal. 57 days later, on February 27th, God opened the door to the ark and told Noah to bring everyone and every living creature out. They did, and immediately Noah built an altar and sacrificed one of every clean beast and fowl to God.

God liked Noah's action and blessed him and his family. Then God told Noah that from that time on, every living animal would be food for him, just like the green plants and herbs. God told Noah to not consume the blood of the animals—only the meat.

Then God made an agreement with Noah. He told Noah that He would never again destroy the world by flood. To seal the agreement, God produced a rainbow in the sky so each time people saw the colorful pattern, they would be reminded of God's promise.

Noah and his family settled near the ark, and Ham, Japheth, and Shem began families with their wives. Ham became the father of Canaan. (Canaan was important in the life of Joshua.)

Within a few generations, the earth was populated again. Even the animals and birds multiplied rapidly on the earth. Green plants and trees returned to cover the land, and streams of water flowed freely across the terrain. A flood that lasted just over a year had destroyed all life on earth except for those in the ark. And now life had returned. It was a new beginning.

But the earth was not the same as the earth Noah and his family remembered. The water canopy was gone. In its place were big puffy clouds and blue sky. The constant humidity was replaced by comfortable dry conditions. The barometric pressure on the surface of the earth was half as high, and the sun was bright. With the water vapor gone, more solar radiation reached the earth. This changed the ecosystem and affected the lifespan of these post-Flood people. Gone were the long 900-year-plus lifespans. After the Flood, most people lived to the "ripe old age" of around 120. Abraham lived longer and died at 175.

The Flood also caused the single continent of Pangaea to split into multiple continents. The whole crust of the earth shifted. All of geology can be explained by this rearranging of the earth's crust by the Flood. Division of the continents occurred rapidly during the 150 years following the Flood (days of Peleg). The word *"archipelago"* for "group of islands" comes from the word "Peleg."

A massive change also occurred in the weather. Instead of serene, constant conditions, now there were storms, rain, hail, and violent winds. With the protective greenhouse canopy gone, Noah and his family could clearly see the bright sun and blue sky during the day and the moon and stars at night from horizon to horizon.

Water is the dominant material on earth. It makes up two-thirds of our planet. The average height of the land is 5,000 feet above sea level. The average depth of the ocean is 12,000 feet below sea level. If all of the land were pushed into the ocean so the earth was level everywhere, water a mile deep would cover our planet.

There are those who dismissed the concept of a worldwide flood. But these skeptics are now learning that there is irrefutable evidence for such a flood. Five years ago, an ancient coastline with boats and pottery was discovered 550 feet below the surface of the Black Sea near Synope, Turkey. After the Flood, the water level did not return to what it was before the Flood.

Today geologists are finding continuous horizontal sediments containing fossils from the Antediluvian Age, confirming a widespread, catastrophic flood. The rich oil fields of the Middle East were produced by the weight of water pressing down the vegetation and mud that existed at the time of the Flood. Yes, the Flood occurred, and our world has not been the same since.

First Rainbow Appears

*I will put my rainbow in the clouds to be
a sign of my promise to the earth.*
GENESIS 9:13

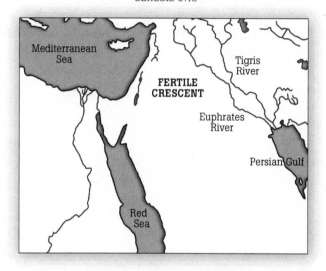

GENESIS 9:8–17; REVELATION 4:3
Location: Fertile Crescent | **Historical Time:** Early Bronze Age – ca 2600 BC
TO VIEW MAPS ONLINE:
Copy this link into your browser and press Enter/Return
www.britannica.com/EBchecked/topic/205250/Fertile-Crescent
ancienthistory.about.com/od/neareast/ss/110708ANE_10.htm

AFTER THE FLOOD, GOD MADE A PROMISE TO NOAH AND
his sons. He said that never again would all life be killed
by a global flood. He made His promise to them, their
descendants, and every living thing that was there with
them, everything that came out of the Ark.

He said, *"This is the sign of the promise I am giving you and every living being that is with you for generations to come."* Then He spoke the words that created the rainbow for all time, *"I will put my rainbow in the clouds to be a sign of my promise to the earth."* He explained that whenever He formed clouds over the earth, a rainbow would appear in the clouds.

God made this promise to all life on earth back then. We've had severe floods since then, but never to the scale that occurred 4,500 years ago.

Egypt Overrun by Frogs

Aaron held his staff over the waters of Egypt.
The frogs came up and covered the land of Egypt.
EXODUS 8:6

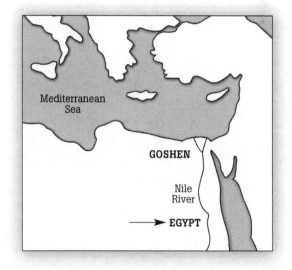

EXODUS 8:1-15
Location: Egypt | **Historical Time:** Late Bronze Age – ca 1445 BC
TO VIEW MAPS ONLINE:
Copy this link into your browser and press Enter/Return
en.wikipedia.org/wiki/File:Ancient_Egypt_map-en.svg

Second Plague

THE NILE RIVER WAS TURNED TO BLOOD IN THE FIRST plague against the pharaoh and the gods of Egypt. The pharaoh refused to let the Hebrews leave to worship outside Egypt. Moses again asked the arrogant pharaoh to let the Israelite people go into the desert to worship. He told the pharaoh that if he didn't agree, God would send a swarm of frogs to inundate everything in his nation.

The pharaoh ignored him, so Moses had Aaron hold his staff over the waters of Egypt. Frogs suddenly appeared and covered the land. They crawled out of the Nile, out from beneath furniture, from under piles of field crops, and from beneath linen clothing. They were everywhere.

This was a direct slap at Heqt, the goddess of birth. Heqt was believed to assist in childbirth, so frogs invading the pharaoh's bedroom and jumping on his own bed was an insult to this god and to the pharaoh. In Egypt the killing of a frog, even if involuntary, was punishable by death.

But the magicians of Egypt also caused frogs to appear. The pharaoh asked Moses to pray to his God to take the frogs away, and then he would let the Israelites go and offer sacrifices to their God. The pharaoh recognized that the God of Israel was responsible for this plague.

Moses asked the pharaoh when he'd like him to pray that all the frogs except those in the Nile leave them. The pharaoh told him to make it happen the next day. Moses prayed, and the next day the masses of frogs on land suddenly died leaving only those in the Nile. Frogs died in the houses, on courtyards, and in the fields. There were heaps of dead frogs everywhere. Soon the bodies began to stink.

But once the pharaoh saw that the plague had gone away, he again became stubborn and reneged on his agreement.

Gnats (Sand Fleas) Suddenly Appear

Aaron held out the staff in his hand and struck the dust on the ground. It turned into gnats that bit people and animals. All the dust on the ground everywhere turned into gnats.

EXODUS 8:17

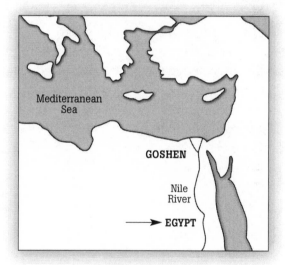

Mediterranean
Sea

GOSHEN

Nile
River

⟶ EGYPT

EXODUS 8:16-19
Location: Egypt | **Historical Time:** ca 1445 BC
TO VIEW MAPS ONLINE:
Copy this link into your browser and press Enter/Return
en.wikipedia.org/wiki/File:Ancient_Egypt_map-en.svg

Third Plague

GOD TOLD MOSES TO HAVE AARON STRIKE THE DUST ON the ground with his walking staff. He did, and suddenly millions of gnats (sand fleas or lice) appeared and began biting the people and animals. There were so many insects inside their clothing and digging under their skin that even the priests of Egypt had to shave off their hair every day and wear a single tunic to keep the lice away.

This was a direct insult to Geb, the Egyptian god of the earth. It was also an insult to the magicians in the pharaoh's court. The first plague made the water in the Nile stink. The second plague made their land stink. This plague directly affected their bodily comfort.

Pharaoh's magicians could not duplicate this condition. According to the sages, they took moist earth, pulverized it, and tried to convert it into lice. They too were getting bitten by the insects from the plague. Humbled, they told the pharaoh that this was the hand of God. Then they became silent, vanquished by the God of Israel and His supernatural power. Still the pharaoh dug in his heels and refused to give in.

Flies (Beetles)
Suddenly Infest Egypt

*Dense swarms of flies came into Pharaoh's palace
and into the houses of his officials.*
EXODUS 8:24

EXODUS 8:20–32
Location: Egypt | **Historical Time:** Late Bronze Age – ca 1445 BC
TO VIEW MAPS ONLINE:
Copy this link into your browser and press Enter/Return
en.wikipedia.org/wiki/File:Ancient_Egypt_map-en.svg

Fourth Plague

GOD TOLD MOSES TO GO OUT EARLY IN THE MORNING AND
stand before the pharaoh while he was on his way to the
Nile declaring that if he didn't listen to his demands, God
would send swarms of insects to cover everything in Egypt

except the region of Goshen up in the Nile delta (where the Israelites lived).

Bible scholars think that the insects were scarab beetles, although in some Bible translations they are called "flies." Egyptians pictured the god Ra as a scarab that pushed the sun across their sky, so this plague was an insult to Amon-Ra, their creator and king of the gods. Drawings of Amon-Ra show this god with the head of a beetle.

Other scholars think these insects were the blood-sucking gadfly or dog fly. Gadflies caused blindness. And dog flies are painful since they attach to the human body like a tick. Regardless, the insects appeared just as Moses warned. They swarmed and entered the pharaoh's palace and every Egyptian home, but none entered the homes of the Israelites in Goshen in the Delta area.

As dense swarms of insects spread all over Egypt, the pharaoh called for Moses. He told Moses that the Israelites could offer sacrifices and worship right there inside Egypt and that Moses should pray for him. He was suffering the bites, too. Moses told the pharaoh that if the Israelites sacrificed within that country, the Egyptians would consider their sacrifices insulting and want to stone them to death. He said he needed to take the people three days outside Egypt.

Moses was given permission, and he prayed to God that the swarms would leave. The swarms immediately left, but then the pharaoh reneged again and wouldn't let the Israelites go.

Locusts Blanket Egypt

They invaded all of Egypt and landed all over the country in great swarms. Never before had there been so many locusts like this, nor would there ever be that many again.

EXODUS 10:14

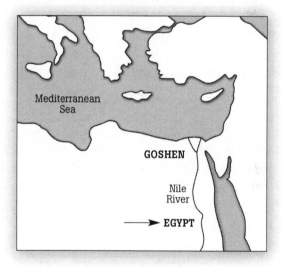

EXODUS 10:1-20
Location: Egypt | Historical Time: Late Bronze Age – ca 1445 BC
TO VIEW MAPS ONLINE:
Copy this link into your browser and press Enter/Return
en.wikipedia.org/wiki/File:Ancient_Egypt_map-en.svg

Eighth Plague

THE EGYPTIAN GOD SERAJIA WAS THE PROTECTOR OF THEIR land, and this plague showed how helpless Serajia and other gods in their deity were against the power of the God of the Hebrews. The other Egyptian gods included Nepri, Ermutet, Isis, Thermuthis, and Seth.

It was March—springtime. Moses again requested freedom and warned the pharaoh of the consequences for not complying. The pharaoh agreed to let the men go, but he refused to let the women and children go. Then he had Moses and Aaron thrown out of his palace.

Outside the palace Moses held out his staff and a wind from the east immediately began blowing. It blew all day and all night. By morning, the skies were filled with millions of locusts. They kept coming in giant swarms that blackened the sky and covered the ground, devouring any vegetation left in Egypt. One couldn't help step on them, and they produced a terrible smell. They flew in the houses and crawled into every building in Egypt. They ate all the green vegetation until no living green plant was left in the country.

The pharaoh admitted that the God of Israel was more powerful than his gods. He asked forgiveness one more time. And he asked Moses to pray to his God to take this plague away.

Moses left the palace and prayed to the Lord. Immediately the winds calmed and then reversed direction—blowing from west to east. The wind picked up the locusts and carried them out over the Red Sea. Not a single locust was left in Egypt. However, the plague did leave destroyed trees and crops, famine, and a growing unrest among the Egyptian people.

But again, once the plague was gone, the pharaoh became stubborn and refused to let the Israelite people go free.

Total Darkness for Three Days

Moses lifted his hand toward the sky, and throughout Egypt there was total darkness for three days.

EXODUS 10:22

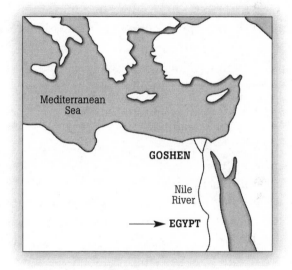

EXODUS 13–21
Location: Egypt | **Historical Time:** Late Bronze Age – ca 1445 BC
TO VIEW MAPS ONLINE:
Copy this link into your browser and press Enter/Return
en.wikipedia.org/wiki/File:Ancient_Egypt_map-en.svg

Ninth Plague

THE SUN WAS WORSHIPED IN EGYPT, AND TAKING AWAY the sun robbed the Egyptians of their supreme god, Ra (Amon-Ra). It also proved the God of the Hebrews to be the supreme power over all other gods.

This time Moses did not repeat his request to have the Israelite nation set free. Instead he raised his hand toward the sky and a darkness immediately enveloped Egypt. There was total darkness for three days. This caused extreme fear and horror among the Egyptians. Yet Goshen up north was not in darkness. It remained in the sunlight.

Some believe the darkness was caused by a dense mass of fine sand that blocked the sun from shining over Egypt. Dust storms are not new to this part of the world. In March each spring, great sandstorms occur over desert regions, blocking out sunlight and blowing away what good soil remains. They have also caused havoc in America.

In 1931 blowing dust in Kansas and Oklahoma became an increasing problem to farmers trying to retain their soil. The blowing dust became so bad that the period 1931 to 1939 became known as the "Dust Bowl" in America. The dust storm on "Black Sunday," April 14, 1935, was the epicenter of the Dust Bowl period. This storm reached from North Dakota to Texas passing into Kansas and blowing dust from the center of the country all the way to the East Coast. That day was described as "hell on earth" and caused many to abandon farms and homes in the plains states. By 1937 the Dust Bowl was passing into history, and by 1939, blowing dust was no longer a problem. But for almost eight years it produced horrible living conditions for people and animals.

In January 2012, a sandstorm off the east coast of Africa covered an area as large as the entire northeastern United States.

Even more recently, the USS Carl Vinson (CVN-70), an American nuclear aircraft carrier, was photographed in the Persian Gulf in March 2012, completely covered by thick dust blowing off Yemen and Oman. The milky sand clouds of dust engulfed the ship and allowed only electronic eyes to see through the obscure scene. Visibility was zero, and all of its aircraft were grounded and kept below on the hangar deck, making the flight deck above look like a dusty desert runway in Nevada.

The storm lasted several days before it blew past out into the Arabian Sea and eventually dissipated.

On shore, Iran, Oman, Saudi Arabia, and Yemen were all affected by the dust. Airports and schools were closed, and hundreds of people packed hospitals as lungs clogged with the fine sand, and breathing was difficult at best. People said the blowing sand stung the body and etched glass windshields.

Perhaps this is why ancient writings say the darkness that engulfed Egypt during the ninth plague could actually be felt. Sandstorms were common that spring when Moses announced it was to occur, but the timing and appearance of this sandstorm was supernatural. It started upon command, and it was directed at Egypt alone. Goshen where the Israelites lived was not affected.

This plague was against the religion and entire culture of Egypt. Besides Ra, the plague was directed against Horus, the god of light, Ptah, the god of the moon, sun, and earth, Atum, the sun god and creator at Heliopolis, Tem, the god of the sunset, and Shu, god of sunlight and air.

It was a horrible experience for everyone in Egypt. For three days people could not see one another. Trade and social life stopped. The darkness was absolute.

Then, as suddenly as it appeared, the darkness faded away and bright sun once again shined over Egypt.

The pharaoh called for Moses and told him that the people could go, but their flocks and herds must stay. Moses said they needed to take everything, and the pharaoh refused, telling Moses to get out of his sight. He said he never wanted to see the face of Moses again. Moses agreed that he would never see his face again. And he didn't.

Sun and Moon Stand Still

*The sun stopped in the middle of the sky
and delayed going down about a full day.*
JOSHUA 10:13

JOSHUA 10:12–15; ISAIAH 28:21
Location: Gibeon and the valley of Aijalon, 8 miles south of Ramalah
Historical Time: Late Bronze Age – ca 1446 BC

TO VIEW MAPS ONLINE:
Copy this link into your browser and press Enter/Return
bibleatlas.org/gibeon.htm
en.wikipedia.org/wiki/Gibeon_(ancient_city)
www.bible-history.com/geography/ancient-israel/ot/gibeon.html
bibleatlas.org/valley_of_aijalon.htm
www.bible-history.com/geography/ancient-israel/ot/aijalon.html

JOSHUA WAS A PERSONAL CONFIDANT OF MOSES. HE WAS
born in Egypt during the late Bronze Age before the Exodus, and he died in the Promised Land at age 110.

He became commander of the army of Moses and led the Israelite nation in a successful battle with the Amalekites in Rephidim shortly after exiting Egypt (Exodus 17).

Joshua was one of the 12 spies who went into Canaan to evaluate the success of a takeover. When Moses and Aaron died, Joshua became the military leader of the Hebrews and led them across the Jordan and into the lands occupied by the Canaanites. He proved himself a brilliant leader and tactician during the seven-year war to take Canaan.

Joshua attacked and destroyed Jericho and then moved on to attack Ai to the west. In this battle, Joshua's army was defeated and 36 Israelite soldiers died. He learned that one of his men, Achan, had taken clothing, 200 shekels of silver, and 50 shekels of gold from Jericho, which he had forbidden. Achan's family knew about this and supported him in his action. But he was caught, and Achan and his family and animals were stoned to death.

The Israelites were in Canaan to take possession of the land for God's glory and not to take the spoils of war. As God said in His Ten Commandments, "Thou shall not covet."

Ai was attacked again by Joshua with 35,000 men, and this time the city was overrun and destroyed.

Joshua's army swept across Canaan and destroyed many other cities and killed idolaters wherever they could be found. The cities and villages all around Jerusalem were about to be attacked by Joshua's army, including the Hivite city of Gibeon (hill city) less than six miles from Jerusalem, 17 miles west of Jericho and five miles south of Ai.

The people of Gibeon knew that they would likely be attacked next, so Gibeonite ambassadors dressed in tattered clothes and worn-out sandals, and carrying split and patched wineskins and dried-out moldy bread met Joshua and his forces coming from the east. They told him they had come from a distant country to make peace and a treaty with him. They said they had heard what the God of Joshua had done to the Amorites east of the Jordan, and were there to tell Joshua they were at his mercy.

Joshua was taken in by their ruse and agreed to keep them safe. He failed to ask God for direction regarding this new development.

Three days later, he discovered that he had been hoodwinked. Nevertheless, Joshua kept his promise to keep them safe, but he reduced the people of Gibeon to servitude. They became woodcutters and water carriers to the nation of Israel. Then Joshua's army moved on and camped at Gilgal.

The Amorite king of Jerusalem heard that Joshua had taken Ai and that Joshua had made peace with Gibeon. He became frightened and decided to form his own alliance. He joined forces with the Amorite kings of Hebron, Jarmuth, Lachish, and Eglon for mutual protection.

The Gibeonites believed that the Amorites would attack them for defecting to Joshua. And they did. The men of Gibeon sent word to Joshua near Gilgal that the Amorite kings who lived in the mountains had united and were attacking them. They urged the Israelites to come quickly to their aid.

Joshua had promised them protection, and the five kings had threatened that vow, so Joshua set out to stop them. His army marched all night from Gilgal and met the five Amorite kings in battle at Gibeon. The Amorites were surprised by the sudden arrival of Joshua and became confused and disoriented. The armies of the five kings fled from the fight, and Joshua's troops chased after them down the slopes of Beth Horon into the valley of Aijalon toward Azekah and Makkedah.

Along the way, huge hailstones rained down on the retreating forces. According to Joshua 10:11, more died from hailstones than from Israelite swords.

Joshua asked God to make the sun and moon stand still so they could finish the battle. The sun stood still in the middle of the sky, and the moon stopped. This appears to be a local phenomenon because the Bible uses the words, "Stand ... upon Gibeon" and in Joshua 10:13 records, *"The sun stopped in the middle of the sky and delayed going down about a full day."* Joshua 10:14 continues, *"Never before or after this day was there anything like it."*

This has been described as the greatest miracle in the book of Joshua. Scientists and other scholars have struggled to understand this event. Even the Jewish historian and adopted Roman Flavius Josephus wrote about the hail and sun and moon standing still in his "Antiquities of the Jews" historical document.

If the sun and moon actually stopped and lingered where they were in the sky, a lot of related issues surface as to how this physically occurred. However, God can do anything, so this is certainly possible from a supernatural power-over-nature perspective.

Others feel that the hail is the key. Hail can occur in swaths up to 15 miles wide and a hundred miles long. And hail of the size described in Joshua 10 could have occurred. It has in recent history. In 1980 hail fell on Orient, Iowa, collecting in drifts up to six feet deep. Ten years later, in 1990, hail fell on Denver, Colorado, causing $625 million in damages and injuring 47 people. Hailstones have been measured almost six inches in diameter and weighing almost two pounds each.

But the aftermath of hailstorms can be significant to our research study. It turns out that hailstorms wash the atmosphere and often leave the sky super clean. At night this can be so clear, people feel as if they can reach up and touch the stars. The moon and stars can make the sky appear like daylight. So there is scientific evidence making the "longest" day possible. If so, this makes the timing and significance of the event a miracle.

Joshua's army marched all night ensuring that their eyes were adapted to nighttime conditions. Then the severe hailstorm occurred. It didn't seem to bother Joshua's troops, but it certainly did the terrified Amorites. Then the sun coming up in a very clear atmosphere and the fact that they were moving west with the sun on their backs made the job of Joshua and his men that much easier.

The five cowardly Amorite kings abandoned their troops and hid in a cave at Makkedah. They were discovered, but refused to come out. So Joshua had large stones rolled over the mouth of the cave. He posted guards at the entrance and told the rest of the army to chase the other Amorites down. The Amorite forces were decisively defeated even though some of them succeeded in getting back to their own fortified cities. This eventful battle sealed the fate of all the cities of southern Palestine.

Then the rest of Joshua's army returned and rejoined the guard force at Makkedah. Joshua had the stones in front of the cave entrance rolled away, and some of his fighting men went inside the cave and dragged the five Amorite kings out.

Joshua told the officers who had fought with him to come forward and put their feet on the necks of these kings curled up on the ground. He told them that before this battle these kings had seemed strong and powerful, but now they were defeated and shown to be weak. Then Joshua had the five kings killed. To add insult to injury, he had their bodies hung on five poles until dark. In the Middle East, hanging a dead body is an additional insult to the person. (This is what happened to the Italian dictator Mussolini during WWII.)

The Israelites captured Makkedah and went on to victories over Libnah, Lachish, Gezer, Eglon, Hebron, and then the whole southern lands, including the Negev desert, the mountains, the foothills, and the slopes. Then they attacked and captured the northern lands of Canaan. When it was over, all of the lands east and west of the Jordan River had been taken except the lands belonging to the Philistines and Geshur. The Canaanite threat was exterminated, and the land was officially dedicated to God.

After this, God told Joshua to have the Israelites draw lots to divide the land as an inheritance for the nine tribes and the half of the tribe of Manesseh.

According to the Book of Joshua, God himself gave the Israelite people all of Israel as it exists today, plus parts of Lebanon, Syria, Jordan, and Egypt. So since 1440 BC, Israel has had a right to exist on the land they now occupy.

Shadow Moves Backwards on Sundial Staircase

Then the prophet Isaiah called upon the Lord,
and the Lord made the shadow go back the
10 steps it had gone down on the stairway of Ahaz.

2 KINGS 20:11

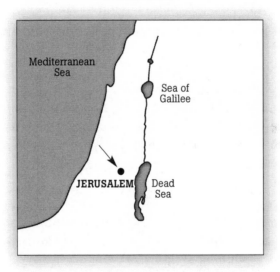

2 KINGS 20:1–11; 2 CHRONICLES 32:24–26; ISAIAH 38:1–8
Location: Jerusalem | Historical Time: ca 680 BC

TO VIEW MAPS ONLINE:
Copy this link into your browser and press Enter/Return
www.sacred-destinations.com/israel/jerusalem-map
www.sacred-destinations.com/israel/israel-map
www.ccel.org/bible/phillips/CP051GOSPELMAPS.htm
bibleatlas.org/jerusalem.htm

A DETAILED DESCRIPTION OF THIS EVENT IS FOUND IN 2 Kings 20 with a lesser description in Isaiah 38 and a mention of the "miraculous sign" in 2 Chronicles 32. Hezekiah was the king of Judah and endured the siege of Jerusalem by King Sennacherib of Assyria. Scholars believe that during Hezekiah's 14th year of reign, he contracted a deadly sickness that was aggravated by the siege. His condition was caused by an abscess and inflamed carbuncle (boil).

These were difficult days for Hezekiah. The Northern Kingdom of Israel had been captured and exiled by the Assyrians 40 years earlier, and now the Southern Kingdom of Judah was being invaded.

And to top it off, he had this festering boil. It had gotten so bad, King Hezekiah was weak and near death.

The prophet Isaiah lived in the city of Jerusalem at the time, and he went to Hezekiah. Isaiah told him to get his affairs in order because he was going to die.

This news was devastating to Hezekiah. He had no children, so he turned his face to the wall, hiding his face in grief and prayed. Isaiah 38:3 reports that he prayed, "Please, Lord, remember how I've lived faithfully and sincerely in Your presence. I've done what You consider right." Then he wept bitterly.

As soon as Isaiah told Hezekiah he would die, Isaiah turned and left the palace, but before he reached the middle court (center of the city), God told Isaiah to go back to Hezekiah and tell him that his prayer had been heard. Isaiah was told to tell Hezekiah that God was going to heal the king. God directed Isaiah to tell the king to go to the Lord's temple the day after tomorrow. Then God would give Hezekiah 15 more years to live, that he would rescue him and defend Jerusalem from the king of Assyria.

Isaiah returned and told King Hezekiah what God had commanded. Then Isaiah said, "Get a fig cake, and put it on the boil so that the king will get well." The placement of a paste of figs was a common remedy in those days to open hard boils and ulcers so infection could drain out.

Hezekiah was pleased with Isaiah's words, but still had doubt because he was so sick. He didn't think he'd be able to go to the Lord's temple the day after tomorrow or if he'd even recover at all.

Hezekiah asked Isaiah, "What is the sign that the Lord will heal me and that I'll go to the Lord's temple the day after tomorrow?"

Isaiah replied that as a sign that God will do as He said, Hezekiah could choose which way he'd like the sun to move on the steps of the sundial outside in the courtyard. Shall the shadow go forward 10 steps or come back 10 steps? (Most versions of the Bible use the word "steps" regarding the sundial. At least one commentary uses the words "degrees.") Since the sundial in the sunny courtyard was a pillar with step markers, I'll stick with "steps. The message is the same using either word.

Hezekiah replied, "It's easy for the shadow to extend 10 more steps forward. No, let it come back 10 steps."

Isaiah called on the Lord and the shadow that had gone down on the stairway built years before by King Ahaz moved back up 10 steps. The reverse movement of the sun's shadow was miraculous.

Hezekiah believed and submitted to medical treatment. A poultice of figs was pressed into a cake and then placed upon Hezekiah's boil. The king's boil healed. He recovered and went to the temple as directed. Three years later a son, Manesseh, was born to him. All went well with the kingdom, and the treasures of Judah increased greatly. Later, Hezekiah would commit a sin of indiscretion during a visit by Babylonians. Hezekiah showed them the treasures Judah had accumulated. When Isaiah heard about this, he told the king that all the treasures of Judah would be taken away by the Babylonians. He was speaking about the exile of the Southern Kingdom of Israel that would occur 100 years later.

In 693 BC, Hezekiah died and his 12-year-old son Manesseh became king. Manesseh was the worst of Judah's kings and the chief cause of God's displeasure with Judah. Manesseh restored idol worship and practiced sacred prostitution and human sacrifice.

Around 650 BC, Manesseh was forcibly removed from Jerusalem by the Babylonians, and the exile of the southern kingdom of Israel to Babylon began. The final destruction of Judah by the Babylonians occurred around 587 BC.

Summary

THIS HAS BEEN AN IN-DEPTH LOOK INTO THE BIBLE'S description of power over nature. You read about the Flood, and the plagues that led to the Exodus out of Egypt. You also read about the sun and moon standing still during battle, and how God reversed the movement of the sun's shadow on sundial steps. In the list below you'll find other incidents involving power over nature. The next chapter will describe God's power over animals.

Relevant Verses in Chapter Five

Incidents Involving Power Over Nature

CLOUD: Pillar/Cloud of Smoke and Fire
Location: In desert during exodus from Egypt
Verse: Psalm 105:39
Cloud pillar provided protective covering during the day and fire to light up the night.

DARKNESS: Instant Darkness
Location: Jerusalem
Verses: Matthew 27:45; Mark 15:33–38; Luke 23:44–49
At the moment Jesus died on the cross at Golgotha, the curtain in the temple ripped in two, the earth shook and rocks were split open. Tombs opened and dead believers came back to life.

DOVE APPEARS: Voice Speaks to Man
Location: Jordan River
Verses: Matthew 3:16; Mark 1:9; Luke 3:21–22
When Jesus was baptized in the Jordan River by John the Baptist, the heavens opened and John saw the Spirit of God coming down in a dove. A voice announced, "This is my Son, whom I love—my Son with whom I am pleased."

DROUGHT: Drought Suddenly Ends
Location: Mount Carmel
Verses: 1 Kings 18:41–46; James 5:18
Elijah prayed and a little cloud appeared in the west and became a hurricane of rain ending a long drought.

FIRE: Fire from Sky Destroys Cities
Location: Sodom and Gomorrah
Verses: Genesis 19:23; Isaiah 1:10–13, 19; Ezekiel 16:49; Jeremiah 49:18; Matthew 10:15; 2 Peter 2:6; Jude 7
Sodom and Gomorrah was destroyed by burning sulfur and fire. Lot was in Zoar.

FLOOD: Catastrophic Flood Kills All Humans except Family of Eight
Location: Northern end of Fertile Crescent, likely modern day Turkey
Verses: Genesis 6:9–8:13; Matthew 24:37–39; Hebrews

11:7; 1 Peter 3:20; 2 Peter 2:5
Canopy surrounding earth
dissolved into rain, and water
flowed out of the ground. Noah
and seven in his family survived
the flood in an ark constructed
of cypress and cedar.

HAIL: Deadly Hail Suddenly
Appears
Location: Egypt
Verses: Exodus 9:13,
Psalm 105:32, 33
Seventh Plague of deadly hail
that killed the Egyptians, not
the Israelites.

PLAGUES: Egyptian Plagues
Described
Location: Egypt
Verses: Psalm 105:26, 27
Plagues in Egypt described
by Solomon.

PLANT GROWS: Plant Instantly
Grows to Provide Shade
Location: East of Nineveh
Verses: Jonah 4
Jonah made a shelter to the
east of Nineveh and sat down
waiting to die. He was angry
that God spared Nineveh
because the people listened to
his warning and the whole city
turned from their wicked
ways. A plant instantly grew
and shaded him from the sun.
At dawn the next day, a worm
attacked the plant and it withered. The sun beat down and
hot east winds blew on Jonah.
Jonah and God had a
discussion about his right to
be angry and why he wanted

to die because the 120,000
people in Nineveh stopped
their wickedness.

RAINBOW: First Rainbow
Appears
Location: Fertile Crescent
Verses: Genesis 9:12;
Revelations 4:3
Rainbow was a sign to Noah of
God's promise to never flood
whole earth again.

SACRED STAR: The Star of
Bethlehem
Location: Jerusalem
Verse: Matthew 2:2
Wise men from east follow
star west and went to
Jerusalem to find the
birthplace of the one "who
was born to be the king of the
Jews." They learned that the
birth was prophesied to be in
Bethlehem of Judea.

SEAS CALM: Voice Causes Sea
to Calm
Location: Sea of Galilee
Verses: Matthew 8:23–26;
Mark 4:35–39; Luke 8:22–24
Jesus calms severe storm on
Sea of Galilee (Lake Gen-
nesaret) when waves were
covering the boat. He was
sleeping and the disciples
woke him up. Jesus stood up
and ordered the wind and sea
to calm. Immediately the
storm stopped and the seas
became calm.

SEAS CALM: Weather Immediately Calms When Man Tossed
into Sea

Location: Mediterranean Sea
Verses: Jonah 1:4–15
Jonah didn't want to go to Nineveh to preach to them about changing their wicked ways. He tried to sail to Tarshish to get away, but the ship was caught in a huge storm. The crew knew he was running away. They asked what they could do to cause the seas to calm. He told them that he was the reason for the storm. He told them to cast him overboard. Jonah was cast overboard during the huge storm and the winds immediately became calm and the seas smooth.

Seas Calm: Wind Stops on Command
Location: Sea of Galilee
Verses: Matthew 14:24–31; Mark 6:45–56; John 6:15–21
Jesus walked on water of Lake Gennesaret (Sea of Galilee). Then Peter walked on water out to Jesus. Wind came up, and Peter lost courage and began to sink into sea. Jesus saved Peter, and then commanded the wind to stop blowing. It did, and the boat continued across the Sea of Galilee to Bethsaida in Gennesaret. There Jesus allowed sick people to touch his clothes, making them well again.

SUN AND MOON STAND STILL:
Sun and Moon Stay in Sky

Location: Gibeon (sun stood still) and in the valley of Aijalon (moon stood still), 8 miles S of Ramalah
Verse: Joshua 10:13
Joshua chased down the fleeing Amorites.

SUN SHADOW MOVES: Sun Shadow Changes Direction of Movement
Location: Jerusalem
Verses: 2 Kings 20:8; Isaiah 38:1–8; 2 Chronicles 32:24–26
Shadow moved backward 10 steps down stairs of sundial, then back up the 10 steps.

WIND, EARTHQUAKE, AND FIRE: Sudden Wind, Earthquake, and Fire
Location: Mount Horeb
Verse: 1 Kings 19:11
Elijah felt and heard the divine manifestations of God as destroying winds, earthquake, and fire on Mount Horeb.

CHAPTER SIX

Power Over Animals

THIS SECTION COVERS BIBLE REFERENCES TO POWER over animals. I found 15 incidents that apply. In the stories to follow I'll elaborate on important examples of this power. At the end of this section, you'll find a list of references to verses covering these and other relevant incidents that were discovered during my research.

Snake Talks
to Woman

"You certainly won't die!" the serpent told the woman.
GENESIS 3:4

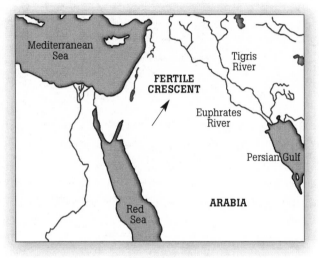

EXODUS 13-21
Location: Fertile Crescent | **Historical Time:** Post Creation
TO VIEW MAPS ONLINE:
Copy this link into your browser and press Enter/Return
www.britannica.com/EBchecked/topic/205250/Fertile-Crescent
ancienthistory.about.com/od/neareast/ss/110708ANE_10.htm

THE STORY OF THE FALL OF MANKIND INTO SIN ILLUSTRATES a number of points, but the one I focus on here is the fact that a serpent was the creature that tempted Eve to sin.

The serpent was possessed by some evil power that remained in the background. The serpent became associated with the powers of darkness. It was the actual tempter. And Genesis 3 suggests that this serpent could walk and talk.

According to Genesis 3:1, the serpent talked directly to Eve and asked, "Did God really say, 'You must never eat the fruit of any tree in the garden?'" Once Eve responded, she was hooked and a dialogue of trickery ensued. The serpent caused her to doubt God's word.

In the center of the Garden of Eden were two trees: the Tree of Life and the Tree of Knowledge of Good and Evil. The evil power in the snake convinced Eve to eat the fruit of the second tree. She gazed at the tree, saw that its fruit looked good, and rather than fleeing from the temptation, she picked some fruit and ate.

She gave some fruit to Adam, and he also ate the fruit from the Tree of Knowledge of Good and Evil.

Immediately sin filled their lives. They felt guilty for what they had done. In a flash they lost Eden and gained a conscience. This haunting sense of shame caused them to sense nakedness. They were naked before, but this was natural and they thought nothing of it. After the fall, they wanted to cover up and took fig leaves to make clothing. Jewish legend says that at the moment of the fall into sin, all the trees in the garden lost their leaves except the fig tree.

When it was evening and cool, Adam and Eve heard God walking around in the garden. They hid among the trees. God called Adam and asked where he was. Adam told God that he was afraid and was hiding because he was naked. God asked him who told him he was naked, and Adam replied, "That woman."

God asked Eve what she had done. She pointed at the serpent and said, "The snake deceived me, and I ate."

Then God cursed the snake more than all the animals. He told the serpent that it would crawl on its belly from thenceforth, that it would take dust into its mouth with its food (Isaiah 65, Micah 7). Sensory input causes snakes to look like they are licking. Licking the dust became a mark of the degradation of the serpent.

The social relationship between the serpent and mankind was also broken. The serpent represented the spirit of revolt from God, and it would continue to tempt man.

God said that from then on, hostility would exist between the snake and the woman. Man and the power of evil would be constantly at odds.

The serpent likely dropped to the ground and slithered off, because we don't find it mentioned in the rest of Genesis.

Then God judged the woman. He said she would have painful childbirth with difficult delivery. According to one Bible commentary, the process of birth is actually easier among the animals.

God also told Eve that although childbirth would be painful, she would still long for her husband, and he would rule her.

Then God told the man that from then on, rather than just keeping the gardens, he would be required to till the ground and raise food. The work would be done under adverse conditions, and there would be thorns and thistles to irritate his life. God said that man would produce food by the sweat of his brow.

In addition, there would be an inevitable certainty of death in their lives, increasing the sadness of their earthly lot. They would not be allowed to eat of the Tree of Life and gain immortality. Now they would die. And when they died, they would return to the dust of the ground because they were taken from it. The party was over, and their lives would never be the same.

Supernatural Force Sends Animals to Ark

*They and every beast after his kind, and all the cattle
after their kind, and every creeping thing that creepeth
upon earth after his kind, and every fowl after his kind,
every bird of every sort. And they went in unto Noah into
the ark, two and two of all flesh, wherein is the breath
of life. And they that went in, went in male and female
of all flesh, as God had commanded him.*

GENESIS 8:14-16

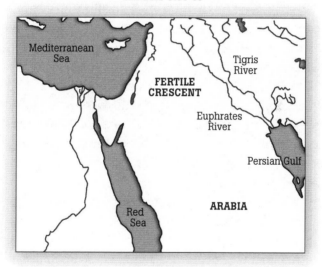

GENESIS 6:10–8:16
Location: Mesopotamia in the Fertile Crescent
Historical Time: Early Bronze Age – ca 2600 BC

TO VIEW MAPS ONLINE:
Copy this link into your browser and press Enter/Return
www.britannica.com/EBchecked/topic/205250/Fertile-Crescent
ancienthistory.about.com/od/neareast/ss/110708ANE_10.htm

MANKIND HAD THRIVED AND SPREAD ALL AROUND THE Fertile Crescent. But mankind had become corrupt and evil. And God was about to annihilate the human race—all but Noah and his immediate family. Noah remained loyal and followed God's directions. He built a huge vessel, an ark. It was to hold eight people and selected creatures from all the animals living on earth.

For 120 years he and his sons labored to build the vessel. As it was completed they probably wondered, "How on earth can we get all these animals here and then into this ark?" Noah simply trusted God to show them the way. And He did.

Seven days before the rains began, animals, birds, and bugs began arriving at the ark there on what today is the Iran/Iraq border. They came in pairs—seven pairs of clean animals (a male and a female to a pair), and one pair of unclean animals, and seven pairs of every species of bird. Recall from the last chapter my discussion about how many species of animals existed. (There are 17,600 unique species today). Why did all these creatures come? Where did they come from? How did they get there? And in what order did they enter the ark?

For those of you who have raised cattle, goats, or pigs, you know the challenges herding these animals. Just think of trying to herd a dozen cats down a street.

Just the fact that these creatures showed up and calmly walked or flew into the ark is a supernatural event in itself.

And think about the tiny creatures—the crawling creatures—some barely an inch long. These were also included in the cast of survivors. How long did it take *them* to get to the ark?

I am consistently amazed that all the animals came in the first place. This is a prime example of God's power over animals. They all listened, and they all responded.

Donkey Talks
To Man

Then the Lord made the donkey speak, and it asked Balaam,
"What have I done to make you hit me three times?"
NUMBERS 22:28

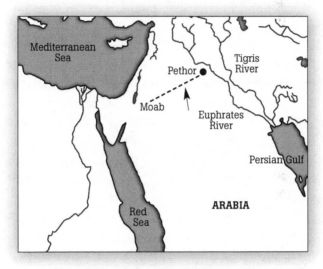

NUMBERS 22:21-34; 2 PETER 2:15-16
Location: On road from Pethor to Moab
Historical Time: Late Bronze Age – ca 1407 BC
TO VIEW MAPS ONLINE:
Copy this link into your browser and press Enter/Return
bibleatlas.org/pethor.htm
www.keyway.ca/htm2008/20080220.htm
bibleatlas.org/regional/pethor.htm

THE KEY PLAYERS IN THIS STORY ARE BALAAM, A PROPHET
living up near Pethor on the Euphrates River, Balak, king
of Moab, who reigned in the region east of the Jordan River
and across from Jericho, and a donkey, a beast of burden.

Moses had led the Israelite nation up through the Arabian Peninsula and the land of the Midianites. The Midianites inhabited northwestern Arabia east of the Gulf of Aqaba, that sliver of water that reached up from the Red Sea. These people descended from Abraham and were also known as Ishmaelites.

The Israelites came to the border of Edom but went around Edom when they learned that they were not welcome to cross. They entered the region of Moab to the east of the Dead Sea. This area is part of Jordan today. Aaron died in this region on Mount Hor. Miriam had died shortly before this time. And Moses was preparing to die and join his ancestors. Like Aaron and Miriam, he would not be allowed to enter Canaan and the Promised Land.

The Israelites set up camp on the plains of Moab east of the Jordan River and across from Jericho. It was here that Moses would die and Joshua would take command of the Israelites for their move into Canaan.

The Moabites in Moab didn't like the Israelites and were afraid of so many foreigners on their lands. (Remember that between one and two million people participated in the Exodus out of Egypt.)

Balak, king of Moab, complained to the leaders of Midian. The Midianites joined with Balak in a conspiracy against the Israelites. They decided to hire the prophet Balaam from up north to come and curse Israel.

Balaam was a prophet for hire. Prophecy was just a business to him. It was not a religion. He believed in the power of curses and incantations and had become a soothsayer. His power to bless and to curse was recognized from Pethor in Mesopotamia all the way down to the Arabian

Peninsula. Balaam was a magician, and he sold his magic skills for money.

People in the Fertile Crescent believed in demons, and they believed that certain individuals had power to control demons using magic spells and incantations. Those with these skills were often hired to discover secrets, foretell the future, and to bless or curse others. Balaam was one of these people.

Initially, Balaam was considered a great prophet, and the accuracy of his predictions had been of great interest to kings. Word of his gifts spread far and wide. However, once Balaam began to covet material things and marketed his gifts for financial reward, God departed from him. Nevertheless, Balaam retained the reputation of a prophet.

King Balak's summons and promise of financial reward proved too much for Balaam. The gold and honor clouded his judgment, and his actions set in motion events that would lead to his own destruction. God would use this semi-heathen soothsayer for His own purposes.

Balaam was at Pethor up on the Euphrates River, 400 miles north of Moab. King Balak sent messengers to Balaam with money to pay him for his service. They told him Balak's message saying, "A nation has just come here from Egypt. They've spread out all over the countryside and are setting up their camp here in front of me. Please come and curse these people for me, because they are too strong for me. Maybe then I'll be able to defeat them and force them out of the country. I know that whomever you bless is blessed and whomever you curse is cursed."

Balaam told them to spend the night and he would tell them in the morning what the Lord tells him. They did. That night God came to Balaam. Balaam told God who the visitors were and why they came. God told Balaam not to go with these princes from Moab or to curse the Israelites because they were blessed.

In the morning, Balaam told the Moabite princes to go back to Moab because the Lord had refused to let him go with them.

They returned to King Balak and told him that the prophet refused to come with them.

So Balak sent a larger group of even more highly respected princes. They told Balaam not to let anything keep him from coming to Moab. They said that King Balak would make sure he is richly rewarded and will do whatever he asks. They repeated Balak's request, "Please, come and curse these people for me."

Balaam asked them to stay the night and he would ask God what he should do. God told Balaam to go with the men, but do only what God would tell him to do. So in the morning, Balaam set off on a donkey with the Moabite princes.

God gave Balaam a warning to do only as He commanded. Balaam was seduced by the promise of the rich reward for cursing Israel, so God reinforced His will on the behavior of Balaam by using the donkey and a Messenger of the Lord.

Balaam loved what his wrongdoing earned him. But he would be convicted of his evil ways when his donkey spoke and refused to allow the prophet to continue his insanity.

The donkey was carrying Balaam along a road leading south toward Moab. Balaam had two servants with him. Suddenly a Messenger of the Lord stood in the path they were on. The Messenger was unseen to Balaam and the others, but the donkey saw it and suddenly swerved off the path and into a field.

Balaam hit the donkey with a switch and it moved back onto the road. The Messenger had disappeared, but it appeared again as the donkey and rider started through a vineyard with narrow walls along the path. The donkey moved over to pass by the Messenger and pinned Balaam's foot against the rock wall, so Balaam struck the donkey again.

The Messenger disappeared only to reappear in a place that was narrower and where there was no room to pass on the side. When the donkey saw the Messenger and no way to go around, it stopped and lay down on the path. Balaam got very angry and struck the donkey a third time.

With that, the donkey began to speak to Balaam. "What have I done to make you hit me three times?" Balaam was surprised. He told the donkey that it had made a fool of him, and if he had a sword, he would kill the animal right there.

The donkey replied, "I'm your own donkey. You've always ridden me. Have I ever done this to you before?"

"No," said Balaam.

At this, the Messenger of the Lord standing in the road with sword drawn became visible to Balaam. Balaam knelt and bowed down with his face touching the road surface.

The Messenger asked Balaam, "Why have you hit your donkey three times like this? I've come to stop you because the trip you're taking is evil. The donkey saw me and turned away from me these three times. If it had not, I would certainly have killed you but spared the donkey."

Balaam told the Messenger that he had sinned, that he didn't see the Messenger of the Lord. Then he offered to go back if the trip was evil.

The Messenger told Balaam to continue on his trip with the princes of Moab, but warned him to say only what he would be told to say.

Then the Messenger disappeared, the donkey got up, and Balaam joined the rest of the group and continued traveling down to Moab.

King Balak met Balaam when he arrived at Ir Moab, in the Arnon Valley on the border of Moab and the kingdom of the Ammonites.

Balak asked the prophet why he didn't come when he was first summoned. Balaam told the king that he was there now but could only say what God would tell him to say.

They went to Kiriath Huzoth where Balak sacrificed animals to his heathen Moabite god. The next morning, Balak took Balaam up to Bamoth Baal where they could view the Israelite camp. Below in the Israelite camp on the plain of Moab, Joshua was planning the invasion of Canaan and an attack on the city of Jericho.

Balaam told Balak to build seven altars and to sacrifice on each. He said he would go to hear from God and come back to tell Balak what he was told.

As you can read in Numbers 23 and 24, Balaam blessed the Israelites instead of cursing them. Balak had altars made in two other places, and Balaam made a total of three prophecies, all blessing the Israelite nation.

King Balak got mad, clapped his hands, and told Balaam to leave and that he would not receive the reward offered to him for his service.

Balaam explained that he told the princes and him that he could only say what God told him to say. Then Balaam made a fourth prophecy and told Balak that a star (brilliant leader) will come from Jacob (David) and a scepter (authority) will rise from Israel and crush the heads of the Moabites and destroy all the people of Sheth. He said Edom will be conquered as will Seir. He finished by telling Balak that Israel will become wealthy and rule from Jacob (David in Jerusalem).

Next Balaam prophesied that the Amalekites would be destroyed and the Kenites taken away to Assyria. Finally he said that Roman ships from Cyprus will conquer Assyria and Eber before these Phoenicians on the Roman Ships are also totally destroyed.

Then Balaam turned and left the presence of King Balak and the Moabites, returned to Pethor and disappeared from the subsequent history of Israel.

Cows Pull Wagon with Ark in God's Direction

The cows went straight up the road to Beth Shemesh.
1 SAMUEL 6:12

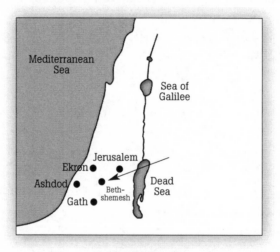

1 SAMUEL 6:1–12
Location: Ashdod, Gath, Ekron, and Beth Shemesh in southwestern Canaan
Historical Time: Iron Age – ca 1050 BC

TO VIEW MAPS ONLINE:
Copy this link into your browser and press Enter/Return
en.wikipedia.org/wiki/Ashdod
www.keyway.ca/htm2001/20010212.htm
bibleatlas.org/gath.htm
www.holylandphotos.org/browse.asp?s=1,2,6,27,122 (Gath)
www.lds.org/scriptures/bible-maps/map-10?lang=eng (shows Ashdod, Gath, and Ekron)
en.wikipedia.org/wiki/Ekron
www.keyway.ca/htm2002/20020805.htm Ekron
en.wikipedia.org/wiki/Beit_Shemesh
www.penn.museum/sites/Canaan/Collections.shtml
bibleatlas.org/beth-shemesh.htm

THE PHILISTINES HAD CAPTURED THE ARK FROM THE Israelites and had taken it to Ashdod on the shore of the Mediterranean. From that moment on, the Ark proved a curse for the Philistines. Philistine people came down with cancerous tumors, statues of heathen gods fell to the ground in the presence of the Ark, and hundreds died from being in its presence.

The Ark was taken from Ashdod 22 miles southeast to Gath (about 10 miles inland), and then 11 miles north to Ekron, but the people of Ekron refused to accept this container. By then, the Philistines had had custody of the Ark for seven months. They decided to return the Ark to the Israelites.

But how should they return it? They called together Israelite priests and people with skills in explaining omens and asked them, "Tell us how to return it to its proper place."

The priests told them to return the Ark with a guilt offering. The Philistines asked what kind of guilt offering they should give.

They were told to produce five gold statues shaped like tumors and five gold statues of mice and place them in a box next to the Ark. The gold tumors and gold mice represented the five Philistine rulers. These rulers and their people had the plague. They were told to put the Ark and the box of gold objects on a new wagon hooked to two dairy cows that had never pulled a cart. Then they should release the cows to pull the cart in any direction they wished.

The priests said if the cattle pulled the Ark toward Beth Shemesh, a city to the west of Jerusalem, then the disaster associated with the Ark was an act of God. If they pulled it somewhere else, then the tumors and plague were an accident.

The cattle began mooing and immediately started pulling the cart up the hill toward Beth Shemesh. They stopped mooing and pulling the cart forward when the Ark reached the field of Joshua of Beth Shemesh. Israelite priests lifted the Ark and box of gold objects and placed them on a large rock there in the field. These priests were not affected by touching the Ark.

The wooden cart was chopped apart to make a fire, and the cattle were sacrificed to God. When the five Philistine rulers saw this, they left and returned to Ekron. And so the Ark was returned to the Israelites on a wagon pulled by cattle in the direction dictated by God.

FOOD FOR THOUGHT:

The priests of Israel were in the lineage of Levi, son of Jacob. The lineage goes from Jacob to Levi to Amram to Aaron. Since the Exodus, the family of Aaron became priests, and served in the temple and cared for the Ark of the Covenant. Many people died by coming in contact with or being near the Ark. Yet the priestly descendants of Aaron were not affected by the power emanating from the Ark. Why not?

Birds Bring Prophet His Daily Food

*Ravens brought him bread and meat
in the morning and in the evening.*

1 KINGS 17:6

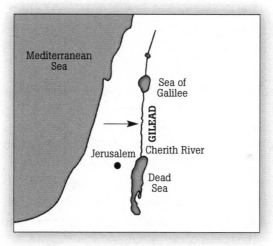

I KINGS 17:2-6
Location: Gilead and then the Cherith River east of Jordan River
Historical Time: ca 874 BC, 870-848 BC

TO VIEW MAPS ONLINE:
Copy this link into your browser and press Enter/Return
bibleatlas.org/gilead.htm
www.keyway.ca/htm2001/20010827.htm
www.bible-history.com/geography/ancient-israel/gerasa.html
www.ibiblemaps.com/m008.html (Brook Cherith)
bibleatlas.org/cherith.htm

HERE'S AN EXAMPLE WHERE THE POWER OF ANIMALS
extended to birds. Ahab, the son of Omri, became king of
Israel and ruled for 22 years in Samaria. He was an evil
man and married an evil woman, Jezebel. They wor-

shipped Baal and set up altars to worship this god. Ahab also had worship poles erected that were dedicated to the goddess Asherah. But the kingdom of Ahab was about to be punished for its sins.

Elijah was a prophet from Tishbe. He settled in Gilead and told Ahab that famine was coming. He said that for the next several years, there would be a severe drought with no dew or rain until he said so. It lasted three years.

Queen Jezebel was cruel and vindictive. She would go after anyone who crossed her. And Elijah had. As the people began to starve for lack of water and food, they prayed to their gods, but found their gods unable to stop the famine.

Elijah knew that Jezebel would try to kill him. So did God, who told Elijah to go and hide alongside the Cherith River to the east of the Jordan. The Cherith is a small tributary stream feeding into the Euphrates River from Syria. 300 years later (570 BC), another prophet, Ezekiel would have his own supernatural experience at the Cherith River.

God told Elijah that ravens would bring him food and he could drink from the stream by the Cherith. So Elijah left Gilead and did what God commanded. He lived by the Cherith River until it dried up. Ravens brought him bread and meat in the morning and in the evening. And he got his water from the stream. The birds sustained him while the famine continued.

After the Cherith became dry, Elijah went to Zarephath near Sidon where he helped a widow and her family with flour and oil to make food during the rest of the famine (1 Kings 17:8).

Man Lives
after Three Days
inside a Fish

The Lord sent a big fish to swallow Jonah.
JONAH 1:17

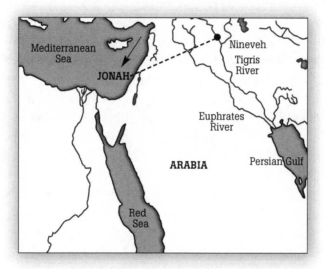

JONAH 1:1–17; MATTHEW 12:40; LUKE 11:29–32, 24–26
Location: Mediterranean Sea, Nineveh | **Historical Time:** ca 793–753 BC
TO VIEW MAPS ONLINE:
Copy this link into your browser and press Enter/Return
www.worldatlas.com/aatlas/infopage/medsea.htm

THIS IS A FASCINATING ACCOUNT ABOUT JONAH, A PROPHET
living in Gath-hepher, near Nazareth. One day God spoke
to Jonah telling him to immediately go to Nineveh and
announce that God can no longer overlook the wicked
things they had done.

Nineveh, the capital of Assyria, was a huge city on the Tigris River about 500 miles northeast of Nazareth. The people there worshipped idols — Nanshe, the fish goddess of freshwater, and Dagon, the fish god, who was half man and half fish. None of the Ninevites worshipped the God of Israel.

The Assyrians were not known to be friendly or hospitable to Israelites, especially those who tell them they are sinful and need to change their lifestyles. Jonah was fearful. He was not about to walk into the capital of Assyria announcing that God was going to punish them unless they straightened up and lived right. He felt they would certainly kill him as painfully as possible.

Jonah felt that God would spare the Ninevites if they repented and changed their ways, but Jonah didn't want them spared. The Assyrians had attacked his own people. Many had died, and Jonah did not want mercy given to the Ninevites.

So he looked for an escape from his assignment and decided to put as much distance as he could between himself and Nineveh. The farthest he could go to the west was Tarshish, on the southwest coast of Spain, outside the Mediterranean Sea past the Strait of Gibraltar and over 2,000 miles west of Palestine. Tarshish was founded by the descendants of Japheth, son of Noah.

Jonah went to Joppa on the coast of Palestine to find a ship to Tarshish. Today we know Joppa as Jaffa, a city adjacent to Tel Aviv, the largest metropolitan area in Israel. Joppa is located on the coast about 30 miles south of Caesarea. The harbor there has been in continuous use since 1400 BC.

At Joppa, Jonah found a ship about to sail for Tarshish. And he secured passage on this vessel.

Shortly after the ship put out to sea, a sudden and violent storm occurred. I've been in the Mediterranean during nasty storms. This body of water is like a giant bathtub. Storms can occur often, and the waves are huge. In nautical terms we call this "sea state." The higher the sea state number, the higher the distance between the top (crest) of the waves and the bottom (trough). The sea state and the size of the boat or ship determine how well the ride becomes. Sailors know how to navigate through high seas, but this storm was different. It came up suddenly, and it tossed their ship about as a cork in river rapids. Psalms 107:23-28 says that the sea state in this storm was such that the waves lifted the ship up to the heavens and then plunged the ship down to the depths.

The ship and the people on board were violently buffeted about, and the ship was in danger of becoming swamped, breaking apart, and sinking. The courage of the sailors melted, and they became terrified. The crew tossed cargo overboard to lighten the ship and help it float higher out of the water to avoid being swamped and sunk.

Jonah knew that he was the cause of the storm, but kept silent. He went below deck and lay down, hiding from God. Soon he was asleep. The captain of the ship found him and woke him up. He asked how Jonah could sleep in that tempest. The sailors had prayed to their gods to save them, but there was no answer. The captain asked Jonah to get up and pray to his God to save them.

While he was below deck talking to Jonah, the crew decided to cast lots to find out who was responsible for bringing this disaster on them. At the time, casting lots referred to tossing small stones or pebbles to see what the pattern showed. Think of them as dice. An analogy is picking straws to see who gets the short straw. This exercise showed them that Jonah was the reason for the storm. Jonah came topside, and the sailors asked Jonah why this storm was upon them. They asked about his country and nationality.

Jonah said, "I'm a Hebrew." According to Strong's Concordance, the term he used refers to a descendant of Eber, the great grandson of Shem, who was the oldest son of Noah. (Interestingly, the great grandson of Noah was Nimrod, founder of Nineveh.)

Jonah continued, "I worship the Lord, the God of heaven. He is the God who made the sea and the land." With these words, Jonah told them he was the reason God sent the storm.

When they asked what they should do, Jonah told them to throw him overboard. Then the sea would calm.

At first the men tried to row the ship back to shore instead, but soon gave up as the storm became a violent tempest. They acknowledged the power of God and cried out to Him asking that they not be held responsible for the death of this man, even if he was a shirking runaway. Then they threw Jonah overboard. Immediately the sea became calm.

This reminded me of an old gospel song that goes: *"Put your hand in the hand of the man who stilled that water. Put your hand in the hand of the man who calmed the sea ..."*

The men were terrified at the awesome power of God. As suddenly as it came, the storm stopped. They offered sacrifices and made solemn vows to the Lord.

Jonah was barely in the water when a huge fish swam up and swallowed him. This was fascinating for me. Could this really happen? If you take the Bible as the true word of God, then "Yes," anything is possible. But, the engineer side of me wanted to find empirical evidence of humans living inside a foreign body like a sea creature. So I began researching this subject. I wanted to know what kind of fish could take a whole man into its mouth, not tear or crush his body, and keep the man inside and undigested? Are there reports to substantiate this condition? Can the Bible itself help in my search?

Some clues are found in the prayer Jonah made from inside the fish (Jonah 2:1-8). He said that seaweed was wrapped around his head. This suggests that the fish was not carnivorous. The fish was a plant eater. The enzymes in it did not digest Jonah.

According to a commentary written by J. Vernon McGee, the *sulphur-bottom whale* (also called a *blue whale*) and the *whale shark* are large enough to swallow a man. Another large fish is the *basking shark*. Blue whales can be 100 feet long. Whale sharks have been found that are 41 feet long, and the basking shark can be 33 feet long. All have huge mouth openings.

These creatures don't have sharp teeth to tear or crush. Instead they act like seagoing vacuum cleaners sweeping along at or just under the surface scooping up seawater, plankton, fish eggs, seaweed, and occasionally small fish. The water is strained out by the gills and these giants of the sea swallow what is left.

I found several reports of humans and animals being swallowed and living inside large fish.

In 1933, a sulphur-bottom whale 100 feet long was found. The mouth was over 10 feet wide and it had a nasal sinus in its head over seven feet high and twice this in length. A man could live in this cavity. It could possibly give the whale a headache, too, causing a massive sneezing session to get the person out of the whale's head.

A pertinent article by Dr. Ransome Harvey was published in the Cleveland Plain Dealer. It described a dog lost overboard from a ship and later being found alive and barking six days later inside the head of a whale.

French scientist M. de Parville wrote about a friend, James Bartley, who was lost at sea on a whale-hunting expedition in the Falkland Islands near South America back in 1891. Two days after Bartley went missing, sailors caught a whale, and inside it they found Bartley alive, but unconscious. According to Parville, Bartley was quickly revived. His skin was wrinkled and bleached white like parchment, but he was alive and went on to enjoy a long life after the ordeal.

Others refute this report and claim it never happened. One group claims it did; and other group claims it didn't. Only God knows.

Whether these reports are accurate or not, the fact remains that sea creatures large enough to swallow a man do exist, so the reality of Jonah being swallowed alive is understandable and certainly possible.

According to the Bible (Jonah 1:17), the prophet was inside the fish for three days and three nights. Then he was spit out on a beach, alive and prepared to complete God's mission regarding the people of Nineveh.

Perhaps he was kept alive inside the sinus cavity of a great sea creature and then sneezed out on a beach on the eastern shore of the Mediterranean. If so, that must have been some sneeze!

He also could have died or gone into a form of suspended animation inside the fish. Then he was "spit" out and revived. The key is that Jonah was alive, and he had a mission to complete.

An analogy has been drawn between the story of Jonah and the resurrection of Jesus. Commentators wrote that Jonah died in that fish and was resurrected on the third day when he was released from his tomb. In Matthew 12:40 Jesus says, *"Just as Jonah was in the belly of a huge fish for three days and three nights, so the Son of Man will be in the heart of the earth for three days and three nights."*

If Jonah died in that great fish and then came to life when he was spit out on that beach, his story follows that of Jesus, who died and came back to life after three days. In both instances, neither body decayed (suffered "corruption").

Once Jonah was placed on shore, he traveled the 500 miles to Nineveh, where he told the people there to repent. Nineveh was a huge city. It took him three days just to walk through (Jonah 3:3). After a day walking into the city, Jonah told the people there, "In 40 days, Nineveh will be destroyed." I'm told this was the shortest revival sermon on record. It worked. From the king down, everyone in Nineveh repented, and the city was saved.

Man Safe after Night in Den of Lions

*So the king gave the order, and Daniel was brought
to him and thrown into the lion's den.*

DANIEL 6:16

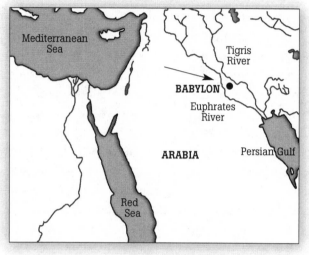

DANIEL 6:1-25
Location: Babylon | Historical Time: ca 515 BC
TO VIEW MAPS ONLINE:
Copy this link into your browser and press Enter/Return
www.keyway.ca/htm2008/20080220.htm

THIS STORY IS ABOUT A JEW WHO WAS EXILED FROM JUDAH
to Babylon near the beginning of the sixth century BC and
became an advisor to Babylonian kings and Persian kings
after them. The story reinforces the resistance of the exiles
to temptations to abandon their faith and the protection
God gave Jews who remained faithful to their roots and
belief in Him.

Daniel had done so well interpreting dreams and advising the Babylonian king Belshazzar that Daniel was made third highest ruler in the kingdom. But King Belshazzar was killed and Darius, the Mede, took over the kingdom. Darius decided to divide the operation of the country with three officials who would manage and rule over 120 satraps. The satraps would report to the three officials, so the king wouldn't be cheated.

Daniel so distinguished himself that Darius was thinking of making Daniel his second in command and putting him in charge of the whole kingdom. The other officials and satraps tried to find something wrong in Daniel such that he could be denied this highest position.

They couldn't, so they looked into his religious convictions. Once they discovered that Daniel prayed to the Hebrew God, they convinced Darius to make a law and decree that anyone who asks for anything from a god or person except Darius himself for the next 30 days would be thrown into a den of lions. Lions were used to kill political and religious criminals. The lions would be starved and then the unfortunate criminal would be fed to them.

The officials and satraps knew that anything Darius made law could not be changed. Darius signed a written decree to this effect, and the word went out to all the people in his realm. Then the evil and deceiving politicians set up Daniel to take a fall. They wanted to permanently remove him from his position and potential for promotion.

Daniel knew about the decree, but he still went to the upper room in his house and got down on his knees and prayed toward the open window in the direction of Jerusalem. He prayed like this three times each day.

During one of his prayer sessions, a group of officials and satraps came in and witnessed Daniel praying. They went directly to the king and confirmed his decree. Then they reported Daniel.

The king was extremely disappointed and tried every way he could to avoid carrying out the decree, but the officials and satraps persisted. They said, "Your Majesty, the Medes and Persians have a law that no decree or statute made by the king can be changed."

King Darius had no choice. He gave the order, and Daniel was brought to him. Then the king told his old friend "May your God, whom you always worship, save you!"

Daniel was thrown into the den of lions, and a stone was placed over the opening. Darius put his seal in wax or clay on the stone using his own ring and that of his nobles. Then he went into his palace and spent a troubled night without food or company. He tossed and turned all night anxiously waiting for dawn.

As the gray of dawn arrived, the king quickly got up and rushed down to the lion's den. As he approached, he called out, "Daniel, servant of the living God! Was God, whom you always worship, able to save you from the lions?"

With relief and delight, he heard Daniel reply, "My God sent his angel and shut the lions' mouths so that they couldn't hurt me. He did this because he considered me innocent. Your Majesty, I haven't committed any crime."

King Darius was overjoyed. He had Daniel taken out of the den. Everyone saw that Daniel was completely unharmed.

Then the king ordered that the officials and satraps who brought the charges against Daniel be brought before him. King Darius had these men, their wives, and children thrown into the same den of lions. According to Daniel

6:24, before these people fell to the bottom of the den, they were attacked by the lions and all their bones were crushed. They died the death they had intended for Daniel. God controlled the lions and taught everyone in Babylon an important lesson in power over animals.

King Darius sent out a decree that all of his subjects should tremble with terror in front of Daniel's God. Daniel was restored to power and prospered greatly during the reign of Darius and the following reign of Cyrus of Persia.

Fish Pays
Temple Tax

Take the first fish you catch.
Open its mouth, and you will find a coin.
MATTHEW 17:27

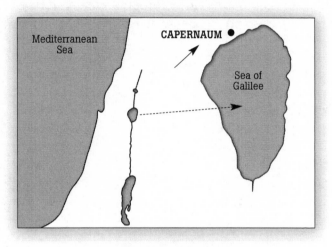

Mediterranean
Sea

CAPERNAUM ●

Sea of
Galilee

MATTHEW 17:24–27
Location: Capernaum | Historical Time: ca 33 AD
TO VIEW MAPS ONLINE:
Copy this link into your browser and press Enter/Return
bibleatlas.org/capernaum.htm
www.bible-history.com/geography/ancient-israel/capernaum.html
www.ccel.org/bible/phillips/CP051GOSPELMAPS.htm

JESUS AND HIS DISCIPLES WERE TRAVELING TOGETHER
throughout Galilee. When they came to Capernaum on the
northwest shore of the Sea of Galilee, they entered Peter's
house. Peter was still outside and was approached by officials regarding collection of the temple tax. Every male
Israelite over 20 was required to pay a half shekel tax

annually toward the maintenance of the Temple. It was usually paid between the 15th and 25th of March (about Passover time). Peter's tax payment was overdue.

They asked Peter, "Doesn't your teacher pay the temple tax?" And Peter replied, "Certainly."

Peter went inside his house. Before he could speak, Jesus asked him, "What do you think, Simon? From whom do the kings of the world collect fees or taxes? Is it from their family members, or from other people?"

"From other people," Peter said.

Jesus replied, "Then the family members are exempt. However, so that we don't create a scandal, go to the sea and throw in a hook. Take the first fish that you catch. Open its mouth and you will find a coin. Give that coin to them for you and me."

Peter went down to the shore and tossed out a line and hook. He immediately caught a fish, and inside the mouth of the fish, Peter found a silver Stater coin. This was worth four drachma or four dinari, equivalent to a shekel— enough to pay the tax for both Peter and Jesus.

As the son of the Heavenly King, Jesus was free from paying the tax. However, to avoid an impression that he was dishonoring the temple, Jesus had Peter pay the tax for both of them, using money provided by a fish.

A Donkey Will
be Found There

You will find a donkey tied there...
MATTHEW 21:2

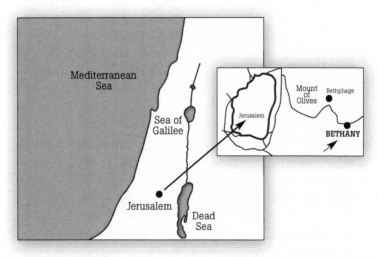

MATTHEW 21:1-9; MARK 11:1-11; LUKE 19:29-44; JOHN 12:12-19
Location: Bethphage and Jerusalem | **Historical Time:** ca 34 AD
TO VIEW MAPS ONLINE:
Copy this link into your browser and press Enter/Return
www.ccel.org/bible/phillips/CP051GOSPELMAPS.htm

IT WAS ALMOST PASSOVER AND JESUS AND HIS DISCIPLES
had left Jericho and were traveling to Jerusalem for His
arrest, trial, and crucifixion. As they neared Jerusalem, they
came to Bethphage and Bethany at the Mount of Olives.

Jesus sent two disciples ahead into the village of Bethphage. He told them they would find a donkey and a colt
tied there for Him. The colt had never had a rider on it
before. It would be used by Jesus to ride into Jerusalem.

Riding a horse would symbolize war, but riding a donkey would symbolize a peace mission.

The disciples found the colt as Jesus said they would. It was tied to the door of a house. As they were untying the young animal, some men there asked why they were taking the donkey. They told them that Jesus had need of it, and they let the disciples take the animal.

The disciples put their coats on the donkey, and Jesus sat on it for the ride into Jerusalem. Others spread their coats on the road in front of the donkey. Along the way people also cut leafy green palm branches and spread them on the road.

A crowd of people and the disciples escorted Jesus into Jerusalem shouting "Hosanna! Blessed is the one who comes in the name of the Lord! Blessed is our ancestor David's kingdom that is coming! Hosanna in the highest heaven!"

Jesus entered Jerusalem and went into the temple courtyard. It was late, so Jesus left with the 12 disciples and went over to Bethany (Mark 11:11).

They stopped for dinner at the home of Lazarus, Mary, and Martha. Martha served the dinner, and Lazarus ate with Jesus and the disciples. Mary put fragrant oil on the feet of Jesus, and then dried His feet with her hair. Both women honored Jesus in their own way.

The next day, Jesus cursed a barren fig tree on His way to Jerusalem where he threw the moneychangers and salespeople out of the temple. When the chief priests heard what Jesus had done, they vowed to kill Jesus. They wanted to kill Lazarus, too, because when he was resurrected, he caused many people to become followers of Jesus.

Every evening, Jesus would leave Jerusalem with his disciples. Jesus entered Jerusalem on a donkey. He would leave a triumphant winner of men's souls.

Fish Fill Net on Right Side of Boat

They threw the net out and were unable to pull it in because so many fish were in it.

JOHN 21:6

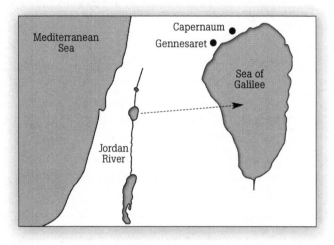

JOHN 21:6-11
Location: Sea of Galilee | **Historical Time:** ca 34 AD
TO VIEW MAPS ONLINE:
Copy this link into your browser and press Enter/Return
en.wikipedia.org/wiki/Sea_of_Galilee
emp.byui.edu/SATTERFIELDB/Galilee/default.htm
www.bible-history.com/geography/ancient-israel/sea-of-galilee.html

THIS INCIDENT COINCIDES WITH THE THIRD TIME JESUS showed Himself to His disciples after His resurrection. Six of the disciples were at the shore of the Sea of Galilee (Sea of Tiberius). It was still dark, and Simon Peter told them that he was going fishing. They all said they would accompany him out on the water.

They put their net over the side and waited. Each time they checked, the net was empty. They were about 100 yards offshore when the sun began to rise in the east.

Then they saw a man standing on the shore. They didn't recognize that He was Jesus. Jesus asked, "Friends, haven't you caught any fish?" They told Him they hadn't caught a thing.

Jesus told them, "Throw the net out on the right side of the boat, and you'll catch some." They pulled in their net from the left side and tossed it out on the right.

Immediately the net filled with fish—so many they couldn't pull it back into the boat. God had total power over sea life and had given the disciples a boatload of fish.

One of the disciples recognized Jesus on shore and exclaimed, "It's the Lord!" Peter jumped into the water and started wading to shore while the disciples stayed with the boat dragging the net behind them up to shore.

When they reached dry land, they saw a fire with a fish lying on the coals. Next to the fire was a loaf of bread.

Jesus said, "Bring some of the fish you've just caught."

Peter went down to the water, jumped into the boat and pulled the net ashore. The net contained 153 large fish, but the net held and did not tear.

Then Jesus said, "Come, have breakfast." Jesus took the bread, gave it to them, and did the same with the fish. He had just shown them God's power over fish.

Summary

THIS HAS BEEN AN IN-DEPTH LOOK INTO THE BIBLE'S description of power over animals. You learned that animals can speak if God wills this to happen. And you learned how God controlled the actions of birds, cattle, lions, and even fish. In the next chapter you'll read about God's power of prophecy.

Relevant Verses in Chapter Six

Incidents Involving Power Over Animals

ANIMALS ARRIVE AT ARK: Mass Migration before the Flood
Location: Mesopotamia near Iran/Iraq border
Verses: Genesis 6:10–7:16)
Supernatural event about selected pairs of clean and unclean animals arriving at the ark to enter and survive the Great Flood

BIRDS FEED MAN: Birds Bring Man Daily Food
Location: Cherith River east of Jordan River
Verse: 1 Kings 17:6
Ravens brought Elijah bread and meat every morning and evening by the brook at the Cherith River.

COWS ACT ON OWN: Cows Pulling Ark in Wagon Take Off in Direction Dictated by God
Location: On road between Beth Shemesh and Gath
Verses: 1 Samuel 6:1–12
The Philistines wanted to return the Ark. They contacted the Israelite priests who told them to put it on a cart pulled by two cows that have never pulled a cart before. They were told to let the cows go at will. If they go toward Beth Shemesh, then God is behind the tumors. If they go in another direction, then the tumors are an accident. The cows immediately began pulling the cart toward Beth Shemesh.

DONKEY: A Donkey Will be There
Location: Bethphage, Bethany, and Jerusalem
Verses: Matthew 21:1–9; Mark 11:1–11; Luke 19:29–44; John 12:12–19
Jesus tells two disciples to go into Bethphage where they would find a donkey and a colt tied up for Him to use.

DONKEY TALKS: Donkey Talks to Balaam
Location: on road from Pethor on the Euphrates River to Moab
Verses: Numbers 23:26; 2 Peter 15–16
Animal speaks to Balaam about treatment. King Balak of Moab wanted the prophet Balaam to curse the Israelites. Moabite princes came to Balaam and offered riches. After

refusing once, Balaam then went with them. The donkey saw the Messenger of the Lord and stops. Balaam didn't and beat the donkey. The animal spoke to Balaam.

FISH FILL NET: Huge Catch of Fish
Location: Sea of Galilee
Verses: John 21:6–11
Jesus told His disciples to put their fish net out on the right side of their boat. They did and caught 153 large fish without tearing the net.

FISH PAYS TAX: Fish Pays Temple Tax
Location: Capernaum
Verse: Matthew 17:27
At Capernaum, the collectors of the temple tax asked if Jesus paid the tax. Jesus told Peter to cast a hook out in the Sea of Galilee and take the first fish caught. In its mouth they found a one Stater coin. This was given to pay the tax.

FISH RELEASES MAN: Fish Spits Man Out on Beach
Location: Beach near road to Nineveh
Verse: Jonah 2:10
Fish took Jonah to shore and spit him out onto beach. Then God told him again to go to Nineveh.

FISH SWALLOWS MAN: Man Swallowed by Big Fish
Location: Mediterranean Sea
Verses: Jonah 1:1–17;

Matthew 12:40; Luke 11:29–32
Jonah was swallowed by a whale–sized fish. He was inside the fish for three days and three nights before being spit out on a beach.

LION AND BEAR KILLED BY BOY: Lone Boy Kills Lion and Bear
Location: Unknown
Verses: 1 Samuel 17:34–37
David killed a lion and a bear that were attacking a helpless lamb.

LIONS DON'T HARM MAN: Man Unharmed after Being Locked up all Night in a Den of Lions
Location: Babylon
Verse: Daniel 6:16
Daniel was trapped by his devotion to God and prayer against a decree that no worshiping or praying to God was to occur for 30 days. He continued his daily prayers and was placed in a den of many lions. They didn't touch him, so the next day he was released and his accusers were placed in the same den. They were immediately ripped apart and eaten by the same lions.

LIVESTOCK DIE: Livestock Suddenly Die – Fifth Plague
Location: Egypt
Verses: Exodus 9:1; Psalm 78:50
Infectious anthrax-like viral plague (murrain) or pestilence killed livestock.

SERPENT SPEAKS: Snake Talks
  Location: Fertile Crescent
  Verse: Genesis 3:1
  A snake talked to the woman and convinced her to eat the fruit of a tree that gave wisdom to recognize good and evil.

SNAKE: Staff of Moses Changes into Snake
  Location: Egypt
  Verse: Exodus 4:2
  Moses' staff turned into a snake. He grabbed it by the tail, and the snake turned back into a walking staff.

SNAKE: Walking Staff of Aaron Changes into Snake
  Location: Egypt
  Verse: Exodus 7:10
  Aaron's staff turned into a large snake. The pharaoh's magicians made their staffs change into snakes, but Aaron's snake ate the snakes of the magicians.

CHAPTER SEVEN

Power of Prophecy

PROPHETIC VISION IS ANOTHER FASCINATING SUB-
ject in my search for things supernatural and
strange recorded in the Bible. To *prophesy* is to pre-
dict or tell what will happen before an event
occurs. And a person who sees the future, foretells
events to come or who can speak for God is called
a *"prophet."* The ability to foretell events is a gift.
The Bible is filled with warnings, predictions, and
prophecies made by a number of prophets. Occasionally ordinary people are made to prophesy.

Both *Nave's Topical Bible* and *Strong's Exhaustive
Concordance of the Bible* provide long lists of prophecies that were made and fulfilled. These prophecies
deal with birth, death, salvation, and destruction. I
found 52 verses in the Bible that deal with prophecy.

In this section I'll elaborate on some important
examples of the power of prophecy. At the end of
this chapter, you'll find a list of references to verses
covering these and other relevant incidents that
were discovered during my research.

Joseph Interprets
Dreams of Prisoners

... both prisoners ... had dreams one night.
GENESIS 40:5

GENESIS 40:1-23
Location: Egypt | Historical Time: Middle Bronze Age – ca 1690 BC
TO VIEW MAPS ONLINE:
Copy this link into your browser and press Enter/Return
en.wikipedia.org/wiki/File:Ancient_Egypt_map-en.svg

JOSEPH WAS IN PRISON BECAUSE HE REFUSED TO BE
seduced by Potiphar's wife, and she lied about him. While
there he hears two other prisoners discussing dreams they
had concerning their future. One was a cupbearer who
tasted each drink before the pharaoh drank to ensure it
was not poisoned. The second man was the royal baker for
the pharaoh. Each man had made a mistake in the pres-

ence of the pharaoh and on command by the pharaoh, they were put in prison by Potiphar, captain of the guard. They were placed under Joseph's care. When they said there was no one available to tell them what their dreams meant, Joseph told them that only God can tell them the meaning. Joseph asked them to tell him about their dreams and he would ask God for the meanings. They did, and Joseph interpreted each dream. He told them that in three days the royal cupbearer would be reinstated in his job. However, the royal baker would be executed in three days. Both prophecies came true.

Joseph Interprets Dreams of the Pharaoh

Pharaoh had the same dream twice.
GENESIS 41:25

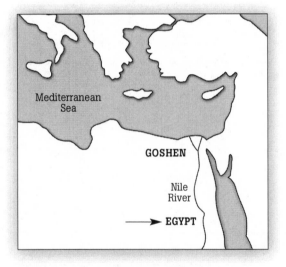

GENESIS 41:1–44
Location: Egypt | **Historical Time:** Middle Bronze Age – ca 1690 BC
TO VIEW MAPS ONLINE:
Copy this link into your browser and press Enter/Return
en.wikipedia.org/wiki/File:Ancient_Egypt_map-en.svg

THE PHARAOH HAD TWO DISTURBING DREAMS AND CALLED his magicians and wise men to come and interpret these dreams. They could not, but the royal cupbearer remembered when Joseph had interpreted his dreams and that of the royal baker. The cupbearer told the pharaoh, and the pharaoh commanded that Joseph be brought to him.

Joseph was taken out of prison, cleaned up, and brought before the pharaoh. The pharaoh demanded an explanation for his dreams. Joseph said he could not give the meanings of the dreams, but God could.

Then the pharaoh described his dreams and Joseph accurately predicted seven years of good crops with plenty of food followed by seven years of famine. This pleased the pharaoh.

Joseph was made second in command to the pharaoh, and he prepared the nation for the next 14 years. The predictions came true.

Seer Tells Saul Where to Find Missing Donkeys

The servant again answered Saul, "Look here! I have one-tenth of an ounce of silver. I'll give it to the man of God. Then he'll tell us where to find the donkeys."

1 SAMUEL 9:8

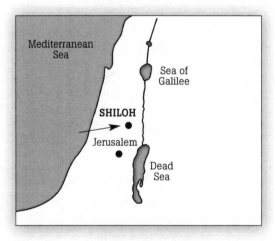

1 SAMUEL 9:3–21; 10:2
Location: Shiloh | **Historical Time:** Iron Age – ca 1020 BC
TO VIEW MAPS ONLINE:
Copy this link into your browser and press Enter/Return
en.wikipedia.org/wiki/Shiloh_(biblical_city)
www.newworldencyclopedia.org/entry/File:Samaria-new.JPG

THIS INCIDENT OCCURRED WHEN ISRAEL CLAMORED FOR a king. For years after they had settled in the Promised Land, judges guided and counseled the various tribes, keeping order as they believed God intended. All the people except the Israelites in the Middle East were ruled by kings, and the Israelites decided they should have the same structure. They wanted a king to rule over them.

Focus in on the land of Benjamin adjacent and to the north of Jerusalem. Saul's father, Kish, of the tribe of Benjamin, had two donkeys that wandered away. He asked his 30-year-old son, Saul, to find them. Saul was the classic image of a perfect male specimen. He was tall, dark, and handsome—the kind of man with features that attracted women. And Saul was someone destined for greatness. He would be king.

Saul and a servant set out to locate the animals. They searched through the mountains of Ephraim and the regions of Shalisha (north of Lydda), Shaalim (in the highlands of Ephraim), Benjamin (area south of Ephraim), and Zuph (near Gibeon), but they didn't find the father's donkeys.

Saul was ready to quit searching and told his servant, "Let's go back or my father will stop worrying about the donkeys and worry about us instead."

Saul's servant knew that Samuel was a seer and suggested they go to him for advice. Samuel knew they were coming and was expecting them. Before Saul arrived, God had told Samuel that he was to anoint Saul king of Israel.

The next day, Saul and the servant arrived, and they were told that Samuel was on his way to the worship site in the city. The people there would not eat until Samuel arrived and blessed their sacrifice.

Saul and his servant met Samuel coming toward them on his way to the city. As soon as Samuel saw the tall Saul, the Lord told Samuel, "There's the man I told you about. This man will govern my people."

Saul asked Samuel where the seer's house was located. Samuel replied, "I'm the seer." Samuel told Saul to go with him to the worship site. He said that Saul would eat with him that day and that he would let Saul go in the morning. Before he could ask, Samuel told Saul not to worry about the donkeys that were lost because they had been found.

Samuel told Saul that he and his father's family would have all that is desirable in Israel. Saul replied that he was a man from the tribe of Benjamin, the smallest tribe of Israel, and his family was insignificant among all the families in the tribe. He could not understand why Samuel was saying such things to him.

Then Samuel had Saul and his servant sit with him in the banquet hall at the head of 30 guests. Saul was given the choice piece of meat, and he ate with Samuel.

That night Saul slept on the roof of Samuel's house. The next morning Samuel told the servant to go outside. He wanted to talk with Saul. Then Samuel anointed Saul's head with olive oil and declared him to be ruler of Israel.

Samuel told Saul that after he left, he would meet two men at Zelzah on the border of the territories of Ephraim and Benjamin. They would tell him the donkeys were found and that his father worried about him. At the oak tree in Tabor, Saul would meet three men going to Bethel. One of them would give him two loaves of bread. Next he would pass a Philistine military post and meet a group of prophets at the city. They will be prophesying, and they will be led by men playing a harp, a tambourine, a flute, and a lyre. Samuel said that at that moment, the Lord's Spirit will come over him and Saul too will prophesy. Then Samuel told Saul to go ahead of him to Gilgal and wait seven days for Samuel to arrive and tell him what to do.

When Saul turned to leave Samuel, his whole attitude changed, and the things that Samuel predicted all occurred. His servant joined Saul and they continued on together. They met Saul's uncle, who asked them, "Where did you go?"

Saul told his uncle that they had gone to look for the donkeys, and when they couldn't find them, they went to Samuel. The uncle asked them what Samuel had said. Saul said, "He assured us the donkeys had been found." But, Saul didn't say a word about Samuel telling him he would become king.

Samuel called the Israelite people together at Mizpah, a city in the tribal area of Benjamin and a few miles from Jerusalem. He said, "This is what the Lord God of Israel says: 'I brought Israel out of Egypt and rescued you from the power of the Egyptians and all the kings who were oppressing you. But now you have rejected your God who saves you from all your troubles and distresses.' You said, 'No! Place a king over us.' Now stand in front of the Lord by your tribes and family groups.'" Then the prophet Samuel had all the tribes of Israel come forward one at a time.

When he got to the tribe of Benjamin, Samuel had them separate and come forward according to family. The family of Matri was chosen, and then Kish and his family were chosen. Then Saul in the family of Kish was called out. But Saul was not to be seen.

They prayed and asked the Lord. He told them Saul was hiding in the baggage belonging to Kish. The people got him and brought Saul out to stand with his family. Saul stood a head taller than all the others. Samuel said, "Do you see whom the Lord has chosen? There is no one like him among all the people."

When they saw Saul, the people shouted, "Long live the king!"

Messengers and King Saul Suddenly Prophesy

God's Spirit came over Saul's messengers
so they also prophesied.
1 SAMUEL 19:20

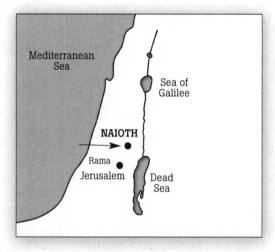

1 SAMUEL 19:20-24
Location: Naioth and Ramah | **Historical Time:** Iron Age – ca 1010 BC
TO VIEW MAPS ONLINE:
Copy this link into your browser and press Enter/Return
bibleatlas.org/naioth.htm
www.keyway.ca/htm2011/20110124.htm

SAUL WAS KING AND FOUGHT THE PHILISTINES ALL DUR-
ing his reign. He was victorious until he failed to follow God's
instructions to destroy all the people and belongings of the
Amalekites. He even allowed the Amalekite king to live.

Samuel confronted Saul on this and told him that he no longer deserved to be king. Saul was repentant, but Samuel said God had decided that Saul was no longer going to be king. They were at Gilgal.

Saul pulled at Samuel's robe, and it tore. Samuel said to Saul, "The Lord has torn the kingdom of Israel from you today." Then Samuel said, "Bring me King Agag of Amalek." With the trembling Agag before Samuel, the prophet said, "As your sword made women childless, so your mother will be made childless among women." And Samuel killed the king. Then Samuel went to Ramah while Saul returned to his home at Gibeah.

At Ramah, God told Samuel to fill a flask with olive oil and go to Bethlehem to anoint one of Jesse's sons king. David was selected by God to replace Saul as king of Israel. From this time on, Saul despised David and tried to kill the heir apparent. But Jonathan, Saul's son, loved David and protected him.

David defeated Goliath and the Amalekites. He made a name for himself in the nation of Israel. When Saul went looking for David, his wife, Mi'chal, helped David escape. David went to Samuel at Ramah. After telling Samuel what Saul had done, Samuel and David went to live out in the pastures around Ramah.

Saul sent messengers to get David, but they saw a group of prophets prophesying with Samuel and they began to prophesy, too. They went back to Saul and reported what had happened. Saul sent another group of messengers, but they also prophesied. A third group was sent, and the same thing happened. So Saul went to Ramah himself. In the city, Saul asked where he could find Samuel and David.

The people in Ramah told Saul that Samuel and David were in the pastures outside town. As Saul approached the pastures, he was suddenly taken over by God's Spirit, and he, too, began to prophesy.

While David fled to find his friend Jonathan, Saul lay on the ground before Samuel and prophesied all day and night.

Seer Tells King David His Son Would Die

...since you have shown total contempt for the Lord by this affair, the son that is born to you must die.

2 SAMUEL 12:14

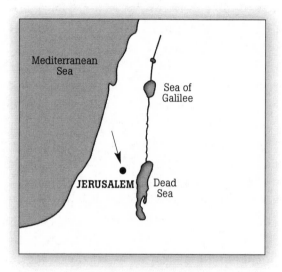

2 SAMUEL 11:2–12:24
Location: Jerusalem | Historical Time: Iron Age – ca 1000 BC
TO VIEW MAPS ONLINE:
Copy this link into your browser and press Enter/Return
www.sacred-destinations.com/israel/jerusalem-map
www.sacred-destinations.com/israel/israel-map
www.ccel.org/bible/phillips/CP051GOSPELMAPS.htm
bibleatlas.org/jerusalem.htm

KING DAVID LUSTED AFTER ANOTHER MAN'S WIFE AND HAD Bathsheba, brought to him. He slept with her, and she became pregnant. When he learned her condition, David tried to get Bathsheba's husband, Uriah the Hittite, to go home and sleep with his wife, but Uriah refused. He told David that he was a military man and at war. Home life must wait until the war was won.

David sent a letter to Joab, the general of the forces, telling him to put Uriah on the front lines and then abandon him so he'd be killed in battle against the Ammonites. Uriah was killed as David planned.

After a suitable period of mourning, David took the widow Bathsheba into his household and made her his wife. She took her pregnancy to term in the palace with David. Bathsheba gave birth to a son, but God considered David's action evil.

The prophet, Nathan, went to David. Nathan told David a story about a rich man taking a poor man's lamb and preparing it for another. David became incensed at the story and said the man who did this must pay back four times the price of that poor man's lamb.

Nathan told King David that he was the man. Then he told David what he had done regarding Bathsheba and her husband, Uriah. David felt remorse and admitted sinning against the Lord. Nathan told David that God had forgiven him the sin, but the son born to them must die. David begged for the life of the child, but immediately the child became sick. After seven days of suffering, the child died.

Man of God Predicts Destruction of Altar

You will see the altar torn apart.
The ashes on it will be poured on the ground.
1 KINGS 13:3

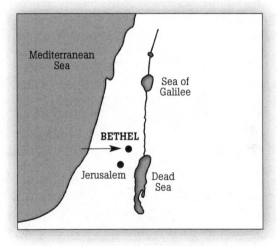

1 KINGS 13:1–3; 2 KINGS 23:15
Location: Bethel | **Historical Time:** ca 931 BC
TO VIEW MAPS ONLINE:
Copy this link into your browser and press Enter/Return
blog.eteacherbiblical.com/wp-content/uploads/2008/01/judah-and-israel.gif

SOLOMON DIED, AND HIS SON REHOBOAM BECAME KING.
Jeroboam, one of Solomon's officers, had rebelled against
Solomon. The prophet Ahijah from Shiloh told Jeroboam
that he would become king of 10 of the tribes of Israel.
Solomon's son Rehoboam would be left with the tribe of

Judah because Solomon had abandoned God and had worshiped Astarte, goddess of the Sidonians, Chemosh, the god of Moab, and Milcom, the god of Ammon.

Before he died, Solomon tried to kill Jeroboam, but Jeroboam had fled to Egypt and stayed there until Solomon died. When Jeroboam heard that Solomon was gone and Rehoboam was now king, he returned from Egypt. Rehoboam invited Jeroboam back, and Jeroboam said if Rehoboam would lighten the heavy load Solomon had placed on them, then Jeroboam and his people would serve Rehoboam.

Rehoboam asked for advice from the older leaders who had served Solomon. They advised gentle treatment for the people of Jeroboam. Then Rehoboam asked the younger crowd with whom he had grown up. They advised harsh treatment of Jeroboam and his people.

Rehoboam ignored the advice of his seniors and answered Jeroboam harshly. He sent Adoram, his officer in charge of forced labor, to the northern tribes of Israel. The people stoned Adoram, and Rehoboam fled to Jerusalem. The nation of Israel split into the northern kingdom of 10 tribes and the southern kingdom of Judah and Benjamin. King Rehoboam ruled the Israelites who lived in the city of Judah. Jeroboam was made king over all Israel except the tribe of Judah (and Benjamin), and ruled the 10 tribes of the northern kingdom.

King Rehoboam gathered all the people of Judah and the tribe of Benjamin to fight against the people of Israel. Shemaiah, a man of God in Jerusalem, told Rehoboam not to wage war against Jeroboam and their relatives from Israel. King Rehoboam listened and backed off on the battle plan.

King Jeroboam rebuilt Shechem in the hills of Ephraim and settled there. But he distrusted King Rehoboam and began to worry that if the people of the 10 tribes under him went to Jerusalem to worship and sacrifice in the temple, they would begin to follow Rehoboam again and abandon his rule. So Jeroboam made two golden calves and placed one in Bethel and the other in Dan. Jeroboam told the people to worship these calves instead of going to Jerusalem to worship. He also appointed men who were not descended from Levi to be priests at these worship sites. He followed the same festival schedule as in Judah, but he had the people pray to the golden calves.

A man of God from Judah came to Bethel. Jeroboam was standing at the altar in the temple ready to offer a sacrifice. The man of God condemned the altar and said that a son will be born in David's lineage. He will be called Josiah and he will sacrifice the priests from these illegal worship sites on that same altar right there in Bethel. He then said, "This is the sign that the Lord will give you: You will see the altar torn apart. The ashes on it will be poured on the ground." Suddenly the altar ripped apart and its ashes poured out on the ground.

As described in 2 Kings 22, years later Josiah became king. He was only eight. When he was 26, the chief priest found the book of Moses' Teachings in the temple. King Josiah read this book and learned how God intended the Israelites to live. Josiah repented and immediately cleared Israel of all the idols and returned the land to proper worship of the Lord. As part of this cleansing, he tore down the altar at Bethel (rebuilt?) and burned the worship site. The ashes were poured on the ground just at prophesied 300 years earlier by the man of God during King Jeroboam's rule (2 Kings 23:15).

Prophet Predicts Isolation of King

You will be forced away from people and live with the wild animals.

DANIEL 4:25

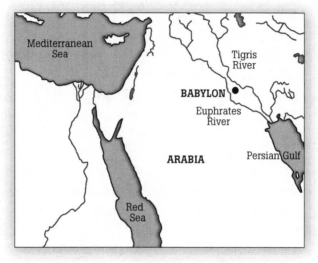

DANIEL 4:1–27
Location: Babylon | Historical Time: ca 605 BC
TO VIEW MAPS ONLINE:
Copy this link into your browser and press Enter/Return
www.keyway.ca/htm2008/20080220.htm

NEBUCHADNEZZAR WAS A CHALDEAN WHO RULED BABY-lon in the 6th century BC (605-562 BC). (In reality, he should be called Nebuchadnezzar II, since the first Neb-uchadnezzar ruled Mesopotamia 600 years earlier [1126-1103 BC], but I'll refrain from using the "II" label since we know this incident with Daniel occurred in the

6th century BC.) The Chaldean period is also called the Babylonian period. This was when Babylon defeated and replaced Assyrian rule in the world. The reach of Babylonian power was great and included what is now called Iraq, Iran, Syria, Israel, Egypt, Turkey, Saudi Arabia, Jordan, Kuwait, Lebanon, and even Cyprus.

For 40 years, Nebuchadnezzar ruled Babylon during the Iron Age when technology was moving from bronze to iron. He was responsible for the famed Hanging Gardens of Babylon.

Like the Egyptians, the Chaldeans were known for their abilities with astrology, fortune-telling, magic, sorcery, and the occult. King Nebuchadnezzar was always seeking the most knowledgeable and capable people in these disciplines to incorporate them into his kingdom. Thus it was that the highly intelligent and gifted Daniel was taken by the Babylonians from Judah to Babylon.

According to Bible historians, King Nebuchadnezzar besieged and took Jerusalem from King Jehoikim of Judah around 605 BC. The Babylonians took the temple treasures to Babylon. Nebuchadnezzar also ordered that some of the brightest and able young men among the royal family and nobility of Judah be brought to Babylon to be trained for the king's service.

Ashpenaz, the Babylonian chief of the court of Nebuchadnezzar, chose promising Israelites for this service. These included Daniel, Azariah, Hananiah, and Mishael (Daniel 1:6). All four were given new names. Thus Daniel was called Belteshazzar and the other three became Shadrach, Meshach, and Abednego (the people in the fiery furnace incident).

These four men were to be trained for three years in the language, literature, and customs of the Chaldeans in Babylon followed by acceptance into service to King Nebuchadnezzar. Daniel had the ability to understand visions and interpret dreams. Daniel would prophesy for 70 years and all through his captivity and life in Babylon.

Nebuchadnezzar was arrogant, proving the adage, "Absolute power corrupts absolutely." And he promoted idol worship throughout his kingdom.

In the second year of his reign, Nebuchadnezzar had a series of repeating dreams after boasting about his great achievements. He dreamed that he saw a tall oak tree in the middle of the earth. The tree reached into the sky and could be seen from everywhere. It had beautiful leaves and produced fruit for everyone. Wild animals found shade under it, and birds lived in its branches.

In his dream the king suddenly saw a holy being, a watcher, come down from heaven. This guardian shouted, "Cut down the oak tree! Cut off its branches! Strip off its leaves! Scatter its fruit! Make the animals under it run away, and make the birds fly from its branches."

Then the holy being announced that the stump of the tree and its roots would be left in the ground, but the tree would be secured in the grass with an iron and bronze chain. It would get wet with dew from the sky, and it would have plants on the ground with the animals. The watcher said the human mind of the tree would be changed into that of an animal. It would remain like this for seven time periods.

The watcher shouted that the guardians, the holy ones, announced this so every living creature would know that the Most High has ultimate power over human kingdoms and can place anyone in charge of them.

Not understanding these dreams, the king gathered magicians, astrologers, and sorcerers, and Chaldeans commanding them to interpret his dreams. They could not.

Daniel came to Nebuchadnezzar and listened to him describe his dreams. Daniel was stunned and told the king not to let the meaning of the dream frighten him. Then Daniel said that the oak tree was the king himself. He said that the king would be forced away from people and live outside with the animals, eating grass and getting wet from dew. Daniel told him that he would live like this for seven time periods until the king realized that the Most High (God) in heaven rules even over him.

Then Daniel advised the king to stop sinning, pity the poor, and live according to the Most High.

The king took all this in, but he did not change his way of living. Twelve months later, he was walking around the royal palace, admiring how great he was and what he had done in Babylon, when suddenly a voice came to him from heaven. The voice told him that his kingdom had just been taken away from him. He would now be forced out of power and be made to live with the wild animals for seven time periods. Immediately this prediction came true. Nebuchadnezzar lost his sanity and was forced out of the palace. He ate grass like the cattle and was wet by morning dew.

In Daniel 4:33, you can read, "... his hair grew as long as eagle feathers and his nails grew as long as birds' claws." An ancient painting shows Nebuchadnezzar crouched and walking on all fours like a wolf. His hair was so long it dragged on the ground.

Some have speculated that the king's malady was caused by a rare psychiatric delusion called *lycanthropy* in which the king thought and behaved like an animal in his altered state of mind. Some even claim he had a form of dementia caused by syphilis. The Bible simply states that Nebuchadnezzar lost his sanity and lived like a wild animal for seven years. At the end of this time, he looked up and thanked the Most High, recognizing His power above all others. The mind of Nebuchadnezzar returned to him, and his honor and position of glory were restored. He never forgot his experience and was a humble ruler for the next 22 years. Nebuchadnezzar died in 562 BC, 24 years after Jerusalem and the temple were destroyed.

Son of Lying Mother Dies as Predicted

When she walked across the threshold of her home, the boy died.

1 KINGS 14:17

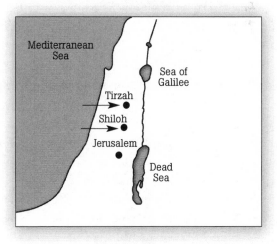

I KINGS 14:1-18
Location: Shiloh and Tirzah | **Historical Time:** ca 930 BC
TO VIEW MAPS ONLINE:
Copy this link into your browser and press Enter/Return
en.wikipedia.org/wiki/Shiloh_(biblical_city)
www.newworldencyclopedia.org/entry/File:Samaria-new.JPG
en.wikipedia.org/wiki/Tirzah_(ancient_city)
www.bible-history.com/geography/ancient-israel/ot/tirzah.html

JEROBOAM WAS AN EVIL KING. HE RULED THE NORTHERN kingdom of Israel. He appointed priests and had them work at illegal worship sites. He had worship poles set up and dedicated to the goddess Asherah.

Ahijah was an old prophet in Shiloh and losing his sight. Nevertheless, he still had the power and vision of a prophet. And Ahijah was outspoken in his condemnation of the actions and activities of Jeroboam and his administration.

One day Jeroboam's son Abijah got sick. Jeroboam worried what would happen to the boy, but he didn't want to visit the prophet Ahijah, himself. So he asked his wife to disguise herself so the prophet would not recognize her as the wife of the king. Jeroboam told her to take 10 loaves of bread, some raisins, and a jar of honey to Ahijah in Shiloh and then ask the prophet about the boy.

God told Ahijah what was about to happen and told him what to say to Jeroboam's wife when she arrived.

As the woman was brought into Ahijah's room, he said, "Come in. You're Jeroboam's wife. Why are you pretending to be someone else?" She was flabbergasted. He knew she was coming before she even got there.

Then Ahijah said, "Tell Jeroboam, 'This is what the Lord God of Israel says: I picked you out of the people and made you a leader over my people Israel. I tore the kingdom away from David's heirs and gave it to you. But you have not been like my servant David. He obeyed my commands and faithfully followed me by doing only what I considered right. You have done more evil things than everyone before you. You made other gods and metal idols for yourself. You made me furious and turned your back to me.'"

Ahijah continued describing what God had said, "'That is why I bring disaster on Jeroboam's house. I will destroy every male in his house. I will burn down Jeroboam's house, and it will burn like manure until it is gone. If anyone from Jeroboam's house dies in the city, dogs will eat him. If anyone dies in the country, birds will eat him.' The Lord has said this!"

Then Ahijah told the wife of Jeroboam to go home. He said that the moment she sets foot in the palace, her child would die. He would be the only one of Jeroboam's family to be properly buried. Ahijah also said that God would appoint a new king over Israel and destroy the house of Jeroboam.

He said that God would uproot Israel from the land and scatter them beyond the Euphrates River because they worshiped idols and put up poles dedicated to the goddess Asherah.

Jeroboam's wife was shaken. She got up and returned to Tirzah. The moment she stepped across the threshold of her home, the child, Abijah, died just as the prophet Ahijah predicted.

Drought Begins as Predicted by Elijah

... there will be no dew or rain during the next few years unless I say so.

1 KINGS 17:1

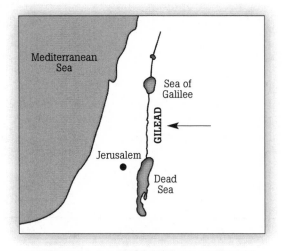

1 KINGS 17:1-7; 1 KINGS 18:41-46; JAMES 5:17
Location: Gilead | Historical Time: ca 875 BC
TO VIEW MAPS ONLINE:
Copy this link into your browser and press Enter/Return
bibleatlas.org/gilead.htm
www.keyway.ca/htm2001/20010827.htm
www.bible-history.com/geography/ancient-israel/gerasa.html

ELIJAH WAS A NO-NONSENSE PROPHET WHO GOT IN THE face of ruling monarchs like Ahab, king of Israel. During the 22-year reign of Ahab, Elijah consistently challenged the king in Samaria about his sins. Ahab's wife, the wicked Jezebel resented being criticized for their sins and executed all the prophets she could find. Obadiah, the man in charge of the palace of Ahab, hid 100 prophets in caves and fed them during Jezebel's search-and-destroy mission in Samaria. Elijah remained untouchable and always evaded the search teams. Obadiah believed that each time Ahab's troops got close, Elijah would be teleported by the Lord's Spirit to an unknown place (1 Kings 18:12).

Then Elijah came to Ahab and told him that a severe drought was coming. He said no dew or rain would appear in Samaria for the next few years unless he (Elijah) said so.

As predicted, moisture in the atmosphere and ground dried out, crops died, and people began to starve. The drought lasted over three years. The details of this event are in the previous chapter (Power over Animals). Ravens fed Elijah twice each day.

The end of this severe drought is described in 1 Kings 18:41-46. Elijah was up on Mount Carmel. He told his servant to check the sky over the sea. After checking eight times, the servant saw a little cloud rising out of the sea in the distance. It looked like a man's hand, but it grew larger until the heavens became black with clouds. Then wind and rain drenched the ground. The drought was over.

Elijah Predicts Death of King Ahab

At the place where the dogs licked up Naboth's blood, the dogs will lick up your blood.

1 KINGS 21:19

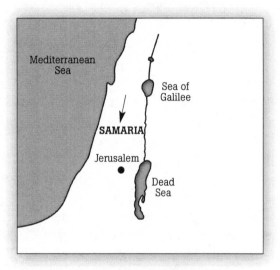

1 KINGS 21:19; 22:38
Location: Samaria | **Historical Time:**ca 870 BC
TO VIEW MAPS ONLINE:
Copy this link into your browser and press Enter/Return
en.wikipedia.org/wiki/Samaria
www.gods-word-first.org/bible-maps/samaria-map.html

IN THIS INCIDENT, AHAB, KING OF ISRAEL, FOUGHT AND defeated King Benhadad I of Aram. Instead of killing him as God commanded, Ahab made a treaty with Benhadad (Benhadad I). *(NOTE: Benhadad I ruled Aram from 885-865 BC; Benhadad II ruled from 880-842 BC, and Benhadad III ruled from 796-792 BC)*

As described in 1 Kings 20:34-43, a prophet told King Ahab that he would lose his life in place of King Benhadad. Upset and resentful, the king of Israel returned to Samaria. Naboth from Jezreel had a vineyard next to Ahab's palace. Ahab wanted the vineyard for a vegetable garden, but Naboth refused saying that he was forbidden by the Lord to give Ahab what he inherited from his ancestors. So Jezebel, the wife of Ahab, conspired against Naboth and caused him to be stoned to death. Then she told Ahab to confiscate Naboth's vineyard.

Elijah was forewarned and met Ahab on his way to the vineyard. Elijah told Ahab, "This is what the Lord says, 'At the place where the dogs licked up Naboth's blood, the dogs will lick up your blood.'" Elijah also prophesied that Jezebel would die and be eaten by dogs inside the walls of Jezreel. Both prophecies came true (1 Kings 22:1-39) (2 Kings 9:30-37).

Isaiah Predicts the Safety of Jerusalem

He will never come into this city.
2 KINGS 19:32

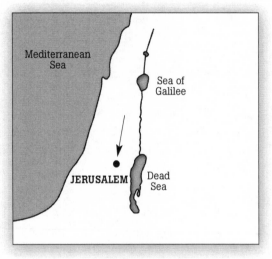

2 KINGS 19:20-35
Location: Jerusalem | **Historical Time:** ca 729 BC
TO VIEW MAPS ONLINE:
Copy this link into your browser and press Enter/Return
www.sacred-destinations.com/israel/jerusalem-map
www.sacred-destinations.com/israel/israel-map
www.ccel.org/bible/phillips/CP051GOSPELMAPS.htm
bibleatlas.org/jerusalem.htm

IN HIS 14TH YEAR AS KING OF JUDAH, HEZEKIAH AND THE
Jews were under siege in Jerusalem by King Sennacherib
of Assyria. As described in detail in Chapter 3 (Power over
Life and Death), King Hezekiah sent Eliakim, Shebna, and
the leaders of the priests to the prophet Isaiah, who was
also there inside the city.

Isaiah told the visitors to go back and tell the king not to worry. He said Jerusalem was safe. He said that God would put a spirit in Sennacherib that would cause him to believe a rumor and return to his own country where he would be assassinated.

Sennacherib was camped with his main forces north of Jerusalem when he heard a report that the Egyptians had mounted an offensive against him and were moving up to meet his forces in battle. In fear he left the area and returned to Nineveh in Assyria where he was assassinated in his pagan temple by his own sons.

The same night Isaiah prophesied about the Assyrian threat, the large contingent of 185,000 troops besieging the city died mysteriously, and Jerusalem and her inhabitants remained safe just as Isaiah had predicted.

Prophecy of Exile and Loss of Judah's Treasures

The days are going to come when everything in your palace, everything your ancestors have stored up to this day, will be taken away to Babylon.

2 KINGS 20:17

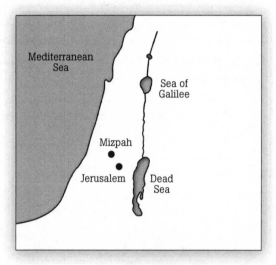

2 KINGS 20:12-20; 25:1-25
Location: Jerusalem and Mizpah | **Historical Time:** ca 720 BC

TO VIEW MAPS ONLINE:
Copy this link into your browser and press Enter/Return
www.sacred-destinations.com/israel/jerusalem-map
www.sacred-destinations.com/israel/israel-map
www.ccel.org/bible/phillips/CP051GOSPELMAPS.htm
bibleatlas.org/jerusalem.htm
www.bible-history.com/geography/ancient-israel/ot/mizpah.html
bibleatlas.org/mizpah_3.htm
www.biblestudy.org/maps/historic-israel-map.html

THE ASSYRIAN THREAT WAS GONE, JERUSALEM WAS SAFE, and Hezekiah remained in power. But he had gotten deathly ill until he prayed for life and was healed. Once back to health, the king became so proud of his accomplishments, he made the greatest error of his life. He boasted. The Babylonians defeated the Assyrians and became the primary power in the land. The son of King Merodach Baladan of Babylon sent letters and gifts to Hezekiah congratulating him on his return to health.

Hezekiah was so happy about his health, he received the messengers of the king with open arms. Then Hezekiah proudly showed the Babylonian messengers his warehouse of gold, silver, balsam, fine olive oil, armaments, and every treasure in the palace and in the kingdom.

When Isaiah heard what Hezekiah had done, he prophesied the successful invasion of Jerusalem and confiscation of all the treasures Hezekiah's ancestors had collected and stored. Everything of value would be taken away to Babylon, including some of Hezekiah's own family.

King Hezekiah agreed with the prophecy, but asked for peace and security for as long as he lived. This was granted, and after Hezekiah had died, Manasseh, Amon, Josiah, Jehoahaz, Jehoiakim, Jehoiakin, and Zedekiah (formerly Mattaniah) ruled the kingdom. In his ninth year of rule, Zedekiah was attacked by the Babylonian forces of Nebuchadnezzar, and Jerusalem was put under siege. For 18 months nothing could enter or leave the city. The famine was severe, and the siege caused widespread starvation in the city.

In the spring of the 11th year of Zedekiah's rule, the walls of Jerusalem were broached and the city fell. Judah's soldiers abandoned their posts, and King Zedekiah tried to escape on the road to Jericho. He was caught and taken to Riblah where his sons were killed in his presence, and then he was blinded, put in shackles, and taken to Babylon as prisoner.

King Nebuchadnezzar of Babylon didn't want Judah to turn into a barren desert, so he appointed Gedaliah, a wise and gentle Jew, to govern those few Jews left in Judah. He set up his office in Mizpah, a few miles from Jerusalem and began a peaceful rule. But he was assassinated by Jewish army commanders of Zedekiah who had fled and escaped the Babylonians.

All the treasures in Jerusalem were taken, and the temple, royal palace, and all the houses in Jerusalem were burned. All the utensils were taken and all the bronze was pulled down and removed. The city was in ruins, and most of the people of Judah became captives and were exiled to Babylon. A few poor farmers remained to work in the vineyards and on the farms around Jerusalem.

So 166 years after Isaiah prophesied about the downfall of Judah, the era of the kings of Judah ended.

Food Prices Collapse as Predicted by Elisha

About this time tomorrow 24 cups of the best flour will sell for half an ounce of silver in the gateway to Samaria. And 48 cups of barley will sell for half an ounce of silver.

2 KINGS 7:1

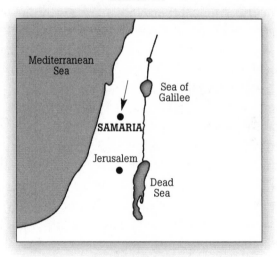

2 KINGS 7:1-16
Location: City of Samaria | Historical Time: ca 850 BC
TO VIEW MAPS ONLINE:
Copy this link into your browser and press Enter/Return
en.wikipedia.org/wiki/Samaria
www.gods-word-first.org/bible-maps/samaria-map.html

THE ARAMEANS HAD BESIEGED THE CITY OF SAMARIA causing widespread famine and starvation. Food had become so scarce, prices skyrocketed. The king inside Samaria blamed Elisha for not getting God to save the people and was considering capitulating to the Arameans. He sent a servant to Elisha. The servant told Elisha the king said "This severe famine is from the Lord. Why should I wait any longer for the Lord to help us?"

Elisha answered, "Listen to the word of the Lord! This is what the Lord says: 'About this time tomorrow 24 cups of the best flour will sell for half an ounce of silver in the gateway to [the city of] Samaria. And 48 cups of barley will sell for half an ounce of silver." Ground wheat flour was more expensive than barley.

When the prices collapsed, a seah (about 12 pounds) of fine flour was 24 cups (about 2.5 gallons) and sold for 1/2 ounce of silver. A seah (about 20 pounds) of barley was 48 cups and sold for 1/2 ounce of silver. One measure of wheat equaled two measures of barley.

This means that while the price of a seah of flour was high, it was still incredibly cheap compared with the prices for the most worthless kinds of food (donkey head and the plant "dove's dung," a bitter plant that was not normally eaten).

King Benhadad of Aram had Samaria blockaded, but rumors began to circulate that the Hittites and Egyptians may have been hired by the king of Israel to attack them. At dusk the Arameans heard the sounds of chariots, horses, and a large army moving their way. They panicked and abandoned their camps with everything intact, including their huge stock of food. They ran for their lives back toward Aram. The road away toward Jordan became littered with clothes and equipment.

When the people in the city heard what had happened, they raced out and collected the bounty. There was so much plunder and foodstuffs that prices plummeted as Elisha had predicted.

Elisha Predicts Death of King Benhadad

The next day Hazael took a blanket, soaked it in water, and smothered the king with it. Hazael ruled as king in his place.

2 KINGS 8:15

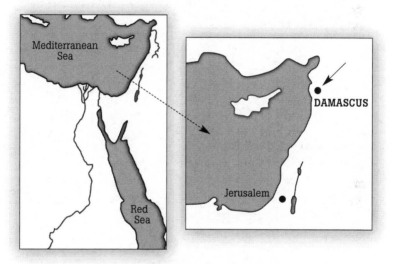

2 KINGS 8:7-15
Location: Damascus | Historical Time: ca 850 BC
TO VIEW MAPS ONLINE:
Copy this link into your browser and press Enter/Return
en.wikipedia.org/wiki/Damascus

KING BENHADAD II OF ARAM GOT SICK AND BEGAN TO DIE. Elisha went to Damascus and the king sent Hazael, his military captain, to visit Elisha and find out if he would recover. Elisha told Hazael to tell Benhadad that he would get better, although the Lord had shown Elisha that Benhadad would die. Elisha also told Hazael that he would become king of Aram.

The next day Hazael smothered King Benhadad II with a blanket soaked in water. Hazael became king in his place just as predicted by Elisha.

Elisha and the Stomped Arrows

Elisha said, "Take the arrows." So the king took them. "Stomp on them," he told the king.

2 KING13:18

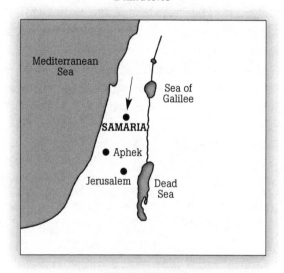

2 KINGS 13:16-19
Location: Samaria and Aphek | Historical Time: ca 796 BC
TO VIEW MAPS ONLINE:
Copy this link into your browser and press Enter/Return
en.wikipedia.org/wiki/Samaria
www.gods-word-first.org/bible-maps/samaria-map.html
bibleatlas.org/aphek.htm
www.bible-history.com/geography/ancient-israel/tower-of-aphek.html
www.biblewalks.com/Sites/Afek.html

THIS EVENT OCCURRED DURING THE REIGN OF KING
Jehoash of Israel (798-782 BC) and as Elisha's earthly life
was coming to an end. Samaria was being oppressed by the

Arameans. Jehoash came to see Elisha before he died, and during this visit, Elisha gave the king one more prophecy. He told Jehoash to get a bow and some arrows. When the king held the bow and the arrows in his hands, Elisha laid his hands on the king's hands and said, "Open the window that faces east." The king did, and Elisha said, "Shoot."

After the king shot an arrow out the window, Elisha prophesied, "This is the arrow of the Lord's victory, the arrow of victory against Aram. You will completely defeat the Aameans at Aphek."

Then Elisha told Jehoash to take the rest of the arrows and stomp on them. The king put them on the floor and stomped three times, then stopped.

Elisha became agitated and angry. He told the king that he should have stomped five or six times, because now he would only defeat the Arameans three times.

Shortly thereafter, Elisha died and was buried. And the fate of Israel and the Arameans happened just as Elisha had said. King Hazael of Aram continued to oppress Israel, but began to lose battles. Then Hazael died, and his son Benhadad succeeded him. When King Benhadad III of Aram attacked Israel again, King Jehoash defeated Benhadad three times and recovered the cities that had been taken from the northern kingdom of Israel.

Eliezer Predicts King's Death and Destruction of Ships

Then Eliezer, son of Dodavahu from Mareshah, prophesied against Jehoshaphat.

2 CHRONICLES 20:37

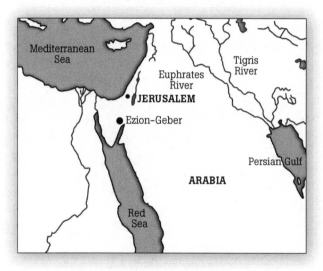

2 CHRONICLES 20:35-37
Location: Mediterranean Sea, Jerusalem, Ezion-Geber
Historical Time: ca 853 BC

TO VIEW MAPS ONLINE:
Copy this link into your browser and press Enter/Return
www.worldatlas.com/aatlas/infopage/medsea.htm

KING JEHOSHAPHAT OF JUDAH ALLIED WITH KING AHAZIAH of Israel, who caused Jehoshaphat to do evil things. They made ships in Ezion-Geber to sail to Tarshish in southern Spain.

But Eliezer, son of Dodavahu from Mareshah, came to Jehoshaphat and prophesied, saying, "The Lord will destroy your work [ships] because you have allied yourself with Ahaziah."

As prophesied, the ships were wrecked and did not sail to Tarshish.

Evil Queen Jezebel Dies as Predicted

They threw her down, and some of her blood splattered on the wall and the horses. The horses trampled her.

2 KINGS 9:33

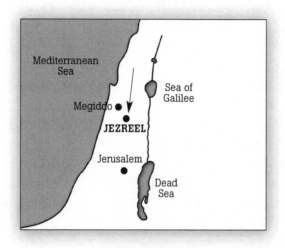

2 KINGS 9:7–37
Location: Megiddo and Jezreel | **Historical Time:** ca 841 BC
TO VIEW MAPS ONLINE:
Copy this link into your browser and press Enter/Return
www.crivoice.org/phototour/pjezreel.html
www.keyway.ca/htm2000/20000515.htm

ELIJAH TOLD AHAB, KING OF ISRAEL, THAT HIS EVIL WIFE would die and be eaten by dogs. Later, Elisha, Elijah's successor, repeated the prophecy as Israel and Judah went to fight Aram.

Joram was Ahab's son. Ahab had ruled Israel from 874 BC to 853 BC. Then Joram became king and ruled Israel (from 852-841 BC). Ahaziah, the son of King Jehoram of Judah, became king, and Ahaziah and Joram joined forces to fight King Hazael of Aram.

Joram was wounded and was taken to Jezreel. Ahaziah went to Jezreel to see Joram.

In 841 BC, while Joram was still king, Jehu was anointed king of Israel by Elisha and told by the prophet that he was to destroy the family of Ahab, and God would get revenge on Jezebel, King Ahab's evil wife, for shedding the blood of the prophets and other servants of the Lord. Elisha prophesied that Jezebel would die and dogs would eat her corpse inside the walls of Jezreel. He said there would be no body left to bury.

So Jehu took an army and traveled to Jezreel. The watchman in the tower at Jezreel saw the troops approaching and had Joram notified. Joram commanded a chariot driver to go out to meet Jehu and ask if everything is all right. The messenger in the chariot didn't return, and the army continued to approach.

A second chariot was sent out, and this one also did not return.

So King Joram of Israel and King Ahaziah of Judah each boarded chariots and drove out to meet Jehu themselves. They found Jehu in the field that was taken from Naboth of Jezreel.

Joram asked Jehu if everything was all right. Jehu answered, "How can everything be all right as long as your mother continues her idolatry and witchcraft?"

Joram whipped his chariot around and began to flee, shouting at Ahaziah, "It's a trap, Ahaziah!"

Jehu took his bow and shot an arrow through the back and out the chest of Joram. Joram slumped over in his chariot, and Jehu had Joram's body thrown on the ground in the field that belonged to Naboth. This fulfilled the prophecy made by Elijah in 1 Kings 21:19.

King Ahaziah fled off down the road to Beth Haggan. Jehu ordered his men to chase Ahaziah down and shoot him in his chariot. They caught up with him at Gur Pass near Ibleam. Mortally wounded, Ahaziah went on to Megiddo, where he died.

Jehu continued toward Jezreel. When Jezebel, mother of Joram and wife of Ahab, heard Jehu was entering the city, she put on makeup, fixed her hair and went to the second-story window to look down at Jehu when he came into the courtyard.

When Jehu came through the gateway, Jezebel called down, "Is everything all right, Zimri, murderer of your master?"

Looking up, Jehu asked, "Is anyone on my side? Anyone?" Some eunuchs appeared in another window and Jehu said, "Throw her down."

They grabbed the struggling Jezebel and tossed her out of the window. She hit the stone courtyard and some of her blood splattered on the wall. Horses trampled on her body.

Jehu went inside the palace and got a drink. Then he said to his men, "Take care of this woman who had a curse on her. After all, she was a king's daughter." (Jezebel was the daughter of Ethbaal, king of Zidon.)

His men went out to get the body, but all they found was her skull, feet, and hands. Dogs had eaten everything else.

Jehu recognized that the prophecy of Elijah so many years before had then been fulfilled (2 Kings 9:10). Jehu commented that Elijah had said, "Dogs will eat Jezebel's body inside the walls of Jezreel." And this was how the life of an evil and wicked woman ended.

Micaiah Tells the King He Would be Killed

If you ever return safely,
the Lord has not spoken through me.

2 CHRONICLES 18:27

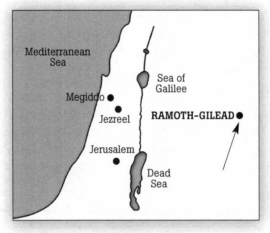

2 CHRONICLES 18:5-34
Location: Ramoth in Gilead | **Historical Time:** ca 853 BC
TO VIEW MAPS ONLINE:
Copy this link into your browser and press Enter/Return
www.oneyearbibleblog.com/2011/07/july-26th-one-year-bible-readings.html
dwellingintheword.wordpress.com/tag/1-kings/

KING JEHOSHAPHAT OF JUDAH HAD AGREED TO JOIN WITH King Ahab of Israel in attacking Ramoth in Gilead, but Jehoshaphat asked that Ahab first find out what the Lord says about this. Ahab called together 400 prophets of Israel and asked them, "Should we go to war against Ramoth in Gilead or not?" To a man they said, "Go!"

But Jehoshaphat wanted to hear from a prophet of Judah. He asked Ahab, "Isn't there a prophet of the Lord whom we could ask?"

Ahab told him that Micaiah, son of Impa, lived here, but Ahab didn't like Micaiah because he always prophesied evil regarding him. Jehoshaphat told him he should not say this.

Micaiah was summoned, and he told King Jehoshaphat and King Ahab that a spirit would cause the 400 prophets to deceive Ahab and encourage him to attack. Zedekiah, son of Chenaanah, went up to Micaiah and struck him on the cheek, taunting Micaiah. King Ahab ordered that Micaiah be sent back to Amon, governor of the city, and to Joash, the prince, directing them to put Micaiah in prison and feed him nothing but bread and water until Ahab returns home safely.

Micaiah calmly said, "If you really do come back safely, then the Lord wasn't speaking through me." Micaiah told the people to remember his words.

Micaiah was put in prison, and King Ahab of Israel and King Jehoshaphat of Judah proceeded to Ramoth in Gilead.

Ahab told Jehoshaphat that he would disguise himself for going into battle, but Jehoshaphat should wear his royal robes. In the meantime, the king of Aram gave orders to the chariot commanders to not fight anyone except Ahab, king of Israel.

When the two opposing forces met at Ramoth, the chariot commanders thought Jehoshaphat was the king of Israel and they surrounded him. He cried out for God to help him, and God made them realize he wasn't the king of Israel.

Just then one of the Arameans shot an arrow into the Israeli-Judean forces at random. The arrow hit Ahab between his scale armor and his breastplate. Ahab shouted to his chariot driver to turn around and get him away from the Aramean troops. He was badly wounded. The battle got worse that day. King Ahab propped himself up in his chariot facing the Arameans. At sundown Ahab died just as prophesied by Micaiah.

Elijah Sends Letter Prophesying King's Death

[Elijah wrote] "You yourself will be very ill with a lingering disease of the bowels, until the disease causes your bowels to come out."

2 CHRONICLES 21:15

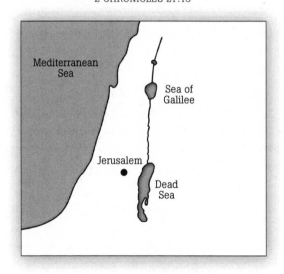

Mediterranean Sea

Sea of Galilee

Jerusalem

Dead Sea

2 CHRONICLES 21:12–19
Location: Jerusalem | **Historical Time:** ca 848–841 BC

TO VIEW MAPS ONLINE:
Copy this link into your browser and press Enter/Return
www.sacred-destinations.com/israel/jerusalem-map
www.sacred-destinations.com/israel/israel-map
www.ccel.org/bible/phillips/CP051GOSPELMAPS.htm
bibleatlas.org/jerusalem.htm

ONCE AGAIN KING JEHORAM OF JUDAH CAUSED THE JEWISH people to become sinful. He created illegal places of worship around Judah, and he encouraged the inhabitants of Jerusalem to worship foreign gods.

Elijah sent Jehoram a letter telling him in no uncertain terms what the Lord God felt about his behavior. Elijah wrote, "This is what the God of your ancestor David says: 'You haven't followed the ways of your father, Jehoshaphat, or the ways of King Asa of Judah. Instead, you have followed the ways of the kings of Israel. You, like Ahab's family, have caused Judah and the inhabitants of Jerusalem to chase after foreign gods as if they were prostitutes. You have killed your brothers, your father's family. Your brothers were better than you. The Lord will strike a great blow to your people, your sons, your wives, and all your property because you did this. You will suffer from a lingering disease of the bowels until your intestines come out.'"

Then God prompted the Philistines and the Arabs near Sudan to attack Judah. They took everything they could find in the royal palace, including Jehoram's sons and wives. Only Ahaziah, Jehoram's youngest son, remained in Judah.

Then, in 843 BC, God struck Jehoram with an incurable intestinal disease. After suffering for two years, his intestines fell out of his stomach and he died a painful death. He was only 40, but he died in 841 BC as prophesied by Elijah. And no one was sorry to see him go.

Famine Predicted by Agabus

Through the Spirit Agabus predicted that a severe famine would affect the entire world.

ACTS 11:28

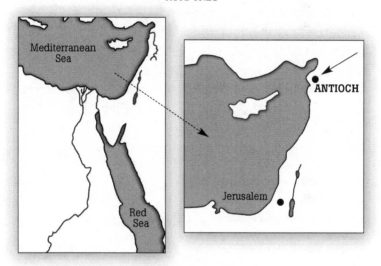

ACTS 11:26–30
Location: Antioch | **Historical Time:**ca 45 AD
TO VIEW MAPS ONLINE:
Copy this link into your browser and press Enter/Return
en.wikipedia.org/wiki/Antioch
www.ccel.org/bible/phillips/CN092MAPS1.htm
www.murraymoerman.com/1christ/scripture/acts.asp
theonlinebibleschool.net/mod/resource/view.php?id=277
www.welcometohosanna.com/PAULS_MISSIONARY_JOURNEYS/0.6antioch.html

PAUL AND A NUMBER OF DISCIPLES WERE AT ANTIOCH IN northern Syria. Prophets in Antioch included Agabus, one of the early converts. It was during this period that the term "Christian" was first used to describe the followers of "The Way."

Claudius was the Roman emperor from 41-54 AD, and in 44 AD Agabus prophesied that a severe famine would occur and drastically affect Judea.

The next year (45 AD) the area from Greece through Judea was affected by a serious famine that devastated crops and food supplies. It happened just as Agabus had predicted.

The disciples in Antioch decided to contribute whatever they could afford to help the believers in Judea who were being affected. Barnabas and Paul were dispatched to take the contribution to the leaders in Jerusalem. This was a classic example of Gentile Christians sharing with and helping Judean Christians.

Jesus Predicts Betrayal

I can guarantee this truth: One of you is going to betray me.
MATTHEW 26:21

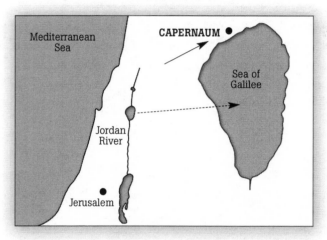

MATTHEW 26:21-25; MARK 14:18-21; LUKE 22:21-23; JOHN 13:10, 13:21
Location: Capernaum and just outside Jerusalem | **Historical Time:** ca 33 AD

TO VIEW MAPS ONLINE:
Copy this link into your browser and press Enter/Return
www.sacred-destinations.com/israel/jerusalem-map
www.sacred-destinations.com/israel/israel-map
www.ccel.org/bible/phillips/CP051GOSPELMAPS.htm
bibleatlas.org/jerusalem.htm

THE EARTHLY LIFE OF JESUS WAS WINDING DOWN, AND HE was preparing to enter Jerusalem for the final showdown. As He was leaving Capernaum on the northwest shore of the Sea of Galilee, He told his disciples that one of them was a devil and would betray Him. He was speaking of Judas, who was about to sell the whereabouts of Jesus to the Jewish leadership for 30 pieces of silver.

As Jesus approached Jerusalem, the disciples were ready to prepare the Passover meal. Jesus told them how to locate a house for them to use to celebrate the meal. They did, and then they prepared the Passover meal.

While sitting at the table with the 12 disciples, Jesus said, "I can guarantee this truth: One of you is going to betray me."

The disciples asked who, and He replied, "Someone who has dipped his hand into the bowl with me." Judas asked, "You don't mean me, do you, Rabbi?" and Jesus replied, "Yes, I do."

Jesus Predicts Donkey Will be There

You will find a donkey tied there...
MATTHEW 21:2

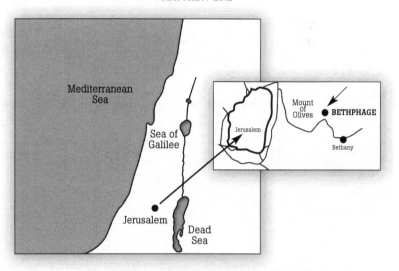

MATTHEW 21:1–9; MARK 11:1–11; LUKE 19:29–44; JOHN 12:12–19
Location: Bethphage and Jerusalem | **Historical Time:** ca 33 AD
TO VIEW MAPS ONLINE:
Copy this link into your browser and press Enter/Return
www.ccel.org/bible/phillips/CP051GOSPELMAPS.htm
bibleatlas.org/bethphage.htm

(See Chapter 6 *Power over Animals*)

Jesus Predicts
Man Will Provide
Room for Meal

*My time is near. I will celebrate the Passover
with my disciples at your house.*
MATTHEW 26:18

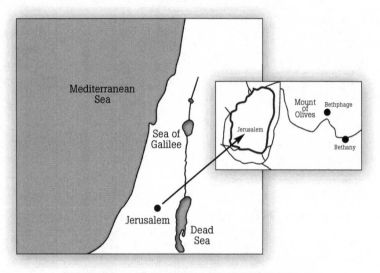

MATTHEW 26:17–20; MARK 14:12–17; LUKE 22:7–17
Location: Jerusalem | **Historical Time:** ca 33 AD
TO VIEW MAPS ONLINE:
Copy this link into your browser and press Enter/Return
www.sacred-destinations.com/israel/jerusalem-map
www.sacred-destinations.com/israel/israel-map
www.ccel.org/bible/phillips/CP051GOSPELMAPS.htm
bibleatlas.org/jerusalem.htm

JESUS TOLD HIS DISCIPLES TO CONTINUE ON INTO Jerusalem where they would meet a man carrying a jug of water. Jesus told them to follow this man to his house and then ask him about the room where Jesus would eat the Passover meal with His disciples.

One of the disciples was directed to tell the man, "The Teacher says, 'My time is near. I will celebrate the Passover with my disciples at your house.'"

When they went on, they found the man as Jesus had described. One of the disciples repeated what Jesus told them to say. The man immediately took them upstairs, where he showed them a large room with a long table. It was the location for the Last Supper—the Passover meal.

Jesus Predicts
Own Death

*Everything that the prophets wrote about the
Son of Man will come true. They will make fun of him,
insult him, spit on him, whip him, and kill him.*

LUKE 18:31-33

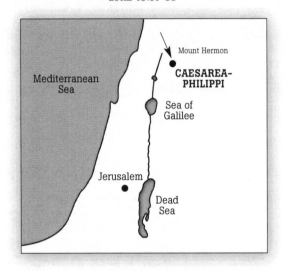

MATTHEW 16:21-23, 17:22-13, 20:17, 26:1-2; MARK 8:31-33, 9:31,
10:34; LUKE 9:22, 9:43-45, 18:31-34; JOHN 11:45-57
Location: Caesarea Philippi by Mount Hermon to Jerusalem
Historical Time: ca 33 AD

TO VIEW MAPS ONLINE:
Copy this link into your browser and press Enter/Return
en.wikipedia.org/wiki/Caesarea_Philippi
www.bibleplaces.com/banias.htm
en.wikipedia.org/wiki/Mount_Hermon

JESUS AND HIS DISCIPLES WENT FROM CAESAREA PHILIPPI
at the southwestern base of Mount Hermon 25 miles south
to the Sea of Galilee and on to Jerusalem. He began to tell

them about His coming death and resurrection. Four times He said He would soon die.

Matthew 16:21-23; Mark 8:31-33; Luke 9:22
Matthew 17:22-13; Mark 9:31; Luke 9:43-45
Matthew 20:17; Mark 10:34; Luke 18:31-34
Matthew 26:1-2; Mark 14:1-2; Luke 22:1-6;
John 11:45-57

Each time He told them, the disciples' emotions progressed from being frightened to being angry, to being in denial, to being sad. In Matthew 16:22, Peter objected to the words of Jesus and was aptly chastised for it. Jesus had difficulty getting the disciples to understand that this was the plan of God, and that He would die and then come back to life after three days.

He talked to them all the way from Caesarea Philippi through Galilee to Jerusalem. And His predictions came true (Thank God).

Jesus Predicts Peter's Denial

Before a rooster crows tonight,
you will say three times that you don't know me.
MATTHEW 26:34

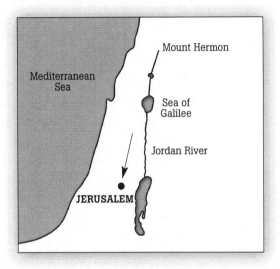

MATTHEW 26:31-35; MARK 14:27-31; LUKE 22:31-34; JOHN 13:36-38
Location: Jerusalem | **Historical Time:** ca 33 AD

TO VIEW MAPS ONLINE:
Copy this link into your browser and press Enter/Return
www.sacred-destinations.com/israel/jerusalem-map
www.sacred-destinations.com/israel/israel-map
www.ccel.org/bible/phillips/CP051GOSPELMAPS.htm
bibleatlas.org/jerusalem.htm

AFTER THE PASSOVER MEAL, JESUS TOOK THE DISCIPLES
to the Mount of Olives. Here He told them that they would
all abandon Him that night.

Peter objected and said that even if the others abandon Him, he never would leave Him.

Jesus curtly rejected Peter's comment and told him that he would deny knowing Him three times before the rooster crowed.

This prophecy came true just as Jesus had said.

Jesus Predicts Resurrection in Three Days

For as Jonah was three days and three nights in the belly of a huge fish, so the Son of Man will be three days and three nights in the heart of the earth.

MATTHEW 12:40

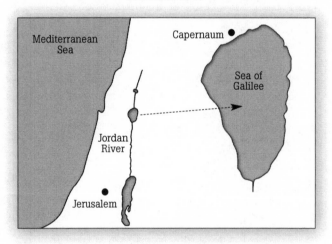

MATTHEW 12:38, 16:21, 17:22; MARK 8:31, 9:31; LUKE 9:22, 9:43
Location: near Capernaum | **Historical Time:** ca 33 AD
TO VIEW MAPS ONLINE:
Copy this link into your browser and press Enter/Return
bibleatlas.org/capernaum.htm
www.bible-history.com/geography/ancient-israel/capernaum.html
www.ccel.org/bible/phillips/CP051GOSPELMAPS.htm

DURING HIS LAST DAYS ON EARTH WITH HIS DISCIPLES, Jesus told His followers that He would die, but then be resurrected from the dead and live again.

The first time He said this was reported in Matthew 12:38. Jesus was asked by the scribes and Pharisees to show them a miraculous sign.

Instead, Jesus told them that the people of that evil and unfaithful era looked for a sign, but the only one they would get is the sign of the prophet Jonah. Just as Jonah was in the belly of the huge fish for three days and three nights, so would the Son of Man be in the heart of the earth for three days and three nights.

The next time He told them was near the Sea of Galilee (Matthew 16:21) (Mark 8:31) (Luke 9:22). After feeding 4,000 people on a mountainside near the Sea of Galilee, Jesus got into the disciples' boat and sailed to the territory of Magadan.

Pharisees and Sadducees came to test Jesus. They asked for a miraculous sign from heaven. Jesus put them in their place and said the only sign they will be given is that of Jonah.

The third time was while Jesus and the disciples were traveling in Galilee. He told them that He would be betrayed and killed, but on the third day, He would be brought back to life. The disciples became very sad (Matthew 17:22) (Mark 9:31) (Luke 9:43).

In each instance, Jesus told the disciples that He would be resurrected in three days, but His disciples heard only that He was going to die.

Jesus Describes
End Times Rapture

One will be taken, and the other one will be left.
MATTHEW 24:40

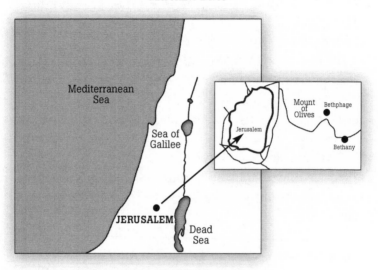

MATTHEW 24:38–44; LUKE 17:22–36
Location: on road to Jerusalem and on Mount of Olives
Historical Time: ca 33 AD

TO VIEW MAPS ONLINE:
Copy this link into your browser and press Enter/Return
www.sacred-destinations.com/israel/jerusalem-map
www.sacred-destinations.com/israel/israel-map
www.ccel.org/bible/phillips/CP051GOSPELMAPS.htm
bibleatlas.org/jerusalem.htm

JESUS HAD JUST HEALED 10 MEN OF A SKIN DISEASE, AND one, a Samaritan, had come back to thank him. He had been traveling along the border between Samaria and Galilee. As Jesus and the disciples began walking toward

Jerusalem, they were constantly followed by Pharisees who kept pestering Jesus with questions.

Some of them asked Him when the kingdom of God would come. Jesus told them that people could not observe the coming of the kingdom of God.

He said, "The time will come when you will long to see one of the days of the Son of Man, but you will not see it." On that day His coming will be like lightning that flashes from one end of the sky to the other. Jesus told them that when the Son of Man comes again, conditions will be like the days of Noah (Luke 17:26). When the Flood began, the people were eating, drinking, and getting married. Then the Flood started and destroyed all of the people except Noah and his family.

He said it will be like the time of Lot (Luke 17:28). People were eating, drinking, buying and selling, planting and building when Lot left Sodom and fire and sulfur rained from the sky destroying all of the people in Sodom.

When He comes again, people should not collect their belongings. And they should not turn to look back as Lot's wife did.

Then Jesus spoke the words that have intrigued Christians for centuries. He said, "I can guarantee that on that night if two people are in one bed, one will be taken and the other one will be left. Two women will be grinding grain together. One will be taken, and the other one will be left."

Regarding this rapture event, they asked where those who disappear will be taken. His only response was, "Vultures will gather wherever there is a dead body."

End Times
Described by Enoch

Enoch, from the seventh generation after Adam,
prophesied about them.
JUDE 14

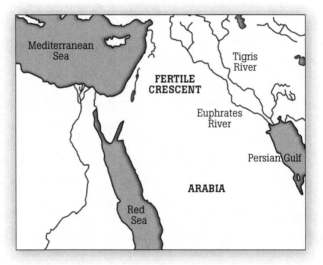

JUDE 14
Location: Fertile Crescent | **Historical Time:** ca 2990 BC
TO VIEW MAPS ONLINE:
Copy this link into your browser and press Enter/Return
www.britannica.com/EBchecked/topic/205250/Fertile-Crescent
ancienthistory.about.com/od/neareast/ss/110708ANE_10.htm

IN THE BOOK OF JUDE, THE BROTHER OF JAMES WROTE about the sinful nature of people and how they will act in the last days.

He said that Enoch, who was born 800 years after Adam, prophesied about these people. He said that in the end times, people will appear and ridicule God. They will follow ungodly desires and cause divisions among people. They will be concerned with physical things, not spiritual things. And they will be judged. The Lord will come with thousands of His angels to judge and convict the ungodly.

End Times
Described by Daniel

*It will be a time of trouble unlike any that has existed from
the time there have been nations until that time.*
DANIEL 12:1

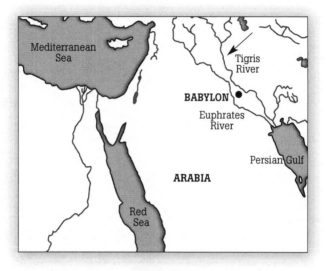

DANIEL 10-12
Location: by Tigris River in Babylon | **Historical Time:** ca 590 BC
TO VIEW MAPS ONLINE:
Copy this link into your browser and press Enter/Return
en.wikipedia.org/wiki/Arabian_Peninsula

WHILE IN EXILE UP IN BABYLON, DANIEL (RENAMED BELTE-
shazzar) had a vision of a great war to come. He was given
a glimpse of the end times by an angel of God.

During his vision, Daniel saw a man (humanoid) dressed
in linen wearing a belt made of gold from Uphaz. His body
was like beryl, his face looked like lightning, and his eyes

were like flaming torches. His arms and legs looked like polished bronze and his voice sounded like the roar of a crowd.

Daniel saw him, but others didn't. However, they felt his presence and began to tremble violently.

Daniel learned of great wars to come and the leadership of the angel Michael in the battles. As the angel spoke to him, Daniel became stronger. The angel described a vicious and violent war between the northern and southern kings and the deceit and corruption that will mark these end times.

He said "At that time Michael, the great commander, will stand up on behalf of the descendants of your people. It will be a time of trouble unlike any that has existed from the time there have been nations until that time." Then he told Daniel that many dead will rise from their sleep and be judged. Some will live forever. Others will wake up and be ashamed and disgraced forever.

End Times
Described by
Zechariah

Their flesh will rot while they are standing on their feet.
ZECHARIAH 14:12

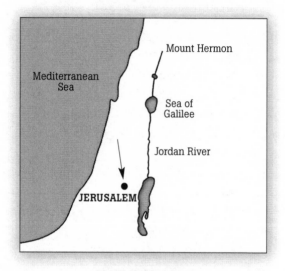

ZECHARIAH 14:3-21
Location: Jerusalem | **Historical Time:** ca 548 BC
TO VIEW MAPS ONLINE:
Copy this link into your browser and press Enter/Return
www.sacred-destinations.com/israel/jerusalem-map
www.sacred-destinations.com/israel/israel-map
www.ccel.org/bible/phillips/CP051GOSPELMAPS.htm
bibleatlas.org/jerusalem.htm

ZECHARIAH LIVED DURING THE REIGN OF THE PERSIAN king, Darius I (550-486 BC). In the second year of the reign of Darius, Zechariah began to have visions and saw the future.

The last chapter of the Book of Zechariah describes a major war in the end days. He said that all nations who have gone to war against Jerusalem will be destroyed. Some of the descriptions are graphic.

In Zechariah 14:12, the prophet writes: "This will be the plague the Lord will use to strike all the people from the nations that have gone to war against Jerusalem. Their flesh will rot while they are standing on their feet. Their eyes will rot in their sockets, and their tongues will rot in their mouths." This sounds like a biologic epidemic of major proportions. Zechariah said that the animals will also be affected.

Panic will spread and people will fight one another. It will be horrible.

End Times
Described by Jesus

*There will be a lot of misery at that time, a kind of misery
that has not happened from the beginning of the world
until now and will certainly never happen again.*

MATTHEW 24:21

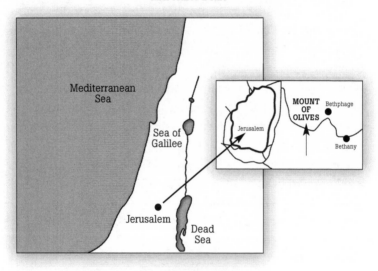

MATTHEW 24:3-32
Location: Mount of Olives | **Historical Time:** ca 33 AD
TO VIEW MAPS ONLINE:
Copy this link into your browser and press Enter/Return
www.frugalsites.net/jesus/gethsemane.htm

JESUS AND THE DISCIPLES WERE SITTING UP ON THE
Mount of Olives. They now understood that He was going
to die shortly. So His disciples asked Him how they could
know that He was coming again.

He told them that there will be wars and rumors of war. There will be famines and earthquakes. And these are only the beginning of the end. Jesus said that people will hate and betray each other, and false prophets will appear and deceive many. Lawlessness will increase, and many will fall out of love. But those who endure to the end will be saved.

Jesus said there will be much misery at that time, a kind of misery that has not happened from the beginning of the world until now. He said that if God does not reduce the number of those days, no one will be saved. But these days will be reduced because of those chosen by God.

Once the good news about God's kingdom has spread throughout the world, then the end will come.

After the misery, the sun will turn dark, the moon won't give light, the stars will fall from the sky, and the powers of the universe will be shaken. He said, "The Son of Man will come again just as lightning flashes from east to west." Jesus went on, "And they shall see the Son of Man coming in the cloud of heaven with power and great glory." This Shekinah cloud will be present at the end of time.

The angels of God will appear with a loud trumpet call. They will go out in every direction and gather those whom God has chosen.

According to Matthew 25:32, the people of every nation will be gathered in front of God and be judged. Those selected by Him and placed on the right will be welcomed into His kingdom and enter eternal life. Those not selected and placed on the left will be cast into the everlasting fire prepared for the devil and his evil angels. They will go into eternal punishment.

End Times
Described by Peter

*By God's word, the present heaven
and earth are designated to be burned.*
2 PETER 3:7

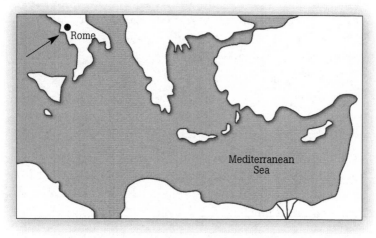

2 PETER 3:3-18
Location: possibly Rome | Historical Time: ca 60 AD
TO VIEW MAPS ONLINE:
Copy this link into your browser and press Enter/Return
www.rome.info/ancient/map/

PETER DESCRIBES THE CONDITIONS LEADING UP TO THE last day and how the world will end. In 2 Peter 3:7, he writes, "By God's word, the present heaven and earth are designated to be burned. They are being kept until the day ungodly people will be judged and destroyed." I found it interesting that Peter states that both heaven and earth will be burned.

He describes a grim future for the planet when he says, "On that day heaven will pass away with a roaring sound. Everything that makes up the universe will burn and be destroyed.

He says that on that day, heaven will be on fire and will be destroyed. Everything in the universe will burn and melt. But God has promised His people will be relocated to a new heaven and a new earth.

End Times
Described by John

A powerful earthquake struck. The sun turned as black as sackcloth made of hair. The full moon turned as red as blood. The stars fell from the sky to the earth like figs dropping from a fig tree when it is shaken by a strong wind. The sky vanished like a scroll being rolled up. Every mountain and island was moved from its place.
REVELATION 6:12-14

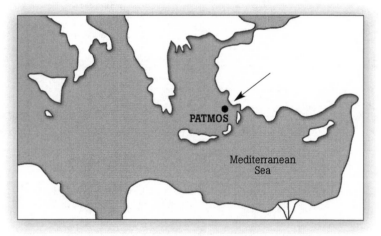

REVELATION 1-22
Location: Greek Isle of Patmos | **Historical Time:** ca 95 AD
TO VIEW MAPS ONLINE:
Copy this link into your browser and press Enter/Return
www.greeka.com/dodecanese/patmos/patmos-map.htm

HERE JOHN HAS BEEN EXILED TO THE ISLE OF PATMOS IN the Aegean Sea east of Greece. Patmos is 10 miles long and 6 miles wide. John spent 18 months here. During his exile, John had a vision of the end times and wrote the Book of Revelation.

The 22 chapters of Revelation all refer to the end of time. Some of the writings of John are more significant. In Chapter 6 verses 12-14, he talks about a powerful earthquake followed by the sun turning black and the moon turning red. He says that the stars will fall from the sky as it vanishes. And every mountain and island will move.

He wraps up by describing the final judgment. Satan will be freed and gather Gog and Magog for war. Their army will be as numerous as the grains of sand on the seashore. This army will surround Jerusalem and the encampment of God's holy people.

Then fire will suddenly come down from heaven and burn the army of Gog and Magog to death. Satan will be thrown into the fiery lake of sulfur, where the false prophet and the beast were already thrown, and these three will be tortured day and night forever.

Next all the dead will be judged before the white throne of God. The sea and death and hell will give up its dead. Books, including the Book of Life, will be opened and the dead judged based on what is written in the books. Anyone whose name isn't in the Book of Life will be thrown into the fiery lake.

Then the first heaven and earth will disappear. The sea will be gone, too. A new heaven and a new earth will appear and a new Jerusalem will come down from heaven. God will live with humans from then on, and there will be no more death, grief, crying, or pain.

End Times
Described by Paul

The Spirit says clearly that in later times some believers will desert the Christian faith. They will follow spirits that deceive, and they will believe the teachings of demons.
1 TIMOTHY 4:1

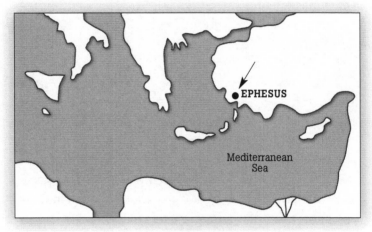

1 TIMOTHY 4:1-3
Location: Ephesus | **Historical Time:** ca 45 AD
TO VIEW MAPS ONLINE:
Copy this link into your browser and press Enter/Return
en.wikipedia.org/wiki/Ephesus

PAUL WAS IN EPHESUS AND PROPHESIED ABOUT THE CONDITIONS leading up to the last days. He said some Christian believers will fall away because they will follow deceiving spirits, and they will believe the teachings of demons.

He said "These people will speak lies disguised as truth." They will discourage people from getting married and will try to stop them from eating certain foods. Paul affirms that everything created by God is good, and nothing should be rejected if it is received with prayers of thanks because the word of God and prayer set these things apart as holy.

Summary

THIS HAS BEEN AN IN-DEPTH LOOK INTO THE BIBLE'S description of the power of prophecy. As you review the list of relevant verses below, you'll discover more incidents where prophesies came true. In Chapter 8, you'll read about other strange and supernatural things associated with the Bible. Here I'll discuss giants, monsters, dragons, dinosaurs, astrologers, magicians, psychics, seers, sorcerers, ghosts, heavens, other dimensions, the unseen, and the Watchers.

Relevant Verses in Chapter Seven

Incidents Involving Power of Prophecy

BATTLE OUTCOME: Stomped Arrows Determine Outcome of Battle
Location: Aphek
Verses: 2 Kings 13:16–19
Elisha told King Jehoash to shoot an arrow out of the east-facing window, then to stomp on the rest of the arrows. The king stomped three times and the Arameans were defeated three times.

BETRAYAL: Jesus Predicts Betrayal
Location: Jerusalem
Verses: Matthew 26:21–25; Mark 14:18–21; Luke 22:21–23; John 13:10; John 13:21
Jesus told his disciples He would be betrayed, and then put to death.

BETRAYAL: Jesus Predicts Betrayal
Location: Capernaum
Verse: John 6:70
Jesus told the disciples that one of them was a devil (Judas) and would betray Him.

CITY SAFE: Prophet Predicts Jerusalem Will Be Safe

Location: Jerusalem
Verses: 2 Kings 19:32; Isaiah 37:21
Isaiah told the Israelite King Hezekiah that King Sennacherib of Assyria would not take Jerusalem.

DEATH: Death Occurs as Predicted
Location: Jezreel
Verses: 2 Kings 9:33–35
Jezebel, King Ahab's evil wife was tossed out of a window to her death. Her body was trampled by horses and then eaten by dogs just as predicted by Elijah and Elisha.

DEATH: Death Predicted
Location: Shiloh or Tirzah
Verses: 1 Kings 14:1–18
Blind prophet Ahijah was visited by King Jeroboam's wife, in Shiloh. She pretended to be someone else. Ahijah told the lying wife her son would die when she stepped across the threshold of her home. This happened as Ahijah foretold.

DEATH: Jesus Predicts His Death
Location: near Bethany and Mount of Olives

Verses: Matthew 26:1–2
Jesus told disciples that He would be handed over to be crucified in two days.

DEATH: Jesus Predicts His Own Death
Location: Jerusalem
Verse: John 16:16
Jesus was at His last supper in the upper room with His disciples. He told them He was soon to die.

DEATH: King Told of Impending Death
Location: Samaria
Verses: 1 Kings 21:19;
1 Kings 22:38
Elijah told King Ahab that dogs would lick up his blood where Naboth was stoned. It happened. Ahab was killed in battle and died on his chariot. Chariot was taken to the Pool of Samaria to be washed out. Dogs licked up Ahab's blood as predicted.

DEATH: Prophet Describes Boy's Impending Death
Location: Jerusalem
Verse: 2 Samuel 12:14
Prophet Nathan told King David his son would die for David's sin with Bathsheba. His son died shortly thereafter.

DEATH: Prophet Predicts Death of King
Location: Jerusalem
Verses: 2 Chronicles 21:12–19
Elijah told Jehoram, King of Judah, that his failure to follow God's laws would cause him to lose family, wealth, and property. And Jehoram would "suffer from a [Chroniclesic] intestinal disease until his intestines came out." Philistines and Arabs attacked Jehoram and ransacked the royal palace. Jehoram got an incurable intestinal disease and died a painful death two years later when his intestines fell out. He was 40 years old.

DEATH: Prophet Predicts Death of King
Location: Gilead
Verses: 2 Chronicles 18:5–34
Micaiah was called before King Ahab of Israel and asked if they would win a battle by attacking Ramoth in Gilead. Unlike 400 other prophets there who all told Ahab he'd win, Micaiah told him he would lose and be killed. King Ahab died at sundown.

DEATH: Prophet Predicts Evil Woman Will Die
Location: Ramoth Gilead
Verses: 2 Kings 9:7–32
Elisha told Jehu, son of Jehoshaphat, that King Ahab's evil wife, Jezebel, will die and be eaten by dogs and Jehu would replace Joram as king of Israel.

DEATH: Prophet Predicts King Will Die
Location: Damascus
Verses: 2 Kings 8:7–15
Elisha told Hazael, the

military captain for King Benhadad of Aram, that he would soon replace the king. The next day Hazael smothered King Benhadad with a wet blanket and became king of Aram.

DEATH: Prophet Predicts King's Death and Destruction of Ships
Location: Mediterranean Sea
Verses: 2 Chronicles 20:35-37
King Jehoshaphat of Judah allied with King Ahaziah of Israel and did Evil. They made ships in Ezion Geber to go to Tarshish. Eliezer prophesied that because Jehoshaphat allied with Ahaziah, their work would be destroyed. The ships were wrecked, and they couldn't go to Tarshish.

DEATH AND RESURRECTION: Jesus Predicts Death and Resurrection
Location: near Sea of Galilee
Verses: Matthew 16:21; Mark 8:31; Luke 9:22
Jesus told His disciples that He would go to Jerusalem to suffer and die, but would rise again on third day.

DEATH AND RESURRECTION: Jesus Predicts Death and Resurrection
Location: Galilee
Verses: Matthew 17:22; Mark 9:31; Luke 9:43
Jesus told His disciples a second time that He would go to Jerusalem to suffer and die,

but would rise again on the third day.

DEATH AND RESURRECTION: Jesus Predicts Death and Resurrection
Location: On road to Jerusalem
Verses: Matthew 20:17-19; Mark 10:33; Luke 18:31-34
Jesus told disciples a third time that He would go to Jerusalem to suffer and die, but would rise again on third day.

DEATH AND RESURRECTION: Predicts Jesus Death and Resurrection
Location: Jerusalem
Verse: Acts 2:29
Peter talked about the prophecy of King David regarding the death and resurrection of Jesus.

DENIAL: Jesus Predicts Peter's Denial
Location: Jerusalem
Verses: Matthew 26:34; Mark 14:30; Luke 22:31-34; John 13:36-38
Jesus told Peter he would deny knowing Him three times before a morning rooster crows.

DESTRUCTION: Destruction of Jerusalem Predicted
Location: Jerusalem
Verses: 2 Kings 22:14-20
Prophet Huldah, wife of man in charge of royal wardrobe, told priests from Temple in Jerusalem that disaster was coming to the city and its

people. The people turned back to God, and the current generation was allowed to live and die in peace without seeing what was coming for Israel. King Josiah instituted religious reform, and there was peace during the days of King Josiah, King Jehoahaz, King Johoaikim, and King Jeholakin of Judah. Then King Zedekiah ruled. Jerusalem fell when King Nebuchadnezzar of Babylon attacked King Zedekiah of Judah and took the city of Jerusalem.

DESTRUCTION OF ALTAR: Altar Destruction Predicted
Location: Bethel
Verses: 1 Kings 13:1–3
"Man of God" told King Jeroboam the altar would be torn apart. It was, and the ashes were poured onto the ground.

DONKEY: Jesus Predicts Donkey Will Be There
Location: near Beth'page and Bethany at Mount of Olives
Verses: Matthew 21:1–11; Mark 11:1; Luke 19:29–34; John 12:12–19
Jesus told disciples to go ahead into Beth'phage and Bethany at Mount of Olives where they would find a young donkey tied there. It would never have been ridden.

DREAM: Angel Appears to Joseph in a Dream
Location: Nazareth
Verses: Matthew 1:20–25

An angel told Joseph that his betrothed Mary was pregnant by the Holy Spirit and would give birth to a son. The angel said the boy was to be called Jesus.

DREAMS: Joseph Interprets Dreams
Location: Egypt
Verses: Genesis 40:1–23
Joseph interpreted the dreams of fellow prisoners, a cupbearer and the royal baker. One prisoner would be restored, but the other will be executed.

DROUGHT: Drought Immediately Starts
Location: Gilead
Verses: 1 Kings 17–1; James 5:17
Elijah told King Ahab that no rain would come unless he said so. Elijah prayed, and a severe drought immediately began – lasted three and a half years.

DROUGHT: Drought Ends as Predicted
Location: Carmel
Verses: 1 Kings 18:41–46
The drought in Samaria ended when Elijah told King Ahab that rain was coming. After checking eight times, Elijah's servant saw a storm developing out at sea. It brought torrential rain to the area.

END TIMES: End Times
Location: Mount of Olives
Verses: Matthew 24:23–31
Jesus describes horror of

unbelievers and salvation of chosen ones.

END TIMES: End Times
Location: unknown
Verses: Luke 21:23-28
Jesus describes horror, miraculous signs and salvation of chosen ones.

END TIMES: End Times
Location: Greek Isle of Patmos
Verses: Revelation 1-22
John describes Judgment Day and the end of the world as we know it.

END TIMES: End Times
Location: Ephesus
Verses: 1 Timothy 4:1-3
Paul describes conditions leading up to the last days. He talked about people who will deceive and follow the teaching of demons. They will speak lies disguised as truth and will try to stop many from getting married and from eating certain foods.

END TIMES: End Times
Location: Possibly Rome
Verses: 2 Peter 3:3-18
Peter describes the conditions leading up to the last day and how the world will end in burning and melting to be replaced by a new heaven and a new earth.

END TIMES: End Times
Location: Jerusalem
Verses: Joel 1-3
Prophet Joel describes the end times and Judgment Day like advancing locusts. He mentions food disappearing before the eyes, fire burning up everything, and the last major battle against the enemy.

END TIMES: End Times
Location: Jerusalem
Verses: Zechariah 14:3-21
Prophet Zechariah describes a great earthquake, a biologic epidemic that rots flesh, eyes, and tongues of enemies who attacked Jerusalem that cause widespread panic and paranoia.

END TIMES: End Times
Location: Unknown
Verse: Hebrews 12:26
Verse explains that when God spoke, the earth shook, but on the last day God will shake not only the earth but also the sky.

END TIMES: End Times
Described
Location: Babylon by Tigris River, Tigris
Verses: Daniel 10-12
Daniel (renamed Belteshazzar) was given glimpse of the End Times by angel of God. During vision by Tigris River, Daniel sees man (humanoid) dressed in linen with belt made of gold from Uphaz. Body was like beryl, his face looked like lightning and his eyes were like flaming torches. His arms and legs looked like polished bronze and his voice was like the roar of a crowd. Daniel saw him, but others didn't; they

felt his presence and began to tremble violently. Daniel learns of great wars to come and leadership of Michael in the battles. As the angel spoke, Daniel became stronger. Angel describes dead rising and being judged.

END TIMES: Peter Predicts End Times
Location: Jerusalem
Verse: Acts 2:18
Peter described miracles, miraculous signs and weather changes that would occur on the last day.

END TIMES: Prediction of Last Days
Location: Fertile Crescent
Verses: Jude 14
Enoch talked about the judgment of God and the angels. The Lord will come with thousands of His angels to judge and convict the ungodly.

EXILE: Exile of Judah Predicted
Location: Jerusalem
Verse: 2 Kings 20:12
Isaiah told King Hezekiah of Judah that because he showed treasures of Israel to Babylonian representatives, the Jewish people and all their treasures would be taken captive to Babylon. They were.

FAMINE: Famine Predicted
Location: Antioch
Verse: Acts 11:27
The prophet Agabus came from Jerusalem to Antioch.

He predicted severe famine would affect the entire world. Claudius was the Roman emperor. The disciples in Antioch decided to contribute to help the believers in Judea who would be affected.

FAMINE: Joseph Predicts Severe Famine
Location: Egypt
Verses: Genesis 41:1-44, 53
Joseph told Pharaoh that a severe famine was coming.

FINDING DONKEY: Seer Told Man Where to Find Missing Donkeys
Location: Shiloh
Verses: 1 Samuel 9:3-21; 10:2
Saul's father, Kish, had two donkeys that wandered away. He asked Saul to find them. Saul and a servant set out to find them, but couldn't. Samuel was known as a seer, so they went to him for advice. Samuel was expecting Saul and told him where the lost donkeys would be found.

ISOLATION: Prophet Predicts Isolation of King
Location: Babylon
Verses: Daniel 4:1-27
Daniel told King Nebuchadnezzar that his dream meant that he would be forced away from rule and would live with wild animals, eat grass like cattle, and be made wet by dew from the sky. His hair would grow as long as eagle feathers and his nails would

grow as long as bird claws. After seven time periods the king would realize the power of God and accept the rule of God. This prediction came true 12 months later.

KING PROPHESIES: King Saul Suddenly Prophesies before Prophet
Location: Naioth
Verse: 1 Samuel 19:23
God's spirit took over Saul's body and mind. Saul prophesied before Samuel.

MEAL LOCATION: Jesus Predicted Man Would Provide Location for Meal
Location: Jerusalem
Verses: Matthew 26:17–20; Mark 14:12–17; Luke 22:7–17
Jesus told disciples to go into Jerusalem where they'd meet a man carrying a jug of water. He told them to follow him to his house and then ask where a room was that Jesus could use to eat the Passover meal with his disciples. The man took them upstairs and showed them a large room.

MESSENGERS PROPHESY: Messengers of King Saul Suddenly Prophesy
Location: Naioth
Verse: 1 Samuel 19:20
God's Spirit gave Saul's messengers the power to prophesy.

POWER: Disciples Told of Great Power

Location: Jerusalem
Verse: John 14:12
Jesus told His disciples they would have power to do greater things than Him with help of the Spirit of Truth. He described how Holy Spirit will guide and lead believers.

PRICE COLLAPSE: Food Prices Predicted to Drop Significantly
Location: Egypt
Verses: 2 Kings 7:1, 16
Elisha predicted that flour and barley prices would collapse dramatically overnight. They did.

PROMISE OF SON: Son Promised to Barren Old Women
Location: Shunem
Verses: 2 Kings 4:14–17
Elisha told the old woman she would have a baby boy.

RAPTURE: Jesus Predicts End Times Rapture
Location: On road to Jerusalem and on Mount of Olives
Verses: Matthew 28:38–44; Luke 17:34–36
Jesus describes rapture to disciples.

RESURRECTION: Jesus Predicts Three Days to Resurrection
Location: Synagogue in Capernaum
Verse: Matthew 12:38
Jesus told the scribes and Pharisees that just as Jonah was in the belly of the fish for three

days, He would be in the heart of the earth for three days.

SHIPWRECK: Angel Warns Apostle about Shipwreck
Location: in Ionian Sea between Adramyttium in Greece and Rome in southern Italy, and in the Mediterranean Sea and the island of Malta
Verses: Acts 27:1–42
Paul was a prisoner on a ship sailing from Adramyttium in Greece to Rome, Italy when the ship is caught in a strong storm. An angel told Paul that the ship would be destroyed but all 276 on board would survive. After 14 days adrift, the ship ran aground and broke up in the rain on the shore of Malta. All on board got safely to shore.

WAR: Prophet Predicts Continuing Wars
Location: Judah
Verses: 2 Chronicles 16:7–10
The prophet/seer Hanani told King Asa of Judah that because he foolishly failed to depend on God during battle, he would have to fight more wars.

CHAPTER EIGHT

Other Paranormal

THIS CHAPTER IS A CATCH-ALL ON OTHER STRANGE and supernatural things mentioned in the Bible. These include giants, monsters, beasts, dinosaurs, dragons, mystics, ghosts, heavens, other dimensions, the unseen, and Watchers. At the end of this chapter, you'll find a list of verses covering these and other relevant incidents that were discovered during my research. I found 280 verses that deal with these subjects. In the stories to follow I'll provide examples.

There Were
Giants in the Land

*The Nephilim were on the earth
in those days—and also afterward.*

GENESIS 6:4

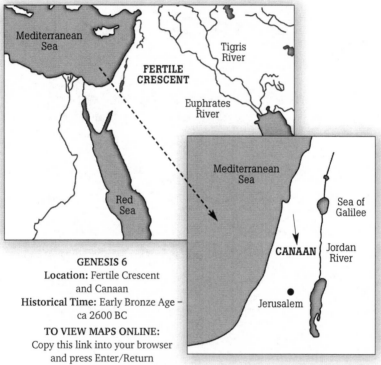

GENESIS 6
Location: Fertile Crescent
and Canaan
Historical Time: Early Bronze Age –
ca 2600 BC

TO VIEW MAPS ONLINE:
Copy this link into your browser
and press Enter/Return

www.britannica.com/EBchecked/topic/205250/Fertile-Crescent
ancienthistory.about.com/od/neareast/ss/110708ANE_10.htm
www.penn.museum/sites/Canaan/Collections.shtml
www.bible-history.com/geography/maps/map_canaan_tribal_portions.html
www.lds.org/scriptures/bible-maps/map-2?lang=eng
ancienthistory.about.com/od/canaanmaps/a/Maps-Canaan.htm

ONE OF THE MOST FAMILIAR STORIES FROM THE BIBLE IS about a small shepherd boy named David, who stood up against a huge Philistine warrior, named Goliath, and won. But is this story just a myth? Was Goliath real? Do giants really exist?

Thanks in part to the Internet a large body of evidence is showing that giants indeed are real, and that Goliath was one of them. In fact, we are now learning that there were many giants who lived throughout history.

Genesis 6:4 begins with *"There were giants [nephilim] on the earth in those days ..."* This sentence introduces the term "nephilim" to the reader. Translated from the original Hebrew, the term nephilim is "gigantes" meaning large. The English changed the word gigantes to "giant." According to Webster's Collegiate Dictionary, a giant is "a person or thing of unusually great size or power." Current interpretation is that a giant is someone who is more than twice your own height.

Another definition of the Hebrew word "nephilim" is "naphal" meaning "to fall." This implies that the nephilim were beings who had fallen out of grace. Were these fallen angels?

Genesis 6 states that sons of God took earthly females and produced offspring. Who were these "sons of God?"

There are two schools of thought regarding this mystery. One holds that the children of Seth interbred with the children of Cain, and their offspring were giants. The second view is that angels (sons of God) intermarried with the daughters of men.

The intermarriage of the godly Sethites with the ungodly Cainites doesn't account for the nephilim. And it's not backed up by references in the Bible.

The second school of thought is based on fallen angels who were kicked out of heaven because they rebelled against God. This is supported by passages such as 2 Peter 2:4 and Jude 6, which mention the binding up of the fallen angels. In addition, Job 1:6, Job 1:38, and Daniel 3:25 mention "sons of God" as angels.

These fallen angels took on human bodies and intermarried with mortal women. Their goal was to corrupt the bloodline of mankind and destroy the boundary between heaven and earth. They wanted to make it impossible for a savior called Jesus to be born. They also wanted to prevent the Israelites from entering Canaan.

So they intermarried and corrupted the people. Because the offspring were large, they became favored in leadership roles. Many became mighty men and women, renowned and wealthy. Both men and women from these unholy unions became very successful in the eyes of the common people, so they were often rich and powerful people of influence. They were the military, government, and business leaders, and they took roles that enabled them to control and guide entire societies. Such people we call "giants" of industry. Nevertheless they were champions of wickedness and harbored evil thoughts continually (Genesis 6:5). And they constantly sought to entrap others in their vice. This sounds like some people today, doesn't it?

Finally, God decided to destroy these beings. The crossbred hybrid race of humans and evil angels died in the Flood. But since angels don't die, some of the fallen angels remained after the Flood. Thus Genesis 6:4 says the nephilim were on the earth in those days *"...and also afterward."* This haunting statement confirms that their existence didn't end with the Flood. After the waters subsided, the nephilim started the cycle of wickedness all over again.

The existence of fallen angels was believed and accepted by the Jewish philosopher Philo of Alexandria (20 BC–50 AD) and Jewish historian Josephus Flavius (37-100 AD). The hybrid creatures called fallen angels or nephilim were also described in writings such as the *Apocrypha*, the *Book of Enoch*, the *Genesis Apocryphon* (*Apocalypse of Lamech*), *Jubilees*, and the *Pseudepigrapha* (noncanonical literature of the Old Testament).

Here's the bottom line: Fallen angels did exist; they do exist today; and they created giant men and women. Nephilim giants lived on earth before Noah. In fact, researchers now believe that Noah and his family were giants themselves. An increasing abundance of evidence suggests that before the Flood, the entire human race was of great stature.

Bible records support the fact that giants lived in early times. The book of Numbers covers a period between 1600 and 1400 BC. Described in this book is an incident where Moses sent 12 scouts into Canaan to spy on the people. Canaan is the area to the west of the Jordan River and along the coast of the Mediterranean. Tribes of giant races lived in Canaan and went by the names Anakim, Emim, Horim, Rephaim, and Zamsummim. The Rephaim lived on the east side of the Jordan.

Some of the people in these tribes were renowned. Arba, father of Anak, and his seven sons (the Anakim) were giants living near Hebron in the south of Palestine. Og, a Rephaim and the king of Bashan was a giant, who slept in a bed 13 feet long. Goliath and his four brothers from Gath were also giants.

God wanted these giants and the cities where they lived destroyed. In Numbers 13:33, the Israelite spies of Moses reported the existence of giants in Canaan, and said they felt like grasshoppers in the sight of these nephilim (giants). Most of the spies were afraid to attack Canaan as God commanded. Joshua and Caleb wanted to follow God's command, but the weakness of the other 10 spies and hesitation by Moses caused God to send the Israelite nation back into the wilderness to wander until that generation (except for Joshua and Caleb) died.

Finally, 40 years after the exodus out of Egypt and wandering in the deserts, Moses and Aaron died, and Joshua led the Israelite nation across the Jordan River into Canaan. In Joshua 11, we read that Joshua defeated the giant Anakims and killed the giants of Anak in the mountains. Only a few giants in Gaza, Gath, and Ashdod were left. These were the only three Canaanite cities taken by the Israelites in which giants still lived. That was 1400 BC, and 400 years later, giants would still exist in the area that was once Canaan.

Turn your focus now to Gath, a city about 30 miles to the west of Jerusalem and about 15 miles from the Mediterranean coast. The giant Goliath was born in Gath. Then look on your map of Israel and locate Bethlehem, about three miles to the south of Jerusalem. David, the man who would be king, was born in Bethlehem in 1040 BC.

In 1027 BC, David was about 13 years old, and Gath was one of the few places where the giant race of Anakim had survived. Goliath grew to a height of almost 10 feet. He had four brothers and they were giants, too. All five of these huge men served in the Philistine army. Goliath was the bully of the group and the champion of the Philistines.

His armored coat weighed 150 pounds, and his spear itself weighed 20 pounds. Goliath was big, and he was powerful. And then there was little David.

According to 1 Samuel 16:11, David was the youngest of the eight sons of Jesse. The family lived in Bethlehem, and three of David's older brothers (Abinadab, Eliab, and Shammah) were serving in the army of King Saul. The Israelites were in a desperate struggle against the Philistines, and things were not going well.

David was too young to be a soldier, so he served as the guardian of his father's sheep. He was small, barely five feet tall, but he was strong, and resourceful. To protect himself and his sheep from the predators that roamed the hillsides back then, he became an expert using a projectile-throwing-weapon called a "sling." He used his trusty sling to kill both a bear and a lion. God was preparing David for the fight of his life.

Each morning and each evening for 40 days, Goliath would step forward and taunt the Israelites across the valley of Elah between Gath and Jerusalem. He challenged the Israelites to send someone to fight him. He said the losing side would become slaves of the other. King Saul offered riches and social status to any person who would kill the giant, but the Israelite soldiers were terrified of Goliath's size and shrunk back from a confrontation with this huge man.

One day Jesse had some bread, roasted wheat, and cheese put into a sack. He told David to take the bread and grain to his brothers on the front and to give the cheese to the captain of the Israelite regiment.

When David arrived, he heard Goliath bellowing across the valley. Feeling that God would help him, David volunteered to fight Goliath. King Saul was astounded. Here was a young shepherd boy offering to fight an experienced Philistine warrior and giant.

But there was no one else to send, so David's offer was accepted. King Saul wanted David to wear protective armor, but David declined. All he would take was his sling.

As David and Goliath approached each other, David reached down and picked up five smooth stones out of a dry creek bed. One stone was for Goliath. Scholars think the other four stones were for Goliath's brothers.

Goliath and David exchanged words and then Goliath moved toward David. David quickly ran toward Goliath swinging his sling. He hurled a stone at Goliath, and the stone sank deep into Goliath's forehead killing him instantly. The 10-foot Goliath fell forward on his face. David took Goliath's own sword and cut off the giant's head. As David returned to the Israelite lines holding Goliath's head by the hair, the Philistines bolted and ran in terror. The Israelite army charged the fleeing enemy. As reported in 2 Samuel 15-22, Goliath's four brothers would also die in combat against the Israelites.

Yes, there were giants who lived way back in time. And others are recorded in recent history.

In old rock strata, archeologists have found human footprints dating to the time of the dinosaurs. These footprints reveal that some of the people back in those days were giants.

In Peru, Inca stone carvings show humans living with dinosaurs. And based on the stone carvings, the people who lived back then were incredibly tall.

Footprints of giant people have been found at Laetoli, in Kenya; near Demirkopru, in Turkey; in the Megalong

Valley near Penrith, and near Kempsey in New South Wales, Australia. They have also been found near Glen Rose, Texas; at Antelope Springs, Utah; near Alamogordo, New Mexico; and in Glen Canyon, Arizona.

The footprints in the Megalong Valley were made by people between 12 and 20 feet tall. The three footprints found near Penrith were made by someone 12 feet tall. And the footprints found near Kempsey were made by a human 17 feet tall.

The Glen Rose tracks were made by humans between 8.3 feet and 11.8 feet tall. The person who made the tracks at Antelope Springs, Utah was wearing a sandal.

Giant bone fossils have been discovered in the "mountain-valley" area of Turkey. One fossilized hind leg is 120 cm long, indicating that this person was over 16 feet tall.

Southwest of Lovelock, Nevada, miners found several mummified remains of red-haired humans, who were around eight feet tall, confirming an old Indian story about red-haired giants called "Si-Te-Cahs."

Skeletal remains of a human twice the size of the largest primate have been found in Java. And petrified remains of giants have been found in South Africa, Australia and China.

In Bathurst, Australia, fossils have been found indicating that these ancient people were between 10 and 25 feet tall, and weighed around 600 pounds. A jaw found at Gympie, Queensland, Australia came from a person 10 feet tall.

A report from 1555 AD said that the emperor of China had 500 giants who served him as archers of his guard.

In 1569 AD, a physician in the area of Belgium treated a youth 9' tall and a woman about 10' tall near his home in Flanders.

A 1719 AD account by Captain George Shelvock, describes Indians living on an island off the coast of Chile. These people were 9 to 10 feet tall.

In 1865 AD, an 8' 2" Chinese giant showed himself in England at the old Egyptian Hall in Piccadilly. He was a courtly gentlemen and an able scholar. And his sister was 8' 4" tall.

A bodyguard of Austria's Archduke Ferdinand was 11 feet tall. As reported in 1887 AD, Josef Winkelmaier lived in Austria and was 8' 9' tall.

And then there's Cornwall in England. Cornwall was known as the "Land of the Giants." The Cornish giants had six toes on each foot and six fingers on each hand. They were typically over 7' tall when the average height in England was barely five foot six inches.

And in 1761 AD, a Cornish miner discovered a stone coffin that held an 11' skeleton. The skeleton crumbled to dust when exposed to the air, but a tooth remained. The tooth was 2.5 inches long.

Excavations are being conducted near the site of Gath. Perhaps one day soon we'll find the remains of Goliath and his brothers, proving once again that the Bible is accurate, and that these Philistine giants really did exist.

Behemoth:
Monster of the Land

Look at Behemoth which I made along with you.
JOB 40:15

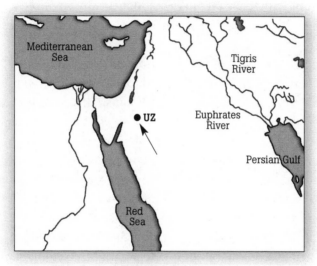

JOB 40:1-24
Location: Northwest Arabia in Uz | **Historical Time:** ca 586 BC
TO VIEW MAPS ONLINE:
Copy this link into your browser and press Enter/Return
bibleatlas.org/full/uz.htm
bibleatlas.org/uz.htm
espliego.files.wordpress.com/2008/03/middle-east-public-domain.jpg
www.visitjordan.com/default.aspx?tabid=63

JOB WAS A PIOUS MAN, WHO EXPERIENCED HORRIBLE
human suffering for over seven years. He lived around 586
BC in the northwest corner of Arabia in the territory of Uz,
near Edom. During his suffering, he evaluated life and
death and spoke about living with hardship and misery.

The Book of Job was likely written after the Flood and the Tower of Babel incident. It contains many references to creation and primeval events. In fact, this Book has many words that occur only once in the Bible.

Job introduces two new creatures, the *behemoth* and the *leviathan*. Both beasts were included in the Book of Job to reinforce the fact that God is all-powerful. The Bible says that He alone created these beasts, and only God can destroy them.

In Job 40, you can find descriptions of the behemoth, a terrifying land monster that lived to the east of the Garden of Eden in a desert invisible to humans. This creature was huge and ate grass on the mountainsides. It had a huge tail that was like a large cedar trunk. This creature was so massive it could walk through raging rivers without being disturbed. Its limbs and bones were strong like copper and iron. The amazing strength of this creature made behemoth the unconquerable, unchallenged beast of the land.

Some have suggested that behemoth was a hippopotamus, a water buffalo, an ox, or an elephant, but it seems more likely that behemoth was some form of dinosaur. It's commonly identified with the *sauropod dinosaur*, a creature that lived during Biblical times. This was the only known animal with a tail that moved like a swinging cedar.

Job described behemoth as a fearsome primeval and colossal beast, yet one that was powerless before the Creator.

Leviathan:
Beast of the Sea

*Can you pull Leviathan out of the water with a fishhook,
or tie its tongue down with a rope?*

JOB 41:1

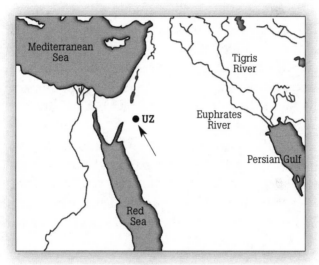

JOB 41:1–34
Location: Job lived in Northeast Arabia in Uz
Historical Time: Early Bronze Age – ca 2600 BC
TO VIEW MAPS ONLINE:
Copy this link into your browser and press Enter/Return
bibleatlas.org/full/uz.htm
bibleatlas.org/uz.htm
espliego.files.wordpress.com/2008/03/middle-east-public-domain.jpg

Webster's Dictionary states that a leviathan is a sea creature of immense size and power. According to Strong's
Exhaustive Concordance of the Bible, this horrible sea
monster is mentioned in four places in the Word of God
(Job 41:1, Psalms 74:14, Psalms 104:26, and Isaiah 27:1).

It's interesting that these Bible references all capitalize the name Leviathan suggesting that only one of these monsters existed.

Leviathan was huge and frightening. It was shaped like a slippery, twisting snake with a large head, a long neck, a large darting tongue, bright red eyes, and terrifying sharp teeth. Its long neck was made of folds of flesh that stuck together. The neck was solid and could not be moved. Even its chest was like a solid rock, and when it rose from the depths of the sea it made the mighty men of the day draw back in fear. The deep sea would boil like a pot and the hot water would stir. As it moved through the water, this monster left a shining path behind causing the sea to appear to have silvery hair.

Its smooth skin enabled it to swim gracefully through the water. On its back were rows of tightly sealed scales locked together and inseparable. On its belly were scales that appeared like sharp pieces of broken pottery. According to Psalms 104:26, the sea was a playground for this monstrous creature. It lived in the Abyss, the deepest part of the ocean.

While this sounds like the legendary Loch Ness Monster, Leviathan was much more. It was like a flame-throwing dragon. When it snorted, it gave out a flash of light. Flames shot from its mouth, and sparks of fire flew from it. In Job 41:20, we read that smoke came out of its nostrils (*like a boiling pot heated over brushwood*). Its breath could set coals on fire.

While fearful, the warriors of the day would attempt to kill this monster. But swords, spears, lances, arrows, and darts could not penetrate its hide. Iron weapons were like straw against it, and bronze weapons acted like rotten wood. Stones flung at it would break apart against its powerful body. Nothing could stop this monster of the deep. It was fearless and looked down in disgust on anyone who arrogantly went up against it.

There is no record of a Leviathan ever being killed by man. Yet according to Psalms 74:14, God smashed the heads of Leviathan and gave its body to the creatures of the desert for food.

According to Jewish legend, a great battle will occur at the end time between Behemoth and Leviathan. They will seem evenly matched so God will slay them both. The skin of the Leviathan will be used to make shelters. The meat of both the Behemoth and the Leviathan will be eaten by the people amid great joy.

Does the leviathan still exist? According to Isaiah 27:1 it does. And it cannot be defeated by man. Only God has the power to destroy this beast. The Bible says that on the last day, God will kill Leviathan, the horrible devil in the sea and rid our world of this frightening monster.

Dragons and Dinosaurs

And I went out by night by the gate of the valley,
even before the dragon well...
NUMBERS 2:13

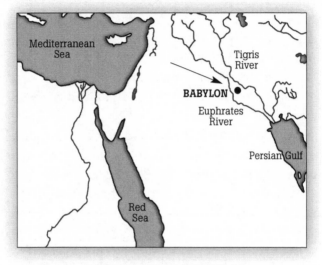

NUMBERS 2:13; JEREMIAH 51:34
Location: Babylon | **Historical Time:** Early Bronze Age – ca 2600 BC
TO VIEW MAPS ONLINE:
Copy this link into your browser and press Enter/Return
www.keyway.ca/htm2008/20080220.htm

RECENTLY I LISTENED TO A FASCINATING CD CONTAINING a report by Bob Dutko, a Christian radio talk show host, who presented 10 proofs that dragons and dinosaurs actually lived at the same time as humans. Dutko is an articulate and intelligent man, who challenges the secular world with Biblical evidence. His comments tweaked my interest and prompted my scientific brain to research his thesis. My research took me into the Internet and deep into various versions of our Holy Bible. What I found is both interesting and enlightening.

First, the books of the Old Testament were completed and preserved on Hebrew scrolls around 500 BC, and the Jewish historical books called the "Apocrypha" were recorded in Greek. Then the books of the New Testament were completed and recorded in Greek on papyrus by the end of the first century AD. This spread the word of God throughout the world. And Bible writers of the time described God's word and their world as they saw it, from their perspective, yet divinely inspired.

The history of our Bible is quite a read. It's been written, translated, and retranslated many times. An Internet search can let you follow the development and translations of this holy book from the codices of 300 AD through the Latin Vulgate in 600 AD, to the Wycliffe Bible of 1380, to Martin Luther's German Pentateuch of 1523 and German New Testament of 1529, to the elaborately illustrated English Tyndale New Testament of 1530, to the Geneva Bible, the first English study Bible of 1560, to the 1611 King James Bible with its 80 books of the Old Testament, Apocrypha, and New Testament (later reduced to the 39 books of the Old Testament and 27 books of the New Testament), to the English Revised Version Bible of 1880, to the American Standard Version in 1901, the New American Standard Version in 1971, the New International Version in 1973, and the English Standard Version in 2002. Throughout history, the Bible has been translated and "updated" by scholars to make it more understandable to Christians of the time.

So what does this have to do with dragons? While attempting to interpret from the original Hebrew and Greek to create "updated" versions of the Bible, some words have been changed based on the prevailing view at the time. As I said, the original writers of the Bible described events and incidents based on the world as they knew it. Today, Bible writers attempt to bring the ancient words into modern perspective. Along the way, some descriptive words were changed, and unfortunately the meanings have sometimes changed with them.

One such word is *dragon*. This word appears in early versions of the Bible. Yet some writers (scribes) of future versions of our Bible replaced "dragon" with the words "serpent," "sea serpent," "jackal," or "monster." However, the word "dragon" has a long and fascinating history and should not be dismissed to modernize today's interpretation of God's Word.

My research revealed that dragons are mentioned in art and literature all through our early history. Just look up the word "wyvern" in your dictionary. It's been said that behind every "myth" is some fact. Politically correct writers may morph the wording, but the fact that dragons existed is evident in ancient carvings, in legends, in artifacts, and in writing ever since man was able to draw and scribe.

The word "dragon" was originally used to describe any fearsome creature that could endanger man or animals. Dragon was often associated with evil and the Devil. In some cases, the word was used to describe land creatures such as the prehistoric *dinosaur* and the flying *pteradactyl* or *pterosaur*. The pteradactyl looks quite similar to the flying dragons so prevalent throughout history. Dragons have been described as winged serpents with two legs and a long knotted or barbed tail. They have also been associated with land creatures like the behemoth described in the Bible, and like dinosaurs and *Tyrannosurus Rex*, and with sea creatures such as the Leviathan from the Bible, or like the *plesiosaurus* and the Loch Ness Monster. Myth, legend, and fact are often blurred in our version of reality.

The term "dinosaur" wasn't used until 1841 when the first skeleton of a prehistoric creature was uncovered, so before this time, descriptions of dragons were from eye-witness accounts. The term dinosaur comes from "dino" (terrible) and "saur" (lizard). Some of these dragons were giant reptilian creatures.

Burial stones from Peru have been found showing carvings of a man riding on the back of what appears to be a prehistoric dinosaur. Cave drawings in France show early man with dragons and dinosaurs. A Mayan sculpture found near Vera Cruz, Mexico shows a serpent bird that lived among the people.

In 450 BC, Herodiatus wrote about winged serpents in Arabia. A description carved around 1200 BC described the Sumerian king Gilgamesh who ruled Mesopotamia around 2600 BC. The inscription says that he "slew the dragon."

Alexander the Great reported in 300 BC that his soldiers were afraid of the dragons in India. And the Vikings had fierce-looking dragon carvings mounted at the bow of their ships. They too knew about dragons.

Ancient Chinese books and art describe how they dealt with these creatures. A Chinese figure from around 25 AD depicts a fearsome dragon. Some Chinese books describe families that kept dragons and raised their young since the Chinese royalty of the time would use dragons to pull their chariots. And the Chinese zodiac shows 12 different animals. Eleven, such as the monkey, are commonly recognized. However, one is a dragon and is evidence that dragons existed when the original zodiac was developed. In 1200 AD, Marco Polo wrote about seeing dragons in China.

Early people weren't all uneducated and of low intelligence. Many were superstitious, but many were also inquisitive. And it is from these people that history developed. The Scientific Revolution began in 1543 with Francis Bacon, Copernicus, Galileo, and Newton. And documenting history was in full swing, including the understanding and acceptance of dragons that had persisted for thousands of years. A French engraving from 1475 shows a dragon attacking a lion. In December 1691, a dragon was reported to live in a cave in the wetlands near Rome. It terrorized the local population. A sketch of the creature still exists today. A 1684 painting from the Netherlands shows a man and a lamb walking toward a dragon and a leopard.

There is a legend from the Crusades describing how a soldier in the Roman army had saved a helpless maiden by killing a dragon in Libya. The soldier became remembered as Saint George and many versions of this story persist. The only consistent theme is that a dragon was killed by this man.

In early editions of the Bible, stories mentioning dragons were common. In Genesis 1:21 of the 5th century Latin Vulgate, one can read "So God created the great dragons." In the King James Bible, the word "dragons" for sea serpents was replaced with the word "whales." Still the King James Bible uses the word "dragon" at least 19 times as shown in Table 1.

TABLE 1

Verse	King James*	1952 Revised Standard	1995 God's Word
Gen 1:21	whales	sea monsters	sea creatures
Ex 7:9-12	serpent	large serpent	large snake
Deu 32:33	*dragons*	serpents	snake
Neh 2:13	*dragon*	jackal	snake
Job 7:12	whale	sea monster	sea monster
Job 30:29	*dragons*	jackals	jackal
Job 40:15	Behemoth	Behemoth	Behemoth
Psm 44:19	*dragons*	jackals	jackals
Psm 74:13	*dragons* in waters	*dragons* on waters	seamonsters
Psm 74:14	Leviathan	Leviathan	Leviathan
Psm 91:13	*dragon*	serpent	snakes
Psm 148:7	*dragons*	sea monsters	large sea creature
Isa 13:22	*dragons*	jackals	jackals
Isa 27:1	Leviathan	Leviathan	Leviathan
Isa 34:13	*dragons*	jackals	jackals
Isa 43:20	*dragons*	jackals	jackals
Isa 51:9	*dragon*	*dragon*	serpent
Jer 9:11	*dragons*	jackals	jackals
Jer 10:22	*dragons*	jackals	jackals
Jer 49:33	*dragons*	jackals	jackals
Jer 51:34	*dragons*	monster	monster
Jer 51:37	*dragons*	jackals	jackals
Eze 29:3	*dragon*	*dragon*	monster
Mic 1:8	*dragons*	jackals/ostriches	jackal/ostrich
Mal 1:3	*dragons*	jackals	jackals

* From *A Reader's Guide to the Holy Bible, King James Version*, Camden, NJ: Thomas Nelson, 1972.

The Apocrypha contains a story of Daniel going up against King Cyrus and a dragon whom the Babylonians worshipped. It was about 400 BC. According to the Apocrypha, Daniel fed the dragon pitch mixed with animal fat and hair. The dragon died and the Babylonian dissenters became enraged. The leaders of Daniel's opponents demanded that either the king or Daniel be put to death. Cyrus had Daniel cast into a lion's den, but Daniel was protected by God and remained alive and well. While in the pit, Daniel was provided food by the prophet Habakkuk. When Daniel was found alive and well in the pit of lions, the king acknowledged the God of Israel and had Daniel removed. Then he had the leaders of the Babylonian dissenters thrown into the same pit. They were killed.

A limestone relief from the 3rd century BC was found in Ebla in what is now Syria. It clearly shows a dragon standing in front of several people. Today this relief is in the Aleppo Museum in northwestern Syria.

From these descriptions we conclude that dragons existed when our Bible was originally written. Later interpreters had difficulty using the terms "dragon" or "monster" in some verses in the Bible. So publishers began writing out the word "dragon" or "monster" in new editions of the Bible. But based on the original writings, the word "dragon" was used. Dragons did exist. And some of these animals could have been dinosaurs.

When God created the creatures of the sea, the flying birds, and the animals described in the Book of Genesis, He could easily have created large flying reptiles, dragons and dinosaurs. Gigantic swimming creatures such as the *plesiosaur* and huge flying reptiles such as the *pterosaur*, and the lumbering 200 foot-long *sauropod* could have co-existed with other living creatures those many years ago. There are some who now believe that these creatures lived at the same time as Adam. When the Book of Job was written a few centuries after the Flood, great land, air, and sea creatures could have been alive and roaming the earth. The reason why these fascinating animals became extinct since Biblical times is still being sorted out. As we search for answers, the distinction between religion and science is becoming less a blur and more a fact we can understand and accept.

Magicians, Psychics, Seers, Sorcerers, and Astrologers

In the morning he was so upset that he sent for all the magicians and wise men of Egypt.
GENESIS 41:8

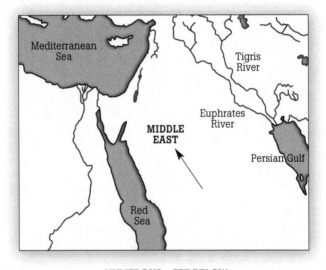

NUMEROUS – SEE BELOW
Location: Middle East | **Historical Time:** All time periods
TO VIEW MAPS ONLINE:
Copy this link into your browser and press Enter/Return
espliego.files.wordpress.com/2008/03/middle-east-public-domain.jpg

SINCE SOME OF THE TERMS ARE INTERCHANGEABLE, I combined all the occult, mysterious, and magical words. Then I looked for every instance where these were mentioned in the Bible. Here are the meanings of each term:

Astrology: *a study of the heavenly bodies (sun, moon, stars, and planets) to determine their influence on human affairs. Astronomy is the science of studying celestial bodies outside the earth's atmosphere.*

Black art: *a forbidden skill using witchcraft, sorcery or other occult practices for evil purposes.*

Conjure: *to affect or influence by or as if by invocation or spell; to effect or produce by or as if by magic; to call upon or command a devil or spirit by invocation or spell; to call or bring into existence by or as if by magic; to call upon or command a devil or spirit by invocation or spell; an act or instance of witchcraft; to invoke.*

Conjurer: *one who conjures or calls up spirits, or practices magic; a magician.*

Divination: *the practice of seeking to foretell future events or discover hidden knowledge by occult or supernatural means.*

Invoke: *to call forth or upon a spirit by incantation.*

Invocation: *the act of invoking or calling upon a deity or spirit for aid, protection, inspiration, or the like; an incantation.*

Incantation: *chanting or uttering words purporting to have magical power; to bewitch; to put a spell on.*

Magi: *the "wise men," who paid homage to the baby Jesus. A class of Zoroastrian priests in ancient Media and Persia believed to be astrologers.*

Magic: *the art of producing illusions by sleight of hand; using techniques such as incantation to exert control over* *the supernatural or the forces of nature. Magic is also called sorcery or witchcraft.*

Magician: *one who performs sleight of hand tricks or other illusions; a sorcerer, one skillful in performing magic.*

Medium: *a person through whom the spirits of the dead are alleged to be able to contact the living.*

Necromancy: *a method of divination through invocation of the dead; magic practiced by witch or sorcerer; a conjuration.*

Seer: *a person who sees or prophesies future events; a person with spiritual insight or knowledge to see the outcome before it occurs; a prophet; a person purported to have powers of divination through crystal gazing or reading tea grounds.*

Sorcery: *the practices of a person who is thought to have supernatural powers granted by evil spirits; black magic; witchery.*

Witch: *a person, esp. a woman, who professes or is believed to practice magic, esp. black magic; sorceress (warlock is a male witch).*

Witchcraft: *the art or practices of a witch; sorcery, magic; witchery.*

Witchery: *witchcraft; magic, magical influence; charm.*

Man has always been a superstitious creature. Since the days of Adam, people struggled to understand events and conditions. This led to the rise of astrology, magic, sorcery, and psychic phenomenon. And individuals began to develop skills in each of these fields.

The problem arose when people who worshiped the Creator were exposed to evil in the form of fallen angels. These evil angels introduced humans to astrology, black art, divination, fortune-telling, incantations, magic, necromancy, sorcery, and every kind of witchcraft. All of these things were intended to draw people away from their belief in God and a complete reliance on Him.

These evil entities caused mankind to worship nature, the earth, the sky, the moon and the stars, the sun, water, animals, and even kings and pharaohs. The people considered them gods. At one time, the Egyptians worshiped over 2,000 gods.

Supernatural events or incidents were explained as the will of the gods. Whenever a king or ruler encountered a mystery or challenging problem, they consulted their astrologers, magicians, seers, and sorcerers. (Many world leaders still do today.)

The astrologers would study the position of the stars and planets and attempt to explain the world and the future based on their belief in this practice. Before there were newspapers with the daily "horoscope," ancient rulers used astrologers to explain how their lives would be affected. Depending on the month they were born, the horoscope with its 12 different signs of the zodiac created a sense of supernatural knowledge. Astrology was designed to move the focus of people away from a single God and encourage them to worship something else—an idol or false god.

The prophets of the Bible condemned this practice and spoke out against it. Isaiah challenged the astrologers to save the Israelites from Babylon and judgment. He mocked them as a doctrine of demons. They failed to prove superiority over the God of Israel, and God proved all-powerful against them and their gods.

In my research, I found 17 references to "astrology" or "astrologer" in the Bible.

Astrology/Astrologer/Starry Hosts

2 Kings 17:16 – *"... bowed down to starry hosts ..."*

2 Kings 21:3 – *"... bowed down to starry hosts ..."*

2 Kings 23:5 – *"... burned incense to ... sun and moon, to the constellations and to all the starry hosts ..."*

2 Chronicles 33:4 – *"... built altars to all the starry hosts ..."*

Isaiah 45:12 – *"... marshaled their starry hosts ..."*

Isaiah 47:13 – *"... Let your astrologers come forward, those stargazers ..."*

Jeremiah 8:2 – *"... will be exposed to the sun and the moon and all the stars of the heavens ..."*

Jeremiah 19:13 – *"... and to all the starry hosts ..."*

Ezekiel 8:16 – *"... bowing down to the sun ..."*

Daniel 2:4 – *"... then the astrologers ..."*

Daniel 2:5 – *"... king replied to the astrologers ..."*

Daniel 2:10 – *"... astrologers answered the king ..."*

Daniel 4:7 – *"When the magicians, enchanters, astrologers and diviners came ..."*

Daniel 5:7 – *"The king called out for the enchanters, astrologers and diviners."*

Daniel 5:11 – *"... appointed him chief of the magicians, enchanters, astrologers and diviners ..."*

Zephaniah 1:5 – *"... bow down on the roofs to worship the starry host ..."*

Acts 7:42 – *"... gave them over to the worship of the heavenly bodies ..."*

I found the words "magic" or "magician" mentioned 20 times in the Bible.

Magic/Magician

Genesis 41:8 – *"... sent for all the magicians ..."*
Genesis 41:24 – *"... told this to the magicians ..."*
Exodus 7:11 – *"... Egyptian magicians also did the same things by their secret arts ..."*
Exodus 7:20 – *"... the Egyptian magicians did the same things by their secret arts ..."*
Exodus 8:7 – *"... magicians did the same things by their secret arts ..."*
Exodus 8:18 – *"... when the magicians tried to ..."*
Exodus 8:19 – *"... magicians said to Pharaoh ..."*
Exodus 9:11 – *"... magicians could not stand before Moses ..."*
Daniel 1:20 – *"... better than all the magicians and ..."*
Daniel 2:2 – *"... summoned the magicians ..."*
Daniel 2:10 – *"... ever asked such a thing of any magician ..."*
Daniel 2:27 – *"... no wise man, enchanter, magician or ..."*
Daniel 4:7 – *"... when the magicians, enchanters, astrologers and diviners came ..."*
Daniel 4:9 – *"... chief of the magicians ..."*
Daniel 5:11 – *"... appointed him chief of the magicians, enchanters, astrologers and diviners ..."*
Acts 8:11 – *"... amazed them for a long time with his magic ..."*
Revelation 18:23 – *"... by your magic spell ..."*
Revelation 21:8 – *"... who practice magic arts ..."*
Revelation 22:15 – *"... who practice magic arts ..."*

I found 23 references to "diviner" or "divination" in the Bible.

Divination

Genesis 30:27 – "... *have learned by divination that* ..."

Genesis 44:5 – "... *the cup my master drinks from and also uses for divination* ..."

Genesis 44:14 – "... *can find things out by divination* ..."

Leviticus 19:26 – "... *practice divination or* ..."

Numbers 22:7 – "... *taking with them the fee for divination* ..."

Numbers 23:23 – "... *no divination against* ..."

Deuteronomy 18:10 – "... *who practices divination* ..."

Deuteronomy 18:14 – "... *who practice sorcery or divination* ..."

Joshua 13:22 – "... *who practiced divination* ..."

1 Samuel 15:23 – "... *like the sin of divination* ..."

2 Kings 17:17 – "... *practiced divination* ..."

2 Kings 21:6 – "... *practiced sorcery and divination* ..."

2 Chronicles 33:6 – "... *practiced sorcery, divination and* ..."

Isaiah 44:25 – "... *makes fools of diviners* ..."

Jeremiah 27:8 – "... *do not listen to your prophets, your diviners, your* ..."

Ezekiel 13:23 – "... *no longer see false visions or practice divination* ..."

Daniel 2:27 – "... *no wise man, enchanter, magician or diviner* ..."

Daniel 4:7 – "... *when the magicians, enchanters, astrologers and diviners came* ..."

Daniel 5:7 – "... *called out for the enchanters, astrologers and diviners* ..."

Daniel 5:11 – "... *appointed him chief of the magicians, enchanters, astrologers and diviners* ..."

Micah 3:6 – *"... without divination ..."*
Micah 3:7 – *"... seers will be ashamed and the diviners disgraced ..."*

I found 13 references to "medium" or "mediums" in the Bible.

Medium/Mediums

Leviticus 19:31 – *"... turn to mediums or seek out ..."*
Leviticus 20:6 – *"... who is a medium or ..."*
Deuteronomy 18:10 – *"... who is a medium or spiritist ..."*
1 Samuel 28:3 – *"... expelled the mediums and spiritists ..."*
1 Samuel 28:7 – *"... woman who is a medium ..."*
1 Samuel 28:9 – *"... has cut off the mediums and spiritists from the land ..."*
1 Chronicles 10:13 – *"... consulted a medium ..."*
2 Chronicles 33:6 – *"... consulted mediums and spiritists ..."*
2 Kings 21:6 – *"... and consulted mediums and spiritists ..."*
2 Kings 23:24 – *"... got rid of mediums and spiritists ..."*
Isaiah 8:19 – *"... to consult mediums and spiritists ..."*
Isaiah 19:3 – *"... will consult the idols and the spirits of the dead, the mediums and the spiritists ..."*
Jeremiah 27:8 – *"... do not listen to your prophets, your diviners, your interpreters of dreams, your mediums ..."*

I found 11 references to "seer" or "seers" in the Bible.

Seer/Seers

1 Samuel 9:19 – *"... Samuel replied, 'I'm the seer.'"*
2 Samuel 15:27 – *"'Aren't you a seer?' the king asked Zadok the priest."*

2 Samuel 24:11 – *"... the Lord spoke His word to the prophet Gad, David's seer ..."*
2 Kings 17:13 – *"... through every kind of prophet and seer ..."*
1 Chronicles 9:22 – *"... David and the seer Samuel ..."*
1 Chronicles 29:29 – *"... in the records of the seer Samuel, the prophet Nathan, and the seer Gad ..."*
2 Chronicles 9:29 – *"... the seer's vision about Jeroboam ..."*
2 Chronicles 12:15 – *"... of the seer Iddo ..."*
2 Chronicles 29:30 – *"... with the words of David and the seer Asaph ..."*
Isaiah 30:10 - *"They say to the seers, 'Don't see the future.'"*
Micah 3:7 – *"... seers will be ashamed and the diviners disgraced ..."*

I found 51 references to "sorcerer" or "sorcery" in the Bible.

Sorcerer

Exodus 7:11 – *"... called the wise men and the sorcerers ..."*
Exodus 7:22 – *"... sorcery practiced by magicians ..."*
Exodus 8:7 – *"... sorcery practiced by magicians ..."*
Exodus 8:18 – *"... sorcery practiced by magicians ..."*
Leviticus 19:26-28 – *"... sorcery forbidden ..."*
Leviticus 19:31 – *"... sorcery forbidden ..."*
Deuteronomy 18:9-14 – *"... sorcery forbidden ..."*
Numbers 22:6 – *"... sorcery practiced by Balaam ..."*
Numbers 23:23 – *"... sorcery practiced by Balaam ..."*
2 Kings 9:22 – *"... sorcery practiced by Jezebel ..."*
Isaiah 8:19 – *"... sorcery denounced ..."*
Isaiah 19:3-11 – *"... sorcery practiced by Egyptians ..."*
Isaiah 19:12 – *"... sorcery practiced by Egyptians ..."*
Isaiah 57:3 – *"... near hither, ye sons of the sorceress ..."*

Isaiah 47:9-13 – "... *sorcery practiced by the Babylonians* ..."
Isaiah 47:9 – "... *for the multitude of their sorceries, and* ..."
Isaiah 47:12 – "... *and with the multitude of thy sorceries* ..."
Jeremiah 10:2 – "... *sorcery practiced by astrologers* ..."
Jeremiah 14:14 – "... *sorcery practiced by false prophets* ..."
Jeremiah 27:9 – "... *nor to your sorcerers, which speak unto* ..."
Jeremiah 27:9 – "... *sorcery practiced by false prophets* ..."
Ezekiel 12:23, 24 – "... *sorcery to cease* ..."
Ezekiel 13:6-9 – "... *sorcery practiced by false prophets* ..."
Ezekiel 13:22-28 – "... *sorcery practiced by false prophets* ..."
Ezekiel 13:23 – "... *sorcery to cease* ..."
Ezekiel 21:24 – "... *messages of false sorcery* ..."
Ezekiel 21:29 – "... *messages of false sorcery* ..."
Ezekiel 21:21, 22 – "... *sorcery practiced by the Babylonians* ..."
Daniel 2:2 – "... *and the sorcerers, and the Chaldeans, for* ..."
Daniel 2:10, 27 – "... *sorcery practiced by the Babylonians* ..."
Daniel 5:7 – "... *sorcery practiced by Belshazzar* ..."
Daniel 5:15 – "... *sorcery practiced by Belshazzar* ..."
Micah 3:6, 7 – "... *sorcery practiced by astrologers* ..."
Micah 5:12 – "... *sorcery to cease* ..."
Nahum 3:4, 5 – "... *sorcery practiced by the Ninevites* ..."
Zechariah 10:2 – "... *messages of false sorcery* ..."
Malachi 3:5 – "... *sorcery denounced* ..."
Malachi 3:5 – "... *be a swift witness against the sorcerers* ..."
Matthew 24:24 – "... *sorcery practiced by false prophets* ..."
Acts 8:9, 11 – "... *sorcery practiced by Simon Magus* ..."
Acts 8:11 – "... *he had bewitched them with sorceries* ..."
Acts 13:6 – "*There they met a Jewish sorcerer and false
    prophet named Bar-Jesus* ..."
Acts 13:8 - "*But Elymas the sorcerer (for that is what his
    name means) opposed them and tried to turn* ..."
Acts 16:16 – "... *sorcery practiced by the damsel at Philippi* ..."

Acts 19:13 – "... *sorcery practiced by vagabond Jews* ..."
Acts 19:14, 15 – "... *sorcery practiced by the sons of Sceva* ..."
2 Thessalonians 2:9 – "... *messages of false sorcery* ..."
Revelation 9:21 – "... *of their murders, nor of their sorceries* ..."
Revelation 18:23 – "... *by thy sorceries were all nations deceived* ..."
Revelation 21:8 – "... *and whoremongers, and sorcerers, and* ..."
Revelation 22:15 – "... *for without are dogs, and sorcerers, and* ..."

I found 4 references to "witch" or "witchcraft" in the Bible.

Witchcraft

1 Samuel 28:7 – "*Saul consulted the Witch of Endor* ..."
2 Kings 9:22 – "... *as long as all the idolatry and witchcraft of* ..."
Micah 5:12 – "... *will destroy your witchcraft* ..."
Naham 3:4 – "... *and peoples by her witchcraft* ..."

From the pharaoh relying on his magicians to duplicate or counter the actions of Moses and Aaron, to Daniel explaining the dream of King Nebuchadnezzar of Babylon when the king's own sorcerers and astrologers couldn't, to King Saul using the Witch of Endor to contact Samuel, the Bible is filled with stories about the interaction of mankind and the mystical.

In 1 Samuel 28 you can read about Saul, the Witch of Endor, and Samuel, the prophet. Samuel had died and was buried at Ramah (Ramathaim-Zophim) about 7 miles northwest of Jerusalem. Saul and his army were camped at Gilboa. He was facing a huge Philistine enemy force camped at Shunem. And Saul was afraid of the outcome of the battle to come.

Saul had banned mystic actions by mediums and spiritists, so he disguised himself and went to visit a mystic woman in the city of Endor . She was a medium who made an illegal living contacting "familiar spirits," who spoke. Some Bible commentators claim she never actually contacted spirits but used ventriloquism to imitate the voices of the dead. Other sources claim she worked with an evil spirit of Satan to deceive clients. This is the more plausible explanation. The "spirit" she contacted was likely an evil spirit imitating the deceased and deceiving her clients. Her clients never actually saw a spirit or apparition. They only heard the voice.

Saul told her to "bring up" the spirit of Samuel so he could consult with it. When she pretended to contact Samuel, she was surprised when Samuel actually appeared. This had never happened to her before.

When Samuel appeared out of the floor, the medium immediately recognized that this was not her familiar deceiving spirit. She was shocked and became frightened by what she saw. God showed His power to the medium and condemned King Saul at the same time.

As I read this report, I made several interesting observations: First, the apparition came up out of the earth. It did not come down from heaven. Second, the medium was genuinely surprised by the appearance. Something appeared before Saul, and it wasn't just a voice.

Samuel told Saul that he would die in battle with the Philistines. According to 1 Samuel 31:4, the next day Saul was in the Battle of Gilboa and the Israelites were losing.

As the Philistines were closing around him, he fell on his own sword rather than be taken alive. His body was hung on the outside city wall of Beth Shan about 17 miles south of the Sea of Galilee. Saul died just as Samuel had said. And Samuel was conjured up from the dead to the complete surprise of the medium who feigned her ability to do just this.

The strong message I took away from this part of my research is the weakness of these choices when people attempt to understand or control the future using fake and false prophets. In every case, people of God demonstrated powers superior to all those who relied on evil forces. Nowhere did I find an instance where evil defeated good (regardless how Hollywood tries to portray this). And Jesus was the undisputed champion over all the demons, deceivers, and evil forces trying to affect the people back then. He still is.

Ghosts in the Bible

When the disciples saw Him walking on the lake, they were terrified. "It's a ghost" they said.

MATTHEW 14:26

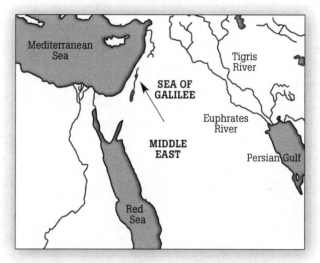

MATTHEW 14:25–27; LUKE 24:37–39
Location: Sea of Galilee and numerous other places
Historical Time: All time periods
TO VIEW MAPS ONLINE:
Copy this link into your browser and press Enter/Return
en.wikipedia.org/wiki/Sea_of_Galilee
emp.byui.edu/SATTERFIELDB/Galilee/default.htm
www.bible-history.com/geography/ancient-israel/sea-of-galilee.html

THE EXISTENCE OF GHOSTS HAS BEEN DEBATED FOR YEARS. People swear to have seen ghosts. Some say they are hallucinations. Others swear ghosts are evil spirits. What are ghosts and are they mentioned in the Bible?

According to Webster's dictionary, a ghost is "the soul of a dead person, a disembodied spirit imagined and wandering, often in vague or vaporous form, among the living and sometimes haunting them." It's also described as "the principle of life; the soul; or the spirit." And the expression "to give up the ghost" means "to die or to cease to function or exist."

When I searched the Bible, I found 18 places where the expression "gave up the ghost" was mentioned. This describes that moment when people died. Since God breathes the spirit of life into us, this spirit is exhaled or breathed out when we die.

Gave up the Ghost
(breathe out, die, or perish)

Gen 25:8 – *"... then Abraham gave up the ghost ..."*
Gen 25:17 – *"... and he gave up the ghost and died ..."*
Gen 35:29 – *"And Isaac gave up the ghost and died ..."*
Gen 49:33 – *"... and yielded up the ghost, and was ..."*
Job 3:11 – *"... why did I not give up the ghost when ..."*
Job 10:18 – *"Oh that I had given up the ghost ..."*
Job 11:20 – *"... shall be as the giving up of the ghost ..."*
Job 13:19 – *"... tongue, I shall give up the ghost ..."*
Job 14:10 – *"... yes, man giveth up the ghost, and ..."*
Jer 15:9 – *"... she hath given up the ghost, her sun ..."*
Lam 1:19 – *"... mine elders gave up the ghost in the ..."*
Matthew 27:50 – *"... yielded up the ghost ..."*
Mark 15:39 – *"... a loud voice, and gave up the ghost ..."*
Luke 23:46 – *"... said thus, he gave up the ghost ..."*
John 19:30 – *"... his head, and gave up the ghost ..."*
Acts 5:5 – *"... fell down, and gave up the ghost ..."*
Acts 5:10 – *"... at his feet and yielded up the ghost ..."*
Acts 12:23 – *"... of worms and gave up the ghost ..."*

And when I searched the Bible for the word "ghost," I found four places where this was mentioned. In the first three verses listed below, the observers thought they had seen an apparition, or ghost.

Ghost

1 Sam 28:7-20 – *"... a ghostly figure of an old man ..."*
Matthew 14:26 – *"'It's a ghost,' they said."*
Mark 6:48-50 – *"... thought he was a ghost ..."*
Luke 24:37-39 – *"... see; a ghost does not have ..."*

I found 90 places in the Bible where "Holy Ghost" was mentioned. The Holy Ghost is not the spirit of someone who is dead. The Holy Ghost or Holy Spirit is one of the three beings comprising the Triune God—Father, Son, and Holy Ghost. So the term refers to the Spirit of God—that being that exists simultaneously in three forms called Father, Son, and Holy Ghost (or Holy Spirit). The Holy Ghost is part of the spiritual realm, unseen but always present.

Holy Ghost

Matthew 1:18 – *"... found with child of the Holy Ghost ..."*
Matthew 1:20 – *"... in her is of the Holy Ghost ..."*
Matthew 3:11 – *"... with the Holy Ghost, and with fire ..."*
Matthew 12:31 – *"... blasphemy against the Holy Ghost ..."*
Matthew 12:32 – *"... speaketh against the Holy Ghost ..."*
Matthew 28:19 – *"... of the Son, and of the Holy Ghost ..."*
Mark 1:8 – *"... baptize you with the Holy Ghost ..."*
Mark 3:29 – *"... blaspheme against the Holy Ghost ..."*
Mark 12:36 – *"... himself said by the Holy Ghost ..."*
Mark 15:37 – *"... ye that speak, but the Holy Ghost ..."*

Luke 1:15 – "... *be filled with the Holy Ghost* ..."
Luke 1:35 – "... *Holy Ghost shall come upon thee* ..."
Luke 1:41 – "... *was filled with the Holy Ghost* ..."
Luke 1:67 – "... *was filled with the Holy Ghost* ..."
Luke 2:25 – "... *and the Holy Ghost was upon him* ..."
Luke 2:26 – "... *unto him by the Holy Ghost* ..."
Luke 3:16 – "... *baptize you with the Holy Ghost* ..."
Luke 3:22 – "... *and the Holy Ghost descended in* ..."
Luke 4:1 – "*Jesus being full of the Holy Ghost* ..."
Luke 12:10 – "... *against the Holy Ghost* ..."
Luke 12:12 – "... *for the Holy Ghost shall teach* ..."
John 1:33 – "... *baptizeth with the Holy Ghost* ..."
John 7:39 – "... *for the Holy Ghost was not yet* ..."
John 14:26 – "... *Holy Ghost whom the Father* ..."
John 20:22 – "*Receive ye the Holy Ghost* ..."
Acts 1:2 – "... *he through the Holy Ghost had* ..."
Acts 1:5 – "... *be baptized with the Holy Ghost* ..."
Acts 1:8 – "... *after that the Holy Ghost is come* ..."
Acts 1:16 – "... *which the Holy Ghost by the mouth* ..."
Acts 2:4 – "... *were all filled with the Holy Ghost* ..."
Acts 2:33 – "... *the promise of the Holy Ghost* ..."
Acts 2:38 – "... *receive the gift of the Holy Ghost* ..."
Acts 4:8 – "*Peter, filled with the Holy Ghost* ..."
Acts 4:31 – "... *were all filled with the Holy Ghost* ..."
Acts 5:3 – "... *to lie to the Holy Ghost, and to keep* ..."
Acts 5:32 – "... *and so is also the Holy Ghost* ..."
Acts 6:3 – "... *full of the Holy Ghost and wisdom* ..."
Acts 6:5 – "... *of faith and of the Holy Ghost* ..."
Acts 7:51 – "... *do always resist the Holy Ghost* ..."
Acts 7:55 – "... *he, being full of the Holy Ghost* ..."
Acts 8:15 – "... *they might receive the Holy Ghost* ..."
Acts 8:17 – "... *they received the Holy Ghost* ..."

Acts 8:18 – *"... Holy Ghost was given, he offered ..."*
Acts 8:19 – *"... he may receive the Holy Ghost ..."*
Acts 9:17 – *"... and be filled with the Holy Ghost ..."*
Acts 9:31 – *"... in the comfort of the Holy Ghost ..."*
Acts 10:38 – *"... the Holy Ghost and with power ..."*
Acts 10:44 – *"... the Holy Ghost fell on all of them ..."*
Acts 10:45 – *"... out the gift of the Holy Ghost ..."*
Acts 10:47 – *"... have received the Holy Ghost as ..."*
Acts 11:15 – *"... the Holy Ghost fell on them, as on ..."*
Acts 11:16 – *"... be baptized with the Holy Ghost ..."*
Acts 11:24 – *"... man, and full of the Holy Ghost ..."*
Acts 13:2 – *"... the Holy Ghost said. Separate me ..."*
Acts 13:4 – *"... being sent forth by the Holy Ghost ..."*
Acts 13:9 – *"Paul, filled with the Holy Ghost ..."*
Acts 13:52 – *"... with joy, and with the Holy Ghost ..."*
Acts 15:8 – *"... giving them the Holy Ghost, even ..."*
Acts 15:28 – *"... it seemed good to the Holy Ghost."*
Acts 16:6 – *"... were forbidden of the Holy Ghost."*
Acts 19:2 – *"Have ye received the Holy Ghost ..."*
Acts 19:2 – *"... whether there be any Holy Ghost ..."*
Acts 19:6 – *"... the Holy Ghost came on them; and ..."*
Acts 20:23 – *"... that the Holy Ghost witnesseth ..."*
Acts 20:28 – *"... Holy Ghost hath made you overseers ..."*
Acts 21:11 – *"Thus saith the Holy Ghost ..."*
Acts 28:25 – *"... spake the Holy Ghost by Esaias ..."*
Romans 5:5 – *"... by the Holy Ghost which is given ..."*
Romans 9:1 – *"... me witness in the Holy Ghost ..."*
Romans 14:17 – *"... peace, and joy in the Holy Ghost ..."*
Romans 15:13 – *"... the power of the Holy Ghost ..."*
Romans 15:16 – *"... being sanctified by the Holy Ghost ..."*
1 Corinthians 2:13 – *"... the Holy Ghost teacheth ..."*
1 Corinthians 6:19 – *"... the temple of the Holy Ghost ..."*

1 Corinthians 12:3 – *"... the Lord, but by the Holy Ghost ..."*
2 Corinthians 6:6 – *"... the Holy Ghost, by love unfeigned ..."*
2 Corinthians 13:14 – *"... the communion of the Holy Ghost ..."*
1 Thessalonians 1:5 – *"... in power, and in the Holy Ghost ..."*
1 Thessalonians 1:6 – *"... with joy of the Holy Ghost ..."*
2 Timothy 1:14 – *"... by the Holy Ghost which dwelleth ..."*
Titus 3:5 – *"... and renewing of the Holy Ghost ..."*
Hebrews 2:4 – *"... gifts of the Holy Ghost, according ..."*
Hebrews 3:7 – *"... as the Holy Ghost saith, 'Today if ...'"*
Hebrews 6:4 – *"... made partakers of the Holy Ghost ..."*
Hebrews 9:8 – *"... The Holy Ghost this signifying ..."*
Hebrews 10:15 – *"... Holy Ghost also is a witness to us ..."*
1 Pet er1:12 – *"... Holy Ghost sent down from heaven ..."*
2 Peter 1:21 – *"... were moved by the Holy Ghost ..."*
1 John 5:7 – *"... Holy Ghost; and these three are one ..."*
Jude 20 – *"... praying in the Holy Ghost ..."*

Although our ancient ancestors believed in ghosts, the Bible says that these apparitions are not spirits of the dead. The Bible says in 2 Corinthians 5:8 that after death, the spirit and soul go to heaven to be at home with the Lord.

When the disciples of Jesus saw someone walking on the surface of the Sea of Galilee, they thought it was a ghost. It was Jesus.

After Jesus rose from the dead, he appeared to his disciples while they were in a locked room. Once again, they thought they were seeing a ghost. They weren't. It was the resurrected Jesus.

During WWII my father had a paranormal experience during combat. He was a gunner on a Navy amphibious landing ship (LST) at Okinawa during 36 hours of intense attack by Japanese kamikaze fighters. It was the worst moments of war, and all the ships off this island were totally involved.

Suddenly, for my dad, the war with its loud sounds and violent explosions was suddenly gone—replaced by whiteness and calm. Directly before him, he saw his grandfather, a man he loved dearly, and who had died several years before the War. According to my dad, his grandfather told him he was going to be wounded, but he would survive and go home. Then the scene evaporated and Dad was instantly back in the chaos and cacophony of battle. Within a few seconds his gun mount was hit and blew up. He and a sailor feeding ammo into the gun were thrown up into the air with torn parts of the gun mount. They landed in a heap on the deck of the ship. After realizing they were both alive, they began laughing. They had been at General Quarters and constantly fighting the enemy for a day and a half, and they were exhausted. But they survived the hit and were alive. The ammo feeder had a piece of shrapnel pass through his wrist, but the wound barely bled. My father had pieces of steel shrapnel imbedded in this back and spent the next six hours on his stomach while medics pulled steel out of his back muscles. Other than numerous wounds like this, and bleeding eardrums, he was fine. He recovered and came home to enjoy 50 more years of family and friends before he graduated out of this life and went off to heaven to be with the grandfather he had seen that day at Okinawa.

So did he see a ghost? What did he see? Does God allow us to see and hear those who've gone on before? Can God talk to us? How do we know that what we see is holy and not evil? This incident with my dad certainly seems good, not evil. How did Mary and Joseph know they were visited by an angel and not by a demon? When people today see Mary the mother of Jesus, are these visions demonic? I suspect not, but God knows.

The Bible predicts that in the last days, demons will become ultra-active as they work overtime trying to distract Christians and other believers in God from total acceptance of God's plan of action. Many people *are* being distracted, and many are experiencing paranormal and psychic events. Often they lead others away from God without knowing what they are doing.

The Bible says that ghosts are actually demons posing as dead people. Their goal is to lure people away from belief in God. When people claim to communicate with ghosts or spirits of the dead, they are deceiving others or are actually communicating with demons and not dead relatives. When people trust a psychic more than God, they open themselves up to demon deception. Increasingly, people are living lives with one foot in the Bible and the other in the world of the paranormal.

The Bible tells us to judge anything supernatural by its fruit. If a being professes Jesus to be the Savior and God, it's probably legit. You can find instructions for testing the spirits in 1 John 4:1. It says, *"Every spirit that confesseth that Jesus Christ has come in the flesh is of God."* If it won't (or can't), it's evil and must be avoided. If a spirit, an ideology, or a person does not hold to the supremacy of God, beware.

Do ghosts exist? Spiritual beings, yes. Spirits of those who have died, no.

The Third
Heaven

*I know a man in Christ who 14 years ago
was caught up to the third heaven.*
2 CORINTHIANS 12:2

*We have a superior chief priest who
has gone through the heavens.*
HEBREWS 4:14

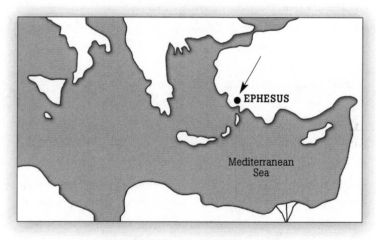

2 CORINTHIANS 12:1-11; HEBREWS 4:14
Location: 2 Corinthians was written while Paul was in Ephesus
Historical Time: ca – 57–65 AD
TO VIEW MAPS ONLINE:
Copy this link into your browser and press Enter/Return
en.wikipedia.org/wiki/Ephesus

WHEN PAUL MADE THE STATEMENT IN 2 CORINTHIANS
12:2 about a man he knew being caught up to the third
heaven, he was talking about himself. This statement
caused me to wonder and have great curiosity. I was

taught early in life that God created heaven and the earth. I understood that the earth is the sphere on which we live, but what was this "third heaven" Paul mentioned?

Through my research I learned that besides earth, there were three heavens created by God.

The first is the immediate atmosphere around earth—what we call "inner space." It's the sky that we see around us. This includes the clouds, the source of rainfall. Psalms 78:23 states, *"He commanded the clouds above, and opened the doors of heaven, and rained down manna on them to eat, and gave them grain from heaven."*

The second heaven is outer space—the starry heaven. It seems to extend staggering distances. This second heaven includes all the stars and planets in our solar system. Genesis 1:14 describes the creation of lights in the sky—the sun, moon, and the stars—the second heaven.

The highest heaven is the "third heaven"—the home of God. This is where the throne of God is found. It's beyond our sight. This is the place Jesus calls, "His Father's house"—a house of many mansions. It's been called "paradise" and the "heaven of heavens." It's where God, the holy angels, and the spirits of righteous humans dwell. This is where you will be when you are in the presence of God.

When Jesus ascended into heaven, He passed through the first and second heavens and went directly into the third heaven to sit next to His own Dad—God the Father Almighty.

Other Dimensions and the Unseen

*So we fix our eyes not on what is seen,
but on what is unseen. For what is seen is temporary,
but what is unseen is eternal.*

2 CORINTHIANS 4:18

*By faith we understand that the universe was
formed at God's command, so that what is seen
was not made out of what was visible.*

HEBREWS 11:3

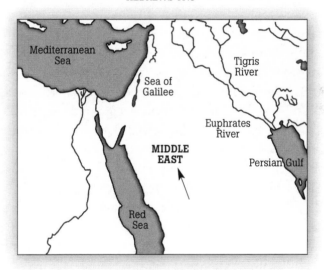

2 CORINTHIANS 4:18; HEBREWS 11:3
Location: multiple | **Historical Time:** ca 65 AD, 1270 AD
TO VIEW MAPS ONLINE:
Copy this link into your browser and press Enter/Return
espliego.files.wordpress.com/2008/03/middle-east-public-domain.jpg

BEFORE I COULD STUDY THE WORLD OF THE UNSEEN, I needed to first research the concept of multiple dimensions. To understand worlds of more than three dimensions (height, width, and depth), I looked and found the history of Nachmanides (1194-1270 AD), a medieval Jewish scholar born in Spain during the Middle Ages and the Crusades. He was both a physician and Torah scholar, and he was a leading rabbi, philosopher, and Bible commentator.

Nachmanides also had a strong mystical bent. His commentaries were the first to incorporate Jewish mysticism (kabbalah). His fascination and wonder about the supernatural side of the Torah (first five books of the Bible) led him to intensely study these writings. What he found in the early chapters of Genesis caused him to conclude that the universe has 10 dimensions. He said four dimensions were "knowable" and six were "unknowable."

His research and writings caused turmoil in the Jewish and Christian communities, and Nachmanides was exiled from Spain to Palestine. He lived the rest of his life in Jerusalem teaching about the mystical contents of the Old Testament. But he was onto something profound.

Since then scientists, physicists, and religious scholars had struggled to understand our universe and how we came to be what we are today. Many physicists look for rational laws defining the state of the universe, but they are gradually acknowledging that there is something incredible about our universe that suggests a supreme being, a God over all. When they cannot understand, they seek solutions in an ever-expanding set of possibilities. This enables mankind to make the next mental leap to a new level of understanding.

In 2009, the Templeton Foundation awarded one million pounds to a French physicist at the University of Paris-Sud for predicting the existence of a hypercosmic god existing outside our physical universe. Research projects on this and other dimensions have grown significantly.

It turns out science can now mathematically prove the existence of multiple dimensions. The first three are width, depth, and height. The Greek philosopher Euclid (330-275 BC) used these to develop *Euclidian* or *plane geometry*. This showed that the angles of a triangle always add up to 180 degrees, and the angles of a rectangle always add up to 360 degrees.

About this same time, the Ionian Greek philosopher and mathematician, Pythagoras of Samos, came up with his *Pythagorean Theorem* relating the sides of a triangle. Knowing the length of two sides, one can easily calculate the length of the third side.

Two thousand years later (1854) Georg Bernard Riemann (1826-1866), a brilliant mathematician and son of a poor Lutheran pastor in Germany, toppled the Euclidean world by showing mathematically that multiple dimensions beyond the first few were not only possible but highly likely. This became known as *field theory*. Reimann's work connected forces in the universe with the geometries of space.

Based on his field theory, Wilhelm Weber, Michael Faraday, and James Clark Maxwell were able to develop *electromagnetic theory* and move the world into new technologies and into the 20th century.

Then in 1905, Albert Einstein expanded on Euclidean geometry and built on Riemann's field theory to define the next dimension—time. Collectively, width, depth, height, and time were called the *space-time continuum*. They are what we can see or easily visualize.

Our understanding of the world is based on scientific method, a process of observing, modeling, testing, and verification through measurements and experiments. What about the world beyond the space-time continuum? What about other dimensions?

Here we enter the world of the spiritual, a world we cannot see directly. A spiritual realm exists that is invisible to human eyes. And it's populated by God, angels, sanctified ancestors, Satan, and evil angels, or demons.

In this world different and unique scientific laws apply, and time flows at a different speed. Studying this takes us into *tensor notation, string theory, singularity, space warp, quantum physics,* and *black holes*—subjects beyond the understanding of most readers. Multiple dimensions and the worlds of the unseen are becoming more understandable as mankind is given the knowledge. Often this is associated with and aided by the appearance of novels and science fiction motion pictures.

As I wrote this section, I immediately thought of an incredibly intelligent author, who addressed the subject of multiple dimensions and God. Clive Staples Lewis (1898-1963) wrote a number of books under the name C.S. Lewis, including *Chronicles of Narnia, The Screwtape Letters,* and *The Lion, the Witch, and the Wardrobe.* He was an academic, medievalist, Christian, lay theologian, novelist, and poet from Belfast, Ireland. He was a strong believer in God and his belief was subtly integrated into all of his writings.

In his *Chronicles of Narnia,* Lewis integrated the concept of Jesus (Aslan) into a world of Narnia with multiple dimensions and passageways into and out of portals. His books have been translated into dozens of languages and over 100 million copies have been sold. His Narnia books stand out among the most beloved classic children's books ever written.

It's said that C.S. Lewis and Sigmund Freud once met to debate Christianity versus atheism. Two weeks after this intense meeting, Freud committed suicide. C.S. Lewis was the man who coined the expression: "You don't have a soul. You are a soul. You have a body."

Scientists now believe there are at least 10 dimensions. (Some actually think there are as many as 26 dimensions.) Entities in each higher dimension can see everything in the lower dimensions, but those in the lower dimensions cannot see beings residing in a higher dimension. Thus we can have an all-knowing God residing in the 10th dimension, easily capable of affecting lives and conditions in lower dimensions (particularly the four dimensions in which we live). From a higher dimension, a being could make changes to people or conditions in a lower dimension.

Thus Elisha actually saw the supernatural warships surrounding the Arameans who were threatening Dothan, although this was unseen to the residents of Dothan and the servant of the prophet until Elisha prayed and enabled others to see this phenomenon as well.

And a hand of an unseen person actually materialized in front of an evil Babylonian king and his party guests, writing on the wall in front of him and predicting the demise of his Babylonian kingdom.

Recall the story of Joshua approaching Jericho. He suddenly saw the Commander of the army of the Lord in front of him holding a sword. This being was unseen before it appeared before Joshua there on the road to Jericho.

And then there's the story of the prophet Balaam riding his donkey on the path from Pethor to Moab. The donkey saw the Messenger of the Lord standing in the way. The Messenger was unseen to Balaam until the donkey spoke.

Entities such as spirits can exist in a higher dimension, completely unseen to those living in the confines of a lower dimension. Once we accept that the unseen actually exist, we can accept that the unseen spirit world controls what we see and feel.

Not only could entities such as angels and Messengers move from one dimension to another, those in higher dimensions could affect what happens in lower dimensions. Therefore, it's much easier to understand how fire could actually come down from another dimension to consume cities, altars, or people, how river and sea waters could be parted so people could cross on dry ground, how food could mysteriously appear, and how teleportation and levitation could actually occur. It's also easier to understand why Bigfoot has been seen but never captured. With knowledge of multiple dimensions, it's easy to see how miracles occurred (and still occur), how people are suddenly saved, how storms suddenly stop, and how raging seas suddenly calm. And we're getting a better glimpse of how prayer can affect outcomes.

The Watchers

*... and behold a watcher and
a holy one came down from heaven.*

DANIEL 4:13

*And whereas the king saw a watcher and a holy one, com-
ing down from heaven and saying, "Chop down the tree and
destroy it, but leave the stump of its roots in the earth, bound
with a band of iron and brass (bronze), in the tender grass of
the field, and let it be wet with the dew of heaven, and let
his portion be with the beasts of the field, till seven periods
of time pass over him."*

DANIEL 4:23

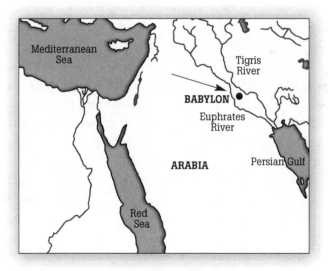

DANIEL 4:13, 4:17, 4:23
Location: Babylon | **Historical Time:** All time periods
TO VIEW MAPS ONLINE:
Copy this link into your browser and press Enter/Return
en.wikipedia.org/wiki/Arabian_Peninsula

WHO ARE THE WATCHERS? ARE THEY GOD'S GUARDIANS of earth? Before I can share what I learned about the *Watchers*, I need to explain *Apocrypha, Pseudepigrapha*, the *Book of Enoch,* and the *Dead Sea Scrolls*. These are all related.

Apocrypha refers to "secret writings" that were rejected for public reading because they were not accepted in either the Jewish Old Testament or in New Testament canons. The Apocrypha is a collection of writings considered uninspired. They were written over a period of 427 years (400 BC – 27 AD) or *Silent Years* when there weren't any prophets around to write words inspired by God.

The earliest Bible was called the *Septuagint*. It was written in Greek and includes the Apocrypha. The Catholic Vulgate Bible written by Jerome in Latin also contains the Apocrypha. The Apocryphal books include *Tobit, Judith, Wisdom of Solomon, Ecclesiasticus, Baruch,* and *1 and 2 Maccabees*.

Other writings of this period may not have actually been written by the author given credit for the work. These falsely attributed works are called *Pseudepigrapha*. The pseudepigraphic books include the *Book of Enoch,* the *Book of the Secrets of Enoch*, the *Book of Giants*, and the *Book of Jubilees*.

Pseudepigraphic works are Jewish and were written between 200 BC and 200 AD. Not all are literally pseudepigraphical. Some are written by a collection of authors in Arabic and were not accepted in the Jewish Tanach or the New Testament. Some appeared to belong in Biblical canons but were still called pseudepigrapha and placed outside the books of the Protestant and Catholic faiths because of their authorship.

One such writing is the Book of Enoch. It was written in Ethiopic script about 300 BC, but parts of it were later found at Qumran among the Dead Sea Scrolls written in Greek and in Aramaic.

This book is important in the history of Jewish mysticism. It describes visits by Enoch to various spirit realms including what's called "the seven heavens" where the angels dwelled, the 5th heaven where the Watchers reside, and up to the "highest" heaven, the throne of God. (The Bible only goes as far as the third heaven.) Enoch was also shown hell, where the wicked were punished.

The Book of Enoch is partitioned into Enoch 1 (chapters 1-36) called the Book of Watchers, and Enoch 2 describing Enoch's visit to heaven after he was made Scribe of God. It's said that he wrote about everything that happened in heaven and on earth. He filled 366 books. It's also said he gave these books to his sons.

In Enoch 1 the *Watchers* are described as special angels assigned to guard the earth and God's people. They had the ability to materialize in our world. The "unknowable" dimensions described by Nachmanides referred to the source of the Watchers. The 5th heaven described by Enoch may be the 5th dimension in Nachmanides' model.

According to Jewish tradition, 200 of these Watchers were sent to earth with specific instructions to serve as sentinels, but not to intermingle with humans. They appeared on Mount Hermon, source of the Jordan River ("place of the descent"), but were found weak and unable to resist the beauty of the women of earth. These beings took the daughters of man and mated with any woman they chose. (Hermon derives from the Hebrew word for curse—*harem*). The offspring of their sinful unions became monstrous giants known as the Nephilim. From the Nephilim came the Anakim and Rephaim tribes of giants.

The evil Watchers (called *Grigori* in Greek) were barred from returning to heaven, but because of their physical size and power, they were worshiped as gods by humans on earth. They could do anything they wanted. And what they wanted was to create chaos and spread evil all over the earth. Along the way they taught mankind how to make weapons of war, cosmetics, enchantments, sorcery, astrology, herbal enhancements, and the signs of the moon, stars, and sun. Based on this knowledge, evil spread everywhere.

The Watchers who remained in heaven and who were obedient to God are known as the *"holy men"* described in Daniel Chapter 4. In the three verses that specifically mention these beings, they were called *"watchers and holy men."* They were organized into a hierarchy of holy archangels that included Michael, Gabriel, Raphael, Uriel, Raguel, Saraqael, Remiel, and Auriel. Hundreds of thousands of other good angels exist to support these eight archangels.

In Enoch 1:6-36, the Watchers are the disobedient or fallen angels. In the Bible, the "sons of God" refer to the descendants of Seth. The "daughters of men" refer to the descendants of Cain. The evil fallen angels became so powerful God decided to rid the world of them through a great flood. So both good and evil watchers existed at the time of Noah and the Flood. Enoch was taken to heaven 669 years before Noah entered the Ark.

According to the Book of Enoch, the archangel Uriel was sent to tell Noah about the pending flood. Raphael was sent to bind the evil Watcher, Azazel, in the desert until judgment day when this evil Watcher will be cast into fire. Gabriel was sent to confuse the evil children of the fallen angels such that they would begin killing each other. Michael was sent to confine the leader and other evil

Watchers in the abyss—bound in "the valleys of the earth" until Judgment Day.

When the hybrid giants born of a Watcher and an earthly woman died, their spirits became demons that tormented mankind because they proceeded from them. Enoch 1 states that these spirits will be punished on Judgment Day. The Watchers are/were punished before and on Judgment Day. The 16th century French theologian Sinistrari wrote that there are beings that exist in a state between human and angels. He called them *demons*.

All of these descriptions were considered myths and just legends until 1947. Then 700 ancient Jewish manuscripts were discovered in 11 caves near Qumran, northwest of the Dead Sea. The manuscripts had been created in the same time period as the Apocrypha and Pseudepigrapha. Most were written in Hebrew with a lesser number written in Aramaic or Greek.

Among the astounding find were 11 fragments of the Book of Enoch written in Aramaic and discovered the next year (1948) in Cave 4. Parts of these fragments are from the Book of Watchers in the Book of Enoch. Manuscript dating showed that these fragments are from the third century BC (around 200-150 BC) around the time of the Maccabean revolt of 167 BC. Suddenly there is a renewed interest in studying Enoch and the Watchers.

In my research, I found another legend concerning a third type of Watcher—one who resides in dark places. These creatures have been described as *"shadow beings."* They are purported to hide in the shadows watching your every move. They are very dark beings—black dark. Their purpose is to spy on, distract, harass, or physically harm humans. These beings are thought to be evil. They too are part of the unseen.

You may see their dark shadows from the corner of your eyes. You may get creepy feelings in certain rooms or in some places where they lurk. You may sense evil and foreboding. And you may feel something brush against you when there is no one nearby. All of these are manifestations of the unseen. It's not your imagination! The unseen are real, and entities from other dimensions are coming into our world. They've been doing so for years. Some of them are good. Others are evil. That is why for each of us, God has assigned a protecting angel. And when need be, our angel can instantly get legions of other angels to keep evil from reaching you.

Most of the time, you will never know about or see the battles that occur in the unseen dimensions or in the skies above. Good and evil are at war constantly, and this war is about you and for you—for your soul. In the End Days all the evil in the universe will come forth for a final confrontation. God and His forces of good will fight the forces of the dark side, the forces of evil. This battle will be worse than all the wars fought in history. Armies of millions will clash. God will win.

And then all of this will be over. The battle will be won. Good will triumph over evil, and all the bad beings, angels, monsters, and demons will be destroyed. From that moment on you'll enjoy peace and comfort in the presence of the Almighty. You'll also be with all those you love and miss. It will be a great life—a great life indeed.

Summary

THIS HAS BEEN AN IN-DEPTH LOOK INTO THE BIBLE'S description of God's power over the paranormal. In this chapter you read about giants and dragons and dinosaurs. You read about Behemoth, the land monster, and Leviathan, the sea monster. You found that astrologers, ghosts, magicians, psychics, seers, and sorcerers are real and are described in the Bible. And you read about other heavens and dimensions in our universe. Finally you read about the Watchers and the unseen. You've learned that God has entities near you, protecting you and nudging you to follow His rules—not those of the evil ones. You have the armor of God around you. Now you're prepared to move forward in your search for truth and reality.

Relevant Verses
in Chapter Eight

Incidents Involving
Other Paranormal Powers

ASTROLOGY: Astrologers –
bowed down to starry hosts
Verse: 2 Kings 17:16

ASTROLOGY: Astrologers –
bowed down to starry hosts
Verse: 2 Kings 21:3

ASTROLOGY: Astrologers –
burned incense to ... sun and
moon, to the constellations
and to all the starry hosts.
Verse: 2 Kings 23:5

ASTROLOGY: Astrologers –
built altars to all the starry hosts
Verse: 2 Chron 33:4

ASTROLOGY: Astrologers –
marshaled their starry hosts
Verse: Isaiah 45:12

ASTROLOGY: Astrologers –
Let your astrologers come
forward, those stargazers
Verse: Isaiah 47:13

ASTROLOGY: Astrologers –
will be exposed to the sun
and the moon and all the
stars of the heavens
Verse: Jeremiah 8:2

ASTROLOGY: Astrologers –
and to all the starry hosts
Verse: Jeremiah 19:13

ASTROLOGY: Astrologers –
bowing down to the sun
Verse: Ezekiel 8:16

ASTROLOGY: Astrologers –
then the astrologers
Verse: Daniel 2:4

ASTROLOGY: Astrologers –
king replied to the astrologers
Verse: Daniel 2:5

ASTROLOGY: Astrologers –
astrologers answered the king
Verse: Daniel 2:10

ASTROLOGY: Astrologers –
When the magicians,
enchanters, astrologers
and diviners came
Verse: Daniel 4:7

ASTROLOGY: Astrologers –
The king called out for the
enchanters, astrologers and
diviners.
Verse: Daniel 5:7

ASTROLOGY: Astrologers –
appointed him chief of the
magicians, enchanters,
astrologers and diviners
Verse: Daniel 5:11

ASTROLOGY: Astrologers –
bow down on the roofs to

worship the starry host
Verse: Zephaniah 1:5

ASTROLOGY: Astrologers –
gave them over to the worship
of the heavenly bodies
Verse: Acts 7:42

BEHEMOTH: Land Monster
Location: Northeast Arabia
in Uz
Verses: Job 40:1–24
Verse confirms presence of
Behemoth, a terrifying land
creature.

DEVIL AND MOSES: Archangel
Michael Argues with the Devil
over the Body of Moses
Location: Mount Nebo at top
of Pisgah
Verses: Jude 9
The archangel Michael argued
with the devil over the body
of Moses. Satan never got
the body of Moses, and Moses
later appeared in bodily
form with Elijah at the
transfiguration of Jesus.

DIVINATION: Diviners – have
learned by divination that
Verse: Genesis 30:27

DIVINATION: Diviners – the cup
my master drinks from and
also uses for divination
Verse: Genesis 44:5

DIVINATION: Diviners – can find
things out by divination
Verse: Genesis 44:14

DIVINATION: Diviners –
practice divination or
Verse: Leviticus 19:26

DIVINATION: Diviners –
taking with them the fee
for divination
Verse: Numbers 22:7

DIVINATION: Diviners –
no divination against
Verse: Numbers 23:23

DIVINATION: Diviners –
who practices divination
Verse: Deuteronomy 18:10

DIVINATION: Diviners – who
practice sorcery or divination
Verse: Deuteronomy 18:14

DIVINATION: Diviners –
who practiced divination
Verse: Joshua 13:22

DIVINATION: Diviners –
like the sin of divination
Verse: 1 Samuel 15:23

DIVINATION: Diviners –
practiced divination
Verse: 2 Kings 17:17

DIVINATION: Diviners –
practiced sorcery and
divination
Verse: 2 Kings 21:6

DIVINATION: Diviners –
practiced sorcery,
divination and
Verse: 2 Chronicles 33:6

DIVINATION: Diviners –
makes fools of diviners
Verse: Isaiah 44:25

DIVINATION: Diviners –
Do not listen to your prophets,
your diviners, your
Verse: Jeremiah 27:8

– 475 –

DIVINATION: Diviners –
no longer see false visions
or practice divination
Verse: Ezekiel 13:23

DIVINATION: Diviners – no wise
man, enchanter, magician
or diviner
Verse: Daniel 2:27

DIVINATION: Diviners – when
the magicians, enchanters,
astrologers and diviners came
Verse: Daniel 4:7

DIVINATION: Diviners –
called out for the enchanters,
astrologers and diviners
Verse: Daniel 5:7

DIVINATION: Diviners –
appointed him chief of the
magicians, enchanters,
astrologers and diviners
Verse: Daniel 5:11

DIVINATION: Diviners –
without divination
Verse: Micah 3:6

DIVINATION: Diviners –
seers will be ashamed and
the diviners disgraced
Verse: Micah 3:7

DRAGONS: Dragons Were
Common
Location: Babylon
Verses: Jeremiah 51:34, 37
The prophet Jeremiah mentions dragons as common in
the Middle East and Babylon.

DRAGONS: A Dwelling Place
for Dragons
Location: between Ananiah
and Ramah in northwest
Arabian desert
Verse: Jeremiah 49:33
Hazor will be desolate and a
dwelling place for dragons.

DRAGONS: By the Dragon Well
Location: Jerusalem
Verse: Nehemiah 2:13
Nehemiah goes out by the
"dragon well" near Jerusalem.

FALLEN ANGELS: Fallen Angels
– Angels who left their proper
position are kept in eternal
chains until Judgment Day.
Verses: Jude 6

FALLEN ANGELS: Fallen Angels
– God bound the angels who
sinned in eternal chains until
Judgment Day.
Verse: 2 Peter 2:4

GHOST: Gave up the Ghost –
then Abraham gave up
the ghost
Verse: Genesis 25:8

GHOST: Gave up the Ghost – and
he gave up the ghost and died
Verse: Genesis 25:17

GHOST: Gave up the Ghost –
And Isaac gave up the ghost
and died
Verse: Genesis 35:29

GHOST: Gave up the Ghost – and
yielded up the ghost, and was
Verse: Genesis 49:33

GHOST: Gave up the Ghost –
why did I not give up the
ghost when
Verse: Job 3:11

GHOST: Gave up the Ghost – Oh that I had given up the ghost
Verse: Job 10:18

GHOST: Gave up the Ghost – shall be as the giving up of the ghost
Verse: Job 11:20

GHOST: Gave up the Ghost – tongue, I shall give up the ghost
Verse: Job 13:19

GHOST: Gave up the Ghost – yes, man giveth up the ghost, and
Verse: Job 14:10

GHOST: Gave up the Ghost – she hath given up the ghost, her sun
Verse: Jeremiah 15:9

GHOST: Gave up the Ghost – mine elders gave up the ghost in the
Verse: Lamentations 1:19

GHOST: Gave up the Ghost – yielded up the ghost
Verse: Matthew 27:50

GHOST: Gave up the Ghost – a loud voice, and gave up the ghost
Verse: Mark 15:39

GHOST: Gave up the Ghost – said thus, he gave up the ghost
Verse: Luke 23:46

GHOST: Gave up the Ghost – his head, and gave up the ghost
Verse: John 19:30

GHOST: Gave up the Ghost – fell down, and gave up the ghost
Verse: Acts 5:5

GHOST: Gave up the Ghost – at his feet and yielded up the ghost
Verse: Acts 5:10

GHOST: Gave up the Ghost – of worms and gave up the ghost
Verse: Acts 12:23

GHOST: Ghost – a ghostly figure of an old man
Verses: 1 Samuel 28:7–20

GHOST: Ghost – "It's a ghost," they said
Verse: Matthew 14:26

GHOST: Ghost – thought he was a ghost
Verses: Mark 6:48–50

GHOST: Ghost – see; a ghost does not have
Verses: Luke 24:37–39

GHOST: Holy Ghost – found with child of the Holy Ghost
Verse: Matthew 1:18

GHOST: Holy Ghost – in her is of the Holy Ghost
Verse: Matthew 1:20

GHOST: Holy Ghost – with the Holy Ghost, and with fire
Verse: Matthew 3:11

GHOST: Holy Ghost – blasphemy against the Holy Ghost
Verse: Matthew 12:31

GHOST: Holy Ghost – speaketh against the Holy Ghost
Verse: Matthew 12:32

GHOST: Holy Ghost – of the Son, and of the Holy Ghost
Verse: Matthew 28:19

GHOST: Holy Ghost – baptize you with the Holy Ghost
Verse: Mark 1:8

GHOST: Holy Ghost – blaspheme against the Holy Ghost
Verse: Mark 3:29

GHOST: Holy Ghost – himself said by the Holy Ghost
Verse: Mark 12:36

GHOST: Holy Ghost – ye that speak, but the Holy Ghost
Verse: Mark 15:37

GHOST: Holy Ghost – be filled with the Holy Ghost
Verse: Luke 1:15

GHOST: Holy Ghost – Holy Ghost shall come upon thee
Verse: Luke 1:35

GHOST: Holy Ghost – was filled with the Holy Ghost
Verse: Luke 1:41

GHOST: Holy Ghost – was filled with the Holy Ghost
Verse: Luke 1:67

GHOST: Holy Ghost – and the Holy Ghost was upon him
Verse: Luke 2:25

GHOST: Holy Ghost – unto him by the Holy Ghost
Verse: Luke 2:26

GHOST: Holy Ghost – baptize you with the Holy Ghost
Verse: Luke 3:16

GHOST: Holy Ghost – and the Holy Ghost descended in
Verse: Luke 3:22

GHOST: Holy Ghost – Jesus being full of the Holy Ghost
Verse: Luke 4:1

GHOST: Holy Ghost – against the Holy Ghost
Verse: Luke 12:10

GHOST: Holy Ghost – for the Holy Ghost shall teach
Verse: Luke 12:12

GHOST: Holy Ghost – baptizeth with the Holy Ghost
Verse: John 1:33

GHOST: Holy Ghost – for the Holy Ghost was not yet
Verse: John 7:39

GHOST: Holy Ghost – Holy Ghost whom the Father
Verse: John 14:26

GHOST: Holy Ghost – Receive ye the Holy Ghost
Verse: John 20:22

GHOST: Holy Ghost – he through the Holy Ghost had
Verse: Acts 1:2

GHOST: Holy Ghost – be baptized with the Holy Ghost
Verse: Acts 1:5

GHOST: Holy Ghost – after that the Holy Ghost is come
Verse: Acts 1:8

GHOST: Holy Ghost – which the Holy Ghost by the mouth
Verse: Acts 1:16

GHOST: Holy Ghost – were all filled with the Holy Ghost
Verse: Acts 2:4

GHOST: Holy Ghost – the promise of the Holy Ghost
Verse: Acts 2:33

GHOST: Holy Ghost – receive the gift of the Holy Ghost
Verse: Acts 2:38

GHOST: Holy Ghost – Peter, filled with the Holy Ghost
Verse: Acts 4:8

GHOST: Holy Ghost – were all filled with the Holy Ghost
Verse: Acts 4:31

GHOST: Holy Ghost – to lie to the Holy Ghost, and to keep
Verse: Acts 5:3

GHOST: Holy Ghost – and so is also the Holy Ghost
Verse: Acts 5:32

GHOST: Holy Ghost – full of the Holy Ghost and wisdom
Verse: Acts 6:3

GHOST: Holy Ghost – of faith and of the Holy Ghost
Verse: Acts 6:5

GHOST: Holy Ghost – do always resist the Holy Ghost
Verse: Acts 7:51

GHOST: Holy Ghost – he, being full of the Holy Ghost
Verse: Acts 7:55

GHOST: Holy Ghost – they might receive the Holy Ghost
Verse: Acts 8:15

GHOST: Holy Ghost – they received the Holy Ghost
Verse: Acts 8:17

GHOST: Holy Ghost – Holy Ghost was given, he offered
Verse: Acts 8:18

GHOST: Holy Ghost – he may receive the Holy Ghost
Verse: Acts 8:19

GHOST: Holy Ghost – and be filled with the Holy Ghost
Verse: Acts 9:17

GHOST: Holy Ghost – in the comfort of the Holy Ghost
Verse: Acts 9:31

GHOST: Holy Ghost – the Holy Ghost and with power
Verse: Acts 10:38

GHOST: Holy Ghost – the Holy Ghost fell on all of them
Verse: Acts 10:44

GHOST: Holy Ghost – out the gift of the Holy Ghost
Verse: Acts 10:45

GHOST: Holy Ghost – have received the Holy Ghost as
Verse: Acts 10:47

GHOST: Holy Ghost – the Holy Ghost fell on them, as on
Verse: Acts 11:15

GHOST: Holy Ghost – be baptized with the Holy Ghost
Verse: Acts 11:16

GHOST: Holy Ghost – man, and full of the Holy Ghost
Verse: Acts 11:24

GHOST: Holy Ghost – the Holy Ghost said. Separate me
Verse: Acts 13:2

GHOST: Holy Ghost – being sent forth by the Holy Ghost
Verse: Acts 13:4

GHOST: Holy Ghost – Paul, filled with the Holy Ghost
Verse: Acts 13:9

GHOST: Holy Ghost – with joy, and with the Holy Ghost
Verse: Acts 13:52

GHOST: Holy Ghost – giving them the Holy Ghost, even
Verse: Acts 15:8

GHOST: Holy Ghost – it seemed good to the Holy Ghost
Verse: Acts 15:28

GHOST: Holy Ghost – were forbidden of the Holy Ghost
Verse: Acts 16:6

GHOST: Holy Ghost – Have ye received the Holy Ghost
Verse: Acts 19:2

GHOST: Holy Ghost – whether there be any Holy Ghost
Verse: Acts 19:2

GHOST: Holy Ghost – the Holy Ghost came on them; and
Verse: Acts 19:6

GHOST: Holy Ghost – that the Holy Ghost witnesseth
Verse: Acts 20:23

GHOST: Holy Ghost – Holy Ghost hath made you overseers
Verse: Acts 20:28

GHOST: Holy Ghost – Thus saith the Holy Ghost
Verse: Acts 21:11

GHOST: Holy Ghost – spake the Holy Ghost by Esaias
Verse: Acts 28:25

GHOST: Holy Ghost – by the Holy Ghost which is given
Verse: Romans 5:5

GHOST: Holy Ghost – me witness in the Holy Ghost
Verse: Romans 9:1

GHOST: Holy Ghost – peace, and joy in the Holy Ghost
Verse: Romans 14:17

GHOST: Holy Ghost – the power of the Holy Ghost
Verse: Romans 15:13

GHOST: Holy Ghost – being sanctified by the Holy Ghost
Verse: Romans 15:16

GHOST: Holy Ghost – the Holy Ghost teacheth
Verse: Corinthians 2:13

GHOST: Holy Ghost – the temple of the Holy Ghost
Verse: Corinthians 6:19

GHOST: Holy Ghost – the Lord, but by the Holy Ghost
Verse: Corinthians 12:3

GHOST: Holy Ghost – the Holy Ghost, by love unfeigned
Verse: 2 Corinthians 6:6

GHOST: Holy Ghost – the communion of the Holy Ghost
Verse: 2 Corinthians 13:14

GHOST: Holy Ghost – in power, and in the Holy Ghost
Verse: 1 Thessalonians 1:5

GHOST: Holy Ghost – with joy of the Holy Ghost
Verse: 1 Thessalonians 1:6

GHOST: Holy Ghost – by the Holy Ghost which dwelleth
Verse: 2 Timothy 1:14

GHOST: Holy Ghost – and renewing of the Holy Ghost
Verse: Titus 3:5

GHOST: Holy Ghost – gifts of the Holy Ghost, according
Verse: Hebrews 2:4

GHOST: Holy Ghost – as the Holy Ghost saith, Today if
Verse: Hebrews 3:7

GHOST: Holy Ghost – made partakers of the Holy Ghost
Verse: Hebrews 6:4

GHOST: Holy Ghost – The Holy Ghost this signifying
Verse: Hebrews 9:8

GHOST: Holy Ghost – Holy Ghost also is a witness to us
Verse: Hebrews 10:15

GHOST: Holy Ghost – Holy Ghost sent down from heaven
Verse: 1 Peter 1:12

GHOST: Holy Ghost – were moved by the Holy Ghost
Verse: 2 Peter 1:21

GHOST: Holy Ghost – Holy Ghost; and these three are one
Verse: 1 John 5:7

GHOST: Holy Ghost – praying in the Holy Ghost
Verses: Jude 20

GIANTS: Giants Appear on Earth
Location: Fertile Crescent
Verse: Genesis 6:4
Sons of God (fallen angels) took any earthly woman they found appealing and produced giant children. These children were giants called Nephilim (Naptha–eem = "giant").

GIANT: Giant Uses Bed over 13 Feet Long
Location: Ashtaroth in Bashan
Verse: Deuteronomy 3:15
Moses and the Israelites are moving against the king of Bashan who ruled in Ashtaroth east of the Jordan River in Moab. All of the cities of Bashan were taken and the people destroyed. Only King Og of Bashan was left. He was a giant man who slept on an iron bed over 13–1/2 feet long.

GIANTS: Giants Frighten Spies
Location: from Desert of Paran through the Negev up to Canaan
Verses: Numbers 13:21–31
Twelve Israelite spies were sent into the "Land of Giants" in Canaan. The men there were the size of Nephilim, descendants of Anak, and made the Israelite spies feel small like grasshoppers.

GIANTS: Goliath Killed by David
Verses: I Samuel 17:1; 1 Samuel 17:4
Giant Goliath was believed to be 9' 6" tall. (The place where the Philistines camped when David fought Goliath is now called modern–day Beit Fased)

GIANTS: Six Fingers Six Toes – David's brother, Jonathan, killed a giant with six fingers on each hand and six toes on each foot. The giant was a descendent of Haraphah, Goliath's father, who lived in Gath
Verse: 1 Chron 20:6

GIANTS: Giant Lahmi is Killed – Goliath's brother, Lahmi, was killed by Elharan.
Verse: 1 Chronicles 20:5

GIANTS: Abisha Kills 300 – Giant Abishai killed 300 men
Verses: 2 Samuel 23:18; 1 Chronicles 11:11, 20, 22

GIANTS: Benaiah Kills Lion – Giant Benaiah kills lion in pit
Verses: 2 Samuel 23:20; 1 Chronicles 11:11, 20, 22

GIANTS: JosHebrews Kills 800 Enemy – Giant JosHebrews uses a spear to kill 800 men
Verses: 2 Samuel 23:8; 1 Chronicles 11:11, 20, 22

HEAVENS: Passing through Heavens – "We have a superior chief priest who has gone through the heavens."
Verse: Hebrews 4:14

LEVIATHAN: Sea Monster
Location: Mediterranean Sea
Verses: Job 41:1; Psalm 74:13
Verse confirms presence of Leviathan, a terrifying sea creature.

MAGICIANS/SEERS/SORCER-ERS: Magicians, Psychics, Sorcerers, and Astrologers Couldn't Interpret Dreams
Location: Babylon
Verses: Daniel 2
King Nebuchadnezzar of Babylon had dream and couldn't explain it. Called for help, only Daniel could explain vision of the future.

MAGICIANS/SEERS/ SORCERERS: Magicians, Psychics, Sorcerers, and Astrologers Couldn't Interpret Dreams
Location: Babylon
Verses: Daniel 2
King Nebuchadnezzar of Babylon had dream and couldn't explain it. Called for help, only Daniel could explain vision of the future.

MAGICIANS/SEERS/ SORCERERS: Magicians and Wise Men – "In the morning he was so upset that he sent for all the magicians and wise men of Egypt."
Verse: Genesis 41:8

MAGICIANS: Magicians – sent for all the magicians
Verse: Genesis 41:8

MAGICIANS: Magicians – told this to the magicians
Verse: Genesis 41:24

MAGICIANS: Magicians – Egyptian magicians also did the same things by their secret arts
Verse: Exodus 7:11

MAGICIANS: Magicians –
the Egyptian magicians did
the same things by their
secret arts
Verse: Exodus 7:20

MAGICIANS: Magicians –
magicians did the same
things by their secret arts
Verse: Exodus 8:7

MAGICIANS: Magicians –
when the magicians tried to
produce ... they could not
Verse: Exodus 8:18

MAGICIANS: Magicians –
magicians said to Pharaoh
Exodus 8:19

MAGICIANS: Magicians –
magicians could not stand
before Moses
Verse: Exodus 9:11

MAGICIANS: Magicians – better
than all the magicians and
Verse: Daniel 1:20

MAGICIANS: Magicians – One
who claims to understand and
explain mysteries by magic.
Verse: Daniel 1:20

MAGICIANS: Magicians –
summoned the magicians
Verse: Daniel 2:2

MAGICIANS: Magicians –
ever asked such a thing of
any magician
Verse: Daniel 2:10

MAGICIANS: Magicians –
no wise man, enchanter,
magician or
Verse: Daniel 2:27

MAGICIANS: Magicians – when
the magicians, enchanters,
astrologers and diviners came
Verse: Daniel 4:7

MAGICIANS: Magicians –
chief of the magicians
Daniel 4:9

MAGICIANS: Magicians –
appointed him chief of
the magicians, enchanters,
astrologers and diviners
Daniel 5:11

MAGICIANS: Magicians –
amazed them for a long
time with his magic
Verse: Acts 8:11

MAGICIANS: Magicians –
by your magic spell
Verse: Revelation 18:23

MAGICIANS: Magicians –
who practice magic arts
Verse: Revelation 21:8

MAGICIANS: Magicians –
who practice magic arts
Verse: Revelation 22:15

MEDIUMS: Medium – turn to
mediums or seek out
Verse: Leviticus 19:31)

MEDIUMS: Medium – who is
a medium or ...
Verse: Leviticus 20:6

MEDIUMS: Medium – who is
a medium or spiritist
Verse: Deuteronomy 18:10

MEDIUMS: Medium – expelled
the mediums and spiritists
Verse: 1 Samuel 28:3

MEDIUMS: Medium – woman who is a medium
Verse: 1 Samuel 28:7

MEDIUMS: Medium – has cut off the mediums and spiritists from the land
Verse: 1 Samuel 28:9

MEDIUMS: Medium – consulted a medium
Verse: 1 Chronicles 10:13

MEDIUMS: Medium – consulted mediums and spiritists
Verse: 2 Chronicles 33:6

MEDIUMS: Medium – and consulted mediums and spiritists
Verse: 2 Kings 21:6

MEDIUMS: Medium – got rid of mediums and spiritists
Verse: 2 Kings 23:24

MEDIUMS: Medium – to consult mediums and spiritists
Verse: Isaiah 8:19

MEDIUMS: Medium – will consult the idols and the spirits of the dead, the mediums and the spiritists
Verse: Isaiah 19:3

MEDIUMS: Medium – do not listen to your prophets, your diviners, your interpreters of dreams, your mediums or
Verse: Jeremiah 27:8

SEERS: Seer – Samuel replied, "I'm the seer."
Verse: 1 Samuel 9:19

SEERS: Seer – "Aren't you a seer?" the king asked Zadok the priest.
Verse: 2 Samuel 15:27

SEERS: Seer – the Lord spoke His word to the prophet Gad, David's seer
Verse: 2 Samuel 24:11

SEERS: Seer – through every kind of prophet and seer
Verse: 2 Kings 17:13

SEERS: Seer – David and the seer Samuel
Verse: 1 Chronicles 9:22

SEERS: Seer – in the records of the seer Samuel, the prophet Nathan, and the seer Gad
Verse: 1 Chronicles 29:29

SEERS: Seer – the seer's vision about Jeroboam
Verse: 2 Chronicles 9:29

SEERS: Seer – of the seer Iddo
Verse: 2 Chronicles 12:15

SEERS: Seer – with the words of David and the seer Asaph
Verse: 2 Chronicles 29:30

SEERS: Seer – say to the seers, "Don't see the future."
Verse: Isaiah 30:10

SEERS: Seer – seers will be ashamed and the diviners disgraced
Verse: Micah 3:7

SORCERER: Sorcery – called the wise men and the sorcerers
Verse: Exodus 7:11

SORCERER: Sorcery – sorcery practiced by magicians
Verse: Exodus 7:22

SORCERER: Sorcery – sorcery practiced by magicians
Verse: Exodus 8:7

SORCERER: Sorcery – sorcery practiced by magicians
Verse: Exodus 8:18

SORCERER: Sorcery – sorcery forbidden
Verse: Leviticus 19:26–28

SORCERER: Sorcery – sorcery forbidden
Verse: Leviticus 19:31

SORCERER: Sorcery – sorcery forbidden
Verse: Deuteronomy 18:9–14

SORCERER: Sorcery – sorcery practiced by Balaam
Verse: Numbers 22:6

SORCERER: Sorcery – sorcery practiced by Balaam
Verse: Numbers 23:23

SORCERER: Sorcery – sorcery practiced by Jezebel
Verse: 2 Kings 9:22

SORCERER: Sorcery – sorcery denounced
Verse: Isaiah 8:19

SORCERER: Sorcery – practiced by Egyptians
Verse: Isaiah 19:3–11

SORCERER: Sorcery – practiced by Egyptians
Verse: Isaiah 19:12

SORCERER: Sorcery – near hither, ye sons of the sorceress
Verse: Isaiah 57:3

SORCERER: Sorcery – sorcery practiced by the Babylonians
Verse: Isaiah 47:9–13

SORCERER: Sorcery – for the multitude of their sorceries, and
Verse: Isaiah 47:9

SORCERER: Sorcery – and with the multitude of thy sorceries
Verse: Isaiah 47:12

SORCERER: Sorcery – sorcery practiced by astrologers
Verse: Jeremiah 10:2

SORCERER: Sorcery – sorcery practiced by false prophets
Verse: Jeremiah 14:14

SORCERER: Sorcery – nor to your sorcerers, which speak unto
Verse: Jeremiah 27:9

SORCERER: Sorcery – sorcery practiced by false prophets
Verse: Jeremiah 27:9

SORCERER: Sorcery – sorcery to cease
Verse: Ezekiel 12:23, 24

SORCERER: Sorcery – sorcery practiced by false prophets
Verse: Ezekiel 13:6–9

SORCERER: Sorcery – sorcery practiced by false prophets
Verse: Ezekiel 13:22–28

SORCERER: Sorcery – sorcery to cease
Verse: Ezekiel 13:23

SORCERER: Sorcery – messages of false sorcery
Verse: Ezekiel 21:24

SORCERER: Sorcery – messages of false sorcery
Verse: Ezekiel 21:29

SORCERER: Sorcery – sorcery practiced by the Babylonians
Verse: Ezekiel 21:21, 22

SORCERER: Sorcery – and the sorcerers, and the Chaldeans, for
Verse: Daniel 2:2

SORCERER: Sorcery – sorcery practiced by the Babylonians
Verse: Daniel 2:10, 27

SORCERER: Sorcery – sorcery practiced by Belshazzar
Verse: Daniel 5:7

SORCERER: Sorcery – sorcery practiced by Belshazzar
Verse: Daniel 5:15

SORCERER: Sorcery – sorcery practiced by astrologers
Verse: Micah 3:6, 7

SORCERER: Sorcery – sorcery to cease
Verse: Micah 5:12

SORCERER: Sorcery – sorcery practiced by the Ninevites
Verse: Nahum 3:4, 5

SORCERER: Sorcery – sorcery denounced
Verse: Malachi 3:5

SORCERER: Sorcery – be a swift witness against the sorcerers
Verse: Malachi 3:5

SORCERER: Sorcery – messages of false sorcery
Verse: Zechariah 10:2

SORCERER: Sorcery – sorcery practiced by false prophets
Verse: Matthew 24:24

SORCERER: Sorcery – sorcery practiced by Simon Magus
Verses: Acts 8:9, 11

SORCERER: Sorcery – he had bewitched them with sorceries
Verse: Acts 8:11

SORCERER: Sorcery – "There they met a Jewish sorcerer and false prophet named Bar–Jesus
Verse: Acts 13:6

SORCERER: Sorcery – "But Elymas the sorcerer (for that is what his name means) opposed them and tried to turn the
Verse: Acts 13:8

SORCERER: Sorcery – sorcery practiced by the damsel at Philippi
Verse: Acts 16:16

SORCERER: Sorcery – sorcery practiced by vagabond Jews
Verse: Acts 19:13

SORCERER: Sorcery – sorcery practiced by the sons of Sceva
Verses: Acts 19:14, 15

SORCERER: Sorcery – messages of false sorcery
Verse: 2 Thessalonians 2:9

SORCERER: Sorcery – of their murders, nor of their sorceries
Verse: Revelation 9:21

SORCERER: Sorcery – by thy sorceries were all nations deceived
Verse: Revelation 18:23

SORCERER: Sorcery – and whoremongers, and sorcerers, and
Verse: Revelation 21:8

SORCERER: Sorcery –
for without are dogs, and
sorcerers, and
Verse: Revelation 22:15

STRANGE: Supernatural
Activities at Mount Sinai
and the Tablets of Law
Location: Mount Sinai
Verses: Exodus 19:16–25;
Deuteronomy 4:5; 5:7–22;
9:8–11; Psalm 68:8; Hebrews
12:18–21

THIRD HEAVEN: Third Heaven –
"I know a man in Christ who
14 years ago was caught up to
the third heaven."
Verse: 2 Corinthians 12:2

UNSEEN: Invisible – for the
invisible things of him
Verse: Romans 1:20

UNSEEN: Invisible – in the image
of the invisible God
Verse: Colossians 1:15

UNSEEN: Invisible – and that art
in earth, visible and invisible
Verse: Colossians 1:16

UNSEEN: Invisible – unto the
King eternal, immortal,
invisible
Verse: 1 Timothy 1:17

UNSEEN: Invisible – as seeing
him who is invisible
Verse: Hebrews 1:27

UNSEEN: Not made of Things
Visible – "By faith we understand that the universe was
formed at God's command, so
that what is seen was not
made out of what was visible."
Verse: Hebrews 11:3

UNSEEN: Unseen is Eternal – "So
we fix our eyes not on what is
seen, but on what is unseen.
For what is seen is temporary,
but what is unseen is eternal."
Verse: 2 Corinthians 4:18

WITCHCRAFT: Witch – Saul
consulted the Witch of Endor
Verse: 1 Samuel 28:7

WITCHCRAFT: Witchcraft –
as long as all the idolatry
and witchcraft of
Verse: 2 Kings 9:22

WITCHCRAFT: Witchcraft –
will destroy your witchcraft
Verse: Micah 5:12

WITCHCRAFT: Witchcraft –
and peoples by her witchcraft
Verse: Naham 3:4

Conclusion

Now it's a Little Clearer

SO THERE YOU HAVE IT! NOW YOU KNOW THAT THE Bible is much more than a history of a people and their relationship with God. By reading this book, you've learned that the Bible is actually a road map for living in both the physical and spiritual realms.

This in-depth look into supernatural powers and strange happenings recorded in the Bible has introduced you to a number of interconnected subjects. You found that giants, dinosaurs, and dragons did exist during Bible times. You discovered that other dimensions do exist, and there is a world of unseen entities out there. You saw how God created and protected His people—still does. You read how God corrected and punished those who disobeyed His commands—still does. And you read how prayer produced awesome demonstrations of the power of God and His team. It still does.

Throughout this examination of the Bible you saw how God provided guides to help His people on their paths through life. These included angels, prophets, messengers, and holy men of God. These guides often demonstrated powers far beyond our own understanding or ability. It's difficult for many people to wrap their minds around these concepts. This is why many religions avoid in-depth discussions about anything supernatural or paranormal. These subjects can be challenging for the layperson. But clarity is coming. *Supernatural & Strange Happenings in the Bible* was written to help you in this process.

God told us that in the end times, many things will be made known to us. They are. Almost daily we are learning more about the events and places described in Scripture. We are also learning more about unseen worlds and other dimensions.

Today there is major turmoil in the field of physics as new evidence surfaces to challenge current presumptions of science. Recent discoveries like the Higgs boson subatomic particle (described in the section under Creation in Chapter 1) are spurning a new era of technological development just as Newton's laws of gravity led to basic equations of mechanics and made the Industrial Revolution possible. God is in charge, and He is making these things happen. What a wonderful time to be a witness to all this!

The Bible is the key to understanding everything I've shared. As I said at the beginning, this is your road map for living. It's your operations manual for life. There are many evils out there, but they are powerless when you fight on the side of God.

As recorded in Ephesians Chapter 6, each of us must put on the whole armor of God so we can stand up to the devil and his demons. We are not fighting against flesh and blood, but against "principalities, powers, and rulers of darkness." God's forces of good help us and oppose those who are unseen and wish us harm. We also battle "spiritual hosts of wickedness in the heavenly places." Protected by God and His army, we can stand firm, and we *will* prevail.

Each day the media describes natural and manmade disasters such as wars, rumors of war, neutron bombs, electromagnetic pulse (EMP) weapons, nuclear, biological and chemical threats, and the collapse of society, the economy, and governments all over the world. These reports make us wonder if we *can* survive. But now, we know we can, and we will if we put our complete faith in He who controls everything. He has power far beyond our understanding, and He has an unbeatable team with Him. So stand by for exciting times. God is on your side, and He *will* cause supernatural and strange happenings in *your* own life. God bless you. And may His force be with you.

Bibliography

References

A Reader's Guide to the Holy Bible, King James Version. Camden, NJ: Thomas Nelson, 1972.

Kaiser, Jr., Walter C. *A History of Israel.* Nashville: Broadman & Holman, 1988.

Lockyer, Herbert. *All the Miracles of the Bible.* Grand Rapids: Zondervan, 1961.

Dickason, C. Fred. *Angels: Elect & Evil, Revised,* N.p.: Moody Publishers, 1995.

Asimov, Isaac. *Asimov's Guide to the Bible: Volume 1, The Old Testament.* New York: Avon Books, 1968.

Baucum, Walter. *Bronze Age Atlantis.* Jerusalem: Russell-Davis Publications, 2008. New York: Robert Appleton Company, 1913.

Easton, Matthew. *Easton's Bible Dictionary, Illustrated Bible Dictionary.* Camden: Thomas Nelson, 1897.

Alexander, David, and Pat Alexander, eds. *Erdmans Handbook to the Bible,* Grand Rapids: William B Eerdmans Publishing, 1983.

Forbush, William Byron, ed. *Fox's Book of Martyrs.* Grand Rapids: Zondervan Publishing House, 1967.

God's Word, Grand Rapids: World Publishing, God's Word to the Nations Bible Society, 1995.

Halley, Henry H. *Halley's Bible Handbook.* Chicago: Henry H. Halley, 1959.

Holman Bible Dictionary. N.p.: Broadman & Holman, 1991.

Illustrated Dictionary & Concordance of the Bible, G.G. Jerusalem: The Jerusalem Publishing House, 1986. []. N.p.: The Gale Group, 2008.

"Patriarchal Palestine." *Journal of the Professional Society of Biblical Archeology*. N.p.: 1895: 1896, xviii. 173 et seq.

Rohl, David. *Legends: The Genesis of Civilization* (1998) and *The Lost Testament* (2002) - mentioned in the context of the Asiatic conquests of . W. Max Müller, "Asien und Europa." 1893

Guinness, Alma, ed. *Mysteries of the Bible*. Pleasantville, New York, Montreal: Reader's Digest Association, 1997.

Nave, Orville J. *Nave's Topical Bible*. Peabody, MA: Hendrickson Publishers, 2002.

New American Standard Bible. La Habra, CA: The Lockman Foundation, 1995.

Pfeiffer, Charles. *Old Testament History*. Washington: Baker Book House/Canon Press, 1973.

Random House Webster's College Dictionary. New York: Random House, 1992.

Taylor, John William. *The Coming of the Saints*. N.p.: Methuen, 1906.

The Holy Bible, English Standard Version. N.p.: Crosway Bibles, Good News Publishers, 2001.

The Holy Bible, International Standard Version. N.p.: ISV Foundation, 2008.

The Holy Bible, New International Version. Grand Rapids: Zondervan Bible Publishers, 1984.

The Holy Bible, New Living Translation. Carol Stream: Tyndale House Publishers, 2007.

Dummelow, J. R. *The One Volume Bible Commentary*. New York: Macmillan, 1908-1964.

Murray, Margaret. *The Splendor That Was Egypt*. New York: Hawthorn Books, 1963.

Standard Bible Atlas. Cincinnati, OH: Standard Publishing, 1997.

Strong, James: *Strong's Exhaustive Concordance of the Bible*. Peabody: Hendrickson Publishers, 2007.

Tyndale Handbook of Bible Charts & Maps. Wheaton, IL: Tyndale House Publishers, 2001.

Unger, Merrill F. *Unger's Bible Handbook,* Chicago: Moody Press, 1966.

Internet: *wiki.answers.com/Q/Who_wrote_the_book_of_Genesis*

Internet: *www.answersingenesis.org/articles/tj/v15/n2/behemoth*

Internet: *www.ancientegypt.co.uk/*

Internet: *www.ancient-egypt.org/*

Internet: *www.angelfire.com/*

Internet: *www.au.af.mil/au/awc/awcgate/gabrmetz/gabr0009.htm*

Internet: *www.av1611.org/genesis.html*

Internet: *archaeologynewsnetwork.blogspot.com/*

Internet: *bible.org/*

Internet: *www.bible.ca/archeology/bible-archeology-exodus-route-rephidim-meribah.htm*

Internet: *bible.cc/2_corinthians/12-2.htm*

Internet: *bibleatlas.org/valley_of_aijalon.htm*

Internet: *www.bibleplus.org/witchcraft/witchcraft.htm*

Internet: *biblestudio.com/weights_and_measures/*

Internet: *www.biblestudy.org/beginner/bible-weights-and-measures.html*

Internet: *www.biblestudytools.com*

Internet: *www.biblica.com/niv/table-of-weights-and-measures/*

Internet: *britam.org/*

Internet: *www.british-israel.ca/Genesis.htm*

Internet: *carm.org/what-does-it-mean-when-bible-refers-third-heaven*

Internet: *www.ccel.org/j/josephus/works/JOSEPHUS.HTM*

Internet: *christianity.about.com/od/whatdoesthebiblesay/a/Ghosts-In-The-Bible.htm*

Internet: *www.crivoice.org/thirdheaven.html*

Internet: *en.wikipedia.org/wiki/*

Internet: *en.wikipedia.org/wiki/Third_Heaven*

Internet: *genesis.allenaustin.net/index.htm*

Internet: *genesis.allenaustin.net/watchers.htm*

Internet: *www.genesispark.com/exhibits/evidence/scriptural/*

Internet: *www.greatsite.com/timeline-english-bible-history/ pre-reformation.html*

Internet: *www.gotquestions.org/sons-of-God.html*

Internet: *www.greeninfluence.org/*

Internet: *www.jewishencyclopedia.com/articles/9841-leviathan-and-behemoth*

Internet: *www.jewishhistory.org/nachmanides/*

Internet: *www.jewishvirtuallibrary.org/*

Internet: *www.jewishvirtuallibrary.org/jsource/Judaism/kabbalah.html*

Internet: *www.keyway.ca/*

Internet: *www.ldolphin.org/*

Internet: *ldolphin.org/eden/*

Internet: *www.letusreason.org/Biblexp130.htm*

Internet: *www.physorg.com/*

Internet: *www.religioustolerance.org/*

Internet: *www.toptenz.net/*

Internet: *weights-and-measures.scripturetext.com/*

Internet: *www.whyangels.com/devil_demons.html*

Internet: *en.wikipedia.org/wiki/Jesus_predicts_his_death*

Internet: *www.biblegateway.com/passage/?search=Mark+8%3A31-38&version=NIV*

Internet: *www.grace4u.org/newtest/matthew/Matt20-17.htm*

Internet: *www.voiceofjesus.org/predictionsofdeath.html*

Internet: *www.4truth.net/fourtruthpbjesus.aspx?pageid=8589952879*

Index

H

About the Author

Who is Robert Brenner?

ROBERT BRENNER IS AN ENGINEER, CONSULTANT, college professor, historical genealogist, and professional speaker with extensive experience in research and information publishing. As a genealogical researcher, he was able to locate and actually visit the German ancestral home of the Brenner family in Trochtelfingen, Bavaria. Accepting a challenge, he spent the last 10 years studying the Bible and researching supernatural and strange events and incidents recorded in Scripture.

A retired naval officer with distinguished service in both nuclear submarines and microelectronic research and development, Brenner holds a bachelor's degree (BSEE) and two master's degrees (MSEE, MSSM).

He has been a guest speaker at over 50 national conferences and symposiums and is a consultant on pricing and the business of desktop service. He is the author of 51 books including *Small Business*

Guide to Pricing, Pricing Web Services, Pricing Tactics, Going Solar: a Homeowner's Experience, and *Supernatural & Strange Happenings in the Bible*. In addition, Brenner has written over 275 articles and has written technical manuals, user manuals and product line literature for numerous companies. He taught technology or engineering subjects at the high school, community college, university, and graduate school levels. A futurist, he enjoys the challenge of research and is currently sharing his findings through his writing and through presentations to the public.

Professor Brenner can be reached by writing him at:

Robert C. Brenner, MSEE, MSSM
Brenner Information Group
P.O. Box 721000
San Diego, CA 92172-1000

Or by email at:
brenner@brennerbooks.com

OTHER USEFUL INFORMATION

Supporting documents have been created to aid in your understanding of this book.

To see these additional references, visit:

www.brennerbooks.com